THE TRIBES AND CASTES OF BOMBAY

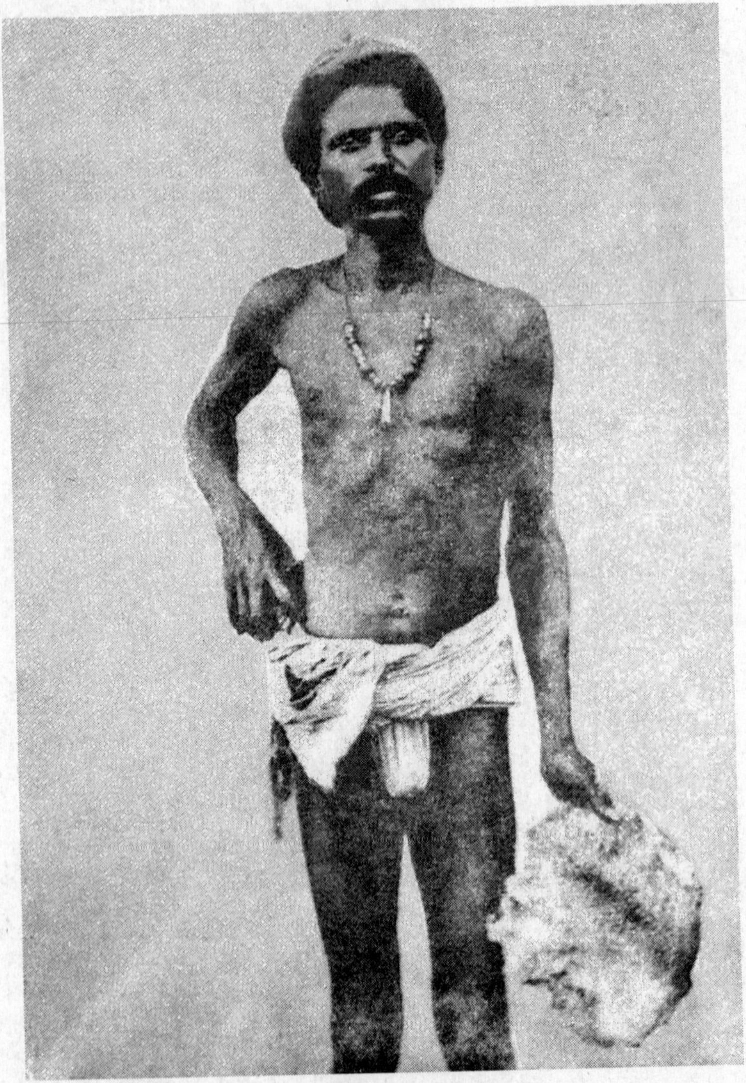

Phanse Pardhi

THE TRIBES AND CASTES OF BOMBAY

R. E. ENTHOVEN

IN THREE VOLS.

VOLUME 1

LOW PRICE PUBLICATIONS
DELHI-110052

Published by
Low Price Publications
A-6, Nimri Commercial Centre,
Near Ashok Vihar Phase-IV,
Delhi-110052
Phones: 011-27302453
e-mail: info@Lppindia.com
url: www.Lppindia.com

First Published 1922
Reprinted in **LPP** 1997, 2008
ISBN 978-81-7536-449-3 (Set)

Printed at
D K Fine Art Press P Ltd.
Delhi-110052

PRINTED IN INDIA

NOTE TO FIRST EDITION.

The present edition is intended for use in India. Vernacular terms such as *panch*, *shraddha*, *lingu*, *etc.*, have been freely used without explanation. It is proposed to issue an English Edition later, in which the results of the Survey will be dealt with in greater detail. The letter 'á' has the sound of 'a' in the word father. Other diacritical marks have been omitted.

NOTE TO FIRST EDITION

The present edition is intended for use in India. Vernacular terms such as *patel*, *shroff*, [illegible], have been freely used without explanation. It is proposed to issue an English Edition later, in which the results of the Survey will be dealt with in greater detail. The letter '[illegible]' has the sound of 'a' in the word 'father'. Other diacritical marks have been omitted.

INTRODUCTION.

History of the Bombay Ethnographical Survey.

Bombay. Madras. Bengal. United-Provinces. Punjab. Burma. Central-Provinces. Assam.

In May 1901 the Government of India issued orders for the commencement of the Ethnographical Survey of the Provinces noted in the margin, and proposed that the enquiries into the origin, social configuration, customs and occupations of the numerous castes and tribes should be spread over a period of four or five years. These enquiries were to follow closely the lines of certain questions approved by Messrs. Nesfield, Ibbetson and Risley at a Conference held in 1885.(1) They were to be carried out by the Superintendents in addition to their ordinary official duties.

It was not found possible to allow more than a few thousand rupees annually to each province for the work of the Survey; and before the work was half done, *i.e.*, in 1909, even this small financial provision was withdrawn. The Survey has since been practically dependent on the voluntary labours of the Superintendent in charge, with such assistance as he was able to secure without the expenditure of funds. This voluntary assistance has been forthcoming from three sources. Certain scholars such as Mr. D. R. Bhandarkar and Mr. B. A. Gupte have placed their knowledge at the disposal of the Superintendent and assisted the work of the Survey in the capacity of Honorary Assistants. A number of gentlemen have furnished valuable materials in the capacity of Honorary Correspondents. Finally, certain local committees organised by the Superintendent during the course of census operations in 1901 for the purposes of investigating and reporting on caste questions have supplied materials of considerable value and interest. With this assistance it has been possible

(1) See Appendix at the end of this Volume.

to complete the Survey of the tribes and castes in the Presidency, excluding Sind, by the beginning of the present year. The work has involved the preparation of nearly 300 articles. These have been published in draft form and circulated for criticism before being finally embodied in the Survey record.

It may at once be admitted that the work could not possibly have been completed, even in this greatly extended period, had it not been for the very full materials available in the pages of the Bombay Gazetteers compiled by the late Sir James Campbell. Much of the work of the Survey has indeed consisted of the re-arrangement of these materials. which were drawn up originally on a district basis instead of dealing with tribes and castes as a whole. When compared with more recent information, the original district accounts have been found to be remarkably accurate in detail. With the assistance described, and in such leisure as was available to the Superintendent, in spite of the pre-occupation of more important official duties, a considerable amount of new information has been collected regarding the tribes and castes of the Bombay Presidency. The ensuing pages thus contain much new matter, though the main source of information has been found in the pages of the Bombay District Gazetteers, which contain accounts remarkable both for their fulness and accuracy.

Scope of the work. At the time of issuing the first of the draft Monographs, of which the complete series is now published in these volumes, I indicated that the tribes and castes recorded in the Census Tables of 1901, and numbering over 500, would be dealt with in three classes :—

Class 1, being those containing one hundred thousand members, were to be described as fully as possible ;

Class 2, being those between one hundred thousand and five thousand, were to be dealt with in less detail ;

Class 3, being those under five thousand, were for the most part to be described merely by rearranging the materials on the lines of the Ethnographical questions.

This scheme has been adhered to. The only important departure from the general scheme outlined by me in 1903 at the time of publishing the first Monograph, dealing with the Ahir, is the omission of the tribes and castes of Sind. This and the following volumes include only tribes and castes found in the Presidency Proper.

Special features of the Survey.

In the course of revising existing materials for the caste accounts a number of new caste divisions have been discovered, both in connection with the groups inside which marriage is essential, and the smaller divisions inside which marriage is forbidden. These are referred to in this work respectively as endogamous and exogamous groups. They are of special interest as the interior structure of a caste is frequently valuable evidence of its origin. It has also been found that certain caste names are synonyms. Castes have in such cases been re-grouped. In connection with castes of converts from Hinduism to Islám, useful information has been obtained from the marriage registers of the *Kázis*, showing the cases in which intermarriage between such castes is allowed. Many Musalmán castes adhere to the Hindu practise of endogamy. Among those Musalmán castes which intermarry are found armourers, butchers, farriers, elephant-drivers, and similar occupational groups which are probably descendants of the camp followers of the Mughal armies. It is interesting to note that contact with the Muhammadan armies has left its influence in the greater freedom with which intermarriage is allowed. The social prejudice which prevents members of many Muhammadan castes from marrying outside the caste is a relic of the previously existing Hindu custom, such castes being clearly traceable to a Hindu origin before conversion.

They are found chiefly in areas where Musalmán rule has stimulated conversion, either by example, as in Bijápur, or by force as in north Kanara, once under the dominion of Hyder and Tipu. A great deal of new information has been obtained regarding the interesting Lingáyat community, which is found to be based partly on religious and partly on caste distinctions. The late Dr. J. F. Fleet, C.I.E., supplied some valuable notes for this article, which forms the basis of a new account of Lingáyats contributed by the Superintendent to Dr. Hasting's Dictionary of Religion. The special interest of the community lies in the fact that it exhibits the process by which a religious movement, starting with the abolition of caste distinctions, develops slowly into a community of which the most recent converts adhere strictly to the non-intermarrying caste distinctions of their Hindu ancestors.

The Survey has brought to light a great deal of new information regarding totemistic divisions in the Deccan and Southern Marátha Country. The identification of Marátha guardians or *devaks* with Kanarese *balis* is an indication of a similarity of origin between certain castes and tribes of the Presidency which has not hitherto been suspected. The subject is one which will repay very careful study.

Tribe and caste

Broadly speaking, the term tribe is used in these pages for a unit based on common descent as opposed to the term caste which is applied to a social unit founded on common occupation, common residence, common language or common political control. A social unit based on religion is described as a sect.

Origin of caste.

A great deal of time and research has been devoted to attempts to arrive at an explanation of the origin of caste. I do not propose in the course of this brief introduction to recapitulate the various theories that have been put forward by numerous scholars to explain the origin and continuance of caste in India. It may, however, be remarked that, given the conditions which have prevailed in this country since the first Aryan invasion, a caste system involving the formation of a number of non-intermarrying groups must from the first have been inevitable.

From the dawn of history India has been subject to invasion by land and sea, and the invaders, who were themselves very probably of mixed origin, have seldom refrained from intermarriage with the heterogeneous population already established in the country. In the Institutes of Manu we find an attempt to classify the resulting units of mixed descent under different names. The process of admixture of blood has continued to the present day. Probably its influence was especially marked during the series of post-Aryan invasions between the third century B. C. and the sixth century A. D. By this time Aryan, Dravidian, and mixed Aryo-Dravidian castes were numerous. Intermarriage with the invading tribes such as the Ahirs, Gujars and other Scythian units must have led to a great complexity of racial types, each naturally tending to preserve itself from further admixture of blood, by forming a marriage group excluded by the purer groups from intermarriage, and itself refusing to countenance unions with those who were members of groups regarded as inferior owing to greater impurity of blood. Racial influence.

To the influence of race, in itself of great importance, would shortly be added the effect of varying occupations as the tribal units passed from the pastoral to the agricultural state, and from that to the practice of arts and handicrafts. Thus true castes were formed; but occupation would not ordinarily obliterate the racial distinctions already referred to. The occupational group would contain various ethnic groups remaining endogamous. In this way, if we start with the idea of descent, we can show the population in tribes divided into groups (castes) following different occupations; or, starting from the occupation, The influence of occupation.

we may show the caste including a number of different tribal groups. The Ahirs and Gujars, immigrant tribes of great importance, are now broken into many caste sections such as those found in the Shimpis, Sonárs, Sutárs, Chámbhárs, etc. We may therefore show Ahirs and Gujars with their occupational divisions as forming part of the tribe, or the castes as a whole, with Ahir and Gujar as sub-castes. In both cases, the sub-divisions are the endogamous units.

Tribe and caste, therefore, are different ways of looking at the same social groups, the tribe being the forerunner of the caste. Unfortunately, the question of the correct classification of such groups is further complicated by other influences besides those of descent and occupation. Of these the principal are religion and domicile.

eligious fluences. The effect of religious movements, such as Jainism, Lingáyatism, Islám and Christianity on social grouping is specially interesting. Jains, found almost entirely in Gujarát and Bombay City, usually form an endogamous division of the occupational caste, though dining with the Hindu element may be permissible. Lingáyatism is more complex. Starting with a repudiation of caste distinctions, Lingáyats have passed through several phases, the earlier converts coming in time to separate themselves from those who joined later; and ultimately, as in the case of Jains, Lingáyats merely form an endogamous division of the Hindu group from which they were converted. This development will be found treated at length in the article on Lingáyats. Islám should not recognise caste; but the practice varies. There are Muhammadan castes that marry with other castes of the same faith. There are many that will only marry within their own caste, though of course not with the Hindu members. Even Christianity has been a source of caste division in places; for there are three caste divisions of Christians in Goanese territory, known as Bráhman, Chardo and Sudra; and certain castes such as Bhandáris,

Kolis and Kunbis contain Christian sections that only marry within such sections.

Domicile and language.

Most important in its effect on caste formation is the influence of domicile and language. A portion of a caste separated by migration from its parent body tends to develop certain differences in customs, occupation or interests. Owing to the common tendency to exaggerate the importance of such differences which is a specially Indian characteristic, marriage with the original body of the caste is frequently abandoned on account of these small differences. In the past, no doubt, the difficulty of communication accelerated this process. Marriages with caste fellows separated by a lengthy and tedious journey from a remote section of the caste would tend to be of rare occurrence, and eventually be looked on as in some way contrary to caste practice, that is to say, as unlawful. The result can be traced in numerous cases where the sub-castes have a territorial name. A reference to the articles on Bráhmans and Vánis will show how numerous local groups of this nature are in Gujarát.

Mr. A. M. T. Jackson has drawn attention to the fact that a change of domicile on the part of a portion of a caste was peculiarly liable to create new sub-castes owing to the powers exercised by Hindu rulers over the caste organizations. As supreme authority, the king must decide questions of caste practice; and he might well do so in such a way as to create local practices at variance with the custom of sections of the caste under another jurisdiction. Here again the proneness of the people to attach undue importance to small points of difference would lead to intermarriage being abandoned between the sections of the caste under different political control. This is no doubt a good instance of the effect of domicile on caste fission. Mr. Jackson's theory will be found to derive much support from the close resemblance between the subdivisions of the two leading castes in Gujarát, the Bráhmans and Vánis, which have many of the same territorial names, and from similar instances quoted in the following pages.

In the Deccan, where in Hindu times political control was more uniform than in Gujarát, castes have retained a greater measure of cohesion. This has been preserved under Muhammadan rule, even though the Deccan was then divided between five, and subsequently three, kingdoms. These territories, unlike the early Gujarát States, were ruled by Muhammadan kings, who did not interfere in caste disputes. That Bijápur, Ahmednagar and Golconda have not given their names to caste divisions is not therefore evidence against the validity of Mr. Jackson's political theory.

The essence of caste.

It will be gathered from the foregoing remarks that caste is in reality a system of 'self-determination' based on the habit of attaching more importance to the differences between social groups than to that which they have in common. Social union is fostered and maintained by attaching importance to all that human beings, whatever their race, occupation or domicile, may have in common with each other. Social cleavage is inevitable when an exaggerated importance is attached to differences of race, occupation or domicile between one group of individuals and another. The barrier of religion may be expected to give rise to groups that will not intermarry, for it is based on fundamentals. But when to this is added an endless series of social fences erected on account of differences in origin, occupation or custom, it is inevitable that society should break into a number of self-contained elements to which there can scarcely be a limit. Too frequently the bar on inter-marriage and inter-dining, which is the essence of caste organization, is based on an assumed superiority of one group of individuals over another, so that, broadly speaking, the Indian caste system might be described as the most complete system of social exclusiveness that the world has ever witnessed. A common sentiment of Indian nationality might provide in time a sufficient motive for pulling down caste barriers. But in India habits and customs, readily formed, are adhered to with great tenacity. An inter-caste marriage law, now under discussion, does not promise to achieve any great measure of success. Recently inter-marriages have been recorded between endogamous castes such as Deshasth and Chitpávan Bráhmans. These, however, are exceptional; and there is no present indication that caste barriers on inter-dining and inter-marriage are likely to be rapidly removed.

Survey plan.

The Survey, therefore, has had to deal with a number of groups which cannot accurately be described as being racial, occupational, sectarian or geographical though one or more of these influences has produced the group in each case. It is almost impossible in such circumstances to avoid cross-divisions when drawing up a list of caste units, particularly in the case of Lingáyats. The aim of the Survey has been to show in each case the groups that form endogamous units, combined for convenience of description under the heading of a major group which must in some cases be religious, *e.g.*, Lingáyats, sometimes occupational, *e.g.*, Vánis, and in rarer instances tribal, as for instance Bhils, Kolis, Káthis, etc.

Caste in process of evolution.

It is of interest to note that when, owing to the influence of the four main causes of caste evolution already described, a group divides into sub-castes the process occasionally has two distinct stages. To commence with, a group that formerly allowed inter-marriage freely between all its members develops a section that for racial, functional or similar reasons hold itself superior in status to the rest of the group. This is shown by the former declining to allow their daughters to marry the sons of the other caste members, but accepting brides for their own sons from the main body of the caste. In the Punjab a great many castes are thus related to each other to the present day, and completely endogamous castes are of rare occurrence. In the Bombay Presidency the practice is less common; but it is found among Rajputs, Maráthás, Lingáyats and even among the lowest castes. Maráthás, who were once one with Kunbis, will still marry Kunbi girls in some parts of the Presidency. Lingáyat Panchamsális are divided into Jangams and Bánjigs, of which the former will marry the daughters of the latter after a process of initiation, though in no circumstances would they allow their own daughters to marry Bánjigs. Two such groups, of which the lower is known technically as hypergamous, will usually tend to develop into completely separate castes in course of time. The marriage of girls from the lower section is abandoned as soon as the breach between the social status of the two sections is sufficiently wide. In the writer's experience, one of the lowest castes of the Presidency, the Mahárs, developed an embryo new caste recently in this way, owing to a number of Mahárs having learnt to drive motor vehicles. The added wealth and prestige that this occupation brought with it showed itself in a "Driver" section, which was disinclined to continue free inter-marriage with the caste as a whole. It only requires time in such circumstances for the caste to develop a completely endogamous "Driver" division.

Primitive and foreign elements in Bombay castes.

In the course of the work of the Survey, it has been possible to accumulate some interesting facts bearing on the extent to which primitive, *i.e.*, pre-Aryan as well as foreign or immigrant elements can be traced in the castes of the Presidency excluding Sind. The result of investigations in the southern portion of the Presidency, where castes are clearly organized on primitive lines, has brought to light a regular system of totemistic divisions of special interest and significance. These divisions are known locally as *balis* and are named after animals such as the elk, the hog deer, the elephant, the monkey, the tortoise, certain fish, and trees or plants such as the banyan, pipal, screw pine, plantain, etc.

There is a division named after the white ant's nest. These *balis* are exogamous, and display the usual totemistic features, *i.e.*, members worship the tree, plant, animal or other object, giving its name to the *bali*, on special occasions such as marriage or the occupation of a new house. They will not cut or injure it in any way, and in no circumstances may those who have a common *bali* be allowed to intermarry. Children appear originally to have inherited the mother's totem. Later this sytem has been modified into one of tracing the totem through the male parent.

Further north in the Presidency we find that many castes show traces of having originally possessed a similar organization. There is a remarkable resemblance traceable between the guardians or *devaks* of the Marátha castes in the Deccan and the *balis* of North Kanara. The same trees as, for instance, the *nágchampa* (Mesua ferrea) and screw pine (Pandanus odoratissimus) are found as *devaks* and as *balis*. In the article on Maráthás information will be found regarding these *devaks*. Being regularly worshipped, carefully preserved, and governing inter-marriages, they appear to possess the leading characteristics of totems. It is reasonable to assume that the *devak* with its suggestive resemblance to the *bali* is strong evidence of the primitive origin of at least an important element in the castes in which it is found. From this assumption very interesting results may follow. It is not possible within the limits of this brief survey to develop the argument to its logical conclusion; but clearly Maráthás contain a much stronger pre-Aryan element than has hitherto been supposed.

We are on more difficult ground when we endeavour to trace the remains of foreign elements in the caste formations of the Presidency. The late Sir James Campbell attached much importance to the survival of the names of post-Aryan invading tribes such as Yávans, Parthians, Ahirs, Gujars and Yádavs, or of the early ruling Indian dynasties, *e.g.*,

Maurya, Kadamba, Chalukhya, among the castes of the Presidency. It has been seen that Ahir and Gujar divisions are still found in many castes. Maurya, Kadamba and Chalukhya survive in the form of surnames, *i.e.*, More, Kadam and Cholke, among Maráthás, Kunbis, Mahárs and Kolis. But it is unsafe to attach much significance to names in India. They probably bear little more signification than the term "Shivajis" which was formerly applied by the English to numerous castes enlisted under the banner of the Marátha hero, that is to say, they indicate subservience to a common leader or dynasty, but do not connote common descent. The Ahir and Gujar elements stand on a somewhat different footing to the surnames ; but it is impossible at the present day to arrive at the exact relation which such sub-castes bear to the original Ahir and Gujar tribes. The subject has been very ably treated by D. R. Bhandarkar in his study of the foreign elements in Hindu society, where both Nágar Bráhman and Sisode Rajput have been shown to have been Gujars originally. It is certain that inter-marriage with local elements has largely obscured the extent to which Ahir and Gujar have contributed to modern caste formations, even in cases where the name survives.

The general impression conveyed by the Survey is that the original foreign element in many of the castes has been greatly obscured by inter-marriage with the indigenous population. Even the Parsis, the most exclusive of immigrant castes, have admittedly mixed with the jungle tribes of Gujarát and the issue, until recently, has been admitted to the Parsi community. Ultimately we may perhaps be prepared to the conclusion that the tribes and castes of the Presidency have far more in common as regards their origin than has hitherto been admitted.

rregular unions.

The pages of the Survey contain much evidence in support of this contention. There is scarcely a caste that is not found to possess a section known as Akaramáshe, Bande, Shinde,

Dasa, Kále, etc., signifying that there has been irregular union either with women of a lower caste or with men of a higher one. The institutes of Manu allow seven generations of marriage within the caste to restore the full status to the issue of such a union. The evidence available tends to show that a much less drastic test was imposed in recent times. The Abyssinian Angria married a Marátha girl; and history equally records instances of Koli chieftains who have been allowed a similar privilege, the children being doubtless classed as Maráthás in both instances. For many years Marátha Kunbi women have served in Bráhman houses in the Konkan, the issue being classed as Shinde under Maráthás.

Birth, marriage and death ceremonies.

A good deal of space is devoted under each of the caste heads to a description of birth, marriage, death and other important social ceremonies. The conclusions to be drawn from a comparison of these ceremonies must await the results of a detailed study. There are certain special ceremonies derived from Dravidian castes in Southern India which tend to occur in the Deccan and thus suggest some connection with non-Aryan elements. Until recently the social status of a caste has been greatly affected by the prevalence of infant or adult marriages, and the existence or prohibition of widow re-marriage. It is of interest to note that, while low-castes have been endeavouring to raise their social status by introducing child marriages and abandoning the marriage of widows, a reform movement among the highest castes is aiming at a return to adult marriage and the re-marriage of widows. The development is one that may have far-reaching effects in the near future.

Tree marriages.

A number of reports have borne witness to the prevalence, among certain wild tribes and low-castes, of the practice of marriage with trees. The occasion selected is when a bachelor desires to marry a widow. In this case the unmarried partner first goes through the ceremony with one of the totem trees, *e.g.*, the *shami* Prosopis spicigera or *rui* Calotropis gigantea.(1) The tree is then cut down and destroyed. It seems probable that the tree bride is intended to form a spirit companion to the widow's first partner, who might, if not so satisfied, devote an unwelcome amount of attention to the re-married couple. This curious custom is in vogue in all parts of the Presidency. It is not to be confused with the ceremony known as *Ark-viváha, i.e.*, marriage with a *rui* bush, prescribed in the Sacred Books for Hindus who lose two wives, before they marry a third time. Most probably the primitive custom gave rise to the Hindu rite, which is restricted to special cases of marriages with third wives; but the original ceremony is clearly a spirit-scaring rite designed to protect a bachelor who marries a widow.

Anthropometrical operations.

In the early days of the Survey a trained operator was employed for a short time, under the direction of the late Sir Herbert Risley, in taking anthropometrical records of some of the leading caste types in Bombay. The number selected for measurement in the case of each caste was very small, and this in itself would render it desirable to view the results with caution. As they stand in their published form, they exhibit such an unexpected jumble of castes and tribes, whether placed by cephalic measurement or nasal index, that it is impossible to deduce from them conclusions of value. Risley was at one time inclined to the view that measurements recorded among the Maráthás afforded evidence of their Scythic origin. He based this conclusion on the discovery of broad-headed people in the Deccan. But measurements which bring together the Bráhman and the Mahár require a great deal of collateral evidence from reliable sources before they can safely be used as the basis of a theory of racial origin. A reference

(1) In some cases this tree must belong to a different village to the bridegroom's which shows that it represents a woman selected similarly from another exogamous section.

to Risley tables[1] will show the Bombay castes or which measurements were taken grouped in the following order:—

A.—By Cephalic Index.	*B.—By Nasal Index.*
1. Deshasth Bráhman.	1. Deshasth Bráhman.
2. Mahár.	2. Nágar Bráhman.
3. Chitpávan Bráhman.	3. Shenvi Brahman.
4. Kunbi.	4. Vánia.
5. Koli.	5. Prabhu.
6. Marátha.	6. Koli.
7. Shenvi Bráhman.	7. Chitpávan Bráhman.
8. Vánia.	8. Kunbi.
9. Nágar Bráhman.	9. Deshasth Bráhman.
10. Prabhu.	10. Marátha.
	11. Mahár.

It will be seen that in the first of these groups a low cephalic index is shared by the Mahár, one of the lowest castes of the Presidency, with the Deshasth and Chitpávan Bráhmans. This is at least disconcerting. The Mahár would not be expected in such strange company. Again, in the case of the nasal index, to which Risley at one time attached so much importance as to hazard the theory that a man's social status would be found to vary in inverse ratio to the mean relative width of his nose, we find the lead rightly taken by three Bráhman castes, which are followed by Váni and Prabhu. After that, the classification is very suspicious. The Koli is found above the Chitpávan Bráhman; the Marátha Kunbi above the Deshasth Bráhman; and both of these are higher in the scale than the Marátha. It is impossible from the known facts to find any satisfactory explanation of these two lists of precedence. Mahárs and Kolis must be as typical representatives of the early types in the Presidency as can well be found. Yet these measurements give them a place close to the Bráhmans, and even above the Deshasth. The Marátha is found below the Koli and

(1) *Vide* The People of India—Appendix IV

the Mahár in cephalic measurement, and placed below the Koli by nasal index. His history and social position would lead to the expectation that the position should be reversed. Unfortunately, it has not been found possible, owing to the withdrawal of financial support from the Survey, to pursue these enquiries and test the recorded data by making additional measurements for each selected caste, or by measuring other typical castes not included in the scope of Risley's observations. This might have thrown some further light on the very curious results already recorded. If any theory at all is to be based on the Risley tables it would seem to be that the tribes and castes of the Bombay Presidency are much more closely connected, racially, from the highest to the lowest, than history, tradition, customs and appearance have hitherto led us to suppose.

Some typical castes.

It is my intention on some future occasion to deal in a separate work with the full results of the Ethnographical Survey. Within the limits of an introductory note space can be found only for a few points of special interest; and these have necessarily been very summarily treated. To illustrate the difficulties in which the classification of the people of the Presidency by tribe and caste is involved I will describe briefly a few typical groups representing important units of the population :—Vánis, Maráthás, Lingáyats, Bhils and Kolis.

Vánis.

The Váni, Banya or Bánjig is a trader corresponding to the Vaishya of the fourfold classification of Manu. As Vaishyas they claim a twice-born status: but here their common interest ceases, for they are divided into a large number of groups that will not intermarry. Of these in Gujarát, the following divisions are common to Bráhman and Váni :—

1. Agarvál.	5. Jhárola.
2. Desavál.	6. Khadáyata.
3. Gujar.	7. Kapol.
4. Harsola,	8. Meváda.

9. Modh.
10. Nágar
11. Nandora.
12. Osvál.
13. Palivál.
14. Porvád.
15. Shrimáli.
16. Sorathia.
17. Váyada.

These being mainly geographical in origin, tend to bear out Mr. Jackson's theory of caste fission to which reference has already been made. These numerous groups contain Jain and Hindu divisions, known as *Shrávak* and *Meshri*, that will not intermarry. They have also divisions known as Visa (20), Dasa (10), Panch (5), Adhich ($2\frac{1}{2}$), representing an increasing admixture of some lower element.

In the Deccan the Váni caste is more homogeneous, only a few divisions being found, owing no doubt to the fact that political control has been more uniform in that area than in Gujarát.

Further South, the Váni is known as a Bánjig, and is generally a Lingáyat. As such, he will not marry with Hindu or Jain Vánis.

Maráthás are the chief unit in the Deccan and Konkan, Maráthás.
probably deriving their name from Maháráshtra, *i.e.*, the Deccan, and representing a tribe with some Northern elements but largely aboriginal. There is probably no substantial difference in origin between the landholding and warrior section, *i.e.*, Maráthás Proper, the cultivators, *i.e.*, Marátha Kunbis, and the numerous local occupational castes such as Marátha Vánis, Sonárs. Sutárs, Parits, etc. Intermarriage is not ordinarily allowed between these groups, although, in remote parts, Maráthás Proper will take girls in marriage from the Kunbi or Kulvádi caste. They will not marry their girls to boys of the Kulvádi caste. The Kunbi, again, is at times recruited from the Koli who settles down to agriculture and acquires a "Kunbi" or cultivator status. The rise of the Marátha power in

the seventeenth century induced the fighting classes (landholders) to claim for themselves Kshatriya rank, and to discourage widow remarriage. It is chiefly on this ground that they claim to be superior to the Kunbis. But by descent the Marátha appears to be one with the Marátha Kunbi and certain other occupational castes in the Deccan.

Lingáyats. Lingáyats are a religious body dating from the eleventh century, when they separated from the Hindu fold by denying the authority of the Bráhman, rejecting the scriptures, and abandoning Hindu ceremonies and pilgrimages. Largely recruited from Jain traders or Bánjigs, these with their priests, known as Jangams, formed originally one body ignoring caste distinctions. Later converts, however, were in course of time relegated to an inferior social status thus giving rise to endogamous groups resembling the ordinary Hindu caste in exclusiveness, though adopting the special religious rites of Lingáyatism. Hindus and Lingáyats do not intermarry, even if they have a common caste name and occupation. The original rejection of caste distinctions has thus, it will be seen, given place to the formation of castes containing Lingáyats bearing the same relation to Hindus in such castes as the Jains in the Váni divisions of Gujarát bear to the Hindu members.

Bhils and Kolis. Bhils and Kolis are aboriginal tribes which probably do not differ at all in origin. They are doubtless the former inhabitants of the greater part of the Presidency, now largely confined to hilly or jungle tracts of country. The common bond between Bhils is one of descent, as is the case with Kolis. Changes of occupation and a certain admixture of foreign blood has led to the formation of a number of divisions in each case. Among Kolis we find divisions with the names of Ahir, Bhil, Dhangar and Marátha. Ahirs and divisions with Marátha names are found among the Bhils. Other primitive tribes besides Kolis, such as

Berads, have Bhil divisions. It has been seen that the Koli, by taking to cultivation, may rise to the position of a Marátha Kunbi. For the most part Bhils and Kolis remain good examples of purely tribal stocks. Intermarriage with inferior Rajputs has in places produced mixed castes from both sources.

During the progress of the Survey the Superintendent has automatically become a tribunal for settling disputes regarding caste precedence. The circulation of the draft monographs led to the formulation of claims such, for instance, as those of Páncháls to be classed as Vishva Bráhmans, of Sonárs to be described as Daivadnya Bráhmans, and of Vádvals to be admitted to rank as Pánchkalshis, or Somvanshi Kshatriyas. Interesting documents have been produced bearing on these disputed points. Mánbhávs have been proved to be entirely distinct from the degraded caste of Mángs with which they were formerly supposed to be connected.[1] The Saváshe Bráhmans have established their appeal against their former classification as degraded Deshasth Bráhmans and have been reclassed as Sahavási Bráhmans. If in the decisions arrived at on these and similar points, the Superintendent's views fail to meet with general acceptance, it may at least be agreed in support of them that the evidence on both sides has been very carefully examined in arriving at these results. Caste disputes.

In conclusion, I would express my grateful acknowledgments to Rái Bahádur B. A. Gupte, Mr. D. R. Bhandarkar, Ráo Bahádur R. C. Artal, Shams-ul-ulma Dr. J. J. Modi, C.I.E., Mr. K. G. Pandit, Ráo Bahadur P. B. Joshi, Mr. M. K. Mehta and Mr. J. A. Saldanha for the valuable assistance they have rendered in compiling many of the draft monographs which form the basis of this work. Acknowledgments.

(1) A very striking resemblance has been brought to light between Mánbhávs and the ancient Christian sect of Manichæans (273 A. D.).

Mr. P. J. Mead, C.I.E., I.C.S., has at intervals held temporary charge of the Survey, and, assisted by Mr. L. J. Sedgwick, I.C.S., has directed the work of compilation recently during my absence in England on duty. I have also received useful materials from Mr. O. Rothfeld, I.C.S., and the Reverend A. Wilkie Brown.

A special tribute is due to Mr. G. M. Kalelkar, who has been my Assistant in the work of the Survey since its commencement, and has carried out the heavy task of drafting caste articles with commendable skill and energy.

R. E. E.

June 30, 1920.

TRIBES AND CASTES OF BOMBAY.

ABDALI.—See under Minor Musalmán Castes.

ABHUVANKAR.—A sub-division of Udámbar Bráhmans.

ABNE.—A sub-division of Mahárs.

ABOTI.—A sub-division of Shrimáli Bráhmans.

ACHARI.—A synonym for Lohár.

ACHARYA.—A sub-division of Audich Bráhmans.

ACHYUTPANTHI.—A synonym for Mánbháv.

ADALJA.—A sub-division of Modh Vániás.

ADHAPRABHU.—A sub-division of Mális.

ADHASHETI.—A sub-division of Mális.

ADIBANJIG.—A sub-division of Lingáyats.

ADIVI.—A sub-division of Koravas.

ADIVICHANCHER.—A synonym for Párdhi.

ADVI.—A sub-division of Gollas.

AGARSINDHVAL.—A sub-division of Bráhmans.

AGARVAL.—A sub-division of Bráhmans and Vániás.

AGARYA.—A sub-division of Vániás.

Name and origin.

AGASAS or Madiwáls are washermen, numbering 25,226 (1901), including 13,099 males and 12,127 females. They are found in all the Kanarese speaking districts and States of the Southern Marátha Country. An alternative form of *agasa* is *asaga*, which seems to be the earlier of the two.[1] The terms *agasa* and *madiwál* mean washerman, and are the Kanarese equivalents of *dhobi* and *parit*. It is thus clear that some confusion is likely to arise in recording the numbers at a census, as in the case of other castes bearing a purely occupational name. In Kanarese districts *dhobis* and *parits* may

(1) *Vide* Buchanan's Mysore, I. P. 337.

be described as *agasas*, and where Maráthi is the common language an *agasa* may be entered as a *dhobi* or *parit*. But, in the mass, all Kanarese speaking washermen would be described as *Agasas*. With this caution the figures quoted above may be accepted as fairly correct. The origin of the term *agasa* is unknown. *Madiwál* is derived from *madi* clean, and indicates the occupation of the caste.

Like the Agasás of Mysore, the Agasás in the south of the Bombay Presidency profess to have a common ancestor Viraghate Madiwál Eshvaram. They also have a tradition that they came into the Southern Marátha Country from the south in the reign of a Chola king.

Endogamous divisions.

Agasás have two endogamous divisions, Hindu and Lingáyat, of nearly equal strength. In 1901 the returns showed

Hindus	..	13,455
Lingáyats	..	11,771

These divisions neither eat together nor intermarry. The caste is very largely represented in Mysore, 90,962 (1901). The Agasás are divided into exogamous sections known as *bedagus*, of which the following are examples: Ambarakul, Adbhigotraja, Bhouparna, Dhautambar, Halagraha, Padata, Rajaka, Rajenami, Romapitra. Telugu, Variduvali.

Marriage.

A member of the caste may marry his father's sister's or mother's brother's daughter. A man may marry two sisters, and two brothers may marry two sisters. Polygamy is allowed and practised, but polyandry is unknown. Girls are married after ten, boys after eighteen. Sexual license before marriage is not tolerated. Girls committing sexual indiscretions are excommunicated.

Among Hindu Agasás the offer of marriage comes from the boy's father, who has to pay a *teru* or bride-price to the girl's father. The day for the marriage is fixed by a Bráhman, who conducts the service. The *Vágnischaya* or the settlement of the marriage is first celebrated, in which sugar is distributed amongst relations and friends. *Simant-pujan* is the reception of the bridegroom in a temple or beyond the village boundary. The *Rukhavat* is a dinner of sweet dishes to the boy's party. The binding portion is the throwing of sacred grains of rice over the bride and bridegroom, and the fastening of a lucky necklace round the bride's neck.

The remarriage of widows is permitted. A widow may marry her father's sister's or mother's brother's son. She cannot marry her mother's sister's son or a member of her late husband's section. A widow remarriage can be celebrated on any auspicious day. It is conducted by a Jangam. The ceremony is extremely simple. The pair put on new clothes, the lucky necklace is fastened to the girl's neck, and the couple then retire for the night. Should a bachelor desire to marry a widow, he is first married to a *shami* bush (Prosopis spicigera).

Divorce is allowed with the sanction of relations and the caste *panch,* if the husband and wife do not agree or the wife's conduct is bad. A divorced woman is allowed to marry again by the widow remarriage form, if the cause of divorce be not adultery on her part. A woman taken in adultery with a member of a higher caste can remain in the caste by paying a fine or giving a dinner to the caste people. If the offence is committed with a member of a lower caste she is excommunicated.

Religion.

The caste follow the Hindu law of inheritance and follow both the Hindu and Lingáyat religions. The chief objects of their worship are Shiva, Kedárling, Sidhái, Yellamma, Bhaváni and Máruti. They observe all the Hindu holidays, and make pilgrimages to Gokarn, Dharmasthal in south Kanara, Tirupati in north Arcot and Saundatti in Belgaum. On holidays and auspicious days goats and fowls are offered to minor gods, which are eaten by the offerers themselves. Images of deceased ancestors are made and installed within a month after death. They are worshipped with offerings of cooked food and articles of dress. The Musalmán saints are venerated. Their spiritual guide is the head of the Smart monastery at Shringeri. In Kanara, their priests are the Havik Bráhmans. In other places the local Bráhmans officiate at their ceremonies. The death and widow remarriage ceremonies are conducted by Jangams.

Death ceremonies.

Those who can afford it burn the dead, others bury. Their death ceremonies resemble those of the Lingáyat Agasás. The *mahálaya* is performed on the corresponding death day in the dark half of *Bhádrapad* for the propitiation of the deceased ancestors.

Occupation.

The Hindu Agasás wash the clothes of Christians, Musalmáns and all Hindus except the impure castes.

Food. They eat the flesh of goats, sheep, fowls and fish, and drink liquor. They rank below the cultivating classes and above the impure castes.

LINGAYAT AGASAS are found all over the Karnátak, the Southern Marátha Country, and the Sátára and Kanara districts. They claim to belong to the *Samudragotra*. The restrictions on intermarriage are the same as amongst other Lingáyats. Girls are married before they come of age, boys at any age. Polygamy is allowed and practised, but polyandry is unknown. The offer of

Marriage marriage comes from the boy's father, who has to pay a bride-price to the girl's father. The day for the marriage is fixed by a Jangam in consultation with a *joshi* (astrologer). The service is conducted by the Jangam only. The ceremonies are as follows :—

Báshtagikárya.—The boy's party go to the girl's house where leading members of the caste are assembled. The girl is bathed and dressed in new clothes presented by the boy's father. She is then made to bow to the house god, sugar and *pan supári* is distributed, and money presents are made to the Jangam by both parties. A feast to the party assembled ends the ceremony.

Yaduragollona.—The girl's party receives the boy's party outside the village boundary and bring them in the village in procession. This is followed by *Rukhavat,* which consists of a feast of sweetmeats given to the whole party.

On the next day the boy and the girl are rubbed with oil and bathed, turmeric paste and red powder are applied to their persons, and they are dressed in rich clothes and ornaments. The boy is then brought in procession to the girl's house. He is taken into the marriage booth, marriage coronets are fastened on his head and the girl's head, they are seated face to face on low wooden stools placed on a square formed of grains, marriage verses are repeated, and grains of rice are thrown on their heads. Next, the boy's mother fastens a lucky necklace round the girl's neck and they are made to bow before the house gods, thus ending the ceremony.

The remarriage of widows is permitted with the restriction that a bachelor is not allowed to marry a widow. The ceremony is conducted by a Jangam who places the widow, dressed in a white robe, on the left of her new husband. The hems of their garments are then joined and they bow to the household gods. Divorce is allowed if the husband and wife do not agree, or the wife's conduct is bad.

A divorced woman is not allowed to remarry. A woman taken in adultery with a member of a higher caste can remain in the caste by paying a fine or giving a dinner to the caste people. If the offence is committed with a member of a lower caste, she is excommunicated. The caste follow the Hindu law of inheritance.

Lingáyat Agasás are non-Panchamsáli Lingáyats without the *ashtavarna* rites. Their family deities are Virbhadra and Párvati. They worship Shiva and Basava and some of the minor Hindu gods. The trees and animals held sacred by the Hindus are worshipped. Images or *lings* are installed in the name of the deceased ancestors and worshipped with offerings of daily articles of food. When an epidemic breaks out, wooden images of the goddesses Durgavva and Mariavva are made and worshipped. Lingáyat Agasás observe almost all the Hindu holidays and make pilgrimages to Gokarn, Yadur, Kedárling, Khidranpur, etc. Religion.

The dead are buried. Those dying of white leprosy are burnt as, if buried, they are supposed to prevent the rain falling. On the third or fifth day after death the castemen are feasted. No ceremonies are performed for the propitiation of the deceased ancestors. Death ceremonies.

These Agasás are the hereditary washermen of the Lingáyat community. They wash the clothes of the Lingáyats only, though they should have no objection according to the tenets of their religion to wash the clothes of other people, even of the most degraded classes. Some of them hold land under the *Rayatvári* and *Bhágdári* system. Some are day labourers and are paid either in cash or in corn. Occupation.

They neither eat flesh nor drink liquor. Food.

AGASA.—A sub-division of Lamánis.

AGERS or saltmakers (from *ágar* a salt-pan), numbering 2,407 (1901), including 1,229 males and 1,178 females, are, with the exception of a few emigrants, found only in the Kanara District. There are no endogamous divisions of the caste. Name and origin.

The caste has six exogamous sections or *balis* known as— Exogamous divisions.

1.	Ajjana bali	.. Agga = fruit of the *ekke* tree (Antiaris toxicaria).
2.	Ane bali	.. Ane = elephant.
3.	Kadvina bali	.. Kadave = elk.
4.	Dyavan bali	.. Dyava = tortoise.
5.	Shirin bali	.. Shire = Gnanodropsis pentaphylla.
6.	Gurvin bali	.. Guruva = a prickly plant.

Those who belong to the second or elephant division worship the elephant, and do not wear ivory ornaments. The elk or *sámbar* group will not kill the *sámbar* or eat its flesh. The tortoise *bali* do not eat the tortoise. The tree and plant giving their names to the remaining divisions are never cut or injured by members of these divisions. It is to be inferred from this very complete system of totem sections that the Agers are a caste of pure Dravidian origin. The *bali* is traced, in their case, through males, both for males and females, and to this extent differs from the more primitive *bali* that is traceable through females, of which instances are numerous in North Kanara.

Marriage. Marriages are prohibited in the same *bali*. A man may marry his maternal uncle's daughter. He is not allowed to marry his father's sister's or mother's brother's daughter. He may marry two sisters. Brothers may marry sisters. The caste head-quarters are at Ankola. Outsiders are not admitted into this caste. Girls are married from the age of six to eleven, and boys from six to twenty-five. Polygamy is permitted, but polyandry is unknown. The negotiations for a marriage are commenced by the boy's father. When a match is settled, the boy's father treats the company present to a rupee's worth of toddy. He has to pay to the girl *hennateru, i.e.*, a bridal portion of Rs. 4. The marriage ceremonies last four days. On the first day the boy's parents go to the girl's father's house and treat the girl's party to a dinner of rice and cocoanut juice. On the second day the marriage takes place. On the third day the bridegroom takes his bride to his house and a feast is given by his father. The festivities end on the fourth day with a feast by the girl's father. The binding portion of the ceremony consists in throwing sacred grains of rice on the bride and bridegroom.

The remarriage of widows is permitted. A widow may marry her late husband's younger brother, but not the elder. With this exception, she cannot marry a member of her late husband's *bali*. A widow's marriage is always celebrated at night during only one month of the year, *viz.*, from the full-moon day of *Bhádrapad* to the full-moon day of *Ashvin*. Only a *budhvant* of the caste is present on the occasion. The ceremony consists in presenting to the widow by her new husband a robe, a nose-ring, and a sum of annas five. The widow has to pay to her late husband's relations the sum of Rs. 4 received by her at the time of her first marriage. A bachelor is not allowed to marry a widow.

A husband may divorce his wife on account of her misconduct. A divorced woman is not allowed to marry again during the life-time of her husband. A peculiar custom of the caste is, that if a divorced woman begets a child, not only is she not excommunicated, but the child is recognized as her husband's legitimate offspring, and he is made to perform its birth ceremonies. If the father of the child is found, he is made to pay a fine of one or two rupees to the caste, which is spent on drinking toddy. If an unmarried widow begets a child, she and her child are allowed to remain in the caste on the widow's paying to the *guru* of the caste a fine of not less than Rs. 12, and an equal amount to the caste.

Religion. The caste follow the Hindu law of inheritance. They are Hindus, and like most Kanara castes chiefly worship Vishnu and his incarnations. Their family god is Venkatráma of Tirupati. They also worship Murkunddev, Sannahossadev, Hulidev (tiger god) and other village gods and goddesses, represented by stones and white anthills. They have much faith in soothsaying, witchcraft, and in the powers of the spirits of the dead. They have no images in their houses. They go on pilgrimage to Tirupati, and occasionally to Gokarn during the *Shivrátra* holidays. They observe almost all the Hindu holidays. Every year on a day in April-May, before the monsoon sets in, offerings of goats and cocks are made to the gods. The heads of the offerings are given to the officiating priests, who are Kumbhárs, a portion being distributed among the village officials, and what remains is eaten by the offerers. Similar offerings are also made once a year to Mariamma, or the cholera goddess. The first of these offerings is known as *gadiávári* and the second as *mariávári*. They are made by most of the lower castes of Kanara—the first to propitiate the god presiding over the rains in the hope of plentiful showers, the second to propitiate the cholera goddess. The caste do not employ Bráhmans for ceremonial and religious purposes. All their ceremonies are conducted by the *budhvants*, or headmen of their caste.

Death ceremonies. The dead are either burnt or buried with their head to the north. About two pounds of rice grains and a pice are buried with the corpse. On every new-moon day and holiday cooked rice and fish placed on a plantain leaf are offered to the crows for the propitiation of the dead. They do not perform the *shráddha*.

Occupation. Their hereditary calling is making salt, and they also work as field labourers. They make palm-leaf umbrellas, which are used in Kanara throughout the year. Like the Buttáls and other field labourers, they are generally indebted to land-owners and work off loans by serving on very low wages.

Food. They eat the flesh of goats, hogs, fowls, rats, and fish. They drink toddy to excess. They eat at the hands of all castes except Mahárs, Chamgárs, Lingáyats, Jains and Halleers. No caste eats with them. They rank below the cultivating classes and above the impure castes.

AGHORI.—A sect of Shiva worshippers.

AGLE.—A synonym for Agri.

Name. **AGRIS**, also known as Agle and Khárpátil, numbered 211,176 at the Census of 1901. They are principally found in Thána (83,733), Kolába (113,115) and the State of Janjira (9,617).

Exogamous divisions. There are no exogamous sub-divisions above families having the same surname and observing common mourning. The following is a list of such families, *kuls* or *gotras* :—

(1) Bhoir.
(2) Chaudhari.
(3) Chaván.
(4) Gharat.
(5) Gulvi.
(6) Jádhav.
(7) Keni.
(8) Máli.
(9) Máhátre.
(10) Mandre.
(11) More.
(12) Mukul.
(13) Navarye.
(14) Pavár.
(15) Shelár.
(16) Shirke.
(17) Vaze.
(18) Yádav.
(19) Kadu.
(20) Mádhovi.
(21) Sare.
(22) Gávad.
(23) Gáikwád.
(24) Khuntale.
(25) Kamáne.
(26) Khanda-ágle.
(27) Dukre.
(28) Ghodinde.
(29) Joshi.
(30) Mohile.
(31) Khárik.
(32) Dasalke.
(33) Khámbalkar.
(34) Kasái.
(35) Bhamber.
(36) Dhumála.
(37) Pángdi.
(38) Kokáti.
(39) Danki.
(40) Gavil.
(41) Shivási.
(42) Kutilkar.
(43) Marikar.
(44) Bholekar.
(45) Varghoda.
(46) Kari.
(47) Dariyácha.
(48) Gondhali.
(49) Sigola.
(50) Kálaj.
(51) Náik.
(52) Pátil.
(53) Thákur.
(54) Kárbhári.
(55) Mukádam.
(56) Kotvál.

Some of these names have apparently been borrowed from Rajputs and Maráthás, some derived from occupations, some are the names of places and some family titles. It is to be noted that these may be distinct *gotrás* bearing the same surnames, members of one of which may intermarry with members of another : *e.g.*, the common names 'Bhoir,' 'Pavár,' 'Jádhav,' 'Mukádam,' which occur all over the Thána District, are borne by families quite distinct one from another, who do not observe common mourning and may therefore intermarry.

There are two endogamous divisions of the caste :— Endo-gamous divisions

(i) Sudh-ágris (pure Agris) who are also called Mith-ágris (salt makers), Jas-ágris (toddy-drawers), Dhol-ágris (drummers), Son-ágle, and Pán-ágle.

(ii) Das-ágris (probably from Dási, a term applied by the Aryans to those of mixed descent or of a different race—see below, where the meaning of the word is dealt with in connection with the Visa and Dasa sections of the Vánis).

The Urap or Varap Agris or Navá Maráthás were originally Agris, but were converted by the Portuguese to Christianity and subsequently reverted to Hinduism. They are not now recognized as Agris and are separately described below.

SUDH-AGRIS are also known as Mith-ágris, Jas-ágris, Dhol-ágris, Son-ágle, Pán-ágle.

The exogamous sub-divisions of Sudh-ágris are the following :

Bhoir.	Mandre.
Chaudhari.	More.
Chaván.	Mukul.
Gharat.	Navarye.
Gulvi.	Pavár.
Jádhav.	Shelár.
Keni.	Shirke.
Máli.	Vaze.
Máhátre.	Yádav.

There are no endogamous divisions of the caste.

There is no marriage within the limits of any one of the subdivisions mentioned above or similar *kuls*, members of which observe common mourning.

A man may not marry a cousin within five degrees of relationship. There is no distinct prohibition against marrying two sisters, but it is not the practice unless the first sister is dead. A man may marry two cousins.

There are no specified prohibitions against marriage with any but those already mentioned, but a well-to-do man does not marry a woman of a poor family, and a man does not go far, *e.g.*, out of the district or even generally out of the *táluka*, for a wife. A Thána Agri would not contract a marriage with an Agri of Khálápur in the Karjat *táluka*, nor with an Agri of the Kolába district.

Agris claim to be Kshatriyas or Khatris, but their small size and dark colour, their love of liquor and their belief in *devs* or un-Bráhman gods are almost marked enough to make them rank as a local or early tribe. The late or Aryan element which they claim and which appears in some of their surnames, according to their story, was introduced into the Konkan from Paithan in the Deccan, when the Deccan was conquered by the Musalmáns at the close of the thirteenth century. Both Mackintosh and Wilson rank them as Kolis.(1)

Origin. The tradition common among them is that they originally dwelt at Mungi Paithan and were transported to the Konkan by Bimbarája, and it is alleged that there are in existence *sanads* given by him to certain persons of the caste. They are not, however, forthcoming.

The following legend is given for what it is worth. Two sons, Agla and Mangla, were born to the sage Agasti; the former the ancestor of the Agris, the latter of the Mángelas (fishermen). The first was told to support himself by the manufacture of salt from the sea, the latter by fishing. The god Parashurám, intending to throw back the sea, was prevented by the intervention of the Agri and Mángela women. At their request he consented to throw it back only 27 miles, and the strip thus formed became the Konkan.

There is another legend to the effect that they are the musicians of Rávan, the demon-king of South India, who in reward for good services settled them in the Konkan.

Each group of twelve villages has a head Pátil or Desái, who settles caste disputes with a *Panch* for that group of villages. The village in which he resides is the chief village of the group. Such are Bhándup and Ovale in the Sálsette Táluka, Sakholi in Bhiwandi, &c.

In Kolába every Agri village has its head or Pátil, who is generally chosen from the oldest, wealthiest and most intelligent families. Meetings of the Agris of one village are called *jamáts*, and when the people of several villages come together the assembly is called *Káshigot* or *Ganga-got*. For the larger meetings invitations are sent in the name of the Pátil or of some other respectable person, and the

---

(1) Trans. Bom. Geo. Soc. I, 491.

guests are told where the meeting is to be held and the reason for holding it. When all have come, earthen jars full of liquor are placed in the middle of the company. One among them fills a small conch-like shell with liquor and presents it to the Pátil or other leading guest and then to the rest. When all have had a draught the discussion begins, and while the discussion lasts liquor is handed round from time to time. After each draught some mouthfuls of parched gram or peas are eaten. In this way as much as Rs. 20 worth of liquor is drunk. The accused, if found guilty, is generally fined from Re. 1 to Rs. 100. If he refuses to pay he is put out of caste. The authority of caste has in no way declined.

The well-to-do live in tiled houses on a stone or brick and cow-dung foundation with walls of stone, brick or reed plastered with cow-dung divided into a main portion round which cows and milch buffaloes are penned, a sleeping room, and a kitchen with a place for the family god; the poorer in huts generally square, sometimes round, on a similar foundation (or one of cow-dung without the raised stones) with reed walls and thatched with grass, rice-straw or palm leaves.

Outsiders are not admitted into the caste.

Marriage is both infant and adult. The husband is generally from 12 to 20 years old, the wife from 7 to 14. **Marriage.**

Polygamy is allowed. A man may have four wives, the same marriage ceremony being gone through in the case of each. The first married is generally the chief wife. Polyandry is unknown.

The marriage ceremony occupies four days. Agris perform the *saptapadi*, or seven steps round the sacred fire, as the binding part of the ceremony.

The betrothal is marked by a present of sugar by the bridegroom to the bride. In Kolába when a match is settled liquor is brought and drunk. After the fixing of the date by the Vatandár Joshi rice is made into *chapátis* and offered to the village and family gods. The first observance is the *Dej* ceremony, when the boy sends to the girl ten *mans* of rice and Rs. 40 in cash. On the second day the bridegroom and bride are covered with turmeric. On the next day the bridegroom goes to the bride's village and the actual marriage takes place. In the night a feast is held, when rice, pulse, one or two vegetables and pulse cakes are served. Little or none of the food is eaten, as the guests pass the whole night in drinking and often become uproarious. On the last day, that after the marriage, the bride's party go and feast at the bridegroom's house and then both go to the bride's father's house.

The essential part of the ceremony is the *antarpát*, a cloth being held between the two and *mantras* pronounced by the priest, followed by an exchange of garlands and the tearing away of the cloth, which completes the marriage.

A Bráhman conducts the ceremony. Rice is the usual offering to the gods, mutton and liquor being given only when the bridegroom is rich. The husband gives ornaments to the wife and her father a *dhotar* (waist cloth) or some small article of clothing to the husband.

Widow-remarriage is allowed, but must not take place till after the *shráddha* ceremony for the late husband. The technical name is *pát* and it is always conducted at night by a Bráhman, *mantrás* being recited by him on the woman and the man's turban, which is then replaced on the latter's head. The couple sit beside each other and their clothes are knotted together, the knot completing the ceremony. *Pánsupári* follows. There is no procession. The widow must marry outside the late husband's *gotra*. It is said that married women whose husbands are alive are not allowed to be present at the ceremony.

Divorce is granted in the case of women having leprosy, sometimes in the event of misconduct on her part. The *Panch* grant a *sod-chiti*. The name for divorce is *kádi modane*, though there is no ceremony of breaking straw. The bond is broken by the *ghatasphot* ceremony. Adultery is usually punished by simple fines if committed with a member of the caste.

The Hindu law of inheritance is followed. A sonless man's property goes to the nephew, daughters having no claim. The widow has a life estate, provided she does not marry.

Religion. In religion they are nominally Smárts and Bhágvats, but some of their death and other customs seem to suggest that they were once Lingáyats. They worship all Hindu gods, particularly Khandoba and Bahiroba, and in their houses have gold and silver embossed plates of their gods and goddesses. In the time of their monthly sickness women are considered impure for three days.

Of late they have become more careful observers of the rules of the Bráhmanic religion. Formerly there were no temples in small villages, but of late several temples have been raised to Máruti and Devi. They now keep religious books in their houses and read them to their wives and children, or go to hear them read and explained by Bráhmans. They have taken to chanting verses in their temples accompanied by music, and perform *bhajan saptáhas*, that is, loud public prayers which last for seven days. They make pilgrimages to

Násik, Pandharpur, Trimbak and Benáres, and in every way show a marked increase in their attention to religious matters.

They worship the usual Hindu saints both of the Vaishnava and Shaiva sect.

Each village has a god or goddess, *e.g.*, Padmábái, Vágheshwar (the two more common), and each family has a god or goddess of the *kulas* above mentioned, *e.g.*, Khanderáo for the Dhamáls, Bhaváni or Shiva for the Bhoirs, the Banyan for the Chaudharis, the Pipal for the Mhátres and Bhoirs, the rays of the sun for the Kenis, etc. It is to be noted that many families have the same god—Khanderáo is a favourite one—and different families of the same name often have different gods, *e.g.*, the Bhoirs in different places have Bhaváni, Shiva, the Pipal, etc.

Offerings are generally rice and milk boiled and mixed. Peacock feathers and flowers are set up at the houses concerned and music is played. Naradeva is worshipped on *Bhádrapad Vadya Amávásya.* Khanderáo is worshipped on *Kartik Vadya Pratipada.* The *naivedya* (rice and milk) is sent to the temple even though the god be worshipped at home, the offering being received by the Bhopi, an Agri. There are said to be no special gods for women and children. Possibly as in other castes, Satvái and Sitala may be worshipped by women.

Bráhmans, usually Palshe, sometimes Deshasth, Golak, Konkanasth or Mádhyandin, are employed for ceremonies connected with marriage and mourning. They are received on terms of equality by other Bráhmans of their castes. In some places Lingáyats are employed to conduct the death ceremonies.

Death ceremonies.

The dead are burnt as well as buried. The ashes of the burnt are collected on the third day and thrown into the sea, a creek, or river. Bones are collected and purified by a Bráhman with *mantras* and put in a bamboo-joint outside the door of the house.

In the case of a death from cholera, or the death of a child under five years old, the body is buried, the head towards the south and the face upwards.

Ancestors are worshipped, the first mourning ceremony being on the eleventh day after death. The *shráddha* ceremony is performed in *Bhádrapad*, yearly offerings of rice and milk boiled and mixed are made (1) to the sea, (2) to the cow, (3) to the crow, (4) to the family god (eaten by the offerer), (5) to Agni (thrown into the fire). These offerings are made both on the death day and in *Bhádrapad* (*Pitar's* day), a Bráhman conducting the ceremony except when a child under five dies, when no Bráhman is called and no anniversary celebrated.

To prevent the ghosts of childless ancestors and men who have died a violent death giving trouble, the only remedy is the giving of a cow to a Bráhman (*Gáyadán*).

In some places they call a Lingáyat priest to conduct their death ceremonies and observe a special rite, *mahebin*, on the second of *Mágh Shudh* (February-March).

The name Agri comes from *ágar*, a salt-pan. The synonym Khár-pátil is also derived from the occupation of working in salt. The original name seems to be Agle. They do not seem to worship any implement or object connected with this production of salt except the sea at times of mourning.

Their family gods or badges are the pine apple and the *hom*, myrobalan, mango, fig and wild mango.

Their *nisháni* (mark employed by those in signing who cannot write) is a plough or a mud hoe. At the first fall of rain the plough is worshipped, a *torana* of five mango leaves and flowers being made. The *ápta* tree is also worshipped at the Dasara. The *tulas* (sacred basil) is worshipped. The mango and young rice are also worshipped, some of the produce being offered to the god before being eaten.

Occupation. Their original occupation is variously stated to be the production of salt and agriculture. Not more than one-eighth of them work at salt manufacture and of the remainder about one-seventh have taken to carpentry, brick-laying and other professions, the main body being agriculturists. A few of them have begun to take Government wood and ferry contracts.

The majority of Agris are registered occupancy rayats paying assessments on their own holdings, or tenants (usually tenants-at-will) of superior holders to whom they pay rent in kind, which generally represents interest on a loan, the superior holders or tenants paying the proportionate assessment according to the *kabuláyat* between them.

A number of the poorer among them are landless day labourers, paid in cash or kind.

Some Agris work as carpenters or brick-layers, and may catch fish though not usually for sale.

Food. Agris drink liquor (*mahua*), eat pork (wild hog only), the flesh of cloven-footed animals (except oxen, buffaloes, bison and nilgái), fowl, fish and abstain from beef, monkeys, crocodiles, snakes, lizards, jackals and rats.

They accept food from Bráhmans, Prabhus, Vánis (the lowest caste), not from Kásárs, Sonárs, Lohárs or Maráthás. There is no distinction between "kachchi" and "pakki".

They can take water from any of the above-mentioned castes, but not from Kolis, Várlis, Thákurs or Nhávis.

They can also smoke with any of those from whom water may be accepted.

Kolis, Várlis, Thákurs and certain other castes accept food from Agris. Vánis are the highest caste that take water from them.

DAS AGRIS differ little from the Sudh-Agris in matters of religion and custom. But the following peculiarities may be noted.

The exogamous sub-divisions of the caste are:

Kadu.	Vaze.
Keni.	Sare.
Gharat.	Gavad.
Madhovi.	

A group of Das Agris is said to have settled near Máhim in the Sháhápur *táluka*. Marriage with this group is prohibited on the ground that its members are ignorant of the proper religious beliefs and practices.

Das Agris, according to their own story the thrum or *dashi*-wearing Agris, but more probably the Agris of impure descent or Dásiputras, are found chiefly along the tidal coast of the Tánsa and Vaitarna rivers east of the Railway line. The local story is that they are the descendants of an Agri's mistress whose children died in infancy. She vowed to the Mahár's god that if her children lived to grow up she would walk from her house to the Mahár's house with a cow's bone on her head and a tag or thrum of wool in the lobes of her ears. Her children grew up and she carried out her vow and was excommunicated.

A Palshe or Golak Bráhman is the priest of the caste.

On marriage occasions two (variously stated four or five) feasts are given at which rice is the principal item, or if the husband is well-to-do, mutton and liquor. The wife's father gives to the husband an article of dress or cooking pots or a cow or buffalo according to his means.

Their sect would seem to be Vaishnava. It is stated that the caste god is Vishnu.

The *mahua* and mango are worshipped in their season.

The supposed descendants of Giri, Puri and Bhárati are regarded as Gurus and visit the Bassein and Máhim *tálukas* once a year, when they are given *dakshina* according to individual means.

The ashes of the dead are taken, if means permit, to Násik or Nirmal.

URAP AGRIS, known also as Varap Agris, are found in several villages in Sálsette and Bassein, and are said to be Christian Agris, who reverted to Hinduism, some in 1820 and others in 1828. According to one explanation the name Urap or Varap is the Persian *urf* or *alias*, and according to another it is the word 'Europe'. Neither of these explanations is generally accepted, and it is thought more likely that the word comes from the Maráthi *orapne* or *varapne*, to scratch or sear with a hot iron, and that they got the name because they had to go through some purifying ordeal when they were let back into caste. This, moreover, is not inconsistent with their having formerly been Christians for a short time and reverted to Hinduism. They are also known as *Nave* or New *Maráthás*. Both in Sálsette and in Bassein the Urap Agris are considered lower than either Sudh or Das Agris, who neither marry or eat with them. They have a separate priest and a separate headman. Their manners and customs are the same as those of other Agris, and they worship the Hindu gods. The chief evidence of their having once been Christians is to be found in their surnames, which are Gomes, Soz, Fernan, Frutad and Minez. It is said that the Bassein Agris who reverted in 1820 had to pay Rs. 1,200. The priest who purified and took them back was Rámchandra Bába Joshi, a Palshe Bráhman. His caste for a time excommunicated him, but he was allowed to rejoin when he ceased to act as priest to the Uraps. One Bhái Mukund Joshi, also a Palshe, succeeded Rámchandra. Like the former he was put out of caste, but when he had a child to marry he did penance and was allowed to rejoin the caste. The name of the priest who admitted the Agris in 1828 (November 12) was Vithal Hari Naik Vaidya, a Palshe Bráhman of Bassein.

AGRI.—A sub-division of Kolis.

AGSALI.—Kanarese term for Sonár.

AGYANA.—A sub-division of Modh Bráhmans.

AHER.—A sub-division of Devángs.

Name.

AHIRS[1] numbered 104,894 at the census of 1901.

The name of the tribe, A'hir or Ahir, is a corruption of the Sanskrit Abhira. The Ahirs are numerous in Khándesh, Násik, Cutch, Káthiáwár and Pálanpur.

In the Census of 1901 the distribution of the Ahirs was shown as follows :—

	Total.	Males.	Females.
Bombay City ..	617	528	89
Ahmedábád ..	483	255	228
Cutch ..	25,854	13,379	12,475
Káthiáwár ..	74,248	37,742	36,506
Pálanpur .	2,629	1,337	1,292

A very few were returned in Khándesh and Poona, where they seem to have concealed themselves under some functional name. There were 24 Ahirs found in Aden.

The Ahirs of Cutch and Káthiáwár differ in many respects from those of the Deccan districts. It is thus necessary to describe them separately. Assuming that they were formerly one tribe, the differences are doubtless to be accounted for by their having a separate domicile and by the influence of the local tribes with which they have thus come in contact.

Exogamous divisions.

In the case of the Cutch and Káthiáwár Ahirs, there appear to be no exogamous sub-divisions except families bearing the same surname. The following is a list of the commonest surnames :—

Abalia, Baradia, Bhadarka, Bhádia, Bhenda, Bhibha, Bhoria, Bhuthar, Chavda, Chetaria, Chhuchar, Chudásame, Gagia, Gogham, Gohel, Goria, Jogal, Kachhot, Kámalia, Kanára, Khava, Khunti, Nandánia, Pidaria, Pithia, Rávaliya, Sanjva, Sindhav, Sisotia, Vádhia, Vasra and Vijva.

Endogamous divisions.

In Cutch and Káthiáwár the endogamous groups are of the territorial type. They are (1) Machhua, from the river Machhu

(1) The materials for this article were collected and compiled by Mr. D. R. Bhandarkar, Honorary Assistant Superintendent of the Ethnological Survey of Bombay.

near Morvi in North Káthiáwár, living in the district of Anjár; (2) Pranthalia, living in Vágad; (3) Boricha in Kanthi; (4) Sorathia, from Sorath in South Káthiáwár, in and about Anjár; and (5) Chokáda, from the Island Chorád in the Ran, living in Adesar, Palánsva, Sanwa, Umiyu, Játáváda, Bela and other parts of Vágád. These sub-divisions do not intermarry, but except the Sorathiás, who are held in disgrace because they once betrayed their chief, Ráo Navghan of Junágad, to the Emperor of Delhi, they dine with one another. In Káthiáwár, they are broken up into the endogamous sections: (1) Gujar Ahirs, who live in towns, and (2) Nesak Ahirs, who live in hamlets or *nes*.

History. According to Manu, Abhiras (Ahirs) are sprung from a Bráhman and an Ambashtha woman; according to the Brahma-Purána, from a Kshatriya father and a Vaishya mother; according to the Bhágvat Purána, from Vaishya parents; and according to an old tradition, from a Rajput slave girl and a Vaishya slave. One authority states that Ahir is derived from *ahi*, a snake, and that the Ahirs are of the family of Ahi of the Nág tribe.

The historians of Alexander (B.C. 325) speak of one Abisares as the ruler of the hills between Murri and the Márgala. It has been held by some that Abisares corresponds to Abhira, and that consequently the king Abisares, referred to by the Greek historians, denotes an Abhira chief. Similarly, the Abiria of Ptolemy (A.D. 150) and the Iberia of the author of the Periplus (A.D. 250), mentioned by them as situated in Upper Sind, have been identified with the Abhira of the Hindu writers. Hence, a theory regarding the southward movement of the Abhiras or Ahirs has been propounded in the Bombay Gazetteer that, in the time of Alexander, they were in the north-west of the Punjab, and that afterwards they migrated as far south-ward as, and were settled in, Upper Sind, about the time of Ptolemy. But this theory cannot commend itself to any one, as the identifications made are erroneous. The Abisares of Alexander's historians, as General Cunningham and Dr. Stein have shown, regularly correspond to Abhisáras, who are mentioned in the Vishnu Purán and Brihat-samhita as a distinct tribe from the Abhiras. Secondly, as rightly maintained by Mr. A. M. T. Jackson, Abiria or Iberia requires to be corrected into Sabiria; and, as a matter of fact, some of the manuscripts of Ptolemy's geography of India present this reading. If this reading is accepted, Sabiria, which, according to the Greek geographers, was in Upper Sind, can at once be recognized to be the Sanskrit Sauvira, which we always find associated with Sindhu, *i. e.*, the modern Sind, in Puránas and in inscriptions.

Another theory put forth by Sir Walter Elliot (Numismata Orientalia, pp. 88—90) is that the Ahirs are the northern section of "a great pastoral race, formerly holding an important place in the political constitution of India," of which the southern section was known as Kurumbas. According to this theory, there appears to have been only one pastoral race in India which was called Ahirs in the north and Kurumbas in the south. But as a matter of fact, we know that there are, at any rate in Northern India, many pastoral tribes other than Ahirs, such as the Gaddis, Ahars, Gujars, Gadainyas, Rewaris and Játs. Besides, if the Ahirs and Kurumbas are one tribe, it is hard to say how they came to be known by different names in the north and the south. The Ahirs are at present found not only in Cutch, Káthiáwár and Khándesh, but also in the Central Provinces, Central India, Bengal and the North-Western Provinces. Though the Ahirs are thus spread over such a large area, they are everywhere known as Ahirs. It is, therefore, inexplicable how the name should have been changed in Southern India, if Ahirs and Kurumbas are one tribe. Again, the Kurumbas or Kurubas are described by Shortt (Imperial Gazetteer, Vol. X, p. 311) as "small in stature, squalid and uncouth in appearance, with wild matted hair, and almost nude bodies. They are sickly-looking, pot-bellied, large-mouthed, prognathous, with prominent outstanding teeth and thick lips." The Ahirs of Gujarát are spoken of as well-made and fair with handsome features. Dalton, in his Descriptive Ethnology of Bengal (p. 315), says that the features of the Mathurábási Ahirs are high, sharp and delicate, and that they are of light-brown complexion. Although, as he further says, the features of the Magadha Gválas or Ahirs are undefined and coarse, and they are dark complexioned, and have large hands and feet, he and, with him, Risley regards them as having originally been Kols, who are quite distinct from the Kurumbas. These differences of features and bodily structure seem to show that the Ahirs and Kurumbas belong to different ethnical stocks.

A third theory held by Mr. Williams and Sir William Hunter traces the Ahir to a Scythian origin. It is alleged that the custom of a widow marrying the brother of her deceased husband, which is prevalent among the Ahirs, indicates a Scythian descent; also that the name Ahir is derived from the word *Ahi*, a serpent, and hence it is argued that the Ahirs, like the Takshakas (Takkas) and Nágas, which also signify snakes, are to be considered as of Scythian extraction, because " serpent-worship formed a typical characteristic of the Indo-Scythian races." These arguments have been ably refuted by Mr. J. C. Nesfield. He has correctly shown that the custom of a widow marrying her deceased husband's brother was not unknown to the Hindus, as Manu and other law-givers distinctly refer to it, and prescribe a law with regard to the division of property affected thereby. Again, snake-worship, as pointed out by Mr. Nesfield, is not peculiar to the Takkas, Nágas or Ahirs, but is prevalent all over India, and the derivation of Ahir from *Ahi*, a serpent, cannot be right, as the original name of the tribe is Abhira. As Ahir is a Prakrit corruption of the Sanskrit Abhira, it is absurd to derive the Prakrit word Ahir from *Ahi*, which is a Sanskrit word.

So far the arguments brought forward by Mr. Nesfield are sound and cogent. But the view he further propounds regarding the Aryan origin of the Ahirs is open to doubt. The traditions of Ahirs, whether in Bengal, the North-Western Provinces, Cutch or Káthiáwár, seem indeed to lend countenance to his view. Thus, the Ahirs identify themselves with the herdsmen (*gopas*) of the god Krishna, and claim Mathura and its neighbourhood as their orginal habitat. The Gujarát Ahirs further allege that they came from Mathura to Káthiáwár with Krishna, who is represented in the Harivansha to have been driven with the Yádavas before Kála-yavana and settled at Dwárka. Again, their sub-divisions Nandabansis, Jadubansis and Goálavansis, which are evidently called after Nanda, Yadu and Gopála (Krishna), seem to indicate their Aryan descent. But there are other considerations of greater weight, which run counter to this view. Thus, to judge from the Páli Játakas, Buddhist scriptures and the Indian epics, the *gopas* or cowherds seem to have settled down into an orderly and peaceable community long before the Christian era ; but the Ahirs, though many of them live as stationary husbandmen, have not yet thrown off their nomadic and predatory habits. Again Dr. Fick, who, for his essay on Indian castes in Buddhist times, ransacked Páli literature, nowhere therein met with the word Abhira. This suggests that the Abhiras were unknown when the Páli literature came into existence. Next, the various Puránas speak of the Abhiras as a tribe. Thus, the Váyu, Márkandeya and Mátsya Puránas locate the Abhiras in the north with the Válhikas, Vátadhanas and Kálatoryas, and in the south with the Shabaras, Pulindas and Vaidarbhas. The Allahabad pillar inscription of Samudragupta also refers to the Abhiras as a tribe, and places them on the frontiers of

Samudragupta's kingdom together with the Málavas, Yaudheyas and Mádrakas. The Abhiras were therefore a distinct tribe as much as the Válhikas, Vaidarbhas, Málavas, Yaudheyas, and so forth. But if the Abhiras had originally signified cowherds, they could scarcely have been described anywhere as a tribe. The cowherds (*gopas* or *gopálakas*), forming part of the Aryan social constitution can be appropriately spoken of only as a caste, just like Sonárs, Sutárs, Nhávis and so forth. Yet the very fact that the Abhiras are mentioned in the Puránas and inscriptions as a tribe, and not as a caste, presumably shows that the word Abhira did not originally mean a cowherd. Next, there is a cave inscription at Násik, which refers to the reign of an Abhira prince named Ishvarasena, son of Shivadatta. Another inscription, found at Gunda and dated 181 A.D., in the reign of the Kshatrapa Rudrasimha, speaks of his general Radrabhuti who is therein called an Abhira. If we carefully consider the names of these Abhiras, it will be seen that their first components, *viz.*, Ishvara, Shiva and Rudra, are all synonyms of the god Shiva. The Ahirs of the present day claim descent from Krishna. But if this really had been a fact, or in other words, if they really had been the descendants of the cowherds (*gopas*), whose hero was Krishna, the names of the rival god Shiva would never have formed components of the names of the Abhiras, whom we find mentioned in inscriptions. Hence the conclusion may be safely drawn that the Abhiras were by no means connected with Krishna and his cowherds even as late as about 300 A.D. to which the first of the two inscriptions mentioned above is to be assigned. Precisely the same conclusion is pointed to by the contents of the Harivamsha and the Bhágvat Purána. The up-bringing of Krishna among the cowherds and his flirtations with the cowherdesses are again and again mentioned in those works, but the word Abhira does not occur even once in this connection. The only words we find used here are *gopa*, *gopi*, and *vraja*. This is indeed remarkable. For the descriptions of the removal of Krishna as an infant to Nanda the cowherd's house, of his childhood passed in playing with the cowherd boys, and of his youth spent in amorous sports with the cowherdesses are set forth at great length, but the word Abhira is not even once to be met with there. From this only one conclusion is possible, *viz.*, that the Abhiras did not originally represent the *gopas* of Krishna. The word Abhira is first given as a synonym for *gopa* (cowherd) in the Amarakosha (A.D. 550), from which it follows that the Abhiras came to be identified with the *gopas* about 500 A.D.

The above remarks indicate that the traditions which are now current among the Ahirs and which connect them with Krishna, Mathura and the *gopas* are only later inventions. If the Ahirs even of the present day are not free from their nomadic and predatory instinct, they must originally have been a nomadic pastoral race, in direct contrast with the *gopas* or *gopálakas* of the period of the Páli literature and the Indian epics, whose habit was doubtless settled. Besides we have seen that the word Abhira did not at the beginning signify a cowherd (*gopa*) and that the Abhiras are described in the Puránas as a distinct tribe. The conclusion is, therefore, irresistible that originally the Abhiras did not come within the pale of Hindu society, but were a non-Hindu, if not a non-Aryan, tribe of shepherds or herdsmen, roaming with their cattle. This conclusion receives support from the Bhágvat Purána and Mahábhárata. In the former (II. 4. 18) the Abhiras are mentioned together with the Kirátas, Hunas Andhras, Pulindas, Pulkasas, Yavanas and Khasas, as the tribes that were purified by Krishna. The Kirátas, Pulindas and Pulkasas are aboriginal races, and the Hunas and the Yavanas are foreign tribes. And as the Abhiras are classed with them, the Abhiras were originally an aboriginal or foreign race. In the Mahábhárata (Musalaparva, VII), Arjuna is represented as coming to Dwárka and burning the dead bodies of Krishna and Balaráma. After the obsequies are performed, he is described as going to Indraprastha in conjunction with the widowed females of Krishna and the Yádavas with immense riches. On his way he was assailed in the Panchanada Desh or the Punjáb by a band of Abhiras, whom he was powerless to resist. They carried away the treasures and the widowed females whom Arjuna had escorted. These Abhiras are described as freebooters and are called herdsmen and Mlechchhas. From this it is evident that the Abhiras were a non-Aryan pastoral race, who combined the character of banditti with that of herdsmen. But it may be asked : how were the Abhiras then incorporated into the Goála or Gavli community ? The influence of fiction on the disintegration of a formerly uniform community or on the amalgamation of different tribes need not be dwelt upon. In process of time, the Abhiras must have, like many other foreign tribes, become Hinduised and adopted Krishna worship. And as community of occupation and religion is often thought to indicate community of origin, the Abhiras, who, like the original Indian *Gopas*, had become Krishna worshippers and were, like them, pursuing pastoral occupations, must naturally have been looked upon as coming from the same stock and soon incorporated with the *Gopas* into one community. Again, it is worthy of note that the Amarakosha gives *Ballava* as well as *Abhira* as a synonym for *Gopa.* In Bengal Pallabs or Ballabhs form an endogamous group, like Ahirs proper, of the Goála or Ahir caste. The Ballavas, therefore, must have originally been like the Abhiras a distinct tribe, who, like the latter, were by uniformity of religion and calling soon included in the Goála caste. Hence there can be little doubt that many other foreign or aboriginal pastoral tribes must have similarly been incorporated into the Goála caste. There is, therefore, much truth in Mr. Risley's assertion that the large functional group, known by the name Goála, comprises several heterogeneous elements.

Now, as regards the migrations of the Abhiras or Ahirs, we have seen above that Arjuna was overtaken and stripped of his possessions by them in the Panchanada country, which is undoubtedly the Punjáb. They are called freebooters and herdsmen. And there are yet many tribes on the frontiers and in Afghanistan, who combine the character of a freebooter with that of a herdsman. The Abhiras, therefore, in all probability entered India from Afghanistan. It is true that there are now few Ahirs in the Punjáb proper. But it must be remembered that of the present pastoral tribes we have in India the Abhiras are the earliest, as we find the Abhira general of the Kshatrapa Rudrasimha mentioned as early as 181 A. D. in the Gunda inscription alluded to above. The Ahirs, again, appear to be the least nomadic and predatory of all the pastoral hordes. Besides, the Ahirs are found much further to the east and the south than any other pastoral tribe. This explains the scarcity of the Ahirs in the Punjáb proper. From the Punjáb they gradually migrated eastward and southward. In the Mirzápur district of the present United Provinces there is a tract called Ahraura, which is equivalent to the Sanskrit Abhiravátaka. To the south of Jhánsi there is another province known as Ahirwár, which also corresponds to the Sanskrit Abhiravátaka. In Mr. V. A. Smith's opinion, the Abhiras, mentioned in the Allahabad pillar inscription, are to be located here. The tract Ahraura and the province Ahirwár, therefore, show that, in their eastward and southward movement respectively, the Abhiras or Ahirs settled there in large numbers and gained a permanent footing. Next, the Puránas speak of the Abhiras as having ruled as paramount sovereigns after the Andhrabhrityas. In confirmation of this, there is one Násik inscription which refers, as stated above, to the reign of an Abhira king called Ishvarasena. From the form of the letters, the inscription is to be assigned to the fourth century. The Abhiras, therefore, must have held sway over Khándesh, Násik, Káthiáwár, Pálanpur and Cutch. With regard to the latter provinces, this will be seen from the fact that, when the Káthis arrived in Gujarát, in the eighth century, they found the greater part of the country in possession of the Ahirs. In Khándesh, however, the Ahirs seem to have been of considerable importance. There is a well-known fort in Khándesh called Asirgad, the name of which, as Ferishta tells us, is derived from Asa Ahir, *i. e.*, the Ahir prince Asa, who built it. Again, in some villages, the original settlement seems to have been supplemented by a complete Ahir community. Further, many artisan classes in Khándesh are of two divisions, simple and Ahir. Thus besides Abhira Bráhmans and Ahirs proper, there are Ahir Sonárs, Ahir Sutars, Ahir Lohárs, Ahir Shimpis, Ahir Sális, Ahir Guravs and Ahir Koli . In some of these classes as among the carpenters, blacksmiths and goldsmiths, the Ahir element has remained distinct. Ahir carpenters and Ahir blacksmiths intermarry, but neither of them marry with the other sub-divisions of carpenters and blacksmiths. In other cases, the Ahir element has merged into the general class, and Ahir has come to be little more than a surname. The Ahirs form so large an element in the Khándesh population that Ahiráni is the local name for the Khándesh dialect of Maráthi spoken by 650,000 (Census 1901) or nearly half of the population. The Ahirs of Cutch and Káthiáwár also have preserved their own dialect, which differs in some respects from the Gujaráti. This indicates that the Abhiras had originally a language peculiar to them. This is in perfect accordance with what Dandin says in his Kávyádarsha about a dialect obtaining among the Abhiras and known as Apabhramsha. [It is not clear whether Dandin here refers to the Abhira tribe or simply the *Gopas*, *i. e.*, Indian herdsmen. But some important considerations show that the Abhira tribe is here in all probability meant. It is an established fact that the principal cause of the corruption of Sanskrit has all along been the inability of the aboriginal and foreign races to pronounce Sanskrit words. The Apabhramsha, *i. e.*, the language of the Abhiras, doubtless contains far greater corruptions than any other Prákrit. If, by the term Abhira used by Dandin, *Gopas* are understood, it is inexplicable how the *Gopas*, who, like the other Hindu castes of the time, formed part of the Aryan community, caused greater corruptions than these latter. These corruptions, therefore, can only be accounted for by supposing that they were caused by some non-Aryan tribes, speaking the *prákrits* that were already in vogue. Hence Dandiṅ must be understood as in all likelihood referring to the foreign tribe Abhira.]

Next, it is worthy of note that, although the paramount sovereignty of the Abhiras, spoken of by the Puráns, did not survive the sixth century, we still find some Abhira princes reigning in later times. Thus a Chudásama prince styled Graharipu and ruling at Vanthali near Junágadh is described in the Dyáshraya-Kávya of Hemachandra as an Abhira and a Yádava. In their bardic traditions as well as in popular stories, the Chudásamas are still called Aheraránás. In a stone-inscription at Amberi, the Bráhman chief Kholeshwar Singhana's general is represented as having destroyed the race of the king of the Abhiras. Again, many ancient remains in the Khándesh district are popularly believed to belong to the period of the Gauli Ráj. From the Archæological point of view, they are to be ascribed to the time of the Yádavas of Devagiri. It is, therefore, not unlikely that, according to popular belief, these Yádavas were Abhiras. This receives some support from the fact that Yaduvanshis even now are one of the most important sub-divisions of the Ahirs.

The widow of an Ahir marries her late husband's younger brother. Children are betrothed at any age, and married between eight and fifteen. Every year on one fixed day Ahir marriages take place. The rules vary in different divisions. Among Prámthalia Ahirs, the day is always the same—*Vaishákh Vad* 13th (April-May). In other sub-divisions the day varies, being fixed by their priests. On the marriage day, the women of the family with singing bring a wooden image of Ganpati, and place it in the marriage canopy. As the bridegroom's party drives up in carts, the bride's relations come out to welcome them with singing. The details do not differ from those observed at other Hindu marriages. During the day, to the sound of the drum *dhol*, the women dance in a circle and the men go through a stick dance, *dándiyarás*, moving in a circle and striking at each other with sticks. Two feasts are given by the bride's party and on the third day the bridegroom leaves, taking his wife with him.

They reverence Tulshishám (Lakshmi and Krishna) in the Gir and the goddess Máta. Of the local deities, they worship Habbáy of the Habba hill, fourteen miles north of Bhuj, and a Rajput saint called Váchara. They are said to observe no special forms of snake worship.

For the marriage ceremony they employ the Parajia Bráhmans who dine with the Ahirs, and are looked upon as a degraded class.

They have gradually given up cattle-herding and are now mostly carpenters, husbandmen and small landholders.

Food. They eat mutton, venison, and other game but not beef, and drink spirits in moderation. In Cutch the eating of flesh and the drinking of spirits though not prohibited is regarded as degrading.

Though they associate with Muhammadans, almost all flesh-eating Hindu castes will dine with them. They dine with Parajia Bráhmans, Rajputs, Rabáris, Anjna Kanbis, Cháraus, Bháts, Parajia Sutárs, Hajáms, Ojha Kumbhárs, Mális, Atits, Darjis, Luhárs and Rávals.

In the case of the Ahirs in Khándesh and Poona, enquiries show that the exogamous sub-divisions of the caste are: (1) Baldárkhám-vále, (2) Bánia, (3) Barodiye, (4) Biloriye, (5) Dhanoriye, (6) Hajáriye, (7) Hinvár, (8) Katáriye, (9) Kookreliye, (10) Moriye, (11) Patháriye, (12) Perwár and (13) Phulsunge. This enumeration does not claim to be complete. The Baldárkhámváles are so called from their peculiar custom of wearing their headdress slanting on one side. The Bániás are traders. The Hajáriyes were military officers under the Mughals, who had a command of one thousand horses. There are signs that these divisions once had totems as follows:—

Division.	Totem.
Baldarkhan	Mango and cotton seed.
Bania	
Barodiye	
Biloriye	
Dhanoriye	Bow.
Hajáriye	Not known.
Hinvar	Deer.
Katariye	Dagger.
Kookreliye	Dog.
Moriye	Peacock.
Pathariye	Mango and cotton seed.
Perwar	
Phulsunge	

The endogamous groups, into which the Deccan Ahirs are broken up, are: (1) Romábans, (2) Goálbans, (3) Dhidamvars, (4) Bharvathiyas, (5) Ghosis and (6) Gujars.

Marriage is prohibited within two degrees both on the male and the female side. There is no prohibition against the marriage of two sisters to the same husband. Two sisters can also be married by two brothers.

Social status, geographical position, difference of religious belief and change of occupation are no bar to intermarriage.

They are said to have once lived at Hyderábád (Deccan). On account of heavy taxation in the Nizám's country, they came with the English army to Ghodnadi at the beginning of the last century, but afterwards separated with the various regiments and went with them to Karáchi, Rájkot, Deesa and Poona.

In addition to what has already been said with regard to the Ahirs being a foreign race, two points deserve to be noticed. The existence of totemistic septs among them, as shown above, unmistakably stamps them as non-Aryan. Secondly, the name Romábans of one of their endogamous sections is worthy of note. Romá the first part of the name, is a regular corruption of the Sanskrit word *Romak*. The name *Romak* is frequently to be met with in Sanskrit works on astronomy, and from the indications therein furnished, it appears to have been the name of a town outside India, where the science of astronomy was cultivated, and from the people of which the Indian writers borrowed a great deal of their knowledge regarding astronomy. The town Romak has been identified by Professor Weber with Alexandria in Egypt; but other Sanskrit scholars demur to this identification. Whatever the correct identification may be, it is not unlikely that the name Romábans points to a foreign horde from Romak having settled in India and subsequently having been incorporated into the Gavli community.

The habit of the caste is settled, so far as the Maháráshtra is concerned. They seem to have no recognized head-quarters.

They do not admit outsiders into their caste.

Boys are generally married between fifteen and twenty. In the case of girls, both infant and adult marriages are in vogue. The adult marriage is mostly prevalent among the poorer classes, and those who can afford it marry their daughters as infants at the age of nine or ten. In the case of adult marriage, if a girl commits sexual indiscretions with a man of her caste but of a different *gotra*, he is compelled to marry her. If he happens to be of the same *gotra*, he is fined Rs. 40 or Rs. 50, with which the caste are treated to a feast. If, however, he is of a different caste, every attempt is made to conceal her sin; but if secrecy is impossible, she is turned out of the caste.

Polyandry is unknown, but polygamy is permitted, if the first wife is barren or is suffering from some incurable disease, such as leprosy. It is also allowed on the grounds of luxury and youth. In theory, a man may marry as many wives as he can afford to maintain. It is rare, however, in actual life to find more than three.

The offer of betrothal generally comes from the boy's family. **Marriage.** The father or the guardian of the boy goes to the house of the girl's father with two or three of his castemen. who inform the latter of the object of the former's visit. The girl's father gives them to understand that he cannot come to any decision unless he takes the consent of his relatives, and that consequently they should call upon him on some other day. The visit is accordingly repeated by the boy's father with the same or different mediators, and the girl's father is asked through them whether he approves of the proposed marriage alliance. This is the first part of betrothal, called *Galikuchi.* The mediators are paid a rupee or two for their trouble, which they spend on drinking. If both the parties have agreed to the connection, then on any day before marriage, the boy's father takes permission from the girl's father through a mediator to perform *Sagái* or the second part of betrothal, and asks him formally, although he himself may know it, where the house of the *nansár* or the girl's mother's mother is situated. On a fixed day in the presence of the caste *Panch* and his and the girl's relatives, the boy is attired in a rich dress, his forehead marked with a pigment spot, and his neck encircled with a flower wreath. The whole party, excepting the boy, then goes to *nansár's* house with liquor and a bag full of *dálmurmura* (parched grain and gram). There in the presence of the *Panch*, the girl's kinswomen throw water dyed with turmeric on the boy's kinsmen, and the boy's kinswomen on the girl's kinsmen. Afterwards *dálmurmura* is divided into as many shares as there are houses of the caste, and the shares of those who are not present are sent to their house. Those who are present take their share at the *nansár's* house and drink of the liquor brought. This *Sagái* may be performed a year, six months or even a week before the marriage.

With the permission of the girl's father obtained through a mediator, a Bráhman is asked to fix a lucky day on which the principal portion of the marriage ceremony is to be performed. On the first day of the marriage, the boy's father, with wool and silken garments, including *angia* bodice, *phadki* upper garment and *langa* robe, proceeds to the girl's house together with castewomen. This is called *Lagan.* At night about ten o'clock, the girl is dressed in these garments and seated in a squatting posture with her feet each on a mango twig, wrapped in a piece of blanket and the wool brought by the boy's kinswomen. Afterwards the castewomen touch one after another the girl's toes, knees, shoulders and head with rice, turmeric and oil and then throw these things to the other side of the girl. This ceremony is known as *Telchadhna.* The caste people who come with the boy's father dine at the girl's house. On the second day in the afternoon a branch of the mango tree is planted in the centre of the wedding booth, and under the branch is placed a red earthen jar smeared with cowdung and with grains of barley sticking to it. *Telchadhna* is repeated twice on this day—in the afternoon and at night, where the mango branch is planted. In precisely the same way, the same ceremony is gone through in the case of the boy at his own house, excepting that the mango branch is planted not in any marriage bower but only in the verandah. At the girl's house it is customary for her father on this day to treat his castemen to bread and *kadi* only. On the third day, the boy's father sends to the girl's house at his own expense a band of musicians, who play music till the *Barát* day is over. The fourth day is the principal day of marriage, called the *Barát* day. At about eight o'clock in the night the boy's father feasts his castemen with ghi, rice, vegetable and split pulse (*Barátki chhák*). In the bath room a square is formed with four brass vessels at the corners. The boy takes his seat in the centre. A cotton thread is several times passed round the brass vessels so as to form a railing. The boy is bathed by *suvásinis* or unwidowed women. Afterwards the boy puts on his wedding dress, which generally consists of a turban, *nima* (a tight tunic), *jáma* (a loose long tunic made of twice as much cloth as the *nima*), silken trousers and *patka* (a scarf of about nine hands in length to make the *jáma* tidy by passing it round the waist and over the shoulders). The boy then sits near the mango branch planted in the verandah. A *tháli* containing red water is placed before him, and his relatives and caste-fellows make him cash presents (*nauta*), which they put in the water. When this ceremony is over, the marriage coronet or *mohor*, made of the leaves of the *shindi* tree with pieces of looking-glass stuck into it, is tied on his brow, and he is seated on horseback holding a *katyár* or dagger in his hand, with which he never parts till the marriage ceremony is completely over. Escorted by his relations and friends and accompanied by torch bearers and musicians playing on drums and instruments, he sets out for the bride's (*Barát*). At the bride's house the procession stops, the bridegroom alights from his horse and is met by the bride's father or brother, who presents him with ear and finger rings (*antya*, *chhápbeda*), and a shawl is thrown over his shoulders. The bridegroom touches the front part of the booth with the point of his dagger. The marriage coronet or *mohor* is then taken off and placed on the booth. The bridegroom is ushered into the marriage hall. The bride's relatives bring sweetmeats for him to eat. When he has partaken of them, he goes out for a walk with his companions, who claim from him *yárána*, *i. e.*, a money present for sweets. The bridegroom afterwards returns, puts on the marriage crown and enters the booth. The bride is dressed in the yellow robe, yellow bodice and marriage coronet, especially brought for her by the boy's relatives with the *Barát* or procession. The bride so clad in her wedding dress is brought into the marriage hall and seated on the left side of the bridegroom, and the *nauta* or cash present ceremony is gone through by the bride's relatives and caste-people, three-fourths of the money so collected being claimed by her father and the remaining one-fourth by the castemen, who spend it on merry-making. The hems of the bridegroom's *patka* and the bride's *chaddar*, which completely hides her face, are tied into a knot (*Galjodä*), and the ceremony of *pámvpujái* is performed in the case of both by the bride's relatives. It is also known as the *dán* ceremony, which consists in bestowing gifts of ornaments, cows or fields on the bride and bridegroom, as contrasted with the *nauta*, where cash presents only are made. As soon as the *dán* ceremony is over, the bride's parents quit the marriage bower and sit in the house, and then comes the turn of *kanyádán*, which forms the essential and binding portion of the whole marriage ceremony. The bride and bridegroom walk six times round the mango branch in the presence of the Bráhman priest and caste-people, who are regarded as witnesses to their marriage. When the sixth turn is completed, some of the castemen go into the house and ask the parents of the bride whether they willingly bestow their daughter upon the bridegroom. When they express their perfect willingness, as might naturally be expected, the castemen return to the marriage hall, and the bride and bridegroom are made to take the seventh and last round of the mango branch, grains of red rice are thrown over their heads, and they become husband and wife. This essential and binding part of the marriage ceremony, known as *kanyádán*, is generally gone through at one after midnight. The kinswomen then take the couple into the house, and the ends of their marriage garments which were tied into a knot at the time of the *Galjoda* ceremony, are severed by a girl, who is paid a pice or two for her trouble. The bridegroom instead of going home rests for the remainder of the night in the house of his father-in-law's neighbour. On the fifth day the *kangna* ceremony is performed at night in the booth near the mango tree. The hems of the bride and bridegroom's clothes are tied together, the wool, brought to the bride's house at the time of *lagan*, is fastened round her wrist with several knots, and the bridegroom is asked to untie them. The time is one of much fun and merriment, the women of the house bantering and taunting the bridegroom, especially when he is long in untying them.

About two hours after *kangna* is over, the bride and bridegroom leave for the bridegroom's house either in a carriage or litter. If in a litter, the bridegroom accompanies her on foot, with the point of his dagger touching it. The next day, *i.e.*, on the sixth day of marriage, the bride is brought back to her father's house by her kinswomen. At night, the bridegroom also goes to his father-in-law's house with his relatives, and the *chála* ceremony takes place. This consists in the bridegroom handing over a glass of brandy to the bride's kinsmen, who conjure him to protect and feed his wife, and honour her relations. On the seventh or the last day the ceremony called *naktora* is gone through at the bridegroom's house. In an apartment where no males are allowed the whole marriage ceremony is imitated from beginning to end by women among themselves, by someone becoming a bridegroom, another a bride, a third a Bráhman priest, and so forth. This closes the marriage ceremonies.

Widow-marriage is permitted and practised. The natural feeling of the relatives of her dead husband is not to allow her to go out of their family, and consequently she is generally married to his younger brother or cousin by her mother-in-law or aunt-in-law. But if she is a grown-up woman, she may not accede to their wish, and may marry any man she likes. If she has a child, the usual practice is for her not to re-marry ; if, however, she is resolved upon re-marrying, no coercion is resorted to, but her children by her first husband are taken from her by his relatives. The form of the marriage ceremony is called *dharávna*, and is performed on dark nights of dark fortnights at about twelve o'clock. She is bathed by widowed women and dressed in a new robe. The ends of her and her new husband's clothes are tied into a knot, and then both are locked together in a room for the night. Marriages by the *dharávna* ceremony are not performed by Bráhmans, and are not attended by unwidowed women. The widow who is married is concealed for two days in the house where the re-marriage takes place, and her face is not seen till after she puts on glass bangles on the third day. If the man who marries the widow be a bachelor, he is first married to a *rui* plant and five stones are placed near it to bear witness to this marriage. This ceremony is known by the name of *áthvar*.

No divorce is allowed, and if the father of the girl refuses to send her to her husband's house, his castemen stop all connection with him. They do not allow him to rejoin the caste, unless he pays a fine of Rs. 100 or submits to the punishment of *chauk*, *i. e.*, a square formed of corn powder, wherein he is seated and beaten five times with a shoe.

Among Ahirs, the father is the absolute owner of the ancestral property, and the son cannot claim any portion thereof during his life-time. The daughter also cannot claim any portion of the *stridhan*, or the ornaments of her deceased mother, which go to the wives of her brothers.

Religion. They worship Shiva, Vishnu and other gods of the Bráhmanic pantheon, but their favourite deities are the goddess Bhavani and the god Krishna. Their preference for Krishna is accounted for by their belief that they are the descendants of the cowherds who were Krishna's companions. On the Janmáshtami day, they paint figures of Krishna on the walls, make offerings and distribute *panjeri* and *batáse*. On the Diváli holidays their daughters worship their cows and she-buffaloes, and are presented with new robes. During the same holidays, in an open space, their Chaudhari sets a cocoanut and betel leaves in the name of Krishna, before which incense and camphor are burnt, and the cows of all Ahirs headed by those of their Chaudhari are conducted in succession over the plain. When the procession is over they go through a stick dance, *tiprya*, first at the Chaudhari's and afterwards at the Bhagat's house. They worship the cobra on the Nágpanchmi day like all other Hindus, but have no special forms of snake-worship. The Hajáriyes have borrowed also the worship of Khandoba and Bahiroba from the Maráthás. The offerings made consist of a goat, rice and cocoanuts, but never a fowl, which they afterwards consume. When their cattle are seized with a pestilence, they propitiate the spirits, who are supposed to send it, by means of a *hom* or sacred fire, wherein are poured blood, flesh and wine, as offerings to them. Afterwards the Ahirs themselves take to drinking. Then a pig is buried underground, with only its head remaining above, and the cattle are made to trample upon it till it dies.

They employ Hindustáni Bráhmans, whom they call Pandes, to officiate at their marriages and register them. But on account of the scarcity of Hindustáni Bráhmans they have begun to invite Bráhmans of Maháráshtra to conduct their marriage ceremony.

They burn their dead, and only those that are not married or at any rate not betrothed, are buried on their backs with their heads to the east.

Death ceremonies. On the death of a person the old practice was for his son to give a feast to his castemen only on the third day. But since their

Bráhmans refused to accept any presents on that day, as it was too close to the day of the deceased's death, they brought into vogue the custom of giving another feast to the caste-people on the thirteenth, when rice and money presents are given to the Bráhmans. In the case of a childless ancestor his nearest relative gives the feasts in the manner just described. The ancestors in general are propitiated on any day in the month of Bhádrapad, as Ahirs are too illiterate to remember the date of their parent's death. They do not appear to observe any ceremony to propitiate a person who has died a violent death beyond that gone through in the case of an ordinary death.

Dhanoriyes, in the first part of whose name may be recognized the Sanskrit word *dhanus*, a bow, show their reverence for the rainbow, by making a bow to it whenever it is visible in the sky. Hinvárs claim to belong to the deer clan, make a bow to the animal whenever it comes within the range of their sight, refuse to eat its flesh, and are always ready to free it from the hands of a snarer by paying him whatever price he may demand for it. Katáriyes are of the dagger clan, as might be inferred from the word *katyár*, from which their name is derived. They are careful never to touch a dagger except on the marriage days, as they believe that by carelessness in this respect they are sure to meet with some accident or other with the dagger.(1) The name Kookreliyes is obviously connected with the Sanskrit word *kukkur*, which means a dog. With regard to these Kookreliyes, it is popularly believed that a person bitten by a mad dog is cured of his hydrophobia if he but goes to a Kookreliye's house and there eats bread prepared by him.(2)

Their hereditary calling is that of cowherds. Very few have departed from this their original occupation. There are none among them who have taken to tillage.

The sign characteristic of their caste is *kávad*, a bamboo lathe provided with slings at each end for holding pitchers, baskets and so forth.

They eat the flesh of goats, sheep and fowls. As northerners, they were formerly averse to eating fowls, like their castemen in other Food.

(1) " The rules not to kill or eat the totem are not the only taboos : the clansmen are often forbidden to touch the totem or any part of it, sometimes even to look at it * * Thus to a man of the Bukuean (Bakwain) or crocodile clan, it is 'hateful and unlucky ' to meet or gaze on a crocodile ; the sight is thought to cause inflammation of the eyes."—*Encyclopædia Britannica*, Vol. XXIII, p. 168.

(2) *Cf.* " Members of the serpent clan in Senegambia profess to heal, by their touch, persons who have been bitten by serpents"—*Encyclopædia Britannica*. Vol. XXIII, p. 469

parts of the country, but by coming in contact with the Maráthás they have taken to eating fowls. They do not eat scaleless fish, and of the scaly fish, they abstain from eating *mus*, *mhaisámachhi* and so forth. They drink liquor.

Maráthás eat *pakki*, *kachchi* and drink with Ahirs. They also smoke from the same pipe as the Ahirs, but the latter will not give them their *sápi* or the piece of cloth tied round the lower end of the pipe. Ahirs, however, will not eat *pakki*, *kachchi*, drink or smoke with Maráthás, but they will do all this with Bráhmans, whether of Northern India or Maháráshtra.

AHIR.—A sub-division of Shimpis, Gavlis, Dhangars, Kumbhárs, Sutárs, Sonárs, Chámbhárs, Kolis.

AHIRWARE.—A sub-division of Kattais.

AHMEDABADI.—A sub-division of Kacchiás, Momins, Desávál Vániás, Kadva Kanbis, Ghánchis, Shrimáli Sonis, Mochis.

AJHRA.—A sub-division of Sonárs.

AJWALIA.—A sub-division of Kachhiás.

AKARMASE.—A term applied to the irregular offspring of a caste. There is an Akarmáse sub-division consisting of such offspring in many castes.

AKSALI.—Kanarese term for Sonár.

AKSHMANGAL.—A sub-division of Bráhmans.

ALIA.—A sub-division of Bohorás.

ALIFSHAI.—A synonym for Benava.

ALIGJA.—A sub-division of Rabáris.

Name and origin.

ALITKARS, also called Pardeshi Alitkars or Sultánkars, numbering 136, including 66 males and 70 females, are found in Ahmednagar, Khándesh, Násik, Poona, and in the city of Bombay. They derive their name from *alita* (lac lodhra), their occupation being the dyeing of goat skins with the *alita* colour. As their synonym suggests, they are not an indigenous caste, but appear to be the descendants of one or two stray families from Márwár. They are quite distinct from the Musalmán tanners known as Sultánkars, except that they have dealings with them in their business of the dyeing of skins. They state that the founder of their caste was Dharmarája, the eldest of the Pándav brothers. The tradition of the caste is that they came from Nagar in Márwár about two hundred years ago to avoid the persecutions of the Pindháris. They regard Márwár, Ujjain, and

Burhánpur as the caste head-quarters. They have come much under the influence of local customs.

Divisions.

There are no endogamous divisions of the caste. Their exogamous sub-divisions are families having the same surname and deity. Their commonest surnames are Butele, Chaván, Khás, Sámbare, Chavale, Pilwál, Bhilwál, Sakune, Nagar, and Tipan. Marriages are prohibited between members having the same surname, and within four degrees of relationship on the boy's side and five degrees on the girl's side. Marriages are also prohibited between families with the same family deity. Marriage with a wife's sister is allowed after the wife's death. Two brothers are allowed to marry two sisters. Marriage is generally infant, though, amongst the poor, girls sometimes remain unmarried till after puberty. Maidens committing sexual indiscretions are excommunicated. If the men involved be castemen, they are fined and made to give a dinner to the caste-people. Polygamy is allowed and practised, but polyandry is unknown.

Marriage.

The offer of marriage comes from the boy's father, who has to pay a *dej* or bride-price of from Rs. 25 to Rs. 100 to the girl's father. The day for the marriage is fixed by a Bráhman, who conducts the service. The principal ceremonies of marriage are as follow :—

(1) *Kunku-lávne* or *Mágni* is celebrated in the same way as amongst the Kunbis, except that the girl's forehead is daubed with red powder by the wife of the caste headman or *Chaudhari*.

(2) *Sagai* or *Soyarik* takes place a week or two before the marriage and consists in the presentation of ornaments and a dress to the girl by the boy's father. A match cannot be broken off after this ceremony has been performed.

(3) *Lagnapuda*, or exchange of pieces of paper (on which the lucky moment for the marriage is written and into which rings are folded), between the fathers of the bride and bridegroom.

(4) *Halad*, or rubbing the boy and the girl with turmeric paste. After this cermony is performed, a marriage coronet is put on the boy's head and a dagger with a lemon fixed to its end is given into his hand. The boy must not part with the dagger till the marriage ceremony is over.

(5) *Máya phiravine*.—This ceremony is peculiar to the caste. It is celebrated on the day before the marriage. The boy is bathed and his head is smeared with red powder. Next, a married pair, with the hems of their garments tied into a knot, go to a potter's under a canopy held by four persons, holding in their hands a winnowing fan

containing uncooked articles of food. They bring from the potter twenty earthen jars of varying sizes and place them in two piles near the *torana-khámb* or chief post of the marriage booth. On each pile are placed five wheaten cakes. Near the jars are placed images of Ganpati and Shivasatidhiáti (a *sati* in the family) and they are worshipped. The boy, some unwidowed women, and other persons then walk seven times round the *torana-khámb* singing songs. While walking, the boy pours water from a jar which he holds in his hand.

This ceremony is also performed at the girl's house, with this difference that the number of jars is twenty-eight or thirty-six and that they are placed in four piles in the four corners of the marriage booth.

On the marriage day the boy goes in procession to the girl's house. At the gate of the marriage booth he is received by an unwidowed woman who holds in her hand a jar filled with water. The boy puts a rupee into the jar and his father pays Rs. 5 to the caste *panch* as their perquisite, and Rs. 3 for treating the party to sugared water. A wooden sparrow is tied to the door of the marriage booth. The boy touches it with the dagger in his hand and enters the booth. The marriage is then performed just after the fashion of the Kunbis, the essential portion being the *saptapadi*.

The re-marriage of widows is permitted. The widow's new husband has to pay Rs. 12-8-0 to the relations of the widow's deceased husband. The widow and her new husband are seated side by side; Ganpati and Varuna (represented by a water-pot) are worshipped; the water-pot is brought in close contact with the pair's heads; the widow's lap is filled; the ends of the garments of the pair are tied into a knot, and they are made to utter each other's names. This completes the ceremony. A bachelor is not allowed to marry a widow. Divorce is not allowed. A woman taken in adultery is turned out of the caste. The Hindu law of inheritance is followed.

The Alitkars resemble the local Kunbis in their religious observances, the special objects of their worship being Bahiroba of Nagar in Márwár and Bhaváni of Tuljápur. Every section of the caste has a separate family deity, that of the Chaváns being Shivasati-Váladhiáti; of the Sávares, Shivasati-Jugandhiáti, and so on. Their priests are the Deshasth Bráhmans. The married dead are burnt, the unmarried being buried with head to the south. The ordinary funeral rites are observed. The *shráddha* and *mahálaya* are performed for the propitiation of the deceased ancestors.

The hereditary occupation of the caste is the tanning of hides and colouring them with the *alita* dye. A few are agriculturists.

They eat the flesh of goats, sheep, fowls, and fish, and drink liquor. Food.

ALIYASANTAN.—A sub-division of Gánigs, Suppaligs, Mogers.

ALKARIS, also known as Shrávagi and Goláláre, numbering 313 (1901), including 142 males and 171 females, are found mostly in Khándesh, a few being residents of Ahmednagar, Násik and the Sátára Agency. The census figures do not appear to represent their number correctly, as many must have been included amongst Rajputs, the caste prefering to be called Rajputs rather than Alkaris. They assert that they are Rajputs, and came into the Deccan when Chitor was conquered by the Musalmáns, to avoid persecution. The only traces of Rajput customs to be found amongst them are the *mánakastambh* (ruby pillar) which is planted in the wedding booth at the time of marriage, and the fact that their family goddess is still the Bhaváni of Chitor. Upon settling in the Deccan, they took to preparing red dye from the root of the *alita* plant (Morinda citrifolia) as a means of livelihood, and thus came to be called Alkaris. From the accounts received, it appears that there is a Jain division of the caste, who abstain from flesh and prohibit widow marriage and divorce. This division accounts for the synonym Shrávagi, apparently a corruption of Shrávak, a common term for a Jain division of a caste. The term Goláláre is possibly a corruption of Galiára, a well-known caste of indigo-dyers in Gujarát, and may have been applied to the caste owing to its being connected with the occupation of dyeing. Name.

According to one account there are two endogamous divisions of the caste, Khárováva and Mithoba; according to another they have three endogamous divisions, Kachhavási, Málábanjári and Jyáphalond; while a third account states that they have two endogamous divisions, Proper and Lodhi Alkaris, who neither eat together nor intermarry. Their exogamous divisions, which are known as *kuls*, are Bhandári, Garode, Hátodia, Kuratiye, Ningote, Pachalore, Pacharatan, Paridhe, Pavayye, Ráyator, Shirodia, Tirole and Telva. Marriages are prohibited between members of the same *kul* and within four or five degrees of relationship. A member of the caste cannot marry his father's sister's, mother's sister's or mother's brother's daughter. Marriage with a wife's sister is allowed during the wife's life-time as well as after her death. Brothers are allowed to marry sisters. Polygamy is allowed and practised, but polyandry is unknown. Endogamous divisions.

Marriage is infant as well as adult. It is stated by some that sexual indiscretions on the part of a girl before marriage are connived at, the girl being excommunicated only if she becomes pregnant. If her seducer be a casteman, he is fined or made to give a dinner to the caste-people. According to another account, a girl accused of adultery with a casteman or a member of a higher caste can remain in the caste by cutting off a lock of her hair, by performing a penance, and by paying a fine or giving a dinner to the caste-people. All accounts are unanimous in stating that girls committing sexual indiscretions with members of lower castes are excommunicated.

Marriage ceremonies.

The offer of marriage comes from the boy's father, who has to pay a sum of money up to Rs. 200 to the girl's father. The day for the marriage is fixed by a Bráhman astrologer. Some of the accounts state that the ceremony is conducted by the caste elders, while others assert that it is conducted by a *pándiji* (a Bráhman priest). The principal ceremonies of marriage are as follows :—

1. *Sagai, Sáyakhada or Sákharpuda* or the betrothal, which takes place a few days before the marriage. The boy's father goes with friends and relations to the girl's father's house and hands over to the girl a packet of sugar and a rupee. Similarly a packet of sugar and a rupee are presented to the boy by the girl's father. Feasts are held at both places and the ceremony concluded.

2. *Mágni or kunku lávane*, in which the girl is presented with clothes and ornaments by the boy's father. The boy is presented with a dress by the girl's father, and feasts are held at both places.

3. *Oil and turmeric-rubbing ceremony.*—This ceremony is performed first on the boy and then on the girl. Unwidowed women sprinkle oil with a leaf over the head of the boy or girl, and throw rice grains thereon. The boy and girl are then rubbed with turmeric paste.

4. *Erection of the marriage booth.*—Four or five days before the marriage, a booth is erected at the girl's house, and a post of mango wood is planted in the booth and rubbed with turmeric paste. This post is called the *mánakastambha* (ruby pillar). All the ceremonies of marriage are performed near this post.

5. *Simantpujan*, or the reception of the bridegroom by the girl's father on the village boundary.

6. *Rukhavat*, in which sweetmeats are taken from the girl's house to the boy's house, and served to his mother.

7. *Bhát bharane.*—On the day following the boy's arrival at the girl's village, he, his parents and his relations are presented with articles of dress by his maternal uncle, a feast is held, and the party go and stay in a garden. There they stop for a day or two, after which the girl's father comes and presents them with articles of dress and takes them in procession into the village.

8. *Lagna* (the marriage proper).—When the bridegroom reaches the entrance to the marriage booth, he is received by five unwidowed women holding jars filled with water over their heads. The bridegroom puts into each of the jars a silver coin, and strikes a stick against a festoon of mango leaves which is tied to the door of the booth. Next the *mánakastambha* is worshipped, the boy and the girl garland each other, and the pair walk five times round the *mánakastambha,* the last act being known as *Chavaribhavari.*

It is stated by some that four yokes (of carts) are formed into a square and filled in with sand. The *hom* or marriage sacrifice is performed on this sand and the bride and bridegroom walk five times round the sacrificial fire.

According to some accounts, the garlanding of the bride and bridegroom by each other is the binding portion of the marriage service. According to others, the striking of a stick by the bridegroom against the festoon tied to the door of the marriage booth is sufficient to make a marriage valid. Some are of opinion that the *Chavaribhavari* is the essential portion, while a fourth party hold that the walking round the sacrificial fire by the bride and bridegroom makes a marriage indissoluble.

The remarriage of widows is permitted. A widow can marry any person whom she could marry as a virgin. A widow remarriage can be celebrated on a dark night, except a new-moon-day, during any month of the year. The widow and her intended husband are seated side by side on two low wooden stools, red powder is applied to the widow's forehead, and the ends of the pair's garments are tied into a knot, which completes the ceremony. Should a bachelor desire to marry a widow, he is first married to a ring.

A husband can divorce a wife if he cannot agree with her, or if her conduct is bad. A divorced wife can marry again by the widow remarriage form. It is said that the man who wants to marry a divorced woman has to pay a certain amount of money to her first husband. A woman taken in adultery with a casteman or a member of a higher caste can remain in the caste by paying a fine or giving a dinner to the caste people. If the offence is committed with a member of a lower caste she is excommunicated. The caste follow the Hindu law of inheritance.

Religion. Alkaris are Hindus of the Shaiva sect. Some are said to be followers of the Várkari and Rámdási sects. Their family goddess is the Bhaváni of Chitor. Goats and fowls are offered to Bhaváni on Tuesdays, which are eaten by the offerers themselves. Offerings to Bhaváni and Khandoba are also made on all days except the Mondays in the months of *Shrávan* and *Chaitra*. They observe all the Hindu holidays and make pilgrimages to all the sacred places of the Hindus. On the eighth or ninth day of the month of *Mágh* a ceremony known as *chakrapuja* is performed. A circle is formed of sixteen kinds of corn, and a dough lamp is placed over it called *Bova*. Near this the *devi* is worshipped with offerings of flesh and liquor. Members of other castes are not allowed to be present at this worship. Images called *virs* are installed in the name of persons who die accidental deaths or in battles. The *virs* are worshipped like gods and carried around in procession on marriage and other festive occasions. When an epidemic breaks out, the goddess supposed to preside over the disease is propitiated with offerings of goats and fowls, and in some places *ghi* or liquor is poured round the whole village affected. Musalmán saints are venerated. The religious teachers of the caste are Gosávis. Their spiritual head is Shankaráchárya. The majority of the castemen state that they have no priests, while a few assert that Bráhmans are employed for religious and ceremonial purposes.

Death ceremonies. The married dead are burnt. The unmarried dead, persons dying of small-pox, leprosy, cholera and snake-bite, and children whose hair is not clipped are buried with head to the north. The bones and ashes are collected and consigned to water on the third day after death. Those who can afford it carry the bones to a sacred river to be thrown into the holy waters. The castemen are feasted on the eleventh or thirteenth day after death. The *shráddha* is performed to propitiate the *manes*. In the case of violent death, as stated before, *virs* are installed in the name of the deceased.

The original occupation of the caste was the preparation of red dye from the root of the *ála* plant (Morinda citrifolia). The introduction of aniline dyes has seriously crippled this industry, and many members of the caste have taken to husbandry and day-labour in consequence. Some hold land under the *rayatvári* system. A few are in Government service.

They eat the flesh of goats, sheep, fowls, deer, partridges and fish and drink liquor. Food.

AMBEKAR.—A synonym for Kabbaligar.

AMBI.—A synonym for Kabbaligar.

AMBIG.—A sub-division of Kabbaligars.

AMIL.—A synonym for Lohána in Sind.

ANALA.—A sub-division of Kanbis.

ANANTKULYA.—A sub-division of Mahárs.

ANAVALA.—A sub-division of Bráhmans.

ANDHARIA.—A sub-division of Kachhias.

ANDHON.—A synonym for Andvan.

ANDVAN.—A sub-division of Mahárs.

ANGIGARA.—A sub-division of Mochis.

ANJNA.—A sub-division of Kanbis.

ANODHIA.—A sub-division of Bráhmans.

ANTYAJA.—A synonym for Mahár.

ARADHIS, or praying beggars, numbering 45 (1901), including 18 males and 27 females, are found in Khándesh, Poona, Sátára and Ratnágirí. They are a mixed class of men and women recruited from all castes of Hindus from Bráhmans to Mahárs and Mángs, and also from Musalmáns. If a man has no child he prays to goddess Bhaváni, and vows that if he is blessed with a child, it will be dedicated to the service of the goddess. Others stricken with dropsy, leprosy or consumption vow that if they recover they will become Arádhis in honour of Bhaváni. Men who are vowed to be Arádhis either by their parents or by themselves marry with women of their own caste. Arádhins or praying girls are considered devoted to their patron goddess and remain single. Name.

When a man wishes to become an Arádhi, he goes to one of the brotherhood and tells him his wish. He is asked whose Arádhi he wishes to become, whether of the Bhaváni of Tuljápur, of Kondanpur, of Rasan, of Kurkumb, of Nhyavar, or of Chatarshingi. He names one of these Bhavánis and is advised to go and visit his patron goddess. If he is not able to undertake the journey he is asked to bring about a pound of rice, turmeric, red powder, betel-nut and leaves, flowers and flower garlands, molasses, a yard of new white cloth, a cocoanut, five turmeric roots, five lemons, five sugarcanes, or in their absence Initiation ceremonies.

five stalks of Indian millet, five dough cakes, frankincense, camphor and money. A few neighbouring Arádhis, both men and women, are called, a spot of ground is cow-dunged and a low wooden stool is set in the spot. Over the stool the white cloth is spread and the rice is heaped on the cloth. On the rice is set a water pot or *Ghat* filled with water, five betel-nuts, ten betel-leaves and one anna to one rupee in cash. The mouth is closed with a cocoanut. Then five sugarcanes or five millet stalks are tied together and made to stand over the stool. At each corner of the stool are placed betel-nuts, lemons, dates, turmeric roots, dry cocoanut-kernels, and one of each is laid in front of the water pot. The presiding Arádhi is termed *Guru* and worships the water pot or *Ghat*. A dough-cake and a flower garland are dropped from the sugarcanes over the water pot, cooked rice and wheat bread and molasses are offered to the god, frankincense and camphor are burnt before it, and the teacher and other Arádhis four times repeat the word *Udava* or arise. The officiating Arádhi places a thick unlighted roll of oiled rags on the novice's head, throws a shell necklace over his shoulder so that it falls on his right, marks his brow with ashes or *angárika* and gives him two baskets to hold in his right hand. After the novice has made a low bow before the goddess and the Arádhi he presents the *Guru* with annas five to rupee $1\frac{1}{4}$, feasts the brotherhood, and is declared an Arádhi.

Arádhis are generally tall, thin and womanish, many of them either being eunuchs or copying eunuchs' ways. They have to beg at least at five houses once a week, on Tuesday, Friday or Sunday, and eat such food as is given them. When they beg, the Arádhi women wear their ordinary dress. The men wear a waistcloth or trousers, and a long coat reaching to the ankles, besmeared with oil. They tie their hair in a knot behind the head like women, use false hair, and deck their heads with flowers and ornaments, generally of brass. They wear nose and earrings of brass and false pearls, brass and shell bangles and wristlets. They wear a garland of *kavadi* shells hanging like sacred thread from the left shoulder down the right side. The shells, which are known as *Bhaváni kavadyás* or Bhaváni's Cowries, are yellow marked with patches of red. The necklace is composed of 35 to 40 shells; besides the necklace they wear shell ornaments round the head, neck, arms and fingers. They carry two bamboo baskets. One of the baskets is small, called Parashrám, with five shells stuck to it, the other is large and has no other name except basket or *Paradi*. From one of their shell necklaces hangs a cloth bag stuck round with shells in which they carry ashes or *angárika*.

which they rub on the brows of the charitable. On their head rests a thick rope of rags soaked in oil but not lighted. Dressed in this way they start begging at six in the morning and beg till noon. When they come near a house they call out *Yemái Tukáicha Jogwa*, *i.e.*, alms in the name of Yemái and Tukái. Sometimes four or five go in a band with drums or *sámel*, metal cups or *táls*, and the one-stringed fiddle or *tuntune*, and their baskets, and beg, singing and dancing.

Arádhis worship all Hindu gods and goddesses and observe all the Hindu holidays. Their priests are Deshasth Bráhmans. Except that their shell necklace and bamboo baskets are laid near the head and burnt or buried with them when they die, their marriage, birth and death ceremonies are the same as those of the caste to which they belong.

ARASINAPATALA.—A sub-division of Devangs.

ARE. A synonym for Marátha; a sub-division of Jogis and Kolhátis.

ARYA DAKSHINI VAISHYA.—A synonym for Kudále Váni.

ARYA VAISHYA.—A synonym for Kudále Váni.

ASADARU.—A sub-division of Mángs.

ASATKAR.—A sub-division of Lamánis.

ASHPURA.—A sub-division of Bráhmans.

ASHTAGARKAR.—A sub-division of Pánchkalshis.

ASSAL.—A sub-division of Dhangars, Maráthás and Mángs.

ATARS, numbering 349 (1901), including 184 males and 165 females, are a small caste of perfumers, found principally in Dhárwár and Sátára.

ATHARVAN.—A sub-division of Deshasth Bráhmans.

ATHAVAR.—A sub-division of Kátkaris.

ATHNIKAR.—A sub-division of Bánjigs.

ATISHUDRA.—A synonym for Mahár.

ATIT.—A sub-division of Bháts.

ATLAI-KHURASANI.—A sub-division of Khojáhs.

ATTE VAKKALS derive their name from *Atte*, an oblong ratten hoop used in carrying loads. They are found in the depths of the Ankola and Yellápur forests in the Kanara district. Their language and other circumstances seem to suggest that they have come under the racial influence of the Kunbis or some other community that emigrated into Kanara from Goa. **Name and origin.**

Their home language appears to be Kanarese corrupted by Konkani and by the addition of words which are neither Konkani nor Kanarese. In dress, organization, religion and customs they closely resemble the Hálvakki Vakkals. Their hereditary calling is *kumri* or wood-ash cultivation and cane plaiting. Since the prohibition of *kumri* cultivation, they work as labourers in betel leaf and cardamom plantations. Any one forsaking this occupation is put out of caste, and is re-admitted only on his giving a dinner to the castemen. Unlike the Hálvakki Vakkals, they do not eat the flesh of tame animals.

AUDICH.—A sub-division of Bráhmans.

AUTKAMBLE.—A sub-division of Mahárs

AVARTIA.—A sub-division of Káthis.

AYAR.—A sub-division of Telis.

AYAVALE.—A sub-division of Holáyás.

AYYA.—A synonym for Jangam.

BABA.—A sub-division of Dublás.

BABAR.—A sub-division of Hajáms.

ame. **BABRIAS,**[1] numbering 5,031 (1901), including 2,665 males and 2,366 females, are found chiefly in Bábriávád in the Sorath Pránt of Káthiáwár and are a mixed tribe between the Káthis and Ahirs, with whom they intermarry. They are called Durbar or Ghardera by the residents of the villages owned by them. All of them are land-holders, some of very large tracts, the head being the Tálukdár of Dedan. Their first settlement was at Thán. Whence they came is not known, nor whether they held Thán before or after the Parmárs.[2] One of their traditions tells of their being turned out of Thán by the Jhálás and of their migration to Bagásara, Amreli and Kundla, whence they were driven out by the Káthis. The district now known as Bábriávád was then in the hands of the Vále Rajputs. These were gradually ejected by the Bábriás with the allied tribe of Ahirs, and their lands parcelled among a number of petty proprietors.

visions. In spite of their small numbers, the Bábriás have no less than twenty-two sub-divisions. The three principal are the Kotilás,

(1) From materials contributed by Mr. K. G. Pandit, B.A., LL.B.

(2) The Tuár Rajput tribe reigned at Delhi for five generations, and, being driven thence, about the time of the Pándavas, Mánpál Tuár came to Thán and there reigned. He supported all the people who flocked thither. In consequence of a great famine the men went in search of work, leaving their wives and children at Thán. These were of different castes, and were hence called Báber or Buber, which in the local dialect signifies mixed. They afterwards left and established themselves in the south of the Peninsula hence called Bábriávád.—Sir George Le Grand Jacob.

Dhánkdás and Varus, under one or other of which all others are included. The Kotilás claim descent from a Jain Bráhman of Sihor, by name Trikam. According to their story, Trikam killed his brother and fled from Sihor. As he was resting at Talája, an Ahir's daughter named Deva Dorela fell in love with him. At that time Ethal Válo, the ruler of Talája, was distributing dowries to the maidens of his realm, and hearing that Deva Dorela was suffering from unrequited love, he persuaded the Bráhman to marry her, promising that his son should be the chief among Bábriás. Trikam's eldest son was called Kotila, presumably from the father's forehead mark or *tila*. He married a Bábria, and his descendants are said to have settled at Thán. As Ethal, the Válo chief, ruled at Talája in the fourteenth century, the introduction of his name shows that this branch had its origin about 500 years ago.

According to the bard, when Trikam was driven from Sihor, Origin
he rested near Talája and prepared his food. Deva Dorela, the daughter of a Talája Ahir, and her sister-in-law, passing to fetch water, saw the stranger clumsily trying to cook. Deva Dorela said "This handsome Bráhman seems in trouble." The sister answered in jest, "You are a maiden, cook for him." Deva Dorela replied, "I do as you bid, you are my eldest brother's wife, and to me as a mother." She filled her pitcher at the well, and as she passed the Bráhman she said, "I am your wife and your are my lord," but he answered not. Then she said, "If you say no, I kill myself." So the Bráhman agreed.

The Dhánkdás and Varus claim an earlier origin. The Dhánkdás state that they are descended from the Pándavas of Hastinápur one of whom took refuge at Anhilváda-Pátan, and, in the third or fourth generation, the representative of the family, called Bábria, migrated to Thán. His great-grandson was named Dhánkdia, a term thenceforth assumed as the patronymic of the clan. The Varus call themselves Jethvás and claim descent from Hanumán through Nagján, the father of Jethvo, the ancestor of the present Rána of Porbandar. Nagján's other son Halman had a son called Mek, who was united to a Dhánkda woman named Mál. Among the children of this marriage was Varu, from whom came the patronymic of the clan.(1) As the Dhánkdás and Varus are both more numerous than the Kotilás, it is probable that they are an older stock. But, beyond tradition, there is nothing to fix the date of their entrance

(1) Varu is said to have been born when the Jethvás ruled at Ghumli, and Ghumli is said to have been destroyed by Jám Bámnioji in the fourteenth century.

into Káthiáwár or of their settlement in Bábriávád. They are now an effete race, having fallen to the rank of peasant propietors and owning only thirty-four villages. Four of these belong to one set of proprietors, the Kotilás of Dedan; the rest are divided among the number of shareholders. For some time before and after Colonel Walker's settlement, the Bábrias lived almost entirely by plunder, and whatever independence they had was destroyed by Prabháshankar, the Diwán of Junágad, in 1792. For long after this they were fugitives. Their villages, sparsely scattered over the country, were mere collections of mud huts, and they levied blackmail on any traffic that passed through their limits. They gave free asylum to outlaws, and cherished their blood feuds more inveterately even than the Káthis. They happened to be settled in a little frequented part of the country, in a border land open to the feuds and rivalries of the Muhammadans of Junágad and the Rajputs of Gohilvád. They never came in contact with the British authorities, and thus retained their barbarous habits long after the people of the more open districts had settled into quiet and orderly ways. They gradually passed under the protection of the Nawáb of Junágad, and in 1864 the district was formally annexed to his dominions.

The Bábriás are a connecting link between the Káthis and the Ahirs. They marry their daughters to Sákháyat Káthis, and take in marriage the daughters of Ahirs. Each of their three divisions (which are exogamous) mentioned above is sub-divided into sections, the chief of which are as follows :—

1. *Dhánkda.*—(1) Bholáni, (2) Hadwáni, (3) Zumpáni, (4) Máyáni.

2. *Kotila.*—(1) Bholáni, (2) Deváni, (3) Fatepura, (4) Katedia, (5) Nandrukia, (6) Ranáni, (7) Shelláni.

3. *Varu.*—Desurka, Hánkáni, Undred.

Some of these sub-divisions are named after the villages originally inhabited by the tribe, *e.g.*, Nandrukia from the village of Nandruk. Others are derived from the head of the family who started them, *e.g.*, Bholáni from Bhol. The Bábriás assert that their *gotra* is Káshyap, that they have three *pravars* (the Kotilás have none) and that they belong to the Mádhyandin *shákha*. Marriages are prohibited between members of the same division and between those of the sub-divisions of which the division is formed. A Bábria can marry his mother's brother's or father's sister's daughter, but not his mother's sister's daughter. A man may marry two sisters simultaneously, or one after the death of the other. Two brothers

Marriage.

may marry two sisters. Boys are married between fifteen and twenty and girls between twelve and fifteen. An early age is generally preferred. Cases of sexual indiscretions before marriage are generally concealed and connived at for the sake of the family reputation, but if the attempts to conceal are likely to prove fruitless the girl is married to some one other than the affianced. Polygamy is allowed and practised, but polyandry is unknown.

The offer of marriage is made by the boy's father through a priest of the Zankhara Bráhman caste. The *des* or marriage present amounts to sums upwards of Rs. 50 according to the means of the boy's father. The marriage ceremonies resemble those of other tribes of Káthiáwár of similar standing.

The remarriage of widows is permitted. But so long as the younger brother of the widow's deceased husband is willing to keep her, the widow must consent to be his wife. If she does not wish to live with him but desires to marry another; the intended husband and the widow's father must pay up such fine as the caste determine, to the brother of the late husband. Subject to this restriction, a widow can marry anybody whom she would wed as a virgin. On an auspicious day the relations of both parties meet together, presents are made to the widow, and molasses are distributed among those present, this concluding the ceremony. The next day early in the morning the widow goes with her face veiled to fetch water. On drawing up the water she unveils her face. This act, it is believed, casts off all evils that might otherwise result from the widow's marriage. On her return home, the husband and wife look at each other's faces in a cup full of liquified *ghi*. This act, it is believed, confers blessings on the children, if any, of the husband by his first wife. Divorce is allowed, either party having the right to claim it. The tribe is governed by Hindu law with slight modifications.

Religion.

Bábriás are Hindus by religion ; some belong to the Rámdási sect, others to Rámánuja, still others to Swámi Náráyan. Vishnu is worshipped by preference though there are some who are Shaivas. Each section has its own tutelary goddess, the most common being Chámunda. The minor gods commonly worshipped are Shinkote, Mahámayi and Khákhuo. Those who can afford it make pilgrimages to Dwárka, Tulshi Shyám and other holy places. Goats are offered to gods on the *Dasara* day. The priests of the tribe are Zankhara Bráhmans, who occupy the same status as the other Bráhmans.

Death ceremonies. The dead are burnt. Children under six years and the leprous dead are buried. The corpse is laid with head to the north. The ashes or unburnt bones are preserved in a vessel and thrown into a pool of Tulshi Shyám near Dedán, round which most of the people own property. The rich send the ashes or bones to the Ganges. The *Shráddha* is performed for the propitiation of ancestors in general. The unmarried dead are propitiated by a mock marriage of a male and a female calf by those who can afford it.

Food. Bábriás eat the flesh of goats, sheep, fowls, deer, scaly and scaleless fish and drink liquor. They eat with Ahirs, Talabda Kolis, Rabáris and Bharváds. The Káthis, Rajputs and Mahiás eat with them.

BAD.—A synonym for Londhári.

BADAD.—A sub-division of Karád Vánis.

BADAKSHANI.—A sub-division of Khojáhs.

BADGI.—A synonym for Lohár.

BADHAIS, numbering 145 (1901), including 85 males and 60 females, are found chiefly in the city of Poona. They are immigrants from the Nizam's Dominions and Central Provinces, and, like their castemen there, are carpenters by occupation.(1)

BADIA.—A sub-division of Vághris.

BADIG.—Kanarese term for Sutár.

BAGADA.—A synonym for Bagaria.

BAGANIA.—A sub-division of Vághris.

BAGARIA.—A sub-division of Vániás.

BAGBAN.—*See* under Minor Musalmán castes.

BAGDE THAKAR.—A synonym for Thákar.

Name and origin. **BAGDIS,** numbering 1,324 (1901), including 734 males and 590 females, are a wandering caste with head-quarters in the Kolhápur State, from whence they range over the adjoining districts of Sátára, Ratnágiri, Poona, Belgaum and the States of the Southern Marátha Country. They describe themselves as Kolis, whom they much resemble ; and it is probable that originally they were Mahádev Kolis of the Western Gháts. Their present occupation is blanket-weaving, fishing and begging, and the women are of irregular habits. The Koli origin of the caste seems to be indicated by their tradition

(1) Census of India, 1911; Vol. X, Part I, page 228.

Bagdis

that they are descended from Válmiki, a hill Koli, before his advance to Bráhmanic rank. The head-quarters of the caste are in Bángrul. There are no endogamous divisions of the caste. The exogamous sections, which are identical with surnames, are Gálphádo, Rasankute, Karande, Bhole, Chaván, Singan, Garad, Sásane, Maráthe, Garane, Sálve, Ambale, More and Chaugule. Persons bearing the same surname cannot intermarry. Sameness of *devak* or marriage guardian is no bar to intermarriage. A member of the caste may marry his father's sister's or mother's brother's daughter. He cannot marry his mother's sister's daughter. A man may marry two sisters, and two brothers may marry two sisters.

Marriage is both infant as well as adult. If a girl commits sexual indiscretions with a casteman she is either fined Rs. 7½ or made to give a dinner to the caste-people. She and the offender are then purified by ashes being put into their mouths. If the man involved belong to a lower caste, the girl is excommunicated. Irregular behaviour on the part of the women, however, seems generally connived at, and is a source of profit to the caste. Polygamy is allowed and practised, but polyandry is unknown. Marriage.

The offer of marriage comes from the boy's father, who has to pay a bride-price of from Rs. 12 to Rs. 25 to the girl's father. The day for the marriage is fixed by a Bráhman who conducts the service. The betrothal, which is known as *sákarpuda* or *mágni*, takes place at the girl's house in the presence of the leading castemen, when red-powder is applied to the girl's forehead, her lap is filled, and a packet of sweetmeats is given into her hand by one of the boy's party. A feast to all assembled ends the ceremony. Three or four days before the marriage, the boy and the girl are rubbed with turmeric paste and oil at their respective houses. They are then bathed, marriage garlands are tied round their heads, and a weapon like a dagger with a yellow piece of cloth tied to its handle is given into the boy's hand, with which he must not part before the end of the marriage. The *devak* is installed on the marriage day after the fashion of the Kunbis, both at the boy's and the girl's house. It consists of the *pánchpálvi*, or leaves of five kinds of trees, *viz.*, mango, *umbar* (Ficus glomerata), *shami* (Prosopis spicigera), *pipal* (Ficus religiosa) and *pipri* (Ficus tsiela). In some places the leaves of the *rui* (Calotropis gigantea) and *jámbul* (Eugenia jambolana) are also used. In the evening the bridegroom is taken in procession to the girl's village and seated in the temple of Máruti. He is received there by a party from the bride's house; a turban is presented to him, and he is taken to the girl's house. He is made to stand in the marriage booth with face to the east; the girl is brought and made to stand in front of him; a cloth is held between them, marriage verses are repeated, and the cloth is removed. Next, the pair are seated on two low wooden stools, and a *kankan* or marriage wristlet is fastened round the right wrist of the boy and the left wrist of the girl. The *kanyádán*, or handing over of the bride, is then performed, in which water is poured on the bridegroom's hands (*i.e.*, the *dháre* ceremony) by the bride's parents and a rupee is paid to the bride's mother by the bridegroom. A dinner to the caste-people brings the marriage ceremonies to an end.

The remarriage of widows is permitted. A widow can marry her father's sister's or mother's brother's son. She cannot marry her mother's sister's son or a member belonging to her late husband's section. A widow remarriage can be celebrated on any dark night except the new-moon day, during any month of the year except *Bhádrapad*. A Bráhman priest and leading members of the caste are present on the occasion. Unwidowed women are not allowed to attend the ceremony. The widow and her new husband are seated on a blanket or on two low wooden stools. The widow is presented with a robe, a bodice, glass bangles and toe ornaments, which she puts on. Red powder is applied to her forehead by the Bráhman priest. A pot covered with half a dry cocoanut kernel containing a betelnut is worshipped by the pair, and the Bráhman priest brings the pot into close contact with their heads. The widow's lap is then filled with wheat, betelnuts, turmeric roots, and dry cocoanut kernel, the ends of the pair's garments are tied into a knot, and they are made to utter one another's names, which completes the ceremony. In some places the tying of the ends of the pair's garments is the only ceremony performed after red-powder is applied to the widow's forehead. On the Poona side a bachelor is allowed to marry a widow after he has first married a *shami* bush. In Sátára and other places a bachelor is not allowed to marry a widow.

A husband can divorce a wife if he cannot agree with her or if her conduct is bad, by paying Rs. 7 to the caste-*panch*. The amount is spent on a dinner to the caste-people. A divorced woman can marry again after the fashion of the widow remarriage ceremony. A woman taken in adultery with a member of a lower caste is put out of the caste.

Religion. The caste follow the Hindu law of inheritance and belong to the Hindu religion. They worship all Bráhmanic gods, but the chief object of their worship is Mhasoba, whom they regard as their family god. They also worship Khandoba, Shidoba, Jákhái, Jokhái and other minor gods. They worship their implements of work on the *Dasara* day, when a goat is killed and eaten. Images of deceased ancestors embossed on silver plates are installed and worshipped on holidays and on marriage and other festive occasions, when a goat is killed and castemen are feasted. Every year in the latter half of the month of *Ashádh* a goat is offered to Mariái or the cholera goddess, and a *gondhal* dance is performed by every family of the caste. When an epidemic breaks out, the deity supposed to preside over the disease is propitiated with offerings of cooked food. They observe all the Hindu holidays, but rarely go on pilgrimages. Their priests are Bráhmans, who are received on terms of equality by other Bráhmans.

Death ceremonies. Those who can afford it burn the dead: the rest bury. The unmarried dead, persons dying of leprosy, and children up to ten years old must be buried. At burial the corpse is seated with face to the east. The bones and ashes of those burnt are consigned to water. A stone is fixed on the spot where a corpse is buried. On the twelfth or thirteenth day after death the castemen are feasted.

The hereditary occupation of the caste is weaving blankets and fishing. They also beg and tell fortunes. Of late a few have taken to agriculture. They are day labourers and are paid either in cash or in grain. They do not catch crocodiles or tortoises.

Food. They eat the flesh of goats, sheep, fowls, doves, hares and fish, and drink liquor. They eat the leavings of the higher castes.

BAGVAN.—A synonym for Bágbán.

BAHMON.—A caste of Native Catholic Christians.

BAHROT.—A synonym for Bhát and Cháran.

BAHURUPI.—A synonym for Bhorpi.

BAIL.—A sub-division of Ods.

BAILGAMMAR.—A sub-division of Kabbaligars.

BAILNE KOMBAR.—A synonym for Ghisádi.

BAILUGAR.—A sub-division of Kabbaligars.

BAINU DIVAR.—A sub-division of Halepaiks.

BAIRAGI.—A term applied to a sect of Hindu ascetics, mostly Vaishnavites.

BAJ.—A sub-division of Vániás; a sub-division of Khedáwál Bráhmans.

Name and origin.

BAJANIAS, or Musicians, also called Dholis or Drummers, numbering 6,869, including 3,510 males and 3,359 females, are found all over Gujarát with the exception of the Surat district. The largest number is found in Ahmedábád, Kaira and Pálanpur State. They claim to take their name from their patron Vajai Máta, and state that the founder of their caste was Shámalia Náyak. They are a class of wandering minstrels and rope dancers, and move about the country during the fair season under a headman or *náik* in gangs of ten to twelve. While on the move, they live in tents, which they carry with their kit on small donkeys. In the rainy season they live in temporary huts, roofed with grass and branches. They remain in each camp for a fortnight. Every gang has certain beats assigned to it. If the members of one gang enter the beat of another, they are excommunicated. In the Ahmedábád district some Bajániás have taken to cultivation and are known as Gám-wáste Bajániás in consequence.

Endogamous divisions.

There are two endogamous divisions of the caste, Bajániás proper and Málvi Bajániás. The latter perform athletic feats on ropes, and are considered for that reason to be the social inferiors of the former. The two divisions eat together but do not intermarry There are three exogamous sub-divisions of the caste—Parmárs Ghodias and Nághors. The common surnames are Ghodia, Rakhera, Bakla, Dasiawala, Devránu, Thori, Shamlani. Marriages are prohibited between members of the same sub-division, and within seven degrees of relationship. A member of the caste cannot marry his father's sister's, mother's sister's or mother's brother's daughter. Marriage with a wife's sister is allowed during her life-time as well as after her death. Two brothers may marry two sisters. Marriage is infant or adult. Both boys and girls are married from six months of age up to twenty years. Sexual license before marriage is not tolerated. If a person is found guilty of cohabiting with a maiden, he is bound to a post and beaten, and may, it is said, be even hung from a tree over a lighted fire. He is also fined Rs. 40, out of which Rs. 8 are spent on treating the caste *panch* to liquor, the remaining sum being paid to the girl's father. The girl is only beaten ; no other punishment is inflicted upon her. Polygamy and polyandry are not allowed.

Marriage.

The offer of marriage comes from the boy's father, who has to pay Rs. 12 to the girl's father. Out of this amount Rs. 4 are spent on purchasing clothes for the bride. The day for the marriage is fixed by both the parties in consultation with each other. The marriages of Bajániás generally take place in the rainy season. Thursdays and Fridays are considered to be the luckiest days for marriage. The service is conducted by the bride's uncle or by an elderly member of her family. On the marriage day the bride and bridegroom are rubbed with turmeric paste at their houses, and the bridegroom is taken in procession to the bride's house. He is received by the girl's mother, and his party are treated to a dinner. Next, the hands of the bride and bridegroom are joined, the skirts of their garments tied into a knot, and they are led outside the house into a square formed by setting empty earthen pots at each corner. They are fed with a dish of *kansár,* and, in the presence of the bride's father or other elder male relation, they are made to walk four times round the square, this being the binding portion of the ceremony.

The remarriage of widows is permitted. A widow cannot marry a paternal or maternal cousin. She may marry a member of her deceased husband's family or his younger brother. Widow remarriages are generally celebrated on Sundays, Tuesdays or Thursdays at the temple of Shikotaria Máta. The *báva* or worshipper of the goddess conducts the service. Before marriage, the widow receives a double share from the earnings of the troop to which her husband belonged, because, they say, the widow of Sámbhai Náik, the patron saint of the caste, was allowed a double share on her husband's death. The *báva* then ties the skirts of the pair's garments into a knot, daubs their foreheads with red powder, and puts rice grains on them. Next, their heads are brought into close contact with one another, and they are made to play a game of odd-and-evens with copper coins. The party then return to the house of the widow's new husband, the knot of their garments is untied. and the ceremony is over.

Divorce is allowed with the sanction of the caste *panch,* if the husband and wife do not agree with each other, or if the wife's conduct is bad. A divorced woman can marry again by the widow remarriage ritual. If a woman is taken in adultery, she can remain in the caste by paying a fine of Rs. 12 to the caste-people. The caste follow the Hindu law of inheritance.

Bajániás are Hindus of the Bijmárgi sect. The special deities of their worship are the Shikotaria and Khodiár goddesses. Their patron saint is Sámbhai Náik, who is said to have lost his life in performing a wonderful athletic feat and is probably a deified ancestor who followed the caste profession. They do not go on pilgrimages. They observe all the Hindu holidays. They believe in witchcraft and evil spirits. When an epidemic breaks out offerings are made Religion.

to the Khodiár *máta*, portions of which are distributed amongst the caste members. Their priests worship the *mátás* and are members of the caste, the marriage ceremony being conducted by the bride's uncle or other elderly member of her family.

Death ceremonies. The dead are buried. The corpses are carried to the burial ground to the beating of four drums. On the tenth and eleventh days after death, rice balls are offered to the deceased. On the twelfth day caste-people are feasted and a cot and some clothes belonging to the deceased are given to his sister's son. No ceremonies are performed for the propitiation of the deceased ancestors.

The Bajániás make their living by playing on drums and flutes at weddings, by carving the legs of country cots, and by selling needles, buttons, wooden ladles and mortars for pounding rice. They also make baskets and ropes of *munj* fibres (Saccharum arundinaccum) and hemp, repair grindstones and work as field-labourers. They carry off cattle and are guilty of other field offences. The Málvi Bajániás earn their bread mainly by performing athletic feats on ropes.

Food. They eat flesh of all kinds, except the flesh of the pig and the cow, and drink liquor. It is stated by some that they eat beef. They eat food cooked by all classes, except Dhedás, Mochis, Pomlás and Musalmáns. They refuse food prepared by Darjis. The reason of this prohibition is, according to the Editor of the Bombay Gazetteer (Vol. IX, Part I, p. 503), that at their weddings Darjis offer their god the image of a cow made of *gol* or molasses ; but the statement seems improbable in view of the fact that members of the caste are commonly alleged to eat beef.

BAJ DARMARIA.—A sub-division of Khedávál Bráhmans.

Name. **BAKADS** or Bákadigs, numbering 442 (1901), including 218 males and 224 females, are found only at Ankola in the Kanara district. According to the Bombay Gazetteer the word *bákad* is said to come from the Hindustáni *bák*, a crop estimate, because their wages are paid in grain and not in cash. But it seems probable that the caste is an outcaste section of the Bánts, recruited to a certain extent from other castes also. Thus the endogamous divisions are known as—

Endogamous divisions.

1. Konkan
2. Jain
3. Kunbi
4. Kare Vakkal
5. Sheragi Vakkal
6. Bánt
7. Marátha

which suggest recruitment from the castes so named. They call themselves Bánts, a Kanarese term for warriors, and state that they came from Bantavál, a village near Mangalore, and that they were once Bánts, the chief middle class of *Shudra* husbandmen in South Kanara, and that they were put out of caste and have no intercourse with the parent stock.

There are no exogamous divisions of the caste. Polygamy is allowed and practised, but polyandry is unknown. Girls are married from the age of five till after they attain puberty ; boys between sixteen and twenty-five. They practise the *dháre* ceremony at marriage.[1] The remarriage of widows is permitted. A husband can divorce a wife on the ground of her misconduct. A divorced woman is allowed to remarry. The caste follow the Hindu law of inheritance.

Religion and ceremonies.

Bákads are Hindus. They worship all village gods and goddesses and the ancestral cocoanuts. The object of their special devotion is Venkataráma of Trupati where they go on pilgrimage. Their chief holidays are *Shimga*, *Dasara* and *Bhánd* or car festivals. They have great faith in soothsaying and witchcraft. When an epidemic breaks out goats, fowls and he-buffaloes are offered to Mareyamma. Their priests are Havik Bráhmans. The dead are either burnt or buried. Their ceremonies are similar to those of the Komárpaiks. Those who have died of small-pox, leprosy and cholera are buried. Male children on whom the hair-cutting ceremony is not performed are buried. Female children are buried up to the age of five. At burial the corpse is laid with head to the south. The ashes of the burnt are collected and thrown in the sea or a river on the third or ninth day after death. Then the chief mourner bathes, cooks rice, and making three balls of the cooked rice, places them on a tender cocoanut. Next, three flags, one yellow, one black and one white, are erected in front of the balls, and plantains and betel leaves are offered to them. Then a jar is filled with water, three holes are made in it, it is placed near the balls, and the chief mourner returns home without looking behind his back. The ceremonial impurity expires on the eleventh day. On the twelfth day a man of the caste is presented with articles of dress, a sickle and a dining plate ; and a feast is given to the caste-people. They are chiefly husbandmen. They eat flesh and drink liquor. They rank with Kotegars and Mukris. Until recently they were known as Holebákads or impure Bákads, whose touch was considered to defile.

(1) The *dháre* ceremony consists in joining the hands of bride and bridegroom and pouring water or milk over them. It seems to be a Southern India practice ; but it is found in many Bombay castes.

BAKADIG.—A synonym for Bákad.

BAKAR KASAB.—A sub-division of Musalmán Kasáis.

BAKHTARGARA.—A sub-division of Mochis.

BALAM.—A sub-division of Bráhmans.

BALDE.—A sub-division of Kumbhárs.

BALE.—A sub-division of Mángs.

BALGAR.—A sub-division of Jogis.

BALHI.—A sub-division of Mahárs.

BALKAMBLE.—A sub-division of Mahárs.

BALSAD MALLAVA.—A sub-division of Mallavas.

BALSANTOSHIS or Children Pleasers, a class of wandering beggars, numbering 36 (1901), including 22 males and 14 females, were recorded in 1901 in Sátára, Kolhápur and the Southern Marátha Country. They are fortune-tellers and weather prophets. They wander about the streets in the early morning, turn into some houses, and shower blessings on the children, always ending with '*Bálsantosh*', *i.e.*, bless the babies. They look and speak like Kunbis and resemble them in food, dress, religion and customs.

BALSARIA.—A sub-division of Dublás.

BAMCHA.—A sub-division of Vághris.

BANAJI.—A sub-division of Dhangars.

BAND.—A sub-division of Kolis.

BANDATE.—A sub-division of Rámoshis.

BANDE.—A sub-division of Bhandáris ; a synonym for Barge.

BANDEKAR VANI.—A synonym for Kudále Váni.

Name and origin.

BANDHARAS or Galiárás, numbering 1,053. including 532 men and 521 women, are found in the five Gujarát districts and in Cambay, Rewa Kántha and Cutch. In Ahmedábád, Broach and Cutch they are known as Bandhárás, elsewhere as Galiárás. Their occupation is dyeing cloth, the name Bandhára being derived from *bándhane* (to tie) owing to the process of tying knots on the cloth to be dyed and thus forming a pattern of the portions that remained knotted and uncoloured. Galiára is from *gali* (indigo), the dye most commonly in use. There are no endogamous divisions of the caste. There are numerous exogamous divisions known as Patoria, Gawaria, Hansotia, Tarsangia, Mandika, etc., named after localities. Marriage is prohibited within seven degrees of relationship. A man may marry two sisters, and two brothers may marry sisters. The caste is believed to have come from Márwár, but it no longer intermarries with the parent stock. They claim a Bráhman or Kshatriya origin, dating from the reign of King Janamejaya, and relate obviously mythical anecdotes of the manner in which they were deprived of their sacred thread. Girls are married up to the age of eleven, and boys at any age. Polygamy is permitted but it is not common. Either the boy's father or the girl's commences negotiations for a marriage, the date for which is fixed by a *joshi*. The ceremony is conducted by a Bráhman. Five or six days before the marriage, Ganpati is installed at the houses of the parties to the match, and they are rubbed with turmeric. Then follow the ceremonies known as *mátristhápan*, the painting of the images of Mátáji and Ganpati on a white-washed wall; *mandap muhurta*, the erection of the marriage booth, when a bough of the *shami* (Prosopis spicigera) and a branch of a mango are installed; *ukardi notarvi*, the drawing of figures on the ground with rice grains to the accompaniment of songs, and other similar ceremonies common to many Hindu castes. Marriage.

The joining of the hands of the bride and bridegroom, before they walk round the sacred fire together, is the binding portion of the ceremony.

The remarriage of widows is permitted. The widow cannot marry her husband's elder brother, but she may marry a younger brother. Such marriages must take place on Tuesday, Thursday or Sunday. Should a bachelor desire to marry a widow he must first be married to a *shami* bush. The ceremony consists in throwing rice at each other and looking at a lamp concealed in an earthen pot. It is believed that if a married woman sees this lamp she will become a widow. Divorce is not ordinarily allowed. The caste follows the Hindu law of inheritance.

Bandhárás are Vaishnavs of the Rádhávallabha sect. On the eighth day of each month they worship the *mátás* or divine mothers, and they also worship the *pipal*, *tulas*, etc. In times of sickness they propitiate the *mátás*. The ordinary Hindu death ceremonies are performed, but the caste has one curious custom, *viz.*, if the corpse of a man who has died a violent death is not found, an image of *darbha* grass is made in his name and burnt. Religion.

Though the caste occupation is dyeing with indigo, some members weave, sell drugs, trade in betelnut and tobacco, and make *chunam*, or copper pots. They are not agriculturists.

Food. They abstain from eating flesh or drinking liquor. They will only take *kacchi* prepared by Bráhmans or Vánis.

Name. **BANDIS** or bondsmen, numbering 7,920, including 3,781 males and 4,139 females, are found in Kárwár and Kumta and along the coast as far as Honavar in the Kanara district. They are either the descendants of slaves, either imported or captured in war, once the property of the landed proprietors, or the offspring of women who have served as concubines or been taken in adultery. The caste is still recruited from the latter source, but a movement is in progress which aims at the adoption of the ceremonies and restrictions of the higher castes, and in this manner the true origin of the caste is likely in time to be obscured. They now style themselves Konkan Devdigs, Bhandáris, Kád Haviks and Kád Konkans, with a view to concealing their real status as Bándis.

The members of the caste now profess to belong either to a particular *gotra* or *bali*, but it seems unlikely, in view of the system of recruitment which prevails, that the majority of members could belong to a *bali* or *gotra* other than that of some outside caste from which they were recruited. Regular exogamous sections do not seem to exist in the caste.

Marriage. Marriage is rare, the girls generally becoming prostitutes. The married women lead irregular lives, though avoiding men of the impure castes. In cases where marriages occur, the offer is made by the boy's father, who has to pay a bride-price to the parent of the girl. The ceremonies are the same as in the case of the Devlis. Divorce is allowed. Succession is through females.

Bándis are Hindus. They worship the Bráhmanic gods and evil spirits and offer blood sacrifices to the latter. Their spiritual teacher is the head of the Smárt monastery at Shringeri. Their priests are commonly Karnátak Bráhmans, but recently priests of the Havik caste have been employed. From the *guru* of the Rámchandrapur *math* a portion of the caste has recently obtained permission to wear the sacred thread. The concession is rewarded by an annual offering to the *guru*. The dead, formerly buried, are now burnt. The *shráddha* is performed.

Bándis are employed as domestic servants by Bráhmans and other high caste Hindus. Their chief work is to clean copper pots and pound rice, cowdung the floor, and bring head-loads of firewood. But some of the men work as carpenters and a few as husbandmen.

Food. They eat fowls, fish, mutton and game, and drink liquor.

BANGAD.—A sub-division of Devángs.

BANIA.—A synonym for Vánia and Lohána.

BANIAN.—A synonym for Bhátia.

BANIANI.—A synonym for Bhátia.

BANJARA.—A synonym for Vanjári.

BANJARI.—A synonym for Vanjári.

BANJIG.—A sub-division of Lingáyats.

BANKAR.—A synonym for Halde Máli.

BANT.—A synonym for Bákad.

BANT HASLAR.—A sub-division of Haslárs.

BARAD.—A sub-division of Audich Bráhmans.

BARADI.—A sub-division of Girnára Bráhmans.

BARAHATTA.—A synonym for Cháran.

BARAMASE.—A sub-division of Joháris and Ghadshis.

BARATH.—A synonym for Cháran.

BARDAS, numbering 20 (1901), including 17 males and 3 females, are found only in the hills to the north-west of the Akráni and Dhedgáon in Khándesh. They are basket-makers and wandering cultivators with more skill than their neighbours. They rank between Bhils and Kunbis.

BARDA.—A sub-division of Bhils.

BARDESHKAR.—A sub-division of Gaud Sárasvat Bráhmans.

BAREKARI.—A synonym for Kabbaligar.

BARGE.—A sub-division of Dhangars.

Name and origin.

BARIS, also known as Pánwáles or Leaf-sellers, numbering 6,696 (1901), including 3,412 males and 3,284 females, are found principally in Khándesh and Thána, a few being residents of Poona and Sholápur. Fourteen were returned as Musalmáns. It is doubtful how far the Census figures are accurate, as Báris are likely to be confused with Támbolis, who are sometimes called Báris on account of the similarity of occupation between the two castes. There are a large number of Báris in the United Provinces, who are described as house-servants, makers of leaf plates and cups, and torch-bearers.(1) The Báris in Behar also sell betel leaves.(2) There is a caste of

(1) Crooke's Tribes and Castes of the North-Western Provinces and Oudh. Vol. I, p. 201.

(2) Risley's Tribes and Castes of Bengal, Vol. I, p. 68.

husbandmen in Thána known as Báris, who are said to have come from Gujarát. Most of their women still speak and dress like Gujarátis. These facts seem to point to the conclusion that the original home of the Báris was in Northern India, whence a small number migrated into the Deccan through Gujarát and Berar, probably in the days of the Mughal Emperors of Delhi.

Divisions. There are three endogamous divisions of the caste, of a territorial type: (1) Deshi, (2) Nemádi, *i.e.*, those living beyond the Ajintha Gháts, also called Kumrawata or Ghátole, and (3) Vaswade.(1)

The exogamous divisions of the caste are known as *kuls*, the chief of which are the following :—

Asápure.	Hage.	Povár.
Arambi.	Ikáre.	Sagure.
Berad.	Kolhe.	Saupure.
Bhagure.	Kálbhánde.	Táde.
Chaván.	Kature.	Telangade.
Dhámane.	Másode.	Vasule.
Gárote.	Musale.	
God.	Panchod.	

Marriage. Marriages are prohibited between members of the same *kul*. A Bári cannot marry his maternal uncle's, paternal aunt's, or maternal aunt's daughter, nor his sister's daughter. Marriages cannot take place within three degrees of relationship. Marriage with two sisters is permitted. Two brothers are allowed to marry two sisters. Polygamy is allowed and practised, but polyandry is unknown. Girls are generally married from two to nine, boys from five to twenty-five. Amongst the poor, girls sometimes remain unmarried till after they come of age. Sexual license before marriage is not tolerated. Girls committing sexual indiscretions are turned out of the caste.

The offer of marriage comes from the boy's father. The day for the marriage is fixed by a Bráhman, who conducts the service. The principal ceremonies of marriage are as follows :—

1. *Sagái.*—The boy's father goes to the girl's house, with a few castemen. In their presence the maternal uncles of the boy and the girl, or their fathers' sisters' or mothers' sisters' husbands, throw a garment on one another's turban and give five betelnuts to one another. This is the betrothal or *sagái*. On this occasion the caste *panch* receive Rs. 2. from the boy's father and Re. 1 from the girl's father, which

(1) These sub-divisions are said to contain 98, 84 and 52 *kuls* respectively.

are spent on a dinner. A match cannot be broken after the *sagái* has been performed. Any one disobeying this rule is put out of caste for twelve years.

2. *Kunku Mágne.*—The boy's father goes to the girl's house and presents her with ornaments, clothes and sweetmeats. Ganpati is worshipped and the caste *panch* are paid Rs. 6 by the boy's father and Rs 2. by the girl's father. This amount is spent on liquor or a feast.

3. *Halad.*—On any day, within five days before the marriage, the boy is seated on an iron tripod and rubbed with turmeric paste by five unwidowed women, singing songs. What remains of the turmeric paste is carried to the girl's and she is rubbed with it similarly. Next *kankans* (cotton rags dipped in oil with betelnuts and pieces of blankets tied on to them) are tied to the wrists of the boy and the girl.

4. *Telan.*—On the day before the marriage the boy and the girl are seated on two low wooden stools at their respective houses, and oil is sprinkled on them, with a leaf, by women singing songs.

5. *Rukhavat.*—The ceremony of sending sweetmeats, accompanied with music, to the boy, on the day before the marriage.

6. *Lagna.*—The girl's father sends a horse to the boy's house and the boy starts in procession, riding the horse, for the girl's house. When he reaches the door of the girl's house, the girl's mother waves round him a wooden pestle and a water-pot, and, throwing a bodice on his shoulder, leads him to the god-room, into the house. There the girl is seated in a basket, facing west. The boy is seated facing her in another basket. The betelnuts of the *sagái* and the marriage epistles (*lagna patrikás*) are put into the basket of each, a cloth is held between them, marriage verses are repeated. When the verses are over, the cloth is removed, and the betelnuts and the marriage epistle in the girl's basket are put into the boy's basket and *vice versa.* At night a dinner is held and Rs. 18 are given to the caste *panch* by the boy's father. On the day following, a dinner is held at the boy's house.

7. *Zálzenda.*—A ceremony in which the boy and the girl are taken on the shoulders by two persons, and a dance takes place to the accompaniment of music. This terminates the marriage.

The marriage ceremonies of the Poona Báris greatly differ from the above. Their marriage guardian or *devak* is their house-goddess. On the day before a marriage they give their house-gods to a goldsmith to clean at his house. When cleaned they bring the gods home with music, and instal them with much ceremony, worshipping them with great pomp, playing music, and offering them abundance of sweet-smelling flowers. Oil-cakes are prepared and a feast is held. The boy and girl are rubbed with turmeric at their houses, either on the same day or on the day after relations and friends are feasted. On the marriage day the boy goes on horseback to the girl's house with kinsmen and kinswomen, friends, and music. At the girl's, water and rice are waved round his head, he is taken into the house and made to stand, either on a low wooden stool or in a bamboo basket, facing the bride, and a cloth is held between them. Bráhmans repeat marriage verses, and at the end throw grains of red rice over the heads of the boy and the girl, and they are husband and wife. The skirts of the boy's and girl's robes are tied together, they are seated in the marriage booth, and the sacrificial fire is lighted. They are then taken before the marriage-gods and bow low before them. Their garments are joined, and the boy and the girl repeat one another's names in couplets. On the following day, presents of clothes are exchanged between the two houses, and, in addition, the boy is given a plate or *thála* of queen's metal, a brass or copper water-pot, and a brass lamp. The relations on both sides throw finger-rings and copper and silver coins into the plate for the girl. The girl's parents take the girl in their arms, and, saying to the boy's parents, "all this while she was ours, now she is yours," place her in the boy's arms. The boy's mother puts a little sugar in the girl's mouth, sticks a rupee on her brow, and looks in her face. The skirts of the boy's and the girl's robes are tied, and they are seated, either on a horse or in a carriage and, accompanied by kinsfolk and friends, go in procession to the boy's house. Before entering the house, the boy's mother waves cooked rice and bread over their heads, and throws the rice and the bread away. The boy and girl go into the house,throw grains of rice over the heads of the household and marriage-gods, bow before them, and retire. On the following day, if well-to-do, they give a feast of sweet cakes or *puran-polis*, or, if poor distribute betelnuts and leaves. This ends the marriage ceremony.

The remarriage of widows is permitted. A widow cannot marry her father's sister's, mother's sister's, or mother's brother's son, or a member of her late husband's section, unless she marry her deceased husband's younger brother. A widow re-marriage can be celebrated on any day of the dark fortnight of a month. A few castemen and relations on both sides are present on the occasion. The widow and her intended husband are seated side by side, facing the east, and betelnuts and dry dates, placed on a heap of rice grains, are worshipped, a Bráhman priest repeating *mantras*. Next the widow holds in her mouth betel-leaves, which are bitten by her intended husband. A stick of raw sugar is similarly bitten off. The widow's intended husband takes the same articles in his mouth, one after the other, and the widow bites them off with her teeth. This completes the union. A dinner is given to the caste people. Should a bachelor desire to marry a widow he is first married to a silver ring. Divorce has been lately introduced. A husband can divorce a wife, with the sanction of the caste *panch*, if he does not like her or if he cannot agree with her. A divorced woman can marry again by the widow remarriage form. A woman taken in adultery is excommunicated. The caste follow the Hindu law of inheritance.

Religio

Báris are Hindus of the Shaiva sect. Their family deities are the Bhawáni of Tuljápur and Khandoba. They worship all minor gods and all the plants and animals held sacred by the Hindus. They also worship their betel-leaf gardens. They go on pilgrimage chiefly to the shrine of Bahirám (the god of the betel-leaf gardens) at Renále in Khándesh. They observe all the Hindu holidays. Goats and fowls are offered to Khandoba on Sundays and to Bhawáni on Fridays and Saturdays. These offerings are generally received by the worshippers of the temples. Stone images are made of those women who die leaving behind many children. These images are installed at the roots of banyan trees, beyond village boundaries, and they are worshipped along with the trees on the *vatapaurnima* day (the full moon day of *Jyeshtha*). Musalmán saints are venerated. When cholera breaks out, the cholera goddess is worshipped every Friday, with offerings of turmeric powder. red powder, bangles, and articles of dress and food. When small-pox breaks out, Kákásat is worshipped, with offerings of water. The *gurus* or religious teachers of Báris are Gosávis of the Giri, Puri or Náth sect. Their priests are Deshasth Bráhmans, but the death ceremonies are conducted by the caste elders.

Death ceremonies.

The married dead are burnt, the unmarried being buried, with head to the south. After the corpse has been burnt the funeral party bathe and return to the chief mourner's house, carrying *nim* (Melia azadirachta) leaves. At the mourner's house a lamp is kept burning on the spot where the deceased breathed his last. The mourners take a look at the lamp, sprinkle *nim* leaves round it and return to their homes. On the next day cow's urine and water are sprinkled on the spot where the corpse was burnt, and a piece of bread, molasses and *ghi* are placed thereon. On the third day, accompanied by a couple of near relations, the chief mourner goes to the burning ground, gathers the ashes, and throws them into the river or stream, sprinkles cow's urine, turmeric, red powder, and flowers on the spot where the body was burnt, burns frankincense and offers parched grain and sweetmeats to the spirit of the dead. He gathers the unburnt bones in an earthen jar, puts them somewhere in hiding, and returns home. The chief mourner is considered unclean for ten days. At the end of ten days he either buries the bones in the jar or throws them into water. The ceremonies to be performed on the tenth day differ in different localities. In Khándesh, the funeral party go to a river, the chief mourner bathes, and is shaved by a barber, and he again bathes and cooks rice. He makes a hole into the bank of the river and places in it a dough lamp, fed with *ghi*. Next, cowdung cakes are placed over the lamp and it is covered with sand. A stone from the river is then taken and worshipped, with offerings of rice balls, and both the stone and the balls are thrown into the river. The party then bathes and returns to the house of mourning. In Poona, on this day, the chief mourner feasts the four corpse-bearers with a dish of wheat and molasses called *thuli* and curry. A flower, dipped in butter, is drawn from the shoulders to the elbow of each of the corpse-bearers, and they retire. In Khándesh the corpse-bearers are feasted on the third day. On the eleventh day the chief mourner goes to the burning ground, sets twelve or thirteen wheat balls in a row, drops red powder and flowers over them, and throws them into water. On the twelfth day, the chief mourner and his family-priest go to the burning-ground and make a three-cornered mound and set three earthen jars on it. Over each jar is placed a small wheat cake and a rice ball, and at each corner of the mound is planted a flag, six or eight inches long. The mourner retires to some distance and waits for the crows to come, and when a crow has come and touched one of the balls, he bathes and goes home. The Bráhman who accompanies him is presented with a pair of shoes, an umbrella, a dining-plate or *tát* and a water-pot or *támbya* and four to eight annas in cash. On the thirteenth day the chief mourner fills a plate with food and throws it in a stream or river. The caste is feasted and treated to a dish of sweet cakes or *puran-polis*. A near relation presents the chief mourner with a turban and the mourning or *dukhavata* is over. The *shráddha* and *mahálaya* are performed for the propitiation of the deceased's ancestors.

The hereditary occupation of Báris is growing betel-leaves and selling them wholesale to retail dealers. The poor amongst them also sell them in retail. A few have taken to other occupations, such as carpentry. Some are day-labourers. The implement, which is characteristic of the caste, is the *nakharda* (an iron nail), with which they cut betel-leaves.

They eat the flesh of goats, sheep, fowls, and all sorts of fish, and drink liquor. The lowest well-known caste with whom they eat, drink and smoke are the Kunbis and Phulmális, who also eat food cooked by the Báris. Food.

BARIA.—A sub-division of Kolis.

BARKAR.—A synonym for Kabbaligar.

BARKE.—A sub-division of Mahárs.

BAROCHI.—A sub-division of Khárvás.

BAROT.—A sub-division of Nágar **Bráhmans**.

BARUNIA.—A sub-division of Dublás.

BARUTGAR.—*See* under Minor **Musalmán Castes**.

BARVASHIA.—A synonym for Bhangi.

BASAVI.—A sub-division of Lingáyats.

BAVA.—A synonym for Bairági.

BAVACHAS, numbering 906 (1901), including 416 males and 490 females, are found chiefly in Ahmedábád with a few families in Kaira, Káthiáwár and Mahi Kántha. In the Baroda State they numbered 1,661 at the Census of 1901. The origin of the term Bávacha is unknown. They are grooms, grass-cutters and camp followers, and are described as such in the Baroda Census Report for 1901. They claim to have been originally Vániás, and allege that they were degraded to their present status by eating the white flowers of the *shiri* or *varshádodi*, a kind of vegetable. They have neither endogamous nor exogamous divisions. Marriages are generally prohibited within seven degrees of relationship. Marriage with a father's sister's, mother's sister's or mother's brother's daughter is not allowed. Marriage with a wife's younger sister is allowed and brothers are allowed to marry sisters. Polygamy is allowed, but polyandry is unknown. Boys and girls are married from the age of seven to fifteen. A girl committing sexual indiscretions is fined Rs. 28 and is made over to her seducer. If a married woman is seduced, she is similarly punished. If, however, her husband desires to retain her, the seducer is fined Rs. 7-8 by the community. Name and origin.

The offer of marriage comes from the boy's father, who has to pay a sum of Rs. 22 to the girl's father. The day for erecting the marriage booth is fixed in consultation by both parties. The service is conducted by the caste headman who is called *kotvál*. Marriages generally take Marriage place on Sundays. Three days before marriage the boy and girl are rubbed with turmeric paste and the goddess Káli is worshipped. The bride is then taken to a house opposite the bridegroom's, and puts on a new dress. The bridegroom is brought in and placed by her side. Next, the relations of the bride and bridegroom carry them on their respective shoulders, and tying the hems of their garments into a knot take seven rounds accompanied by women singing songs. These women are presented with a bottle of liquor. In the evening the party go to the bridegroom's house, where a cock is killed in honour of the occasion, the bridal pair are taken to the seat of the goddess in the house, and rice grains are thrown over their heads. On the following day kinsfolk and castemen are treated to the flesh of the cock killed on the previous day, with sweets and liquor.

The re-marriage of widows is permitted. It is generally celebrated on Sunday. The widow's intended husband has to pay Rs. 12 to her father. The widow is taken to his house, a lamp fed with *ghi* is lighted, the pair are seated by the side of the lamp on a low wooden stool, their wrists are tied together with a cotton thread, red powder is applied to their foreheads, and grains of rice are thrown over their heads, thus completing the ceremony.

Divorce is allowed, with the sanction of the caste *panch*, if the husband and wife cannot live in harmony. The wife's intended second husband has to pay a sum of Rs. 22 to her parents. Out of this sum a piece of cloth worth Rs. 1-4 is bought, and thrown over the woman. A piece is then cut from the end of the cloth and is thrown into the house of the woman's intended husband. The woman puts on the cloth and goes to his house, thus completing the divorce. In some places, when a husband wants to divorce his wife, he cuts off a piece of her garment and sends her to her father's house with Rs. 5 and some rice. A woman taken in adultery is fined Rs. 7 or Rs. 8. The Hindu law of inheritance is followed.

Religion. Bávachás are Hindus of the Bálásundri sect. They observe all the Hindu holidays. On the *Dasara* day they offer a goat to the goddess, and the flesh is distributed among all castemen. When an epidemic breaks out, the goddess Kákábaliá is propitiated. They have no priests. All their ceremonies are conducted by the caste *kotváls*.

The dead are generally buried with head to the south. Castemen are feasted on the third day after death. No ceremonies are performed for the propitiation of the deceased ancestors.

The main occupation of Bávachás is selling grass and working as grooms. Some are labourers.

They eat the flesh of goats, sheep and fowls and drink liquor. Food. They eat food cooked by all castes except Dheds, Bhangis and Musalmáns. Formerly they thought themselves polluted by contact with Dheds, but the feeling is dying out as they constantly work in stables with Dheds and Bhangis.

BAVAN.—A sub-division of Mahárs.

BAVANE.—A synonym for Bávan ; a sub-division of Mális.

BAVISA.—A sub-division of Audich Bráhmans.

BAVISE.—A sub-division of Mahárs.

BAVKULE.—A sub-division of Vánis.

BED.—A synonym for Berad.

BEL.—A sub-division of Mahárs.

BELE.—A synonym for Bel.

BELIA.—A synonym for Bel.

BELIM.—*See* under Minor Musalmán Castes.

BELLA.—A synonym for Musalmán Vágher.

BEN.—A sub-division of Mahárs.

BENAVA.—*See* under Minor Musalmán Castes.

BENE-ISRAELS, that is children of Isráel, numbering 10,864 Distribution. (males 5,465, females 5,399) at the 1901 census, are chiefly found in the City of Bombay, the Kolába and Thána districts and the Janjira State between Kolába and Ratnágiri. They are also known as Yahudis or Jews (though they used to dislike the name), and, because they keep Saturday as a day of rest and some of them press oil, as Shanvár Telis or Saturday Oilmen.

Nothing definite is yet known about the origin of the Bene-Isráels. Origin. According to views accepted in the Bombay Gazetteer they came to India either from Aden or from the Persian Gulf. If from Aden, they are believed by some writers to be partly descended from the Jews of the remnant of the tribe of Judah, who after the taking captive of the rest of the tribe by Nebuchadnazzar migrated to Egypt, and were there captured by Darius Hystaspes (B.C. 521—485) and deported by him to the Hejáz in Arabia.[(1)] In the first century before Christ one of the Tubbaa or Hemyarite dynasty of Aden kings (B. C. 100—A.D. 525) came under the influence of their descendants, and was converted to Judaism and introduced the Hebrew faith into South Arabia.[(2)] The settlements of Jews in South Arabia were also probably increased after the dispersion of the Jews of Palestine by Titus (A.D. 79—81) and Hadrian (A.D. 117—138), and the defeat of Zenobia by Aurelian[(2)] (A. D. 270—275). The Jewish Hemyarite princes of the Yemen continued in power till early in the sixth century (525). One of them, Dhu-Nawás, by his cruel treatment of the Christians of Nejrán provoked an invasion of the Ethiopian king Eles Baan, who defeated Dhu-Nawás and fiercely persecuted his Jewish subjects.[(3)] Either at this time or about a hundred years later, when they were hardly used by the prophet Muhammad (A.D. 570—632), a body of Jews may have left Aden and sought safety in Western India.

If on the other hand our Bene-Isráels came from the Persian Gulf they would be Babylonian. The Babylonian Jews were the descendants of the Jews who were carried from Palestine to Upper Mesopotamia by Pul in B. C. 770 and by Shalmanesar about fifty years later. They always remained a large and powerful body. In the third century after Christ, under their leader, the Prince of the Captivity, and again in the fifth century (427) when the Tálmud was compiled, they were in great power. In the beginning of the sixth century the revolt of Rabbi Meir brought on them the wrath of Cavade, the king of the Persians,[(4)] and they continued to suffer severely, till, in 638, the Persian dynasty was overthrown by the Arabs.[(5)] At any time during the sixth century a body of Jews may have sailed from the Persian Gulf to India. It is hard to say from which of these countries the Bene-Isráels have come. In favour of an Arabian origin there is said to be in their appearance some trace of Arab

---

(1) Price's Arabia, 99.

(2) De Sacy, Mem. de Litterature, xlviii, 735—753.

(3) Milman's History of the Jews III, 77—79, 87-88; Wilson's Lands of the Bible II, 657-658.

(4) Basnage's History of the Jews, 535, 563—566. The city where the Prince of the Captivity lived was plundered and the Prince and the President of the Council hanged. For thirty years their doctors did not dare to appear in public.

(5) Basnage's Jews, 570.

blood, they are said to use some Arab words, and there is the modern connection with Arab teachers. On the other hand the close trading connection of the Persian Gulf and India in the sixth century and the fact that Jews bearing the surname of Bene-Israel are still found in Muskat favour the descent of the Western India Bene-Israels from the Jews of Babylon.(1)

Though there is no certainty as to the date when they came to India, it seems probable that it was in the sixth century. Their own tradition, for they have no records of any kind, states that they came to India about fourteen hundred years ago from the north, and that they were wrecked off Návgaon a little to the north of Thal, at the southern entrance to the Bombay harbour, and only fourteen—seven men and seven women—were saved. Two mounds(2) near Návgaon village were said to be the sepulchres where the shipwrecked bodies were buried.(3) Of the history of the Bene-Israels in Kolába nothing is known. They would seem to have lived quietly both under Hindu and Musalmán rulers, like other immigrants almost certainly marrying with the women of the country, to a great extent losing the knowledge of their special history and religion, and adopting the beliefs and practices of the people around them. Several centuries ago a Jewish priest, David Rahabi, coming to Bombay from Arabia, heard of the Jews in the country close by, and going among them won them back from many Hindu observances and taught them the chief tenets and practices of the Hebrew faith. He also introduced the knowledge of the Hebrew language. Since then the leaders of the Bene-Israel community have shown themselves anxious to revive the worship of their forefathers. Synagogues have been built and many Hebrew copies of the law introduced and most of the leading Jewish observances and feasts attended to. This revival owes much to the establishment of British rule in India, to the representatives of which the Bene-Israel from their origin and history, from their skill and

---

(1) Welsted's Arabia, 21.

(2) Now apparently disappeared.

(3) The Rev. J. H. Lord—"The Jews in India and the Far East"—Bombay—1907—suggests that the original Bene-Israel simply came in the course of commerce to the ancient port called "Chemula" in the Kánheri Caves inscription, identified with the "Timulla" or "Simulla" of Ptolemy (A.D. 150), the "Simulla" of the author of the "*Periplus Maris Erythraci*" (A.D. 247), the "Tchi-mo-lo" of the Chinese traveller Hwen Thsang (A.D. 642), the "Chivil" of a Russian traveller, Athanasius Nikitin (A.D. 1470), and finally with the modern village of Cheul or Chaul near Revadanda in the Kolába district.

trustworthiness as craftsmen and clerks, and from their discipline and valour as soldiers, have always been the objects of special interest and goodwill.(1)

Appearance. Bene-Isráels are generally above the middle height and strongly made, and in many cases have an expression of much intelligence and strong character. The men are of about the same colour as Maráthás, perhaps a little fairer. Their eyes are dark brown and their hair black. Their hair is generally close cropped; they wear the moustache; of late some of them shave their chins, but a greater number of them have short beards. In former times they used to wear long side locks, like the Pársis, but now the custom has died out.

The women are generally good-looking and fair; some of them have a ruddy tinge in their cheeks, and have lively black eyes, straight noses and thin lips. Like Hindus they wear the hair tied in a knot behind the head, and deck their heads with flowers.

Dress and ornaments. In the early part of the last century the dress of a Bene-Isráel was partly Musalmán, partly Hindu, a turban or cap, a Hindu coat, trousers or a waist cloth and Hindu shoes. The present tendency is to adopt the English style of dress, and it is possible that before long most of them will wear it.

Till recently Bene-Isráel women dressed like Kunbis in a full robe and loose bodice, passing one end of the robe between the feet and tucking it into the waist band behind and the other over the head. Of recent years there has been a considerable change, some of the young women having begun to dress like Pársi women, but a few copying the English style. Their ornaments are generally the same as those worn by middle and low class Hindus of the same rank.

Language. The home tongue of Bene-Isráels is Maráthi. They have two peculiarities; *r* takes the place of *l* (a peculiarity which also marks the Pársi pronounciation of Gujaráti), and several Arab words are in common use. They pray in Hebrew. The Hindu fashion husbands and wives do not address each other by name. The husband addresses the wife with the phrase *age* (2) and the wife speaks of her husband as the house master or *gharkari*, or formerly if he was an officer in the army, by his rank as *subhedár*, *jamádár* or *haváldár*.

---

(1) The Bene-Isráel owe much to the philanthropic work of Dr. John Wilson in the early part of the 19th century. He devoted much time and energy to improving their condition and his name is still affectionately remembered.

(2) The common Maráthi vocative exclamation when addressing a woman — possibly the Skt. *akka*, itself a word of uncertain origin.

The names in common use among the Bene-Israéls are taken from the Old Testament. Dr. John Wilson says in his Lands of the Bible,[1] "Each of the Bene-Isráel generally speaking has two names, one derived from a character mentioned in scripture and another which has originated in deference to the Hindu usage. The Hebrew names current among males are Abraham, Isaac, Jacob, Reuben (which is said most to abound). Joseph, Naphtali, Zebulun, Benjamin, Samson, Moses, Aaron, Eliezer, Phineas, David, Solomon, Elijah, Hezkiel, Daniel, Ladik, Haim, Shalom, Nashin. The name ***Judah***, it is to be remarked, is not to be found among them". . . . . . "Sarah, Rebecca, Leah, Sephira, Milcah, Zilcah, Miriam, Hannah are the Hebrew names given to the women. Esther, the favourite Jewish name, does not occur among them." Formerly, in addition to these names men were given also such Hindu names as Hasáji, Báláji, Eloji[2], and women Ládubái, Yesubái and Sakubái. But this practice is no longer followed. The names Judah and Esther are now quite common, and some among the educated classes have begun to adopt European, more particularly English, names, such as John, Edward, Albert, etc., for males, and Alice, Amy, Annie, Maud, etc., for females. The terms of respect for men are Azam and Murhabi and for women Amá-sáheb and Bái-sáheb. Their surnames are village names marking former settlements, as Divekar, Návgaonkar, Thalkar and Zirádkar, called after villages in the Kolába district. But here also a change has been gradually working, these old fashioned place surnames being gradually dropped and the name of some distinguished ancestor adopted instead. In some cases the old surnames are modified so as to sound like the English, *e.g.*, Walker for Wakrilkar; but such instances are rare.[3]

Social divisions.

Bene-Isráels have two endogamous divisions, Gore or fair and Kále or dark. According to their story, the Gores are the descendants of the original immigrants and the Káles, of converts, or of the women

(1) Vol. II, page 669 (1847).

(2) The Rev. H. Lord (op. cit. p. 18) points out, however, that these names are sometimes only Hinduized forms of Hebrew names—Hasáji (Ezechiel), Eloji (Elijah) and many others. Báláji, however, he cites with some others, as a case of genuine Hindu name.

(3) This instance is given by Samson (manuscript in records of Ethn. Survey). An examination of the surnames given in the Communal Directory of the Bene-Isráel Year Book, 1918-19, shows that almost all names are either place names or Hebrew names. Four exceptions noted are Worsely (possibly Wasrulkar), Aston (possibly Ashtivkar), Pingle (probably the Konkanasth Bráhman surname) and Siddick (which may be either Muhammadan or modified Hebrew, *cf.* Zadkiel, Zadok, etc.).

of the country. The Gores and Káles, though the same in religion and customs, neither eat together nor intermarry.(1)

Ceremonies. The chief ceremonies among Bene-Isráels are birth, circumcision, marriage, a girl's coming of age, and death. Formerly their ceremonies were quite as important and complicated as those of Hindus and had a special interest from the curious mixture of Hindu and Jewish customs. But the tendency of late is to do away with the old customs and to have as few forms as possible. Nevertheless, on account of their residence in India for several centuries, they possess certain customs which differentiate them off from the Jews of the rest of the world. These customs are fully discussed by the Rev. J. H. Lord(2) and the following is in the main merely a summary of his account:—

(1) *The use of frankincense.*—While the Jews of other countries have not since the burning of the second temple used incense, the Bene-Isráels did so until the middle of the last century. This practice might have been either a relic of pre-Talmudic Jewish customs or a late imitation of Hindu ritual.

(2) *The Nazarite vow.*—Such vows are generally made by a woman without male issue. In the event of her bearing a son thereafter he would be kept with head uncropped till the age of six or seven. Then his hair would be clipped off and weighed against gold or silver, according to the vow, and the equivalent money distributed in charity (or in recent times handed over to the synagogue funds). The clipped hair instead of being burned (Num. VI, 14) is thrown into the sea or any other water. This latter divergence Lord attributes to the imitation of Hindu customs.

(3) *The use of "subjah".*—This plant (apparently *Ocimum basilicum var thyrsiflora* Benty. Cooke Fl. Bom. Pres. II 442) is according to Lord used in many ceremonials. He suggests that it was used as the nearest approach to the hyssop. On the other hand it is of course closely allied to the Hindu *tulsi* (*O. sanctum L*).

---

(1) The division into fair and dark is more marked and more rigid amongst the Jews of Cochin. Dr. J. Wilson (Manuscript in records of Ethn. Survey) held that the black Jews of Cochin are the original immigrants, and that the white Jews are descendants of a second immigration from Jews of Spain driven out by Ferdinand and Isabella and from Jews of Central Europe. This view is accepted by the Rev. J. H. Lord (op. cit. pp. 73—95). This writer provisionally recognises three colours among the Malabar Jews, *viz.*, "brown," the original settlers, "white," the later immigrants, and "black" proselytes from the indigenous natives and persons of half-caste descent.

(2) Op. cit. pp. 22 ff.

(4) The *use of "malida"*.—This is a sweet cake made of rice, milk, *gul*, butter, etc. It is used according to Lord in many ceremonies. The point is that the word is Persian and specially used of offerings at the tomb of a Muhammadan *Pir*.

(5) *The practice of giving cooked liver of a fowl or goat to the officiating priest.*—For this no origin is as yet suggested

(6) *The "cup of blessing"*.—The name is Dr. Wilson's. The ceremony consists of the handing round in the synagogue of a cup of wine previously blessed. Lord considers it a modification of the ceremony of *Habdalah*, or ceremony marking the separation of a holy day from an ordinary one.

(7) *The "kiss of peace."*—At the close of the service in the synagogue the kiss is started by the chief minister and passes thence from him to the elders and so right through the congregation. The bestower of the blessing as between any pair holds out both hands. The receiver first places one hand between the two hands of the bestower and then his other hand over the same. Each then withdraws his hands and kisses the tips of his own fingers. Lord mentions that the practice is in vogue among the Syrian Christians of Malabar, the Nestorians of Kurdistan, and the "Assyrian Christians".

Circumcision

As among Jews of other countries, the male child is circumcised and named on the eighth day after birth. This is one of those customs which has been kept up by the Bene-Isráels from the very beginning, and its observance led David Rahabi to consider that they were the descendants of Jews. There is no fixed rule as to when female children must be named, but usually they are named on, or after eight days from, birth.

Marriage.

Till about thirty years ago boys and girls were married at a very early age, but at present the marriageable age for a boy is about twenty to twenty-two and for a girl fourteen to sixteen, or even later.

The offer of marriage generally comes from the boy's side. The engagement ceremony is performed at the girl's house in the evening, when the girl is presented with a ring or a small golden ornament. The marriage is celebrated on some subsequent Sunday. On the preceding night, which is called "*Halad Mendi* night" the boy and girl, at their respective houses, are rubbed with turmeric paste and moistened powder of the leaves of the *mendi* plant (*Lawsonia inermis*). On following morning a feast is given to relatives and friends at both houses. In the evening, either before or after sunset, the marriage is celebrated at a synagogue or any other convenient place and the married pair are then taken to the house of the bride. In the evening of the next day the pair are taken to the bridegroom's house, and a few days later feasts are given to the nearest kinsfolk at both houses. This ends the marriage.

A necessary function of the marriage ceremony is the execution of the marriage contract by the bridegroom. The contract is attested by the officiating priest and by two or more other persons present, and is handed over to the bride, who gives it to her parents for safe custody.

The Bene-Isráels, though not prevented from practising polygamy, have as a rule only one wife. A second wife is married only in case the first is barren; but even this custom is rapidly dying out.

The marriage covenant is generally rigidly observed. However, in cases of violation of the contract, the innocent party is allowed a divorce, and the liberty of remarriage; but cases of divorce are rare. Intermarriage with alien women is discouraged. The children born of such unions necessarily pass into the Kále endogamous group, even though the Bene-Isráel parent was of the Gore.

Religion. The Bene-Isráels worship one god and use no images. In their synagogues they have manuscript copies of the Old Testament and consider it of divine authority.(1) They do not attempt to proselytize. The essence of their faith is given in the Hebrew sentence: The Lord, our God, He is one Lord.(2) All through life this text is in the Bene-Isráel's mouth. When he repeats it he touches the right eye with the right thumb, the left eye with the little finger, and the forehead with the three middle fingers. Besides the belief in one god, the Bene-Isráel's confession of faith includes thirteen articles(3) :— That God is the Creator and Governor of the universe; that He was, is and will be their only God; that He is without form and without change; that He is beginning and end of all things; that He alone should be worshipped; that the Old Testament is the only true Scripture; that Moses excelled all the prophets, and that his laws should be obeyed; that the law in their possession is the same law as was given by God to Moses; that it will never change; that God knows all men and understands their works; that God will reward the just and will punish the unjust; that the promised Messiah is to come, and that the dead will rise and glorify Him.

---

(1) When worn out, their manuscripts are buried or sunk in deep water. Their loss is mourned as the death of a man (Bom. Gaz., Vol. XVIII, Part I, page 512).

(2) Deuteronomy, vi. 4.

(3) These thirteen articles are those formulated by the Spanish Jew Maimonides and as such are probably of very modern adoption.

Bene-Isráels observe various Jewish fasts and feasts. These do not in all cases correspond with those observed by Jews in other parts of the world ; and even where they correspond in date and name there is sometimes divergence of details as well as ignorance of origin. Taking the months in consecutive order we find the following :—

Tishri (September-October).—(1) *Rosh Hoshána,* New Year feast or Feast of Trumpets, more often called by the Maráthi name *Navyácha San.* (2) *Som Gadalya,* or fast in commemoration of the murder of Gedaliah (II Kings xxv 25, Jer. xli 2). According to notes by Mr. Samson (Manuscript in files of the Ethn. Survey) this is the fast which the Bene-Isráels call " *khiricha roja* " from the preparation of *khir* or sweet rice then eaten. However, this latter is called " *khiricha san* " by the Rev. J. H. Lord (op. cit. p. 34) and identified with the Feast of the Tabernacles. (3) *Kippur* or Fast of the Atonement. This is also called by the Bene-Isráels " *dár fálnicha san* " or festival of " door-closing," because they used to shut themselves up within doors for the whole day. (4) *Sukkoth* or Feast of Tabernacles, lasting for nine days, of which the last is called *Simhath Torah.*

Tebett (December-January).—(1) *Hanukha,* or commemoration of the purification of the temple by the Maccabees. (2) *Sabábi Roja* or Fast in commemoration of the siege of Jerusalem by Nebuchadnezzar. (This is mentioned only by Lord, op. cit. p. 38.)

Shebath (January-February).—*Eliáhu Hannabicha Urus,* or Fair of the Prophet Elijah. This is peculiar to the Bene-Isráels. The site of the fair is, or was, a village named Khandála in the Konkan where the prophet was reputed to have appeared to their ancestors.

Adar (February-March).—On the 13th a fast is held when the story of Lot is read from the " *mejilla* " or parchment.[1] On the 15th *Purim.* According to Lord (op. cit. p. 35) this feast is among the Bene-Isráels also called the *Holicha San,* probably simply from its coinciding in date roughly with the Hindu *Holi.*

Nissan (March-April).—*Passover.* This among Bene-Isráels is also known as the *Anási Dhánkanyácha San* or " Feast of jar-closing from *anás* an earthen jar. The explanation is that these jars contained a sauce (*anási*) which being the nearest approach to leaven was substituted for it.

Sivan (May-June).—*Pentecost,* or the Feast of weeks. Lord says no trace can be found among the older observances. It seems

(1) Only mentioned in the *Bombay Gazetteer,* Vol. XVIII, Part I, page 515, and not in Samson's Manuscript or Lord's work. Hence it may have died out.

clear therefore that this feast had fallen into oblivion until revived in imitation of the later Jewish immigrants of Bombay.(1)

Tammuz (June-July).—*Tammuz,* on the 17th of the month, said by the Gazetteer and Samson Manuscript to be in commemoration of the breaking of the tables of the law by Moses, but by Lord (op. cit. p. 39) of the breach in the wall of Jerusalem.

Ab (July-August).—*Tishabe-áb,* or Fast in commemoration of the burning of the temple. This is also called by the Bene-Isráels "*birdyácha san* from *birda* or half fermented shoots of pulse and other plants which are eaten.

Elul (August-September).—*Selichoth.* A series of days of prayer and optional fasting, which may continue right up to the feast of the Atonement (see above).

The Bene-Isráels have no priests as such, but in former times there were certain families who used to officiate at all religious ceremonies and were called "Kázis." These *Kázis* used to receive fees for their services. But the *Kázis* who were instructed in the rites and ceremonies by David Rahabi and their descendants do not appear to have been able to read the Hebrew language with ease, and therefore when regular service in Hebrew began to be held among the Bene-Isráels, they had to employ other persons for the purpose. These persons were called *Hazzans* and were allowed to perform the ceremonies formerly conducted by the *Kázis.* Thereafter the services of the *Kázis* were less in demand, and now the office is practically extinct though in former times they were looked upon as hereditary priests and had great influence over the community.

Death. The dead are buried without coffins in graves about six feet deep with head to the east. A burial cannot take place after sunset on Fridays, before sunset on Saturdays. Similarly interment is not allowed from 5 p.m. on the day before the day of Atonement till after sunset on that day. Mourning is generally observed for three days in the case of a child and for seven days in the case of an adult during which time flesh is eschewed. The mourners visit the grave on the third day after death in the case of a child and on the seventh day in the case of an adult, and offer prayers for the soul of the deceased. On the same day prayers are also offered at the house of the deceased and a feast is given to those present. Such ceremonies are also held at the end of a fortnight, a month, three months, six months, and eleven months after death. During the period of mourning the relatives of the mourners used to carry cooked food to the

(1) It is also not given in the Calendar in the "Bene-Isráel Year Book," 1918-19.

house of the mourners and to share it with them; but this custom has now almost died out.

Bene-Isráels are chiefly husbandmen, oil pressers, carpenters, but some are schoolmasters, hospital assistants, shopkeepers and cart-drivers. Formerly a large proportion of the regiments of Bombay Foot were of this caste, and an especially large proportion of the Native officers. But conditions no longer exist in which it is worth their while to take up this profession. A large number are turners and fitters in Bombay and many have availed themselves of English education and taken up clerical appointments. A good many women become nurses and midwives. **Occupation.**

Bene-Isráels eat the flesh of animals, fowl and fish, as admissible under the Levitical Law. It was this observation and the dietary laws enjoined in Leviticus that convinced David Rahabi that they were the descendants of Jews. **Food and drink.**

The following very interesting story of their identification is current among them. One day David Rahabi, to test conclusively whether the ancestors of the Bene-Isráels were the descendants of Jews, bought different sorts of fish in the market and gave them to his hostess. The house-wife, who was a very simple woman, was greatly astonished to find that the learned Rabbi had brought some kinds which they were forbidden to eat, but considered that there was some mistake on his part. She selected only such as had fins and scales and threw away the rest. The Rabbi on seeing this was convinced that those among whom he lived were the descendants of Jews. This test, it will be seen, was necessary, to differentiate them from the Muhammadans who like them circumcised their male children.

Among four-footed animals they eat only such as chew the cud and have divided hoofs. They so abhor swine's flesh that "pig-eater" (*suvar kháu*) is their grossest term of abuse. Of birds the rule is that only those may be eaten which do not hold their prey in their feet, and of fish, only those with fins and scales. They drink liquor, both country and European.

No man can be admitted as a member of the Bene-Isráel community without being circumcised. Before a man (or woman), who has been put out of caste, is again received, the back is stripped bare, he is seated on a plate filled with cold water and the priest gives him thirty-nine gentle lashes with a twisted handkerchief or *korda*.

Distribution. **BERADS,** Bedars or Beds, numbering 177,082 (1901), including 88,344 males and 88,738 females, are found principally in Belgaum, Bijápur, Dhárwár and the Southern Marátha Country and also in all the districts and States in the Deccan and Konkan. In the Belgaum district, they are found mostly in Pachhápur about twenty miles north of Belgaum and in the surrounding villages. They are also found near Sutgati on the Belgaum-Poona road in the hills bordering the Ghatprabha. In Bijápur, they are found over the whole district, but are especially common in Badámi in the south. They are found in all parts of the Dhárwár district.

Name. The term Bed (*pl.* Bedaru)[1] seems to mean hunters, from *bete*, hunting. The Maráthás know the tribe as Berads[2] and the Musalmáns as Bedars.[3] The members of the tribe themselves prefer to be called Naikmakkalu, which means chief's children. They are also often called Náikwádis, presumably because they hold the office of Náikwádis (*i.e.*, village police) in many villages. Another synonym is Talwar, which means a village watchman, many of the tribe being hereditary village watchmen. They also call themselves Válmikás after the author of the *Rámáyan*, whom they claim as a caste-fellow. Like Mahárs, Mángs and others who serve as village watchmen, they are sometimes called and sometimes call themselves Rámoshis, which suggests some connection with the great Deccan tribe of that name. It seems probable, indeed, that the Rámoshis and Berads have a common origin and have become separate by the barriers of residence and language. The connection must have been close when a Dravidian tongue was spoken in the Deccan. They follow similar occupations, they both style themselves Náiks and Válmikás, and a common division of Halge is found in both.

Origin. The tribe is largely represented in Madras, Mysore and Hyderabad. In Madras, they number 62,273, in Mysore 245,001 and in Hyderabad 156,586. Some have penetrated as far north as Berar, where they number 4,927. The Telugu Boyas and the Támil Vedáns appear, like the Rámoshis, to be allied to this tribe. The Boyas are hunters by profession. They numbered in Madras 397,189 at the Census of 1901. They call themselves Válmikás and Dorabiddás (children of chiefs) like the Berads, and say they are descended from the sage Válmik

---

(1) In Kanarese the common pronunciation of Beda is Byada, and hence Buchanan (I, 358) styles them Baydaru.

(2) Bérad appears to be derived from Bedar by transposal of the letters d and r.

(3) Campbell, *Bombay Gazetteer*, Vol. XXIII, p. 91, gives 'fearless' as the meaning of the name. This is an obvious pun from *be-der*, Hindustáni, without fear.

and from the Poligars. The Vedáns, who numbered 25,519 in Madras in 1901, are a Támil-speaking, hunting and labouring caste, the members of which were formerly soldiers and subsequently dacoits. They claim descent from Kannayya Náyanar like the Bombay Berads who consider Kannayya to be the founder of their tribe. According to tradition current among the Berads of Bombay this Kannayya was a fowler and hunter, a devout worshipper of Shiva. Pleased with his devotion, Shiva and his consort appeared to him and offered him a choice of boons. Kannayya prayed Shiva to make him and his descendants sure shots and to make his and their lands grow corn without much labour or water. The god granted his prayer, and all Berads are good marksmen and live by hunting and fowling, growing only the *rabi* crops which want neither much water nor much care.

According to Buchanan[(1)] the Kadambás of Banavási were Bedars. He notices[(2)] that in East Mysore the Bedars were strongly Telugu and that near Verul on the crest of the Eastern Gháts the Telugu language was called Bedari. They ranked[(3)] among the left-handed classes. He notices[(4)] that in South Kanara the Bedars were a savage race who ate cats, and with great propriety were called murderers. History relates that after the fall of Vijayánagar the Bedars plundered the town for many days.[(5)] Wilks[(6)] makes the Boyas and Bedars the same. He describes them as wonderfully enduring[(7)] and by their admirable staunchness to their chiefs winning the admiration of Hyder Ali, who turned them into Musalmáns and formed battalions of the Bedar Boyas or *chelás*. Mr. Rice[(8)] gives them a strength of 260,000 ; calls them Bedars or Náyaks and also Kirátakas, Bárikas and Kannaiyas. Some are Karnátás and others Telingás. They have family stocks or *bedagus*. Most Mysore Poligars or petty chiefs are Bedars. Medows Taylor, in the *Story of my Life*, describes the Bedars as the ruling tribe in the State of Sholápur in the Nizám's territory.

Under the Peshwas the village of Chikkadine, about twelve miles north of Belgaum, was the centre of a small Berad State. At the time of the British conquest of the country in 1817 they had a strong organization under a *náik* or chief. In the early years of British rule they caused some trouble, but were reduced to order in 1820. They were still very unwilling to settle to regular work, and preferred to sub-let their land even at a small rent rather than be put to

(1) *Mysore*, Vol. III, p. 163.
(2) *Id.* Vol. I, p. 29.
(3) *Id.* Vol. I, p. 77.
(4) *Id.* Vol. III, p. 6.
(5) *A Forgotten Empire*, Sewell, p. 207.
(6) 1810, *South of India*, Vol. I, p. 447.
(7) *Mysore*, Vol. II, p. 190.
(8) *Mysore and Coorg*, Vol. I, p. 331.

the trouble of farming it. In 1829 there was a great Bedar outbreak under a famous leader named Ráyappa of Sangoli, who was a Kuruba by caste. So successful was he that for a time the fort of Belgaum was believed to be in danger. As recently as 1895 the tribe gave trouble in this district by committing numerous dacoities.

The Berads are an aboriginal tribe of the Kanarese districts. Although they have adopted many customs and usages from castes of a different social standing, the fact that a large number of them still feed on beef is evidence of their primitive origin. Their dark complexion, flat noses and frizzled hair are also proof of their non-Aryan origin.

Admission. Berads are recruited from many other castes, such as Kurubs, Kabbaligars, Vakkals, etc., who are superior to the Berads in the social scale. Members from lower castes such as Vaddars, Koravs, Dheds, etc., and Musalmáns are not admitted. The member to be admitted, if a male, is clean-shaved and bathed. Next, a stick of burning cotton plant is brought in contact with his tongue as a symbol of burning his *kriyákarma* (past actions) and the tribesmen are fed. In the case of a female wishing to gain admission the same ceremony is performed, omitting the shaving. The males thus admitted are relegated as a rule to a special Mallava subdivision and the females to the Gujjal exogamous subdivision. A common ceremony in initiating new members of the caste is the burning of a straw hut, which indicates the commencement of a new life. A similar ceremony is found in the Vaddar tribe.

Appearance, dress and ornaments. As a rule Berads are dark and muscular, and of middle height, with round faces, thin lips, flat noses, round high-boned cheeks, and lank or frizzled hair. The men wear a head-scarf, a waist-cloth or breeches, a coat or shoulder-cloth and shoes or sandals. A few men have their head shaved but most let the head hair grow. Their ornaments are *uddurs* (waist-girdles), *khade* (gold or silver bracelets) and *muruvás* (gold ear-rings). Women tie the hair in a loose knot at the back of the head, and dress in a bodice with short sleeves and in a robe the skirt of which is not passed back between the feet and the upper end of which is drawn over the head. They wear *vánkis* (gold or silver armlets), *karipatti* (gold neck-ornament), *gajjitikke* (gold neck-ornament), *dále* (gold or silver waist-ornaments), nose-rings, wristlets and ear-ornaments.

Tattooing. Girls are generally tattooed at the age of four or five or even later. The tattooing is done by members of the Kiliket tribe, on the middle of the forehead, on the corners of the eyes, near the temples and on both forearms. The common designs are ornamental creepers, flowers, leaves, the *linga*, etc.

Berads have the following endogamous divisions :— Social organization.

1. Proper, known also as Náik Makkalu and Válmika.
2. Bhil or Kiráta.
3. Bile or Halge.
4. Jas, Nas, Myas or Kavalettu.
5. Kakarmundi or Hesi.
6. Kare or Durgámurgi.

The Bile division do not eat the flesh of buffalo, bullock or pig, and do not allow their women to follow prostitution, and hence are known as Bile or white. The Kare or black division have not these distinctive features. They are also known as Durgámurgi as they travel about carrying an image of the goddess Durgámurgavva in a box on their heads.

The exogamous divisions of the tribe which are known as *bedagas* are as follows :—

Anagalawa.(1)	Gujjala.(1)	Metkuppi.(1)
Badakla.	Jampala.	Minagala.(1)
Ballelá.	Kingála.	Motmalna.
Bandla.	Kurlyana.	Mumbudla.
Bhulla.	Mallava.	Nágalna.
Gabbela.	Musagyana.	Phodena.
Gorla.	Metkar.	Sutala.(1)
Gosala.		

These *bedagas* are said to possess their own bards, one for each *bedaga*.

Marriages are prohibited between members of the same sub-division. A member of the tribe may marry a woman of the division to which his mother belongs though not a near relative of his mother such as her sister or her sister's daughter. He may also marry a woman of his paternal grandmother's section and maternal grandmother's section, subject to similar limitations. Children of sisters married to persons of different sections cannot inter-marry. A man may marry his sister's daughter. Adoptive brotherhood is practised and there- Marriage rules.

(1) These divisions are also found among Mysore Berads (see *Ethnographic Survey of Mysore*).

after marriage with a member of the section adopting is prohibited. It is customary among the members of the tribe for parents to exchange daughters, each marrying his son to the other's daughter. Marriage with a wife's sister is allowed during the wife's lifetime as well as after her death. The daughters of widows by their second husbands marry sons of widows by their second husbands, and daughters of first husbands marry sons of first husbands. Polygamy is allowed and practised, but polyandry is unknown. Marriage is generally infant. Sexual license before marriage is neither recognized nor tolerated, though there is no objection to keeping girls unmarried and making them prostitutes. Such girls are taken to a *guru*, who brands them with a stamp. Next they are taken to a temple of Máruti, where a *táli* (lucky necklace) is tied round their neck in the name of the god. They then become eligible for prostitution and are known as *Basavis*. Females dedicated to the goddess Yellamma act as prostitutes and are known as *Jogatis*.

Language. The home tongue of the Berads is a corrupt Kanarese. In Sholápur they speak Maráthi with others and among themselves a dialect of their own. The names in common use among men are—Bala, Bhima, Dásà, Durga, Fakira, Hanma, Kankanna, Kara, Ráma and Yella, and among women—Bhima, Durga, Fakira, Hanma, Ninga, Ráma, Ranga and Yella. The Kanarese word *appa* or father is added to the names of men, and *avva* or mother to the names of women.

Community. The social disputes of the tribe are enquired into and settled by their headmen or *kattimanis*, whose decisions are enforced by putting out of caste anyone who neglects them. When the headman sits to settle a case he calls some respectable members of the tribe, and with their consent delivers judgment. In Belgaum, their headman is called *nádigye* and in Sholápur *náik*. If a woman is put out of caste, either for adultery or for eating with a member of a lower caste, before she is allowed back, her head should be shaved in the presence of the *kattimani*. The present practice is to cut off five hairs of her head with a razor and for the caste officer or *mallavva* to touch her tongue with a live torch of *rui* wood. A little liquor is also given her to drink, as liquor is held to purify the body. When a man is guilty of incest with a kinswoman of his own stock he has to purify himself by shaving off his moustaches, beard and top-knot, by bathing in cold water, and by drinking a small quantity of liquor in the presence of the *guru* and caste-people.

After the birth of a child the midwife cuts the navel cord, bathes the child and mother in warm water, and lays them on a cot in a retired part of the house. The mother is given a mixture of molasses, dry cocoa-kernel, dry dates, dry ginger and pepper, and is fed on boiled rice, wheat puddings and boiled millet mixed with molasses and clarified butter. A woman remains unclean for five days after child-birth. During each of the five days her head is annointed with clarified butter, her body is rubbed with turmeric powder mixed with oil, she is bathed with warm water, and an earthen pot with burning cowdung cakes is laid beneath her cot. The child is rubbed with oil and bathed with warm water. From the sixth to the thirteenth the mother and child are bathed every second day. The child is named and cradfed on the thirteenth, and mil.et, wheat, gram, beans and pulse mixed together are served to all present. In Belgaum, on the fifth day after the birth of a child, they worship the goddess Pánchavi, and feast three or four relations. On the twelfth or nineteenth day the child is cradled and named, and a few relations are feasted. In Dhárwár, the goddess Sathi is worshipped on the fifth day and the child is cradled and named on the twelfth. In Sholápur a woman is impure for ten days after child-birth. On the fifth the house is cowdunged, balls and millet or wheat flour biscuits are made and offered to Satvái, and in the evening a feast is held. The babe, if a boy, is named on the thirteenth, and if a girl, on the twelfth. On the naming day women guests cradle the child and rock it, singing songs. When the singing is over, they are given wheat and *jowári* and their hands and faces are rubbed with turmeric powder; near relations present the child with new clothes, and the guests retire. In Bijápur, the hair of a child, whether a boy or a girl, is cut for the first time either during the first or the third month after birth. In Belgaum, when a child, male or female, is a year old the maternal uncle cuts five hairs with a pair of scissors and asks the barber to cut the rest. In Sholápur, if the child is a boy its hair is clipped when it is six or twelve months old.

Birth ceremonies

The offer of marriage comes from the boy's parents, who have to pay a bride-price of Rs. 100 to the girl's parents. This sum varies according to the means of the parties. When a match is proposed, the boy's father with friends goes to the girl's house and gives the girl's mother Rs. 2 and three-quarters of a pound of sugar, putting a little sugar in the girl's mouth. He dec.ares in the presence of caste-women that the girl is betrothed to his son. He is then treated to two meals—one on the first and another on the next day.

Marriage ceremonies.

After the second dinner he returns home with his party after fixing a lucky day for the wedding. At a lucky hour, with the help of a Bráhman astrologer, the boy's father goes to the girl's to perform the *báshtagi* or betrothal, taking with him a robe worth Rs. 5, *five* bodice-cloths worth Re. 1 each, a cocoanut, *five* dry dates, *five* betelnuts, *five* turmeric roots and *five* plantains, or some silver or gold ornaments. These things are laid before the girl's house-gods. The bridegroom's father tells the girl to put on the robe and the ornaments he has brought, and seating her on a black blanket, lays in her lap the cocoanut and other articles along with a handful of rice. The guests are given betel leaves and betelnuts and sugar. To this betrothal the village officers as well as Lingáyat priests are called. The boy's father and his friends are treated to a feast of sugar dumplings or *kadabus* and clarified butter, and next day to sugar rolly-polies. Within a year or two after the *báshtagi* the marriage is celebrated. On the lucky day fixed by an astrologer, the bride and her friends come to the bridegroom's, where she and her mother alone remain, the rest of her party being lodged in a separate house. Soon after she comes, the bride and bridegroom are rubbed with turmeric paste and bathed in water. The bathing water is taken from two pots round which a square or *surgi* has been drawn, and a pot is set at each corner of the square, which is enclosed by a cotton thread running round the neck of each pot. After his bath the bridegroom puts on gay clothes and the bride is dressed in a white robe and white bodice with green bangles, and both go and bow before the house-gods. On returning they are served with a meal of cooked millet, pea-soup or *sár* and clarified butter. Next day *five* married men go beyond the village border and return to the village boundary or to the village Máruti's temple, bringing two saplings—one for the *hálgambh* or milk post, the other for the *handargambh* or marriage booth post. At the temple a married woman washes their faces and waves a lighted lamp round their heads. They then come in procession to the bridegroom's and drive the saplings into the ground in front of the house to form the main posts of the marriage booth which is afterwards built and in it a marriage altar. In the evening they are given a dinner of cooked millet. After supper the goddess Airani or Lakshmi is worshipped. Four clay buckets each able to hold about a quart, a pitcher and a small pot are brought in procession from the potter's house, who is given undressed food enough for a good meal. In the small pot two little sticks are laid with two betel leaves tied to them by a cotton thread. These two sticks are called *rámbáns* or Rám's arrows. The bridegroom and bride with *five* married women bathe in water from a *surgi* or a pitcher and dress in haste. They bow to the house-gods and are fed on vermicelli or *shevaya* and the guests on sweet cakes or *polies*. On the third day the bride and bridegroom are again bathed and dressed and taken to bow before the family gods. Some men belonging to the bride's party put vermicelli in a bamboo sieve, cover it with a new cloth, and take it to the bridegroom's. This present is called the *surgi bhum* or square earth-offering. It is touched by the bridegroom and eaten by *five* men, three belonging to the bridegroom's party and two to the bride's. The bride and bridegroom are mounted on a bullock, the bridegroom wearing the marriage coronet and the bride a flower-net on her head. They bow before the village Máruti, break a cocoanut, and each pays one anna to the priest, who names their *gotras* or family-stocks. Meanwhile, four men, sons of women by their first husbands, stand at the corners of a square and pass round a cotton thread moistened with clarified butter and milk, take it off, and twist it with a five-fold plait. It is coloured red by a mixture of lime and turmeric powder, and, with a piece of turmeric tied to its end, is wound round the bridegroom's wrist. A similar thread is prepared and tied round the bride's wrist. Meanwhile a Bráhman draws a lucky Jain cross or *svástik* in red paste in the centre of a newly washed sheet. On their return from the temple of Máruti the bride and bridegroom are put facing each other, the bridegroom standing on a stone seat and the bride in a new basket with millet in it. The Bráhman priest holds a cloth between them and repeats marriage verses. At the end of each verse the priest throws rice on the heads of the boy and girl, and the guests join in the rice throwing, which is the binding part of the ceremony. The bride wears a coloured robe and bodice; turmeric root with rice is placed in a fold of the bride's robe and bridegroom's *dhoti*. The priest tells the bridegroom to touch the *mangalsutra* or luck-giving necklace, and fastens it round the bride's neck, and *kankans* or wristlets are also tied to the bridegroom's right wrist and to the bride's left wrist. Bráhmans and Lingáyat priests, both of whom attend, are given money gifts, and the officiating priest, who is a Bráhman, is paid Re. 1-2-0 in cash. The bride's father treats the caste-people to a dinner and the bridegroom's father gives them a supper. After this the bride and bridegroom rub each other *five* times with turmeric paste. Between nine and twelve at night the bride and bridegroom are mounted on a bullock and led to the local temple to bow to the idol, where they break a cocoanut and each pays the priest one anna for naming their family stocks. When the procession reaches the bridegroom's house, a cocoanut is waved round the married couple and broken as an offering to evil spirits. The bride and bridegroom are then led or, if young, are carried to the god-room to bow to the house-gods, where they eat the *bhum* or earth-offering supper with three married women and two men. After supper the bride and bridegroom are seated on a blanket on a *basakki* or rice-seat. At the end each of them says the other's name, the tinsel chaplet is taken from the bridegroom's head and the flower-net from the bride's, and the bride's party are treated to vermicelli or *shevaya.* Next evening comes the *nágvali* or snake-worship, when a *nágvali bhum* or snake-worship earth-offering feast is given to the five married women who brought Lakshmi's jars from the potter's house. The bride's mother hands her daughter to the mother-in-law, asking her to treat the girl as her own daughter. The rice, with which the bride's lap was filled at the *varát* or return procession, is cooked, offered to the house-gods, and eaten by the house-people with friends and relations. This ends the marriage, and next day the wedding guests leave for their homes. Some take the bride to the bridegroom's on the day after this feast and some after a few days. The girl remains there for a day or two, but she does not go to live with her husband before she comes of age. The bridegroom gives a feast to his caste-fellows in honour of his marriage.

The Berads of the Sholápur district have a *devak* consisting of the *pánchpálvi,* which is worshipped and offered the sacrifice of a sheep. Their marriage ceremonies resemble those of local Kunbis.

When a girl attains puberty, she is seated in a *makhar* (a wooden frame), more or less richly decorated according to the means of the parties, and her lap is filled with rice grains, fruit and betel leaves, to the accompaniment of music, for several days. The consummation ceremony is performed on any day from the 5th to the 11th day of menstruation in the first or subsequent months.

Widow re-marriage. The remarriage of widows is permitted. Among the Kanara Berads widows are not allowed to marry, but they are taken as concubines. A widow may marry any member of her late husband's section except a brother or near cousin or a member of her father's section. A widower or one who has once married and has a wife living can only marry a widow. When the parties agree, the intended husband pays to the widow Rs. 2 for bangles and toe-rings and the widow's party give a feast to the husband. A week or two after, the remarriage ceremony is performed. The widow's intended husband has to pay a sum of about Rs. 100 to her parents. The ceremony is conducted by a Lingáyat Mathpati, who must be either a widower or widow remarried man, but not a bachelor. In the absence of such a priest a widow or remarried woman of the Mathpati caste conducts the service. As a rule unwidowed women are not allowed to take part in widow remarriages. On the day appointed for the marriage the widow is presented with a robe and a bodice worth about Rs 10, which she wears. The Mathpati then ties a gold bead with a thread on the neck of the widow, and knots together the ends of the pair's garments, and the couple salute the *Panch*, this being the binding portion of the ceremony. This completes the marriage. A feast at night to the community ends the ceremony. In some places the ceremony is as follows. The widow to be married is taken to Máruti's temple accompanied by her relations and some members of the tribe. She is seated in the temple with a sword under her arm and a lucky necklace is tied round her neck in the name of the intended husband, which ends the ceremony. A married widow cannot bear on her brow the red powder mark, the emblem of unwidowed married life.

A husband can divorce a wife on the ground of the wife being unchaste, sickly, or even ugly. A wife can divorce her husband if he is impotent. When both parties consent, divorce is freely allowed. The ceremony for divorce is for the wife to sever the lucky necklace round her neck and break the bangles on her wrists; and for the husband to tear the broad end of her robe. A divorced woman may marry by the widow remarriage form. The price paid for her by her first husband is refunded to him wholly or partially according to means at the time of the remarriage. The tribe follow the Hindu law of inheritance. Divorce

Berads either belong to the Hindu religion and are followers mostly of the Vaishnava sect or are animists. A few are Shaiváites, and according to one account, some also wear the *linga* like the Lingáyats. The family deities of the Bijápur Berads are Durgava, Mallikárjuna, Máruti, Venktesh and Yellamma, whose images, made either of copper, brass or silver, they keep in their houses. The chief god of the Dhárwár Berads is Hanmappa, whose shrine is at Navalgund. In Sholápur, they chiefly worship Ambábái, Jotiba and Khandoba; and in Poona, Janái, Jokhái and Khandoba. The favourite god of the few Berads found in the Sávantvádi State is Ganpati. They also worship the cobra (*nág*), holding it sacred and never destroying it. Besides the gods mentioned above, Berads worship all Hindu gods, especially local and village gods and goddesses, of whom Religion.

their favourite are Máruti, Lakkavva, and Venktesh. They claim Válmiki, the author of the *Rámáyan*, as a caste-fellow. As Válmiki was devoted to Ráma, the seventh incarnation of Vishnu, the Berads identify every god with Ráma, and begin their worship by uttering the word Rám. The patron saints of the tribe are Manappaya and Kannappaya. They keep most Hindu holidays, chiefly *Dasara*, *Diváli* and the *Ashvin* and *Márgashirsha* new moons, on which, like the Raddis, they perform the *dangora* (field-rite). Like Raddis they also hold *charags* or field-feasts in honour of Lakshmi. They fast on all Mondays in *Shrávan* and on all ordinary Saturdays and Tuesdays, when they take only one meal in the evening. Besides food cooked after bathing, on all big days they offer the gods cocoanuts, dry dates, sugar, molasses, camphor and incense. They also at times offer chickens, goats and buffaloes to the goddesses Durgavva and Dyamavva. They have faith in soothsaying, astrology and sorcery. They have an hereditary married *guru* or religious teacher, who belongs to their own caste and is the religious and social head of their community. Their priests are Bráhmans. In some places, Lingáyat *Mathpatis* are employed to conduct the death ceremonies.

Death ceremonies.

The dead are either burnt or buried. The dead bodies of those who have been branded with a religious seal by the *pujáris* (worshippers) of Yelgurdappa (Hanumant Dev) of Yelgur on the Krishna in the Bágevádi táluka of the Bijápur district must be buried. At burial the unmarried dead are placed in a lying position with head to the south, and the married in a sitting position with the face towards the east. The body is washed and dressed, the brow of a dead man is rubbed with ashes and the head of a dead woman is decked with a flower-net. They carry their dead on a bier, except the poor, who carry them in an old blanket. After burning or burying the body the funeral party bathe and return to the house of mourning. On the third day the mourners take rice, *kánolás* or semi-circular cakes and water to the burning ground in a small new earthen pot and lay them near the spot where the deceased was burnt or buried. They wait till a crow touches the offering. If no crow comes to eat, the chief mourner promises to take care of the deceased's children. If, even after this, the crows refuse to eat, they give the food to a cow and go home. A dinner is given to the corpse bearers, and mourning is ended by smoking together. On the seventh, ninth or eleventh day the ashes and the bones of the deceased are gathered up and thrown into water, and friends and relations are feasted. At the end of a month friends and relations are asked to a feast, at which goat's flesh is served. In Belgaum, a Mahár always goes with the dead body and is paid one anna. On the twelfth day the chief mourner brings water from the village Bráhman, sprinkles it in the house, and, if the deceased was married, a silver plate impressed with the deceased's figure is brought from a goldsmith for annas 4 or 8. On the thirteenth day the relations of the deceased worship the silver plate which is kept in the house and worshipped once in a year. For the propitiation of the deceased ancestors a dinner is given to the tribesmen by every family on the new moon of either *Bhádrapad*, *Ashvin* or *Phálgun*. The ceremony of *shráddha* is not performed.

Occupation.

Berads were formerly a warlike and dangerous class, notorious as thieves and highway robbers. In the Belgaum district, even now, some of them are clever thieves, skilful in eluding search and hiding stolen property, and are much feared by travellers. They steal cattle with such cleverness, and send the stolen animals such long distances, that the greatest energy and caution often fail to find any trace of them. The owner has to go and ask the Berad's help, and if he promises a reward, the animal is found and restored. If an animal is missing it is almost sure to have fallen into the hands of the Berads. As a class they are orderly, hard working, hospitable and free from crime. Some are husbandmen, some village watchmen or *talvárs* holding free grants of lands, some are *pátils* and *shetsanadis*, some are labourers, some are hunters and snarers, and some are cartmen. Many hold lands under the *Rayatvári* system. The *pátils* and *shetsanadis* hold *watan* lands. The Berads observe all the field rites and ceremonies of local Kunbis.

Food and drink.

The staple food of Berads is bread, split pulse, millet and vegetables. They eat flesh as often as they can afford it, except on Saturday, which is sacred to Máruti, or on Tuesday, which is sacred to Yellamma. They are excessively fond of drinking. Some drink liquor daily, and most drink at the Moharram time. The Bijápur Berads do not eat the flesh of the cow and the pig. The Dhárwár, Belgaum and Sávantvádi Berads eat the flesh of cows, buffaloes and pigs. The Berads of Bijápur consider themselves superior to Golars and Vaddars because the latter eat jackals and rats which the Berads do not. The lowest well-known caste from whom Berads can take cooked food is Kabbaligar. The highest well-known caste who will eat, drink or smoke with the Berads is the Korava. Musalmáns do not eat out of the hands of Berads, but Berads have no objection to accepting food from Musalmáns.

The Bijápur Berads rank themselves with Marátha Kunbis and other field-working classes, and look down on Holiás, Madigs and other impure classes, and even on Vaddars and Lamáns. High class Hindus rank them below Musalmáns. In Kolhápur, they rank below Kunbis and above Mahárs and Mángs. In Sávantvádi, they rank themselves under Musalmáns but much above Mahárs, never touching nor dining with the latter.

MUSALMAN BERADS are scattered in small numbers over Sholápur, Belgaum, Dhárwár and Bijápur. They are said to have been converted by Hyder Ali Khán (1762-1782), from whom they have taken the title of Khán. They were in the service of both Hyder Ali and Tipu, who had great trust in their Bedar soldiers.(1) They came to Sholápur and Dhárwár in 1803 with Colonel Wellesly's army. They are mostly traders, servants, messengers and constables. They do not form a separate community and do not differ in their manners and customs from ordinary Musalmáns, and marry among any of the Musalmán communities. They are Sunnis of the Hanafi school and are generally religious and careful to say their prayers.

BERAD.—A sub-division of Rámoshis.

BERAK.—A sub-division of Jogis.

Name and origin.

BHADBHUNJAS, numbering 1,752 (1901), including 966 males and 786 females, are found in small numbers in all the Gujarát districts and in the Deccan. More than half reside in the Surat district. The term Bhadbhunja is derived from *bhad* = an oven and *bhunj* = to parch, meaning a class of men who parch grain. The endogamous divisions are Gujaráti, Maráthi and Pardeshi, separated by difference of language and domicile. The Gujarát Bhadbhunjás claim to be Káyasths. It is alleged that they were brought into the province by Todarmal, the finance minister of Akbar, from Northern India through Násik, to work as writers. It is said that the Káyasths and Bhadbhunjás have a common *gotra*. According to the Bombay Gazetteer, the Pardeshi Bhadbhunjás came originally from Cawnpore Lucknow, Mathura and Bareilly in Upper India and have been residing in this Presidency for the last hundred years. They are also known as Bhujáris or Shri Bastam (*i. e.*, Vaishnava) Káyasths. None of these divisions intermarry, the common bond among them being that of grain parching and selling.

---

(1) Buchanan's Mysore, I, 123.

The Gujarát Bhadbhunjás are the most numerous. The following particulars apply to them.

There are neither endogamous nor exogamous divisions of the caste. They have two *gotras*, *viz.*, Káshyap and Válmiki, but their marriages are not regulated thereby. Marriage with a father's sister's daughter and mother's sister's daughter is not allowed till five generations have passed. Marriage with a wife's sister during the wife's life-time is not allowed. Two brothers may marry two sisters. Bhadbhunjás in Gujarát have formed certain groups of villages, and, as a rule, a man from a particular group must marry a girl of the same group. The habits of the caste are settled. They do not admit outsiders into their caste. Girls are married before they are eleven. Boys are married from five to fifteen. Sexual license before marriage is neither allowed nor tolerated. Polygamy is permitted, but polyandry is unknown. The offer of marriage generally comes from the boy's father, who pays to the girl's father from Rs. 50 to Rs. 150 as dowry. But the girl has a claim to this sum when she becomes the mother of one or two children. The sum is termed *palla*. A Bráhman priest fixes the day of marriage and conducts the service. The marriage ceremonies do not differ from those of local Kanbis. The *Saptapadi* is the binding portion of the ceremony. **Marriage.**

Widow remarriage is allowed. A widow cannot marry her mother's sister's son, maternal uncle's son or father's sister's son. She can marry the younger brother of her deceased husband or any other member of his family. Widow remarriage can be performed in any month on Sunday, Tuesday or Friday. A Bráhman priest leads the new couple to the worship of Ganpati and the *Navagrahas*. The Ganpati is made of wheat flour and the *Navagrahas* are represented by betelnuts. The Bráhman priest then ties the ends of the widow's and her new husband's garments into a knot, and a matron throws rice grains over their heads. The priest then marks their brows with red powder. A lamp fed with clarified butter, lighted at the time of worshipping Ganpati, is taken by the couple and placed on the border of an adjoining well. The throwing of rice grains is the binding portion of the ceremony. A bachelor wishing to marry a widow is first married to a *shami* (Prosopis spicigera) tree.

Divorce is not allowed.

They observe the Hindu law of inheritance.

Bhadbhunjás are Hindus by religion and belong to the Vaishnav sect. The Vaishnavs are again sub-divided into Swámi Náráyan, **Religion.**

Rámánand, Vallabhácharya and Kabirpanth, many belonging to the minor sects. The reason which they give for their preferring the Vaishnav faith is that it is the religion of the Káyasths and they were originally Káyasths. They go on pilgrimages to Dwárka, Dákore, Badrináth, Jagannáthpuri, Benares, Gaya, Trimbak, Násik, etc. They observe all Hindu holidays. Their religious preceptor is the Gosvámi Mahárája of the Vallabha sect. They worship the sweet basil tree, cow and cobra. They worship their account books and their working tool known as *dhákni*. When there is sickness in a house, and they think that it is owing to the ill-will of one of their ancestors, they prepare an idol of rice flour and burn it with all the forms of a funeral. They also observe mourning for ten days and perform funeral rites in the name of the dead. This is known as "*puttal vidhán*." The second form of mourning consists in preparing two images of *darbha* grass and performing the *shráddha* ceremony in the month of *Kártik*. They take a vow for this performance. The one image represents dead ancestors and the other the sage of their *gotra*. The sage is worshipped in order that he may influence their dead ancestors and keep them under their control. In this observance the ancestors are feasted with fried cakes and sweetened milk. They perform a regular *shráddha*, the *pindas* being made of wheat flour. Bráhmans are feasted when this ceremony is over. They worship Muhammadan saints, and make offerings of clothes, sweetmeats, etc. When diseases such as cholera and small-pox are raging, they worship Ambábái, Bechráji and the Sitala goddess. Some adore Baliákáka and Agni. If a person suffering from cholera recovers, they sometimes offer the person to a deity, when, by paying a sum of money, he is repurchased. They burn their dead. Children not more than 15 to 18 months old are buried with their heads turned towards the north. The ashes and bones of the dead are thrown into a river or a watery place.

Death ceremonies.

The caste trace their origin to Káyasths, and say that they were originally writers. They are parchers and sellers of parched grain and pulse. Very few are servants.

Food.

A majority of this caste eat the flesh of goats, sheep, fowls and fish. They drink liquor. They eat *kachhi* and *pakki* at the hands of Kanbis and Kolis. Vánis and Káyasths eat *pakki* at the hands of this caste.

The following particulars apply to Marátha Bhadbhunjás.

The surnames among the Marátha Bhadbhunjás are Gáikwád, Jádhav, Powár and Sinde, who eat together, but families with the same surname do not intermarry. They look like Maráthás, speak Maráthi and live in houses similar to Marátha houses except for the furnace or *bhatti* and a shop in the verandah. In religion, customs and community they closely resemble Maráthás. In addition to parching and selling grain and pulse, they sometimes serve as day labourers, entrusting their shops to their wives and children.

BHAIBUND.—A synonym for Lohána.

BHALAVALKAR.—A sub-division of Gaud Sárasvat Bráhmans.

BHALIA.—A sub-division of Dheds, Kolis and Rávals.

BHALVI.—A sub-division of Bráhmans.

BHAMTAS,(1) also called Uchlias, Takáris and Ghantichors, numbering 2,886 (1901), including 1,446 males and 1,440 females, are a wandering tribe and were found chiefly in Poona, Sátára, Khándesh, Belgaum, Bijápur and Kolhápur State at the time of the last census. The census figures are, it is to be feared, misleading, owing to the fact that many of the caste do not disclose their identity as Bhámtás when the census is taken, but prefer to return themselves as Maráthás or other more respectable castes. They are also occasionally styled Khisa-Kátra (pocket-cutters), Vadaris, Kal Wadars, Tudug Wadars(2) and Kámátis. They take their names Ghantichor and Uchlia from their profession of stealing and picking pockets. Their home speech, which is a broken Telugu, and their names, which have a southern or eastern form, seem to show that they have come from the Telugu districts either of Madras or of the Nizám's country. They have no idea why and when they left their native country, and no memory of having belonged to any other class of Hindus. The author of the Bombay Gazetteer considers that the Poona Bhámtás are not true Bhámtás, and asserts that the proper Bhámtás come, not from the east or south-east, but from the north, and are of Rajput descent. They adopt many disguises in pursuit of their livelihood. At times they keep to some particular disguise for years and travel hundreds of miles, entering and stealing from the houses of the class of people whose dress they adopt.

Name and origin.

Bhámtás consist of two exogamous sub-divisions, Jádhav and Gáikwád. Marriages are prohibited between members of the same sub-division and within four degrees on the boy's side and three degrees on the girl's side. A member of the caste may marry two

(1) Much of the information in this article has been supplied to me by the Police Department through the courtesy of Mr. Michael Kennedy.

2 Kal Wadar and Tugud Wadar mean the thieving Wadars. Wadar is probably a form of Od or Vadda. *See* OD.

sisters, and brothers may marry sisters. With the exception of such castes as Mángs, Mahárs, Chámbhárs, Dhors and Buruds, Bhámtás admit all Hindus of the upper and middle classes, such as Vánis, Márwáris, Sutárs, etc., into their tribe. Muhammadans and Berads are also admitted. They also adopt children of other castes and bring them up to their own profession. Adopted boys are called "Konnad" or "Golyad," girls "Konnadi." It is also said that Uchliás will go so far as to give shelter, in certain cases, to a woman who has got into trouble and belongs to a respectable family. When the child is born, the Bhámta keeps it and sends the mother home with a *sári* and a rupee or two. There are many well-known cases of Bráhmans, Márwári Vánis, Sonárs, Shimpis and other upper and middle class Hindus joining the Bhámtás. The candidate to be admitted passes through two ceremonies—admission to the caste and adoption into a family of the caste. The admission takes place in the presence of the castemen, when the candidate has to pay an admission fee varying from Rs. 10 to Rs. 25. Next, he is bathed and dressed in new clothes, music is played and one of the elder members of the caste drops sugar and turmeric into his mouth. A feast follows, during which two or three of the caste elders sit with the novice and eat from the same plate with him. The candidate is then adopted by one of the castemen and becomes a member of the sub-division to which he belongs.

In every village they have a headman of their own, who is usually the oldest resident Bhámta. He is designated "Pátil," "Taldaru," "Talmad," or "Kattimani," and is the spokesman for the Bhámtás of the village, presides at caste meetings, and is socially respected. "Honour among thieves" is apparently at a discount among them, seeing that there is a well-established trial by ordeal, styled the "*Tel-rawa*" for the purpose of ascertaining the truth in cases of infidelity among the women and withholding of profits on any member's part. On his return from a thieving expedition a Bhámta in the Deccan has to pay a tax of 2 annas in the rupee to the Pátil (also called "Talmad") of his caste.

Marriage. Boys are generally married between ten and twenty; girls between ten and sixteen. If a girl commits sexual indiscretions with a casteman, the latter is fined and made to give a dinner to the castepeople, while the girl is married to a recently joined member of the community, after the widow remarriage fashion. If the offence is committed with a member of a lower caste, the girl is excommunicated; if with a member of a higher caste, it is connived at. Polygamy is allowed and practised, but polyandry is unknown. It is said to be a rule among Bhámtás not to give a girl in marriage till the intended husband has proved himself a dexterous thief.

The offer of marriage comes from the boy's father, who has to pay Rs. 50 to the girl's maternal uncle and Rs. 100 to Rs. 200 to the girl's parents. The day for the marriage is fixed by the boy's parents without consulting an astrologer. The ceremony is conducted by elderly members of the caste. First, the boy and the girl are rubbed with turmeric paste, when a Holár beats a drum and women sing songs. In the evening of the same day the boy goes in procession to a temple of Máruti, and thence to the girl's house. The boy and the girl are then bathed in the marriage booth, dressed in new clothes, and seated on a blanket on a rice-traced square. The brows of both are decked with tinsel chaplets, and thread wristlets or *kankans* are tied round their wrists. Next, the girl's father ties together the ends of the pair's garments, and yellow grains of rice are thrown over their heads by the party assembled, which completes the union. At night a *gondhal* dance is performed before the family god, a goat is killed, and castemen are feasted. After dinner the boy and the girl untie their *kankans*. On the third day the boy returns to his house with his bride and party, which terminates the marriage.

The *devak* or marriage guardian of the Gáikwáds consists of the leaves of the *jámbul* (Eugenia jambolana), a knife and an axe, that of the Jádhavs, of an ear of *jowári* and a cocoanut. The *devak* is tied to a post of the marriage booth at the commencement of the marriage.

The remarriage of widows is permitted. A widow can marry a member of her late husband's section. She may marry his brother, but is not compelled to do so. The ceremony consists in presenting to the widow a robe and bodice, and in tying round her neck a necklace of black glass beads by her new husband. Should a bachelor desire to marry a widow he is first married to a *shami* bush. A husband can divorce his wife on the ground of her misconduct. A divorced woman can marry again after the fashion of the widow remarriage ceremony. If a woman is taken in adultery with a casteman, both are taken to a river bank and the man's face and the woman's head are shaved ; and the man is made to give a dinner to the caste-people.

The caste follow the Hindu law of inheritance and belong to the Hindu religion. Some are followers of the Várkari sect. They worship all the Bráhman gods, but their favourite deities are Bahiroba, Bhaváni, Khandoba, Mhasoba, Vetál and Yellamma. They observe all the Hindu holidays and make pilgrimages to Alandi, Pandharpur. Religion.

Jejuri, Bhimáshankar, or wherever there is likely to be a crowd. They do not ask Bráhmans to officiate at any of their ceremonies. All their ceremonies are conducted by leading men of the caste.

Death ceremonies. The married dead are burnt, the unmarried being buried in a lying position with head to the north. The bones and ashes are consigned to water. On the fourteenth day after death the flesh of a cock and boiled rice are offered to crows on a *rui* bush. For the propitiation of the deceased ancestors, castemen are feasted every year on the new moon day of *Bhádrapad*. The *shráddha* is not performed.

Occupation. Bhámtás follow ordinary rural avocations and occasionally the more well-to-do trade in a small way as merchants or *sávkárs*. Some cultivate land on a large scale and labour in the fields during harvest time. But mostly those who own land rent it to others, not infrequently to the village headman. Some are rich in land and cattle.

Comparatively recently Bhámtás have taken to burglary and even robbery, forming gangs of a dozen or more for the purpose. Originally, it seems, Bhámtás were pick-pockets pure and simple, fairs and bazars and the like offering a large field for their activities. It was also a rule among them not to commit, on pain of expulsion from the caste, crime between sunset and sunrise. All this is, however, now altered.

Both sexes are adept at thieving whether on the railway or in crowds, but the women do not travel so much or so far afield as the men.

Food. They eat the usual kind of animal food and also the flesh both of the tame pig and wild boar. They drink liquor to excess. They will eat with or from the hands of those of other castes who are admissible into their own. Instances of intermarriage between Kaikádis and Bhámtás are not unknown.

BHAMTA.—A sub-division of Kaikádis.

BHANDS, numbering 149 (1901), including 89 males and 60 females, are found chiefly in Káthiáwár. They come from Márwár and gain their living by begging. Some are mimics and ventroloquists. They are Hindus and believe in Chaturbhuj. They allow widow marriage and burn their dead.

Name and origin. **BHANDARIS**, also known as Bhávagunas, numbering 168,667 (1901), including 82,194 males and 86,473 females, are found in almost every district of the Presidency, and in most of the Native States, but chiefly reside in Ratnágiri, Kanara, Kolába, Thána, Bombay City and the State of Sávantvádi. They are called

Mádkárs to the south of the Gangávali river in the Kanara district. Their occupation is drawing toddy from palm trees, and their name is probably derived from the Sanskrit *mandhárak*, a distiller (Bom. Gazetteer, Vol. XV, Part I, p. 286). The caste members prefer to derive it from *bhándár*, a treasury, on the ground that they formerly acted as treasury guards. There is much historical evidence that they were once largely employed as foot soldiers by the Maráthás and the British. From Fryer onwards they are mentioned in Bombay Island under the name of 'Bandareens'. The famous *Hetkaris* of Shiváji were Bhandáris. There is in some respects a striking resemblance between Bhandáris and the Marátha Kunbis. Tradition asserts that during the days of Rajput supremacy in Northern India an army of Rajputs defeated a rising in the Deccan and were consequently called *Bandári*, *Bandhári* (Bhandári),(1) quellers of rebellions. To keep the rebels permanently in check, the army was ordered to remain in the Deccan. Thus in course of time these Rajputs became domiciled in the country and were the ancestors of the Bhandáris. The reign of Allauddin Khilji is given as the period in which the alleged Rajput invasion occurred. But the whole story appears to lack historical foundation.

In a paper read by Mr. Murphy(2) before the Geographical Society he refers to the early settlement of Bhandáris in Bombay Island. As their numbers increased, they carried on war with the Musalmán kings, in which they were helped by the Bhandáris of Champavati or Chaul. It appears that about 1295 A. D. Bimb Rája or Bhimarája took possession of Bombay with the help of the Bhandáris. The immediate successor of Bhimarája was dispossessed of his authority by a Bhandári chief, Shetya of Chaul, who in turn was dispossessed by Musalmáns, Upon the arrival of the Portuguese the Bhandáris were once more in power and assisted the invaders against the Musalmáns. Thereafter at Máhim a Bhandári kingdom was established by Bhongules or Bhandáris. With the help of the Portuguese several petty kingdoms seem to have been established by the Bhandáris on the western coast, and they had for a long time the right of carrying regal ensigns. In this regard a few quotations from Mr. Murphy's paper may be given here :— History

"Of the Bhandáris the most remarkable usage is their fondness for a peculiar species of long trumpet called Bhongulee,

(1) This derivation for the word *Bhandári* appears to have been invented by those anxious to assign a higher origin to the caste than it can probably claim, as no compound can be found of a Sanskrit and Prakrit word. The word *band* is Prakrit, while *ari* or *hári* is a Sanskrit word. *Bandhári* is not a possible compound.

(2) Robert Xavier Murphy, Interpreter of the Supreme Court of Bombay, and prominent member of B.B.R.A.S. in 1830.

which, ever since the dominion of the Portuguese, they have had the privilege of carrying and blowing on certain state occasions. Fryer, in a letter written from Bombay between 1672 and 1681, describes the Bhandáris as forming a sort of honorary guards or heralds to the Governor, and even to this day they carry the union flag and blow their immense trumpet before the High Sheriff on the opening of the Quarter Sessions. This singular privilege receives considerable illustration from a fact stated in MS histories that shortly before the Portuguese occupation of Bombay a race of Bhongulee or trumpeter chiefs seized upon and maintained the Government of Máhim to which Bombay and Salsette were then subject. This, then, would appear to have been a dynasty of Bhandári princes whose humble representatives are still to be seen blowing their trumpets and carrying their standards in the pageants of another royalty.

"We next have a dynasty of Bhongulee or trumpeter chiefs whom there is every reason for believing to be Bhandáris, since they retain the Bhongulee trumpet and the name of Bhongulees to this day and still have some privileges in public pageants which seem the faint shadows of former power. The Mahomedans are described as overthrowing the Bhongulees and again becoming ascendant, and I am to suppose that on the arrival of the Portuguese the Bhongulees or Bhandáris sided with the latter for the expulsion of the Mahomedans and thus perhaps retained those privileges to which here has been no interruption since the dominion of the Portuguese."

It is stated by some that the recognized head-quarters of the Bhandáris are in a village named Mitgávana in the Rájápur *táluka* of the Ratnágiri district, and this statement is corroborated by the practice prevalent among all of them of giving first honour to Mitgávana guests at marriage ceremonies. Some say that certain places in the Goa territory are regarded as the chief seats of their patron deities. The greater number of the caste, however, is to be found settled on the sea coast.

The Bhandáris in the Ratnágiri district admit illegitimate children to the caste, provided that both the father and the mother belong to their caste. This question of admission is decided in a meeting of the leading castemen of the locality, convened for the purpose. Generally, a feast is given to the caste-people, and the person to be admitted is made to sit at the bottom of the row. After the meal is over, he is required to remove the plates and clean the floor.

This admission does not entitle him to be ranked on an equal footing with the castemen for purposes of marriage until the seventh generation.

The Bhandáris include the following endogamous divisions :— Endogamous divisions.

(1) Kitte	(5) Kálan
(2) Bherle	(6) Thale
(3) Gávade or Gaude	(7) Shinde
(4) Bhande	(8) Kirpál

The Bherle Bhandáris tap the *bherla* (Caryota urens). Bandes or slaves are the out-caste section for those who have transgressed caste rules, including illegitimate offspring. Kirpáls, found in Thána, are Christian Bhandáris who have reverted to Hinduism. It is alleged that the Shinde and Gávade Bhandáris in the Thána district occasionally intermarry.

The exogamous divisions of the caste are *kulas*, many of which bear names found even among the Maráthás, *i.e.*, Jádhav, Kadam, Chaván, More, Surve, Bhosle, Ráne, etc. Members of such *kulas* cannot intermarry. They bear names derived from places, such as Ambolikar, Bárdeshkar, Karambalkar, etc. ; and names suggesting positions of authority, such as Pátil, Subhedár, Kotwál, etc. But for purposes of marriage the *kula* name alone is considered. These *kulas* show reverence for *devaks*, such as the banyan, *pipal*, *kadamba* tree (Anthocephalus cadumba), *umbar* (Ficus glomerata), and mango, and are referred to by the names of such trees, *viz.*, the *Vadáche kul* or banyan family, etc. They abstain from burning, cutting, or in any way injuring such *devaks*, which they hold in great respect. The ceremony of installing the *devak* is part of the ordinary marriage ceremony of the caste. Some Bhandáris now claim to belong to the Bráhmanic *gotras*, Vashishta, Atri, Durvas, etc. ; but this seems to be a recent innovation. It is reported that the significance of the *devak* is of varying importance, and that in some places members of *kulas* having the same *devak* do intermarry without objection being raised to the union on this score. Elsewhere such a proceeding would not be tolerated. Descendants of brothers cannot marry so long as a common ancestor can be traced, and the children of two sisters are also forbidden to marry for three generations. Marriage with a wife's sister is permitted even during the life-time of the wife. Polygamy is allowed and practised, the number of wives a man may have at a time being generally two. Polyandry is unknown. Marriage is both infant and adult. Sexual license before marriage

Exogamous divisions.

is neither recognized nor tolerated. In Kanara, girls are married as a rule before attaining puberty.

Marriage.

The offer of marriage generally comes from the boy's father. In Kanara the boy's father has to pay a *teru* or bride-price of from Rs. 12 to Rs. 40 to the girl's father. The day for the marriage is fixed by a Bráhman priest who conducts the service. On the morning of the marriage day the bridegroom goes in procession to a near wood, and cutting a branch of the tree representing his *devak*, brings it home and fixes it in a new earthen pot filled with rice grains covered with a cocoanut, and places the pot near the household gods. The *devak* is then worshipped, and a lamp is kept burning near it for four days, that is, up to the end of the marriage. On this day the pot containing the *devak* and the marriage coronet worn by the bridegroom are carried to a clean spot away from the house, and the pot, the *devak*, and the marriage coronet are left there. The rice and the cocoanut are brought back and thence a dish is prepared and eaten by the members of the family. This ceremony of installing the *devak* is also performed at the girl's house.

A few hours before the marriage takes place the bride and bridegroom at their respective houses are rubbed with oil and bathed under a triangular frame made of three branches of the *sávar* tree (Bombax malabaricum). While they are being bathed, the mother or another female relation of the party walks round the frame with a light in her hand and a basket on her head, containing sweetmeats. The moment the bathing is finished, a male relation of the party cuts down the frame with a knife, unseen by the bride or bridegroom. The sweets in the basket are distributed amongst Mahárs or beggars.

After the bath is over, *Punyáhavachana* (Holy-day-blessing), worship of Ganpati, and other ceremonies observed by the higher castes at the time are performed at the houses of both the bride and bridegroom, and turmeric paste and oil are carried in procession by unwidowed women from the bridegroom's house to the bride's, and are applied to her person. A dinner is held and the party retires. Then comes the marriage proper, which is performed exactly after the fashion of the local Bráhmans, the binding portion consisting in the *saptapadi*. In Kanara they have the *dháre* ceremony, which is the essential portion.

Another peculiarity of the marriage ceremony of the Kanara Bhandáris is that, on the marriage day, before wearing the *báshing* or marrige coronet, the bridegroom has to worship the *kadamb* (Anthocephalus cadumba). On the second and third day feasts are exchanged, and certain games are played by the bride and bridegroom which are common to all the local higher castes. On the fourth day the marriage coronet is removed from the boy's head and he returns home in procession with his bride, which terminates the marriage.

The remarriage of widows is permitted with the sanction of the caste *panch*. In Kanara the permission of the widow's late husband's relations is also necessary. If it is obtained, the widow hands over to them the ornaments received from her deceased husband ; if not, she places the ornaments at the root of the sweet basil plant in front of the house and walks away, after which she becomes eligible for remarriage. A widow is not allowed to marry her father's sister's or mother's sister's son, or a member of her late husband's or father's section. The ceremony is performed at night in an unoccupied out-house. The details vary in the different localities according to local usages. In the Ratnágiri district, where the caste is most numerous, it is celebrated as follows :—

The ceremony of *ovâlani* (waving a platter containing lighted wicks, a pice, a cocoanut, rice grains, and a cock) is first performed by a *Bhagat* (exorcist) in order to free the widow from the dominion of the spirit of her deceased husband, who is supposed to haunt her. The materials of the *ovâlani*, except the cock, which is taken by the Bhagat, are carefully packed together and sent to the house of the widow's deceased husband in order to be lodged at the root of the *tulsi* (sweet basil) plant in front of the house, as it is supposed that these *ovâlani* materials collected together carry back with them the spirit of the deceased husband. The *Bhagat* himself is possessed of his favouring spirit while performing the ceremony. Thus possessed, he promises good to the pair, and conjures the spirit of the widow's deceased husband by means of the *ovâlani*. Thus freed, the widow is presented to her new husband by another widow who acts as her bride's-maid. She applies paste made of flour of *udid* (black gram) to the left knee of the latter, and puts some grains of rice on it. Next, the widow's new husband presents her with a new dress and ornaments which she puts on in the presence of the assembly. This completes the ceremony. A dinner is then held, and a present of Rs. 5 is made to the caste *panch* who sanctioned the marriage. On the following morning before day-break the widow's new husband, accompanied by his friends and followed by her, leaves the house to return home. The widow takes a cock under her arm. When the procession reaches the boundary of the village the cock is immolated, and its head together with a lock of hair from the widow's head and a bit of the new robe worn by her are buried under a rock. The body of the cock is taken away and eaten by the *Bhagat*, who accompanies the pair till they reach home. This ceremony is also performed by the *Bhagat* and is intended to be an offering to the guardian spirit of the village resident on the boundary, who is expected to take charge of the spirit of the deceased husband. Not unnaturally the deceased husband is believed to be very jealous of the second husband, and all the efforts of the *Bhagat* are directed towards annihilating his influence, in case he may be hovering near in the spirit with evil intentions.

The widow remarriage ceremony observed in Kanara is not so elaborate. As amongst most other castes in the district, it consists in the wearing by the widow of new glass or metal bangles and a new robe presented to her by her new husband. Next, rice grains are applied to her forehead by male members on both sides, which completes the ceremony.

Widow remarriage is not looked upon with favour by this community. Unwidowed women are not allowed to attend the ceremony, and the remarried widow is not allowed to cook or be present on auspicious occasions. As a rule a bachelor is not allowed to marry a widow. But if he is unable to meet the expenses of a first marriage he is allowed to marry a widow after he has first married a *shami* (Prosopis spicigera) bush.

A husband can divorce a wife on the ground of her misconduct, which has to be proved before a meeting of the caste *panch*. It is also said that divorce can be effected by mutual consent. In the former case the divorced woman is excommunicated. In the latter she is allowed to remarry after the fashion of the widow remarriage ceremony. Among the Bande Bhandáris adultery or prostitution does not entail loss of caste. They do not object to admit into their subdivision such members of the higher sections of the caste as may have lost their caste by misconduct. Some women among the Bande Bhandáris remain unmarried and follow prostitution as a calling. They are called Kasbins. Kalávants and Bhávins are also recruited from Bhandári women. In the eighteenth century the palace concubines at Sávantvádi were Bhandári women.

Religion. Bhandáris follow the Hindu law of inheritance and belong to the Hindu religion. They are followers of the Shaiva sect. They worship all Bráhmanic and local gods, observe all the Hindu fasts and feasts, and make pilgrimages to all the sacred places of the Hindus. Their family gods are Mahádeva, Rawalnáth, Nágnáth, Rámnáth, Shejjeshwar, Shivanáth, Mahámáye, Kálika, Chandika, Kolamba, Mahákáli, etc., whose shrines are in Goa, Vengurla, Ratnágiri, Rájápur, and other places in the Southern Konkan. Their spiritual guide is the Shankaráchárya of the Shringeri monastery.

The Kanara Bhandáris are the disciples of Gosávis of the Giri sect. On an auspicious day a Gosávi is taken to the house with great pomp and he initiates all the male members of the family into his creed by whispering into their ears a *mantra* or mystic words. He is treated to a dinner of mutton, fish, and liquor, and while he is eating, a dance is performed before him to the accompaniment of cymbals.

The priests of the Bhandáris are Konkanasth, Karháda, or Karnátak Bráhmans.

Death ceremonies

As a rule Bhandáris burn their dead, though burying is not regarded as objectionable, and is not uncommon in the case of poor people. At burial the corpse is either seated or is laid with head to the south. The bones and ashes are thrown into the sea or a river in the vicinity. Those who have the means carry a few of the bones to a sacred river to be thrown into the holy waters. The ordinary funeral rites are observed. For the propitiation of the deceased ancestors the *mahálaya* is performed in the latter half of *Bhádrapad* and the *shráddha* on the anniversary of the deceased.

Occupation.

The hereditary occupation of the caste is believed to be palm-juice drawing and distilling, but since the rise in the palm-tree cess (1877) many have become husbandmen and labourers. Some are traders and contractors. Some have taken to carpentry, masonry, and tailoring, and some are sailors. A few own ships. Coir and cordage are chiefly manufactured by the Bhandáris. Many are employed in the police and infantry. They occasionally own land or occupy it as inferior holders. Many are landless day labourers and are paid either in cash or in kind. The implements which may be said to be characteristic of the caste are a cutting instrument called *káti* in some parts and *áut* in others and a gourd-vessel called *kunda*. Those who abstain from tapping are considered to be raised in social estimation above those who do not.

Food.

The staple food of the caste is rice. They eat the flesh of goats, sheep, fowls, hares, deer, wild boars, and fish. They drink liquor, but it is not used on auspicious occasions, except at the worship of the goddess Durga. They take *kacchi* and *pakki* from the hands of Bráhmans, Vánis, and Maráthás. They do not eat from the hands of Deolis and Bándis though except in Kanara they have no objection to taking water or smoking the hubble-bubble with them. In the social scale they rank next to the Maráthás. The latter maintain that they cannot and do not partake of food with the Bhandáris. The Bhandáris state that the Maráthás formerly ate with them and tell a story to account for the latter's stopping the practice, which runs as follows :—

There is a village named Varavaden near the town of Rájápur in the Ratnágiri district. The Maráthás and Bhandáris of this place lived in great intimacy and on terms of equality. According to the local custom the cocoanut tree to be burnt at the *Holi* festival was carried to the place of burning by the Maráthás and Bhandáris jointly, the former holding the top of the tree and the latter the bottom. One year the Maráthás objected to the Bhandáris holding the bottom of the tree, and a quarrel arose which led to bloodshed. In the struggle many Maráthás and Bhandáris fell. Tradition relates that the wife of one of the Bhandári victims named Párkar peformed *sati* on this occasion. A temple was erected on the spot in her memory, which, it is told, is still in existence, and held in great reverence by the people. On this day the Maráthás vowed never to drink water at the hands of the Bhandáris, and the vow has been strictly observed up to the present day. This incident is said to have taken place about 400 years ago.

BHANDI.—A sub-division of Ods.

BHANDI SANTAN.—A sub-division of Mallavas.

BHANDU.—A synonym for Musale Kolis.

Name and origin.

BHANGIS or Bhangiás, numbering 81,094 (1901), including 41,497 males and 39,597 females, are found in almost every district of the Presidency and in Native States, but chiefly reside in Bombay City, Ahmedábád, Broach, Kaira, Panch Maháls, Surat, Cambay, Káthiáwár, Mahi Kántha, Pálanpur, Rewa Kántha and Poona. In Gujarát, they are also known as Halálkhors, Olgana, Bárváshia, Metariya, Jamphoda and Mela, and in the Deccan and Karnátak as Halálkhors. As a caste of scavengers and sweepers they are the dregs of Hindu society, and contain an admixture of outcastes who have fallen to this level owing to offences against the social code of higher castes. Being open to continual recruitment in this fashion their customs are confused and uncertain. Bhangia is generally supposed to mean broken. Of the origin of its application to the Bhangias three explanations are given. According to one theory it means the broken or outcaste people;[1] according to a second it means the scrap-men or livers on broken meat; and according to a third it means the bamboo splitters. This third derivation derives some probability from their occupation, in certain areas, of plaiting baskets and other articles of split bamboo. According to Campbell,[2] if a Koli is asked in Kaira to split a bamboo he will say: "Am I to do Bhangia's work?" According to Crooke,[3] it is usually derived from the Sanskrit *bhánga* (hemp) in allusion to the drunken habits of the tribe. Nesfield would derive it from the same word in the sense of "interruption", as a Hindu must give up whatever he is doing when he is touched by a sweeper. The Benáres sweepers say that the word is a corruption of *sárbhanga* (*sarva-bhanga*). in the sense that, while part of the Hindu community, they are isolated from it. The term *mehtar* or prince is a honorific title of the heads of several castes, and was commonly applied to the servants of the Emperor Humayun. The term *halál-khor* is derived from the Persian *halál* (clean or lawful) and *khor* (eater), apparently because to them everything is lawful food. This euphemistic title is said to have been introduced by the Emperor Akbar. They are called Bárváshiás because they live outside a village. "Mela" means night-soil, and so the sweepers of it are known as "Mela." The meanings of the terms Olgana and Jamphoda are not known.

Traditions of origin.

According to their own story, Bhangiás are the descendants of a Bráhman sage who carried away and buried a dog that died in the midst of a Bráhman assembly. Their surnames Chohán, Chudásama, Dáfda, Jethva, Makwána, Solanki, Vághela and Vádhiya may possibly shew recruitment from the outcastes of these Rajput clans, while Dhedva, Kumbhár, Máru and Purbiya suggest a mixture of castes. According to Hindu books, they are the offspring of a Shudra father by a Bráhman widow. Their traditional founder is Suparnakha who belonged to one of the eighty-four castes. These the god Rám once invited to a feast given by his wife Sita who had cooked different dishes with her own hands. Suparnakha, instead of eating each dish separately, mixed all the dishes into one mess and ate it in five mouthfuls. Annoyed by his want of manners Sita said to him: "You will henceforth eat food mixed with dirt; you will live

(1) Rev. J. Wilson, *Aboriginal Tribes.*

(2) *Bombay Gazetteer*, Vol. IX, p. 334.

(3) W. Crooke, *Tribes and Castes, North-Western Provinces and Oudh*, Vol. I, p. 260.

on the refuse of food thrown into the street; you will take to the lowest callings; and instead of associating with you, people will shun you." In Gujarát, though the Bhangiás are held to be lower and more unclean, they are viewed with kindlier feelings than the Dhedás. Bhangiás were never forced to wear dishonouring badges. To meet the basket-bearing Bhangia is lucky, and the Bhangia's blessing is valued. Formerly, before attempting the dangers of the Mahi crossing, a Bhangia's blessing was sought. Still, according to Campbell, if a Government officer goes into a Bhangia hamlet, the men with hands raised in blessing say: "May your rule last for ever."

Social divisions.

In the Deccan, the Bhangiás are divided into Bhasods, Chajgadis, Helas, Lálbegis, Makhiyárs and Sheikhs. Of these, Lálbegis and Sheikhs eat together but do not inter-marry and are considered higher than the other four, who do not inter-marry or eat together. Sheikhs profess to be Musalmáns, and Lálbegis are half Hindus and half Musalmáns. In Poona, the Lálbegis and Sheikhs eat together and intermarry. Helas are also found in the United Provinces as an endogamous division of the Bhangiás. The Lálbegis[1] are a totemistic section who refuse to eat the flesh of a hare because Lálbeg, their religious head or *guru*, was suckled by a female hare. In the United Provinces, the Lálbegis have three such totemistic divisions, the hare being a totem of the Kharaha division. It thus appears that the Lálbegis of this Presidency belong to the Kharaha (*kharaha* = hare) division. Many Bhangiás in the northern part of the Presidency appear to be immigrants from the United Provinces. It seems probable that in many cases Bhangiás originally came to this Presidency as camp followers with the armies from the north.

Language.

In Gujarát, the Bhangiás speak Gujaráti and understand Urdu. In Ahmednagar, Sholápur, Kolhápur, Belgaum and Kanara they speak Hindustáni both at home and abroad. In Sátára, they speak Hindustáni and Maráthi and in Poona, their home speech is a mixture of Hindustáni, Gujaráti and Maráthi.

Community.

Bhangiás are bound together by a strong caste feeling and have their headmen to settle social disputes. In Gujarát, breaches of caste rules are punished by forbidding the offenders the use of water and fire, and offenders are re-admitted into caste on paying a fine. In the Ahmednagar district, the offenders who cannot pay the fine have to carry round a tobacco pipe for the caste-people to smoke,

(1) W Crooke, *Tribes and Castes, North-Western Provinces and Oudh*, Vol. I, p. 272.

and are pardoned. In Poona, an adulteress is fined Rs. 40, and if she is discovered to be pregnant she is fined Rs. 60. Before he is allowed to marry a widow, the husband has to give the caste Rs. 14. If a marriage is broken off after a settlement has been made, the offending party has to pay the caste a fine of Rs. 5, and on every marriage there is a caste fee of Rs. 4. A woman who leaves her husband and lives with another man has to pay Rs. 20. In the Ahmednagar district, persons are allowed to join the Bhangi caste from all Hindu classes except Mahárs, Mángs and Chámbhárs. In Kanara, they admit outcastes from all castes and creeds.

Marriage is generally forbidden among relations within six or seven degrees either on the mother's or on the father's side. Marriage with a wife's sister is allowed during the wife's lifetime or after her death. Two brothers may marry two sisters. According to the means of the parent, boys and girls are married between twelve and twenty. Sexual license before marriage is neither allowed nor tolerated. If a girl commits sexual indiscretions before marriage, she is fined from Rs. 25 to Rs. 100 and is made to walk the streets with shoes on her head. Polygamy is permitted, but polyandry is unknown. Marriage.

The offer of marriage comes from the bride's or bridegroom's father, and the proposals are carried through an intermediary known as *panchatia* or *bhánjgadia*. He is paid one rupee for his services. The father of the bridegroom pays up to Rs. 60 to the bride's father, which the latter spends in defraying the marriage expenses. A Bráhman is asked to fix the marriage day and is paid a copper or two for his trouble. In South Gujarát, a priest of their own caste officiates at all these ceremonies; in Central Gujarát, the priest is a Gáruda, that is, Dheda Bráhman. Three or four days before the marriage, the bride and bridegroom, each at their own house, are rubbed with turmeric, the women singing and making merry. On the marriage day, at the entrance to the girl's marriage booth, the bridegroom is received by his mother-in-law; the boy and girl are seated in the central square or *chori* of the marriage booth, facing each other, and between them a fire is lighted, a cotton thread is wound round them, their hands are joined, they make four turns round the *chori* and feed each other with *kansár*, a mixture of boiled wheat flour, clarified butter and molasses. When two rounds are taken by the bride and bridegroom the marriage knot is tied and the ceremony is brought to a close. The tying of the knot is the binding portion of the ceremony.

Widow re-marriage. Widow re-marriage is allowed. A widow is not allowed to marry her mother's sister's son, maternal uncle's son or her father's sister's son. She may marry the younger brother or any other member of her deceased husband's family if she chooses to do so. A widow re-marriage is celebrated on a Sunday, Tuesday or Thursday, at night. The ceremony consists in tying the ends of the widow's and her new husband's garments into a knot. A bachelor is not allowed to marry a widow.

Divorce. Divorce is allowed. The husband may divorce his wife, with the permission of the headmen of the caste, when she bears a bad character. Divorce is known as *talak*. The husband tears a piece of cloth from his head-dress and gives it to his wife, and the wife takes off her glass bangles and puts them into the husband's lap. This done, the divorce is complete. A woman divorced for infidelity to her husband is allowed to marry a second time, and her marriage is conducted in the form of widow re-marriage. A woman excommunicated for immoral conduct is re-admitted by paying a fine.

Inheritance. Bhangiás follow the Hindu law of inheritance. After his death the father's property is divided equally among all the sons, except that, among the bamboo workers, the knife and other tools belong to the eldest son. In the absence of heirs, a Bhangia's property goes to the caste funds.

Religion. Bhangiás are Hindus by religion. They honour almost all Bráhman divinities, and their favourite objects of worship are : in Central Gujarát—Hanumán, Meldi and Shikotri, and in South Gujarát—Ganpati, Devi and the *basil* plant. As they are not allowed to enter Hindu temples they bow to the idol from a distance. Many Bhangiás are followers of the sects of Kabir, Rámánand and Nának. Some of them keep in their houses an image which represents some woman of the family who has been possessed by a spirit. They honour the *Navarátri* or nine-night festival in *A'so* (October). Some teachers or *gurus* of their own caste yearly visit the Bhangiás and receive 8 annas to 1 rupee from each house. There have been several Bhangia saints or *bhagats*, of whom the chief are Chiko, Dhiro, Harkho, Kipro, Lallo, Manor and Válo. Their leading holidays are *Sankránt* in January, *Holi* in February-March, *Akhátrij* in April-May, *Diváso* in June-July, *Sitalásátem* and *Gokuláshtami* and *Balev* in July-August, *Dasara* in September-October, and *Diváli* in October-November. They go to Báchucharáji, Dákor, Dwárka, Shukaltirth and Unái, where they pay their respects to the idols from a distance or content themselves by worshipping the banner which flies from the top of the temple.

They honour Musalmán saints, and some of them are Lálbegis, that is, disciples of the Musalmán saint Lálbeg. In South Gujarát, their great day is the *chaddi* or dark ninth of *Shrávan* in August. The day is marked in honour of a certain Záhir Pir (Záhir Pir lived in the Hissár district of the Panjáb during the reign of the Emperor Firuz Shah, A.D. 1350-1390), who, besides by Bhangiás, is held in esteem by many Gujarát Hindus and Pársis. On this day the Bhangiás form a procession and carry a model of the saint's tomb. In front of the tomb the more devout dance and sing, beating themselves with heavy iron chains but by the power of the saint receiving no harm. When small-pox is raging they worship the Kákábalia deity. They respect Bráhmans, who tell them lucky days, and Gárudás or Dheda priests, who, except in South Gujarát, conduct their marriage ceremonies.

Death. The poor bury and the well-to-do burn the dead. The body is washed, perfumed and covered with a clean cloth, and is laid on a bier, from each corner of which a cocoanut hangs. One of the relatives carries fire before the body in a black earthen pot, and the bier is carried by four men who sing hymns as they go. On their way, near the burying ground, the bearers stop and rest the bier. On reaching the burying ground the body is laid in a pit with its head turned to the north, a copper is thrown in and the pit is filled with earth. When the body is burnt or buried the mourners bathe and return home. At the house of mourning, when the funeral party return, one of the relations of the deceased places an upturned basket over the spot where the head of the deceased lay. On the second day an earthen pot full of water is placed at the spot where the bearers halted near the burning ground, and is allowed to remain there for ten days. The upturned basket in the house is also allowed to remain for ten days. On the eleventh day the basket is set right, the earth underneath the basket is scraped away, and the basket is given to a priest of their own caste. If the body is buried, for ten days after the death one of the family lays a tooth-twig or *dátvan* on the grave, and a little opium if the deceased was an opium-eater. Some Bhangiás do, and others do not, consider themselves impure for ten days after a death. All perform death ceremonies on the eleventh, twelfth and thirteenth. Balls of wheat flour are offered, the clothes of the deceased are given to the officiating priest, and caste-people are feasted on the twelfth and thirteenth.

Occupation. Most Bhangiás, both men and women, are scavengers and night-soil-carriers. They also sweep the roads, winnowing the dust in the hope of finding fragments of gold and silver, make baskets and do other bamboo work, and bury dead animals, cattle excepted. Some serve as trackers, messengers and letter-carriers. A letter telling of a death was formerly brought by a Bhangia. They also serve as night-watchmen, town-criers, drummers, trumpeters, and hangmen. A few Bhangiás cultivate in addition to their regular work. In North Gujarát, except the dragging away of dead cattle, all menial village work falls on the Bhangia. Besides sweeping the roads and carrying away all dead animals, except cattle, the Bhangia watches, shews the road, arranges for supplies and points out boundaries. In municipal towns as scavengers men earn Rs. 8 to Rs. 20 a month and women Rs. 5 to Rs. 10. The winding sheet or cloth that covers the deceased is given to the Bhangia. In the case of the rich this covering is a worked shawl worth Rs. 50 to Rs. 100. The Bhangia also gets the pot in which fire has been carried before the corpse when, as is not uncommonly the case with the rich, the pot is of metal. One of the Bhangia's chief harvest times is an eclipse, either of the sun or the moon. According to Bráhman ideas, Ráhu the tormentor and eclipser of the sun and moon is a Bhangia, and, by pleasing the Bhangiás, Ráhu's fierceness against the sun or moon is tamed. It is therefore right to make presents of clothes, grain and money to Bhangiás. No Bráhman will take gifts during an eclipse. As soon as the darkening sets in, the Bhangiás go about shouting :—eclipse gifts *grahandán*, clothes gifts *vastradán*, silver gifts *rupadán*. When a Hindu dies, his widow breaks her bangles or slips them off and gives them, including one or two whole ones, generally to a Bhangia woman.

Food and drink.

Bhangiás eat the cow, buffalo, goat, sheep, camel, deer, hare, hen, partridge, quail, peacock and dove. They do not eat the dog, cat, monkey, ass, jackal, squirrel, crow, parrot or kite. Some Bhangiás do not eat the wild pig, and the Panch Maháls Bhangiás do not eat the horse. Except in Kaira, where flesh eating is avoided on holidays, they eat flesh whenever they can get it, and, except in Surat, Bhangiás eat the flesh of animals which die a natural death. They eat the leavings of other castes. They drink liquor.

No caste will receive anything at the hands of this caste. They will eat at the hands of all castes except Bajániás and Vághris.

The Deccan Bhangiás

The following customs are peculiar to the Bhangiás of the Deccan :—Their commonest surnames are Aráya, Baráya, Chan, Madya, Manji and Memdábádi. There are no exogamous divisions above families bearing the same surname. They marry their girls between seven and twelve and their boys before they are twenty. The asking comes from the boy's house, and when the match is settled, both fathers put sugar into one another's mouths. A few days before the marriage the girl's father gives a feast to the boy's relations, when sugared rice or *sákharbhát* is prepared. The girl is presented with a new robe and bodice and a flower garland is hung round her neck, betelnut-leaves and tobacco are handed round, and the guests retire. A couple of days before a marriage a dough image of Ganpati is made. This is put in a new earthen jar and worshipped by the house women, and hung in a coir sling somewhere in the house. An image of Ganpati is traced with red paint on a wall in the house and worshipped by the women. The boy and girl at their respective houses are seated on low wooden stools and rubbed with turmeric by the women of their family. The day before the marriage, a feast is held at both the boy's and girl's houses, and a *gel* fruit (Gardenia dumetorum) is tied to the right wrists of both the boy and girl. On the marriage day, the boy, accompanied by kins-people, friends and music, goes either on horseback or on foot to the girl's, where her mother marks his brow with red powder or *kunku,* throws grains of rice over his head, leads him into the marriage porch, and seats him on a square mango bench or *macholi*. The girl is then led out by her mother and seated on a quilt close to the boy. In front of them a square is traced, a new earthen jar is set in each corner of the square and cotton thread is passed five times round the jars. The priest lights a sacrificial fire in front of the boy and girl, and the boy and girl throw grains of rice over the fire and jar. The mother or other elderly woman ties the hems of their garments together, when they go round the earthen jars four times and take their seats as before. The priest repeats marriage verses or *mangaláshtaks*, and, when the verses are ended, closes the ceremony by throwing grains of rice over the heads of the bride and the bridegroom. A feast is held and the boy and girl are seated on horse-back and taken in procession to the boy's house. Here the boy and girl sit in front of the house gods and worship them by throwing flowers and grains of rice over them. Next day the boy and girl go on foot to the girl's house and, after washing their mouths, tooth powder or *dátvan* is rubbed on their teeth and they are made black. A dish of vermicelli or *shevaya* is prepared, and the boy and the girl feast. The boy leaves the girl at her parents' and returns home. A couple or four days after, the girl is taken to the boy's house, and the boy's mother puts glass bangles round her wrists. The marriage festivities end with a feast at the boy's house.

In religion they are half Hindu, half Musalmán, going to mosque and repeating prayers and at the same time having as family deities Khoriyal of Gujarát, Khandoba of Jejuri, Khajapir, Baba Makdumba, Bahiroba, Jotiba and the goddesses Janái, Kalsari and Ghochati. They pay equal respect to Musalmán saints and to Hindu gods, and offer them fowls of which the throat has been cut by a Musalmán. Of Hindu feasts they keep *Shimga* in March, *Dasara* in September-October and *Diváli* in October-November. They fast on the lunar elevenths or *ekádashis* of *Ashadh* or July and *Kártik* or October, on *Gokuláshtami* in August and on Shiva's night or *Shivarátra* in February. Their priest, a Husaini Bráhman, conducts their marriages. Sheikhs profess to be Musalmáns, do not keep Hindu holidays or fasts, and ask the *kázi* or Musalmán priest to officiate at their marriages, and to circumcise their sons.

Death ceremonies.

When a Halálkhor dies, if a man, the body is washed at the burying ground, and, if a woman, at home. The body is carried on a bamboo bier on the shoulders of four near kinsmen. On the way to the burial ground the bier is rested on the ground and a gram and sugar or *bundi* ball and copper coin are placed at the road-side, they say, for the spirit of the dead. They dig a grave, seat the deceased in it, and making a small hole in front of the body, place a lighted dough lamp in it. The chief mourner, followed by others, pours a little water into the deceased's mouth, and, after the chief mourner has thrown in a handful of earth, the rest fill the grave, bathe and go to the deceased's house. At the house each takes a mouthful of water, and, after rinsing his mouth, goes home. On the third day the chief mourner's moustache is shaved, he goes to the burial ground, lights a dough lamp, burns frankincense and lays a flower garland on the grave. On his return he lights another dough lamp, burns frankincense and lays flowers on the spot where the deceased breathed his last. They mourn twelve days, during which they are considered impure and do not touch their caste-fellows. On the morning of the twelfth day seven dough and seven rice balls are prepared and worshipped and thrown into a stream or into a pond. A caste feast at the end of a month completes the death ceremonies.

Food.

They do not eat animals which have died a natural death, but have no objection to eat beef. As a rule all Bhangiás, except Sheikhs, eat no flesh during the month of *Shrávan* or August. They do not eat from the hands of Mahárs and Mángs, but neither do Mahárs nor Mángs eat from Bhangiás.

BHANGIA.—A synonym for Bhangi.

BHANSALIS or Vegus, numbering 15,774 (1901), including 8,112 males and 7,662 females, are found principally in Cutch, Káthiáwár and Sind. The name Bhansáli or Bhansári is said to be derived from a mythical king Bhanusál, but a more favoured derivation is from 'Bhánu' the sun, Bhansális claiming to have been formerly Solankis of the solar race. The name has been lately adopted by the caste, the former name being Vegaos or Vegus, meaning mixed race, which is still applied to them by members of other castes. About A.D. 1200 they had a fort named Vegugad in the Ran, north of Lakhpat, of which traces still remain. They have ninety-six exogamous sections. Marriage is generally adult. Widows are allowed to remarry, Divorce is not permitted. Though Bhansális belong to the Vaishnava sect, some worship the goddesses. They chiefly reverence the Mándvi saint, Sádhu Láldás, to whom they yearly make presents of money and grain. Their family goddess is Hingláj near Karáchi in Sind. Their priests are Gujarát Sárasvat Bráhmans, who eat with them. They are generally labourers, but also cultivate land. They are vegetarians and eat *pakki* and *kachhi* with Lohánás, Khatris, Kansárás, Depálás, and Káyasths. In ceremonies and customs they follow Lohánás, with whom they seem to be closely connected. In appearance they are fair and well made.

BHANSARI.—A synonym for Bhansáli.

BHARADIS, also called Daure Gosávi, numbered 4,353 at the census of 1901. They are chiefly found in Khándesh (1,310), Poona (1,074), Ahmednagar (782), Násik (596), and Thána (554). **Name.**

There are no exogamous sub-divisions above the family. Members of the caste bearing the same surname cannot marry each other. The commonest surnames are :— **Divisions**

Aher.	Harál.
Chaván.	Jádhav.
Devgune.	Rájle.
Dhárde.	Sinde.
Gaikwád.	Váble.
Gund.	Vámne.

Some well known Rajput and Marátha names will be recognized in this list. Their presence suggests the possible Rajput or Marátha descent of members of the caste, though, as we have seen in the case of the Mahárs, Bhils, Bhandáris and Maráthás, too much cannot be inferred from the use of well-known names.

There are three endogamous divisions of the caste :—

(1) Bharádis proper.

(2) Mendjogis or rude beggars.

(3) Sáli Mális.

Of these, Bharádis proper are again divided into (1) God, literally sweet, that is pure, and (2) Kadu, literally bitter, that is bastard, Bharádis, who eat together but do not intermarry.

Bharádis must marry within the caste.

They generally contract marriages with households residing within twenty to fifty miles from their homes. But if they leave their homes and wander in search of employment, they settle wherever they can maintain themselves and form marriage connections there.

Bharádis say they are Marátha Kunbis who were put out of caste when they joined the Náth sect and became followers of Gorakhnáth. It is also related that the caste was founded by a sonless Kunbi who vowed that if he had sons he would set apart one of them to the services of the gods. They are wandering beggars who sing the praises of the gods, particularly of Ambábai of Saptashringi, and dance and play on the *daur* or hourglass-shaped drums. They have no memory of any former home and seem to have lived in the districts where they are found for many generations.

The habit of the caste is settled. In times of scarcity or famine they wander begging through the Southern Marátha Country, the Berars or wherever there are good crops, and after a time return to their homes. They live in poor one-storeyed houses with mud walls and thatched roofs ; but while wandering they live in temporary huts which they pitch in the fields near villages.

The Bharádis or Daure Gosávis are said by Grant-Duff to have formed part of the original Deccan village community, being the seventh of the twelve Alutedárs or village servants entitled to a share in the produce.(1)

Bharadis can admit Maráthás only to their caste. The admission of new members to the caste is made only when the parents make a vow to offer their sons to the god Bhairava. The person to be offered to the god is taken to Sonári near Paranda, where there is a temple of Bhairava. Here the head-man of the Bharádis is feasted.

(1) Grant-Duff—*History of the Maráthas*, page 15, footnote.

He then initiates the boy into the caste by performing the *Mudra* ceremony on him which is as follows :—

The *Mudra* or wearing of the ear-ring, as a rule, is allowed before marriage, the ceremony being performed both on boys and on girls between five and eight. On the day of the ceremony the religious teacher is asked to the house and is seated ; the child is made to sit before him and a hole is cut in his ear lobes with a knife, so that some drops of blood fall on the ground. Brass or horn rings called *Mudrás* are passed through the holes, and a brass or horn pipe or *shingi* is tied to a string and put round the child's neck to be blown before worshipping the gods or taking his food.

When this ceremony has been performed the child is given a *Dabara* (a tabour shaped like an hourglass) to beg in the name of Bhairava, and he is warned not to eat with low castes, exhorted to sing the praises of the god Bhairava and directed to perform "*Gondhal*" at the houses of those persons only in whose families the practice of having a *Bharád* performed by a Bharádi prevails.

Marriage is infant as well as adult. Girls sometimes remain unmarried even after puberty up to their twentieth year, but they must be married as soon as possible after this age is reached. Marriage.

Polygamy is permitted and practised, but polyandry is unknown.

The marriage ceremony of the Bharádis is conducted after the fashion of the Kunbis.

The marriage of widows is permitted.

Divorce is permitted, and a divorced woman can marry again.

The Hindu law of inheritance is followed.

The religion of the Bharádis is Hinduism. They belong to the Náth sect. They do not worship any of the regular Hindu deities, their gods being only Jotiba and Bhairava.(1) Religion.

Their family deities are Bhairavnáth of Sonári in Ahmednagar ; Devi of Máhur and Tuljápur, both in the Nizám's country ; Jotiba in Ratnágiri ; and Khandoba of Jejuri near Poona. They make pilgrimages to these places as well as to Pandharpur and keep the regular fasts and feasts.

Their priest is a village Joshi, whom they ask to conduct their marriages. Their religious teacher is a *kánfátya* or slit-ear Gosávi, whose post is elective and falls to the worthiest disciple.

---

(1) They are also said to worship all Bráhmanic and local gods. (*See* Bombay Gazetteer, Vol. XVII, p. 190.)

Death ceremonies.

Bharádis bury their dead. After death the body is carried to the funeral ground encased in a bag. The chief mourner walks in front with an earthen fire pot and the bearers follow with other mourners blowing the brass or horn pipes called *shingis*. On reaching the burial ground the body is seated in the ready dug grave with its face turned towards the east, cow-dung ashes or *bhasm* are rubbed over it, flowers and *bel* leaves are laid on it, and the chief mourner dips the skirt of his clothes in water and squeezes the water into the dead mouth. The chief mourner sprinkles earth on the dead and the other mourners fill the grave. The chief mourner lays cow-dung ashes or *bhasm* and flowers on the grave, burns frankincense before it, walks three times round it and beats his mouth with his right palm. The funeral party walk round the grave, return to the house of mourning, chew *nim* leaves, wash their mouths and go to their homes.

On the third day after death the mourners go to the burial ground, set flowers, *bel* leaves, cow-dung ashes and food on the grave, and rub the shoulders of the corpse bearers with oil that their fatigue may be removed, and treat them to a dinner. They do not hold the nearest kinsmen of the dead impure. The mourners rub their brows with cow-dung ashes and are purified. Bharádis do not perform the ten-ball ceremony or keep the death day of the dead, but ask the caste-people to dine at the house of mourning on any day between the third and the eleventh after the death.

Bharádis are called Daure Gosávi because they play on the *daur*, which they worship.

Occupation.

The chief and hereditary calling of Bharádis is begging alms at the houses of their rich neighbours and performing the *Gondhal* dance. They find their calling badly paid and a few have taken to tillage, but few, if any, are day labourers or house servants. Husbandmen pay them yearly grain allowances for performing the *Gondhal* dance at the village temples during the *Navrátra*, that is, the nine nights before *Dasara* in September. Worshippers of Devi also ask them to perform the *Gondhal* dance in honour of their goddess and pay them about Rs. 2 a night. The dance usually begins at sunset and lasts till dawn. They first sing ballads or *pavádás* in praise of Devi and secondly of Bhairavnáth to the beat of their double drums or *samel* accompanied by the one-stringed fiddle or *tuntune* and two metal cups or *táls* and amuse the audience with a number of short merry tales about the Hindu gods and heroes. The house-owner gives them free grants of food on the day they dance, and they earn

Rs. 5—6 a month. Their services are in demand during the fair season, but they find little employment during the rains. Besides minding the house, the women spin wool and hemp and weave girdles or *káchás*.

They eat flesh except beef and pork and they eat fish at the houses of Maráthás only. Some declare that they eat flesh only when they are called by a devotee to perform a *Gondhal* and he offers a goat to the gods as a portion of the offering and not otherwise; but this is doubtful. They cannot eat "*pakki*" and "*kachhi*" with any caste lower than Maráthas, nor can they take water from or smoke with a caste inferior to Marathás. Food.

BHARGAV.—A sub-division of Bráhmans.

BHARTHANA.—A sub-division of Bráhmans.

BHARTHARIS or Náths, numbering 546 (1901), including 287 males and 259 females, are found in the five Gujarát districts and in Cambay, Mahi Kántha, Pálanpur and Rewa Kántha. Nearly half the number recorded in 1901 were resident in the Ahmedábád district. The Bhartharis are a caste of beggars and call themselves Sárangi Bhartharis as they play on a *Sárangi* (fiddle) while begging. Outsiders call them Náths. The habits of the caste are settled. They sometimes leave their homes to wander about begging during the month of *Shrávan* (September) and in harvest time. Name and origin.

There are no endogamous or exogamous divisions of the caste. Divisions.

Marriage with father's sister's daughter, maternal uncle's daughter, mother's sister's daughter or wife's sister is not allowed. Two brothers may marry two sisters. Polygamy is permitted but polyandry is unknown. Boys and girls are married between 5 and 10. Sexual license before marriage is neither allowed nor tolerated. The offer of marriage is made by the bride's or bride-groom's father. The bride-groom's father pays a sum of Rs. 28½ to the bride's father and this is spent by the bride's party and the castemen in feasting. The marriage ceremonies resemble those of the local Hindu castes. Widow remarriage is allowed. A widow cannot marry her mother's or father's sister's son or her maternal uncle's son. She is allowed to marry any member of her deceased husband's family. During the ceremony either a caste priest, or in his absence a leading member of the caste, ties threads to the wrists of the couple. Divorce is allowed. A divorced woman can marry again, but her marriage is conducted after the fashion of a widow remarriage. Marriage.

Bharthâris follow the Hindu law of inheritance. They are Hindus by religion and show preference for the worship of Shankar. The preference is based upon the fact that both are ascetics (Yogis). They also worship Rám, Vishnu and his incarnations. They observe all Hindu holidays. They revere Gorakhnáth as their religious preceptor. They worship the *sárangi* which is known as *Ravan Hathho.* They do not worship any minor gods. On the *Shivrátri* day they worship Shivá's *linga* and make offering of *bháng* and *gánja.* When small-pox is raging they worship Baliákáka deity. They employ Bráhmans for religious and ceremonial purposes.

Death ceremonies.

They bury their dead. The deceased is placed in a grave in a sitting position and a cocoanut is put into his hand. The caste perform *shráddha* ceremony for the propitiation of the dead during the *Mela* (fair) held at Sidhpur. The hereditary occupation of the caste is begging alms and playing on the *sárangis.* Some are labourers.

Food.

They neither eat flesh nor drink liquor. They eat at the hands of all castes except Kolis, Vághris and similar low castes.

BHARUCHI.—A sub-division of Bhárgav Bráhmans ; a sub-division of Ghánchis.

BHARUTIA.—A sub-division of Chodhrás.

Name and origin.

BHARVADS(1) or Gádariás,(2) numbering 95,832 (1901), including 50,256 males and 45,576 females, are found all over Gujarát.

According to one story, the Bharváds are of the same caste as the Mehers, to whom Krishna's foster father Nand Meher belonged. According to another story, they are the descendants of a Vaishya father and a Sudra mother. Their original home is said to be Gokal Vrindávan near Mathura. From Gokal they are said to have moved to Mewár, and from Mewár to have spread into Gujarát, Káthiáwár and Cutch. They are closely related to the Rabáris with whom they eat but do not intermarry.

Appearance, dress and ornaments.

The men are heavily built and of middle size. Except when it is tanned red or brown, the skin, though rough and coarse, is somewhat fair. The face is square and the features irregular. The eyes are brown, seldom black, occasionally light brown. The expression is sturdy tending to heaviness; the head and face hair is black, some-

(1) The following account is taken from the Bombay Gazetteer, Vol. IX, Part I, pp. 267—285.

(2) That section of the Bharváds which tends sheep only is known as Gádariás from Gádar, meaning a sheep. (Baroda Census Report, 1901, Vol. I, p. 470.)

times brown; the chest is hairy. The women are middle-sized, square-shouldered and strong, with a flowing stride in walking. The skin is coarse and dusky, but sometimes fair, tanning a bright brown. The eyes are brown or black, not infrequently nearly closed by heavy drooping eyelids. Sometimes a clearcut face with a soft refined expression redeems a group; but as a rule the features are irregular, the expression hard, the voice strong and tending to harshness. Few Bharvád women are neat or clean. They are not fond of bathing, their heavy woollen clothes make washing troublesome, and their coarse crisp hair is seldom oiled or smoothed. The true Bharvád dress for men is three blankets of undyed wool, one wound in broad bands round the head, a second tied round the waist reaching the knee, and a third thrown across the shoulder. A woman's dress consists of a petticoat, a brown woollen headscarf hanging loose from the head with yellow or red spots, and a bodice open behind, loose-fitting in front, and carried down within an inch or two of the waist of the skirt. Unmarried girls wear a headscarf and a petticoat of cotton generally bright in colour. Some Bharvád men, especially young men, wear in the upper left ear, occasionally in both ears, a gold button called *bhungri*, through a hole in the centre of which is passed a gold ring called *ver*. Some wear a necklace of coins or of coinlike circles and a handsome bracelet of heavy filagree work called *randir*, with a flower and very small box-like cylinders welded on to it. Some men also wear silver finger rings. In the upper left ear, sometimes in both upper ears, young women wear a hanging ring with a silver cylinder or *akota* set at right angles to the ring. Old women wear from the upper ear hanging silver ornaments called *loriyer*, and in the lower ear hollow silver hangers called *nangli*. The chief necklaces are the silver called *sánkli*, and the *kánthilo*, a garland of rupee-like silver circles falling below the breast in a heart or tongue shaped pendant called *jibro*. The bracelets are either a double ring of white or red ivory called *chindi*, or a heavy silver ring called *kanchio*, the inner half flat, the outer half cut in deep cogwheel sections. On the left little finger they wear a ring called *keida* and on the left ring finger a plain ring. The anklet is a round ring of silver drooping at each side called *kami-kadla*. On the great toe a silver guard called *ananata* is worn and on the second and little toe a silver ring called *vinchhia*. Some boys wear a silver necklace and a bracelet or *khan*, a plain heavy ring on whose end are stamped the petals of a flower.

Almost all classes of villagers talk of Bharváds as Bhuts, that is, evil spirits. The Bharváds do not quarrel with the name. We are

Bhuts, they say. If a villager is asked why are Bharváds Bhuts, he answers: they are so stupid. Their wildness, their sudden and weird appearance among their sheep, a small heap of blankets rising into a huge figure, give point to the nickname. Their fitfulness is also uncanny, suddenly bursting from stolid dulness to frantic rushings and the oddest shouts, yells and calls. Moreover, they are unclean, seldom bathing, seldom washing their blanket clothes. Finally, they are sin-laden or *pápi*, selling their sheep to be slain. The Bharváds admit their sinfulness. 'So evil are we, our Bráhmans cannot support the burden of our guilt. Of our Audich Bráhmans, all are gone except one, and she is a childless widow.' Their greetings are hearty. Male acquaintances at meeting shout a cheery Rám! Rám! or they clasp right hands and touch the chest and shoulders. Relations, both men and women, who live in distant villages, when they meet, fall on each other's necks, the elderly women taking to themselves the younger's ill-luck either by waving *valva* their hands in front of the person saluted or by *baláilena*, that is, evil taking, by touching the temples of the saluted with their finger-tips and then pressing the knuckles of their hands against their own temples till the joints crack.

Language. Their home tongue is Gujaráti, though in the Panch Mahâls some speak Málvi.

Birth ceremonies. As Bharvád children are often born when their parents are moving from place to place, no ceremonies are performed on the birth, on the sixth day after a birth, or on giving the child cooked food for the first time. In some parts, the mother is not held impure after child-birth, and does all her household work from the day after the child is born; in other places, the mother remains impure for fifteen days.

Marriage Bharváds have a large number of surnames of which forty-six are known as under—Bábaria, Bajuva, Bámbhava, Bosaria, Botaria, Budia, Chuchra, Dámka, Dámker, Dhanga, Dhángia, Dupda, Fángalia, Fátaria, Galia, Gamária, Hádkarda, Jadab, Jhápda, Juthál, Karir, Kátodia, Khánt, Kharagia, Khoda, Lámbaria, Lámpka, Mánga, Mánkuda, Mátiad, Meváda, Mudhava, Munjva, Ráeka, Ranva, Rátadia, Regia, Savasia, Shiar, Sindhat, Susra, Taria, Thuga, Varu, Verái and Veshra. The marriage customs of the Bharváds of North Gujarát, Káthiáwár and Cutch are peculiar. Like Kadva Kanbis, Bharváds celebrate their marriages only once in twelve, fifteen or twenty-five years on a day in *Vaishákh* (May) and all the Bharváds of the neighbourhood hold their marriages in the same place. The marriages are held in open ground on the skirts of the village. The richest Bharvád among those who wish to get their daughters married buys the ground where the marriages are to be celebrated. This is necessary because the ground cannot be used a second time for marriages, but is kept as pasture, and an ornamental wooden post, called the marriage pillar, is set up and preserved to show that the ground has been used for marriages. The ground is first surrounded with a fence of bamboo poles and a booth is built. A branch is cut off a *shami* or *khijda* (Prosopis spicigera) tree and taken in a cart to a carpenter, who forms it into a square post with the image of Bhaváni set on its top. The post is then taken to the booth and planted in the ground. While it is being planted, the women drink large quantities of milk and butter which so excites them that they become frantic, singing lucky songs, breaking down hedges and spoiling the crops. In the centre of the booth a square or *chori* is railed off with bamboo posts and coloured earthen jars are piled at the four corners. Shortly before the marriage hour the several brides with their relations and one Bráhman priest meet in the booth. At the hour fixed for the marriage all the bridegrooms come to the booth one after the other, and are received by the wife of the man who bought the ground and paid for the booth. In receiving each bridegroom the hostess shows him a miniature plough, arrow and churning stick. The bridegrooms pass into the booth, and each sits besides his bride; the several pairs of brides and bridegrooms then go to the part of the booth where the *khijda* post is planted. The hands of the several pairs are joined by the Bráhman priest, and each pair walks round the post, bows to it, and offers it a cocoa kernel. They are next taken to the central square or *chori*, where the hems of their clothes are tied together, and they walk round a fire which is lighted in the middle. This completes the marriage ceremony. The man at whose cost the booth was built feasts the assembled Bharváds for three days. He partly repays himself by levying a tax of Rs. 12½ from the father of each bridegroom.

Among the Bharváds of Central and South Gujarát marriages are performed with little or no ceremony. The usual practice is for the bridegroom to dress in a yellow coat and, sword in hand, to go to the bride's house and seat himself near the bride. A Bráhman or a Darji, or in their absence one of the members of the bride's family, officiates at the marriage.

Widow marriages are allowed, the younger brother of the deceased husband having the first claim to wed his sister-in-law.

Except in some parts of North Gujarát, divorce is easy.

Religion. Except a few who are Rámánandis, Bharváds are followers of mothers or Mátás, who are figured on silver and copper plates. In Rewa Kántha, they call themselves the followers of Jhálábápji and Baldev, whom they describe as two holy Rajputs. The names suggest a connection between the Bharváds and two tribes of Jhálás and Bálás or Válás. Jhálábápji is their special object of worship, to whom they offer vows when their animals sicken. In parts of South Gujarát the owners of sheep and goats worship on Tuesdays or Sundays and on *Káli Chaudas* in October any she-goat or ewe which keeps aloof from the males and is barren. The festival held most sacred by the Bharváds is the *Navarátri* or nine nights in September-October. All fast on the bright eighth of *Aso* in October, and a few fast during the first nine days of that month. *Akhatrij* in April-May is their sheep-shearing day. Most of them believe in, and many are supposed to practise, sorcery and witchcraft. They have three famous holy men or *bhagats*, Ambo, Bhulo and Rághav.

Death ceremonies. Bharváds burn the dead. The chief mourner performs the *shráddha* ceremony on the eleventh day after death with the help of a Káyatia Bráhman. Caste-people are feasted on the eleventh and twelfth days.

Among Bharváds a few are husbandmen and labourers, but the bulk are shepherds or cattle-keepers. Their flocks of sheep and goats are kept in the outskirts of villages and are driven into the grass and bushlands by day and brought back at night. Between November and June they move about the country in search of pasture. They sell goat and cow's milk and weave and sell woollen blankets. They are also paid in grain or in cash for penning their flocks in empty fields as the manure is highly valued.

Instead of sheep and goats, many Bharváds keep cattle, both cows and buffaloes, and make their living chiefly by selling clarified butter and whey.(1)

Food. They live chiefly on milk and millet cakes, though a few in Cutch and Surat eat the flesh of sheep and goats. Except in Surat they do not drink liquor.

BHARVATHIA.—A sub-division of Ahirs.

BHASOD.—A sub-division of Bhangis.

---

(1) For further and very complete details regarding Bharvád customs and ceremonies, see the Bombay Gazetteer, Vol. IX, Part I.

BHATS,[1] numbering 31,882 (1901), including 17,048 males and 14,835 females, are found all over Gujarát and the Deccan, a few being found here and there in the Konkan and the Karnátak. They are numerous in Ahmedábád, Kaira and Káthiáwár and the Native States of Gujarát. Of the above number, 744 were returned as Musalmáns at the 1901 Census. As has been rightly recognized by Steel and Sherring, the Bháts of the Bombay Presidency are to be distinguished as Bháts Rajput and Bháts Marátha. The head-quarters of the former are in Ahmedábád and its neighbourhood, there being in all eleven settlements or *vádás* of them in North Gujarát. Three of the *vádás* are in Ahmedábád, one being in the city itself, five in neighbouring Gáikwár villages, two in Kaira, and one in Cambay. The Marátha Bháts are numerous in Sátára and Kolhápur, once the centres of the Marátha power. Name and origin.

The Rajput or Gujarát Bháts are also known as Báhrots, which appears to be a corruption of the Sanskrit word Bhárata. The other synonyms are Ráo, Kavi (poet) and Dasundi. The last comes from *dasham* tenth and *dáya* part, *i.e.*, one entitled to a tenth part, for it was customary for a chief or his *bhayad* to give his Bhát or bard a tenth part of his own income.

In regard to the origin of the Bháts, the Brahma-Vaivarta asserts that they sprang from the intercourse either of a Shudra father and a Vaishya mother, or of a Kshatriya male and a Bráhman female. The Játiviveka identifies the Bhát with the Mágadha, and traces his descent from a Vaishya father and Kshatriya mother. According to one account, Bháts are sprung from the creator's brain; according to another, they were created from the sweat of Shiva's brow, and driven out of heaven, because of their persistence in singing his praise and his consort's, and hence not unoften the word Bhát is derived from *bhál* the forehead and *alta* born. "According to the fable of their origin," says John Malcom, "Mahádev first created Bháts to attend his lion and bull; but these could not prevent the former killing the latter, which was a source of infinite vexation and trouble, as it compelled Mahádev to create new ones. He therefore formed the Cháran".

The Gujarát Bháts, however, repudiate any connection with the Mágadhas, or the Suta Mágadhavanshis as they are called, and give a different account of their origin. The gods Brahma and Rudra once performed the Váruna sacrifice, from whose pit of fire

(1) From materials supplied by Mr. D. R. Bhandarkar.

arose three Rishis called Bhrigu, Angiras and Kavi. From these Rishis sprang the Bhárgav, Angirasa and Kavivanshi Bráhmans. And it is with these last that the Gujarát Bháts identify themselves. They further assert that there are many Bháts in the Punjáb who trace their pedigree to the sage Kavi, and are known as Kavivanshi Bráhmans. Thus, according to the account given by the Gujarát Bháts of themselves, they appear to be Bráhmans. And this seems, on the whole, to be the correct view. Local inquiries seem to show that the Gujarát Bháts were originally Bráhmans from Allahabad and Márwár, who settled in Ahmedábád and its neighbourhood. That some at least came from North India appears from the existence of the Kanojia Bháts both in Káthiáwár and Cutch. Traces of their Bráhman origin survive in their wearing, however irregularly and carelessly, the sacred thread, and in their having such *Shákhás* as Harmáni, Káshiáni and Parvatáni. The suffix *áni* of these names might perhaps tempt one to take it as an indication of their connection with the Kshatriya tribes of Sind, many of whose clans have names ending in *áni*. But this has little weight inasmuch as the suffix *áni* has been distinctly declared by Pánini, the Sanskrit Grammarian, to denote the *gotra* division, and the names Harmáni, Káshiáni and Parvatáni are in all likelihood equivalent to the Sanskrit Dhárenyáyani, Káshâyani and Párvatáyani. Further, in support of the Bráhman origin of the Gujarát Bháts, it may be added that the word Bhát is a regular corruption of the Sanskrit word Bhatta, which is a term of respect applied to none but the Bráhmans. The name Brahma-Bhát of one of their sub-castes points to the same conclusion. Again, the immense respect paid to the Gujarát Bháts and the inviolability attaching to their person, which are far above that accorded to the other Gujarát or Rajput Bráhmans, are inexplicable except on the supposition that they are Bráhmans. Historical evidence also can be adduced to show that these Bháts are Bráhmans. A Turkish traveller named Sidhi Ali Kapudan (A.D. 1533), while writing about the Bháts of Gujarát and their occupation, speaks of them as "a tribe of Bráhmans." The poet Chande (Sk. Chandra) was the *purohita* (priest) as well as the bard of the well-known Rajput prince Prithviràja Chohán. The office of a *purohita*, especially of such a distinguished and powerful sovereign as Prithviràja, could not have been conferred upon any one but a Bráhman. The bard Chande must, therefore, have been a Bráhman. Bhukhandás, another Bhát, who composed the well-known *Shivarájabhushana*, which is surcharged with the sentiment of heroism, says therein that he was a Bráhman, and even specifies his *gotra* and *pravar*. It may, however, be asked, and undoubtedly with some force, how it is that the Bráhmans could ever stoop to serve the Kshatriyas and lavish panegyrics on them. But the study of Sanskrit literature will easily convince us that instances of Bráhmans turning eulogists of Kshatriyas are not wanting. Limmer, in his work Altindisches Leben, tells us that, in the Vedic times, there were many Bráhman families of singers who lived as parasites of kings and extolled their deeds. Such were Vasishtha to the Tritsu, and Vishvámitra to the Bharata, royal dynasty. In the Máhábhárata too, as was first pointed out by Mr. J. C. Nesfield, Yudhishthira is represented as being accompanied by eulogists and bards, in his triumphant march from Kurukshetra to Hastinápur, after his battles with the Kauravas for paramount supermacy had ended. And these eulogists and bards are explicitly stated to be Bráhmans. Nothing, therefore, precludes us from holding that the Gujarát Bháts are Bráhmans. In the south of the Bombay Presidency, the term Bhat is used to designate the local Bráhman to this day. There can, however, be no question that these Bháts are looked upon by other Bráhmans as degraded. The Bháts explain it by saying that, as they always accompanied the kings to battle, and by reciting heroic poems with spirit and jesture, incited them to valour, the kings, being pleased, bestowed upon them many *jághirs*; but this excited the jealousy of the other Bráhmans, who spitefully lowered them in the Bráhmanical heirarchy. This explanation, however, is one-sided, and can hardly claim our credence. The true explanation of their degradation appears to be that as their calling of bards and eulogists compelled them always to associate with the Rajputs, whether in court or in battle, they gradually lost touch with their Bráhman community, seceded from the Bráhman standard of purity, and adopted many Rajput customs. Thus, though many of them wear the sacred thread, there are not a few who are indifferent to it. Most of them allow widow marriage and have no objection to eat food cooked by Vániás and Kanbis; and some of them even dine with the Rajputs. Excepting the Brahma-Bháts, all drink liquor. Their personal names again are Rajput in form, the men's ending in *sing* and the women's in *ba*; and a good many of them dress like the Rajputs. It is this violation, or at any rate relaxation, of the strict Bráhman rules of social purity necessitated by constant intercourse with the Rajputs that in all likelihood led to the Bháts being lowered in the estimation of the other Bráhmans.

Appearance. Except the genealogists or family heralds, Bháts look like Bráhmans, Vániás and Kanbis. Heralds look like Rajputs. The men wear long curled moustaches and whiskers and shave the hair at the temples. Some wear beards. Unlike Rajput women, the wives and daughters of Bháts, who are tolerably fair and handsome, appear in public. The dress of the men varies according to their profession and the part of the country in which they live. The bards of Rajput chiefs wear trousers, a Rajput turban, a waistband with a dagger(1) stuck in it, and a short cotton coat with four chins or plaits. In former times, instead of the short cotton coat, they wore a full skirted coat that fell to the ankles. The Ránimanga Bháts, instead of a turban, wind a woman's robe round the head. The Sádhu and Atit Bháts dress like Atit and Sádhu beggars. Other Bháts dress like other middle class Hindus except that in Central Gujarát they wear very full petticoats of fifteen to twenty cubits of cloth.

Language. The Bháts speak Gujaráti. Their personal names are Rajput in form, the men's ending in *sing* and the women's in *ba*. Social disputes are settled by a few respected castemen. Except in some parts of Central Gujarát, the Bháts have no hereditary headmen. In Godhra, the common headman is called Ráo and like a few respectable men of the caste in other parts of the Province, he has power to fine and excommunicate for breaches of caste rules. In Cutch the caste levies a small fee on every betrothal, marriage and caste feast.

Divisions. In North Gujarát and Káthiáwár, the Bháts are broken up into thirteen endogamous divisions, which are as follows :—

1. Atit.
2. Brahma-Bhát.
3. Devalvakia.
4. Kankália or Bhund.
5. Kanojiya.
6. Kápdi.
7. Lávania.
8. Mágan.
9. Nagári.
10. Pálimanga or Mádhavia.
11. Ránimanga.
12. Sádhu.
13. Vahiváncha.

None of these divisions eat together or intermarry. In Cutch, they are split up into (1) the Brahma-Bháts and (2) the Dongras. They were both originally Kanojia Bráhmans, but now the latter do not wear the sacred thread. Of all these divisions the Brahma-Bháts stand highest in the social scale. Some of them have been careful to keep the Bráhman rules of social purity. They wear the sacred thread, do not allow widow marriage, and though in Cutch they dine with

(1) A bard seldom appears without the *katár* or dagger, a representation of which is scrawled beside his signature and often rudely engraved upon his monumental stone or *páliya* in evidence that he died in the sacred duty of *trága* or self-sacrifice—Rás Mála II, 265.

Lohánas and Khatris, in North Gujarát and in Káthiáwár they do not dine with Vániás and Kanbis as the other divisions of Bháts do. Each of the above divisions except the Brahma-Bháts is again divided into two divisions—*Kuliás* or of good family, *i.e.*, those who do not allow widow marriage, and *Akuliás* or of no family, *i.e.*, those who allow widow marriage. A *Kulia* eats with an *Akulia* but does not give him his daughter in marriage.

The Brahma-Bháts are said to belong to the Bhárgav *gotra*, the others to the Bháradwája *gotra*. They are stated to have the five *pravars*.

The Brahma-Bháts are split up into the following sections :—

1. Devluk.
2. Harmáni.
3. Indráni.
4. Káshiáni.
5. Kundanpuria.
6. Messana.
7. Parvattáni.
8. Rana.
9. Rao.
10. Sodáni.

The names of some of the sections to be found among the other divisions are as follows :—

1. Dhánáni.
2. Gadhia.
3. Ghedia.
4. Meghpuria.
5. Nakláni.
6. Sadávarti.
7. Sindwa.
8. Sudhpuráni.
9. Waloya.

Marriages are prohibited between members of the same section and between those of the allied sections. Harmáni, Káshiáni and Parvattáni are allied, having had a common ancestor, so also Indráni and Devluk. Now the first three cannot intermarry nor the last two, though any one of the first group can marry among either of the second. A Bhát cannot marry his father's sister's, mother's sister's or mother's brother's daughter. In Cutch, contrary to the general custom, the children of the Bhát and his sister are allowed to marry. Two sisters can be taken as co-wives, the first married being the elder. Two brothers may marry two sisters. Infant marriage is generally prevalent, but partly owing to the heavy expense of the marriage of a daughter and partly owing to the distinction between *Kulia* and *Akulia*, some girls, even twenty-five years of age, remain unmarried. Sexual intercourse before marriage is, however, strongly reprobated, the girl committing it being turned out of the caste. Polygamy is allowed and practised, but polyandry is unknown.

Birth ceremonies. No ceremonies are performed on the day of a birth. On the sixth day the goddess Chhatti is worshipped, while in North Gujarát, Káthiáwár and Cutch, besides a reed pen and an inkstand, a dagger is laid before the goddess. On the sixth day or on any day fixed by the astrologer, the child is named by the father's sister. After childbirth the mother remains impure from twenty to forty days When a child is a year old, the first giving of cooked food takes place. The practice of wearing the sacred thread is not uniform. Sacred threads are worn by three classes. In the first class come the boys whose thread ceremony is performed according to Bráhman rites when they are from seven to eleven years of age and who continue to wear the thread till the end of their lives; in the second class come those whose thread ceremony is nominally performed on the marriage day and who either continue to wear the thread or discard it after the marriage ceremony; in the third class come those who have no chance of marrying and whose thread ceremony is performed when they are twenty to twenty-five years of age. Of the last class some continue to wear the thread and others discard it.

Marriage. The marriage ceremonies of Gujarát Bháts do not differ from those of Kanbis. Their marriage expenses are heavy, and, strangely enough, it is the bride's parents who have to purchase the bridegroom, an expensive commodity if the connection sought is good. Many poor families, whose means were as inadequate as their pride was great, used, therefore, to practise female infanticide, the victims being suffocated in basins filled with water and milk.[1]

Widow remarriage is allowed among all divisions of the Bháts except the Brahma-Bháts. A widow cannot marry her father's sister's, mother's sister's or mother's brother's son, or a member of her late husband's section. One account states that she may marry a younger brother of her deceased husband or a member of his section. A widow remarriage can be celebrated only on a Sunday, Tuesday or Thursday. The widow, taking on her head two water jars filled with water, goes to the house of her intended husband. Ganpati is installed, a lamp is lighted, and the pair are seated in the front of the god. Each of the pair then ties a cotton thread round the wrist of the other, their brows are marked with red powder, the skirts of their garments are knotted, they are made to play the game of odd and evens, molasses are distributed, and the ceremony is over. Among the Káthiáwár Bháts, the intended husband has to pay a sum of Rs. 100 to the widow. The ceremony of the marriage is of the standard type prevailing in Káthiáwár.

---

(1) The usual formula for the order for suffocation was "*dudh piláo*," *i.e.*, give milk to drink. The infant was then put, head foremost, into the milk and so drowned.

R. E. E.

Divorce is allowed among most of the Bháts. Where it is allowed the right accrues to both the husband and wife. If the husband seeks it, he calls his wife his *mother* or *sister* and tears off a piece of cloth from his turban. If the wife seeks it, she gains it by calling her husband her *father* or *brother* and tears off a piece of cloth from her *odhani* or upper garment. A divorce does not require the consent of the community. A divorced woman is allowed to remarry by the widow remarriage form. A woman taken in adultery is excommunicated, but received back into the caste on payment of a fine above Rs. 50. But such cases are rare. The caste follow the Hindu law of inheritance.

In religion Bháts are Rámánujas, Shaivas and Vaishnavas, and worshippers of Amba, Bahuchráji and Kálika. In Káthiáwár some are Jains, and of late years some have become Kabirpanthis, Parinámis and Sváminaráyans. They worship in their houses the images of Ganpati, Máta, Shiva and Vishnu, and visit village temples. Those who have the means make pilgrimages to Dwárka, Benares, Ayodhya, Mathura, Jagannáth and other holy places. The house Máta is represented by a cocoanut set in a niche, before which a lamp fed with clarified butter is kept burning during the time of worship. Among Brahma-Bháts Chámunda is the tutelary deity of the Messanna, Rao and Rána sections, and Kálika of Káshiáni, Parvattáni, Harmáni, Indráni and the Devluk sections. So also Bhaváni is the family goddess of Nakhláni, Brahmáni of the Walloya and Dhanáni, Khodyar of Sindwas, Wágheshvari of Godhia, and so on. The Islám Pir is revered and cocoanuts are offered to him. When an epidemic prevails in a village, by way of propitiating the deity supposed to preside over it, cows are fed or a sacrifice is performed. If an ancestor have died while doing a warlike deed, his image is made in a riding posture and worshipped on the *Diváli* day, and the officiating Bráhman is given rice, wheat flour, ghi, molasses and some cash. The Bháts observe all the Hindu holidays and believe in exorcism, sorcery and omens. Their priests are Audich, Modh, Prashnora or Shrimáli Bráhmans, who officiate at all their ceremonies. Religion.

The dead are burnt except lepers and children under eighteen months old, who are buried in a lying position with head to the north. There is nothing peculiar in their funeral ceremonies. Death ceremonies

Bháts are professional genealogists, bards and singers, and find employment at the courts of native princes or in the families of private gentlemen. Every Rajput chieftain and landed proprietor has a Bhát attached to his family, and each Bhát has a certain round, which Occupation he goes every year. While moving from house to house, the Nagári Bháts beat a *torki* or drum, the Kunkális carry a trident, and the Pálimangas a knife. The Bhát is welcomed on arrival at the chief's house, and is entertained during his stay. He brings his book of chronicles and from it recites all the memorable deeds of the clan, and traces their genealogy to the heroes of old. He also enters in the family record any birth, marriage or death that has taken place since his last visit. He receives a fee for all the entries he makes, and a yearly present according to the liberality of the chief. Bháts had, some years ago, a ready way of extracting money or the fulfilment of pledge made to them. If a man refused to keep a promise made to them, they committed *trága* as it was called, *i.e.*, brought a girl or an old woman of their own family to the house of the defaulter, and threatened to kill or actually did kill her ; and if these means failed, the Bhat used to proceed to plunge a dagger into his heart. The disgrace of these proceedings, and the fear of having a bard's blood on their head, generally reduced the most obstinate to reason. Not a century ago the faith placed in the word of a Bhát was perhaps the only means of obtaining the requisite feeling of security necessary to conduct business of any kind. All men from the prince to the peasant trusted the Bhát, that he would keep his word or die. No deed or transaction was, therefore, considered valid until it had been countersigned by a Bhát. All the security bonds taken by Colonel Walker from the chiefs of Káthiáwár in 1807 were signed by Bháts or Chárans. They were also largely used as treasure escorts, for their passes were held sacred, and the mere threat of a Bhát that he would wound himself was enough to scare any band of robbers and preserve valuable goods untouched. Except in Native States, Bháts are badly off. Poverty compels some of them to beg from the middle classes. Under British rule they have lost their power and means of earning a livelihood. Many Bháts have abandoned their hereditary calling, and have become husbandmen, bankers, moneylenders and traders ; some are of necessity domestic servants and messengers. A few among them are beggars. Some are engaged in their hereditary calling in addition to agriculture during the rains. Many of them hold state grants, and a few are landless day-labourers.

Food. In Cutch and Pálanpur, all Bháts except the Brahma-Bháts eat fish and flesh, and drink liquor. In other parts they are vegetarians, living on the ordinary food-grains.

In North Gujarát and Káthiáwár, the members of all the sub-divisions, except the Brahma-Bháts, eat food cooked by Vániás and Kanbis, although they neither eat together nor intermarry. In Cutch, the Dongras dine with the Rajputs and the Brahma-Bháts with Lohánás and Khatris, quite unlike their castemen in Northern Gujarát and Káthiáwár, who dine neither with Vániás and Kanbis nor with other sub-divisions of Bháts.

The following particulars refer to the Marátha Bháts.

MARATHA BHATS are called Goan Bháts in the Násik district. They do not, like the Rajput Bháts, appear to have been originally Bráhmans. They themselves claim a Kshatriya origin. But they look like, and rank with, the Marátha Kunbis, and do not differ from them in religion and customs. The Marátha Bháts must have sprung into existence with the rise of the Marátha power, to serve as genealogists and bards to the Marátha chiefs, who were disposed to adopt the manners and customs of Rajput princes. Though the habit of the caste is settled, not a few among them are wandering beggars, having no houses and living in temples and rest-houses.

In Khándesh, their endogamous groups are the Pardeshis, Maráthás and Kunbis. In Belgaum, they are split up into the divisions of Marátha or Bráhman Bháts and Thákar or Joshi Bháts. The former repeat the name Brahma before beginning to sing; the latter foretell the future. Marriage is generally infant, polygamy and widow marriage are allowed and practised, but polyandry is unknown.

Boys are girt with the sacred thread before marriage, and generally Rs. 20—25 are paid to the girl's father. A day before marriage, a feast is given in honour of the family gods, and, on the wedding day, the bride and bridegroom are rubbed with turmeric and bathed, and are seated on a blanket spread on a raised seat. The village astrologer comes, repeats texts and throws red rice on the pair, and women sing marriage songs and wave lighted lamps round their faces. The next day the couple are seated on horse back and taken to the temple of their goddess Durga, where they offer the goddess a cocoanut, plantains and betel, and go home. The chief points in which their marriage customs differ from those of the Maráthás are: they have no marriage altar in the bride's booth, they bring no clay jars from the potter's, the boy does not visit any temple on his way to the girl's, and they hold no *antarpat* between the boy and girl at the time of marrying them. Unlike Maráthás, they drive a five or six feet long teakwood pole into the ground in the centre of the booth, and after

Marriage.

the couple have walked seven times round the pole, the marriage is over.

Some of the Marátha Bháts are Shaivas and some Vaishnavas. Their favourite gods are Bálâji, Krishna, Vithoba, Mahádev and Máruti ; and in their houses are the images of Sidhoba and Máyaráni. Their chief goddesses are Dyámava, Ambábái, Durgava and Yellamma. The Vaishnava Bháts of Sátára have a religious head, who is an ascetic or *Bairági* of their own sect, and who whispers a sacred verse into the candidate's ear at the time of the initiation. They believe in soothsaying, witchcraft, and lucky and unlucky days. A few days after child-birth they go into the jungle and offer a goat to the goddess Mukiáyi. They also sacrifice sheep and fowls to their goddesses Durgava and Yellamma, and eat their flesh. In the Thána district, they perform their own ceremonies. In other places, Bráhmans officiate at their marriages.

Some bury, and some burn, their dead. Those that bury lay the head to the south and the feet to the north. In Sátára, they burn their dead. In Dhárwár, after a death the body is seated decked with new clothes, flowers and ornaments, and taken in a car-shaped bier to the burial ground and buried.

Formerly the Rájás of Sátára and many of the nobility had Bháts in their service, who had a minute knowledge of their patrons' family trees, and composed and repeated poems with much spirit and gesture. Since the fall of the chiefship, they have been forced to follow other means of livelihood. Most of them are now hereditary beggars, and their chief calling is to praise any one they meet, and beg for money and clothes. In Poona, the Bháts are usually asked to join Mális and Kunbis in their thirteenth day death feast, where their duty is to call out the names of those who make presents to the chief mourner. In Thána, they go about playing the drum and the fiddle, and attend Mahár weddings. In Násik and Sholápur, they appear on marriage occasions, repeat Hindustáni verses called *bánis* and *kavits* with great force and eloquence, and recite stories. Many of them also work as masons and house servants, and some even go fishing. Not a few have taken to tillage. Some hold grants or *vatans*, and are called Thákurs. Some are cultivators, and some are landless day labourers.

Food. They eat fish, crabs, mutton, fowls, wild game, pigeons, partridges and all other kinds of meat, except beef and pork, and drink liquor. In Sátára, they are not allowed to use liquor.

MUSALMAN BHATS are said to have been originally Brahma Bháts. About seven generations ago a quarrel arose among the Brahma Bháts over a land dispute at Janjmer near Talaja under Bhávnagar which resulted in a split in the community, and a few families went to Goga, which was then under Musalmán rule, the Governor being Dawud Khureshi. This Governor promised to bestow *inám* lands on them, provided they embraced Islám. They consented and became Musalmáns.

The Musalmán Bháts are known as Ránes, and are to be found mostly in Broach and Kaira districts and the Baroda State. They do not admit other Musalmáns into their caste. They marry only among themselves and have two divisions, one of which allows widow remarriage, and the other not. These divisions eat together, but do not intermarry.

The Musalmán Bháts are Sunnis in religion. They follow Muhammad and his immediate successors in the Khalifat, and observe all the Musalmán religious ceremonies They have retained only one of their former religious customs, that of offering cooked food to the family deity and worshipping her at the time of the first shaving ceremony of a child. Their religious preceptor is the Kádri Sayad of Surat. Some of them study the Korán, though imperfectly. Almost all of them are hereditary landlords. A few serve as clerks and school masters.

BHAT.—A sub-division of Meváda Bráhmans.

BHATELA.—A sub-division of Anávala Bráhmans.

BHATI.—A synonym for Bhátia.

BHATIAS(1) numbering 28,332 (1901), including 14,775 males, and 13,557 females, are found principally in Cutch, Káthiáwár, Sind and Bombay City, but are also scattered in small numbers in all the trade centres of the Presidency. Numbers of them are found in the Punjáb, Rájputána and United Provinces and the Tehri villages in the Himalayas. But no satisfactory proof is forthcoming to show that they really belong to the Bhátia community. In remote times they were found in Muttra, but at present their number is very limited. Besides a few of them are found in Dharangaum and Vejapur near Tevla in the Manmád district. Bhátiás are called Vaza Goherens by the Baluchis, Banians by the Arabs, Bániánis by the Negroes and Vánia Bhátiás by the Pársis. They are also known as Bhátis, **Name and origin.**

(1) The materals for this article were in part prepared by Mr. D. R. Bhandarkar and in part supplied by the Bhátia community in Bombay.

Yádavs, Kshatriya Yaduvanshis, Krishnavanshis, Vrishnivanshis, Chandravanshis and Thakkars. The Baluchi term Vaza Goheren means a merchant. Banian and Béniáni are probably derived from the Punjabi *banaj* or Sanskrit *vánijjya* meaning trade, the chief occupation of the caste. Yádav means a descendant of Yadu, from whom the Bhátiás claim descent. The Bhátiás of Muttra are known solely by this name. The Bhátiás of the Himalayan villages of Tehri are known by the names of Yaduvanshi, Vrishnivanshi and Krishnavanshi. Yaduvanshi, like Yádav, means a descendant of Yadu. Vrishnivanshi means a descendant of Vrishni, son of Madhu, one of their supposed ancestors. They are called Krishnavanshi after Krishna, also of the Yádav stock. The appellation Thakkar appears to be a corruption of Thákor meaning a ruling chief, and suggests the Kshatriya origin of the caste.

Bhátiás claim to be Bháti Rajputs of the Yádav stock, who under the name of Bhattis or Bhátiás are the ruling tribe in Jesalmir in North Rájputána. In support of their Rajput origin, it may be mentioned that the Bhátiás are generally well made, active and fair with handsome regular features, and that all of them wear the sacred thread. According to General Cunningham, Bhátia comes from *Bhat*, a warrior. They are also held by Wilford and Elliot to be so called either after Bhat, one of the sons of Shálivéhana, or Bhupat, the grandson of Sáni.

The original habitat of the Bhátiás appears to have been the Lahore and Multan districts of the Punjab, where are still to be found in considerable numbers Bhátis, many of whom are non-vegetarians. According to the accounts of the Punjab Bhátis, their earliest capital was at Gajnipur (B.C.600), supposed by Colonel Tod to be the modern Ghazni, and by General Cunningham to have been not far from Rawalpindi. From Gajnipur, the latter thinks, they were driven in the first century A.D. a little to the south-east before the Indo-Scythians, who killed their king, the father of their most renowned sovereign Shálivåhan. The further progress of the Indo-Scythians was, however, checked by Shálivåhana, who routed them at the pitched battle of Karhor (Korur). His son Rásalu, the founder of Siálkot, also successfully resisted their inroads, but after his death, the Indo-Scythians again pushed forward, and reduced the Bhátis. It appears from this account that the indigenous rulers of the Bhátis were originally Shálivåhana and his predecessors. This seems to receive corroboration from what Wilford says about them. He tells[1] us that

(1) Asiatic Researches, Vol. IX, pp. 218—22.

some tribes of the Bhátis strongly insist on their descent from Sháliváhan, call themselves Vanshyas of Sháliváhana, Shaka-Rája-Vansás, or Shaka-Ráj-Kumárs, the offspring of Shak or Sháliváhana, and consider their chief the representative of Sháliváhana and an incarnation of Vishnu.

If we compare these legends with what we know as history, we find therein nothing but confusion. In the first place, Sháliváhana was not the name of an individual prince; and secondly, Shak can by no means be connected with Sháliváhana. Western India cave inscriptions inform us that there was an indigenous royal dynasty, and not an individual king, called Sháliváhana or Shátaváhana, otherwise known as Andhrabhrityas. Next, from inscriptions as well as Sanskrit literature, we learn that Shak was the name of a foreign race. The Sháliváhans cannot, therefore, be regarded as Shaks. Again, the same inscriptions tell us that the rule of the Sháliváhana dynasty was confined only to Southern India, and that, although at one time they had succeeded in seizing a part of North India, held by the Shaks, the latter soon regained their lost possessions. It is, therefore, inconceivable how the name Sháliváhana has come to be connected with the legends of the Punjab. This much, however, is certain that the accounts of the Bhátis, so far as they are concerned with Sháliváhana and Shak, are to be relegated to the province of pure myth.

As regards their southward movement, Tod mentions[1] that in the eighth century, the Yadu Bhátis were driven south of the Sutlej. But it would seem from the accounts of the third expedition (A.D. 1004) of Mahmud of Ghazni that there was still a small Bhátia kingdom at Bhátia or Bherah on the left bank of the Jhelum near the salt range. And it was probably by the later Muhammadan invaders that the Bhátiás were driven south into the desert and Sind. In Sind, some of the Bhátiás still eat fish and drink spirits. Probably most of them have settled in Cutch and Káthiáwár since the establishment of Jádeja power (circa 1350 A.D.).

An account of their origin prepared by the caste traces the Bhátiás from Indraprastha through Surapura, Muttra, Prayaga, Dwarka, Judo-dang, Bahara, Gujni to Salpura in the Punjáb and eventually to Jaisalmer, where they were almost exterminated by the Musalmáns in 1295 A.D.

---

(1) Western India, p. 154.

Appearance. The Bhátiás are well made, tall and active. They are a little darker and less regular in features than other Gujarát Hindu traders, though in Cutch they are a remarkably fair and handsome race. Their women are generally fair and handsome. In dress and ornaments they do not differ much from the Vániás.

Language. The home tongue of the Bhátiás of Cutch and Bombay is Cutchi. In Hálár and part of Káthiáwár they speak Hálái, which closely resembles Cutchi. In Gujarát and Káthiáwár they speak Gujaráti, and in Sind, Sindi. In olden times the names of males ended in *sing*, *ráj* or *mal* indicative of their Kshatriya origin, *e.g.*, Lálsing, Rámsing, Hansaráj, Jethamal, etc. Such names are still in use in Northern India. The ending *sing* or *sey* which is a corruption of *sinhá* still survives in such modern names as Thákarsey, Tersey, Nánsey, etc. In Cutch, according to the custom of the Thákarais (petty chiefs), the names commenced to end in *ji* for the last century and a half, and they are not uncommon even now. Instances of such names are Bhánji Bhimji, Kánji, Mulji, Prágji, etc. Later on when the authority of the Vaishnav Mahárájás became all powerful, names ending in *dás* came into vogue. Such names are Lakshmidás, Vallabhadás, Náráyandás, Mádhavdás, etc. Boys whose elder brothers have died in infancy are given such opprobrious names as Gábho and Nathu. Such a boy, immediately after birth, is taken to a cow-pen and allowed to lie there for a couple of minutes, and is dubbed Gábho meaning calf, under the belief that the mother cow would protect him. Sometimes, at a very tender age, the nose of the boy is pierced and a nosering is put into it. He is then called Nathu or Nathio after *nath* nosering, which is an ornament used only by females.

Divisions. Formerly the Bhátiás had many endogamous divisions such as Dasa, Diváni, Panja, Visa, Sindi and Trágadi. At present they have only two main divisions (1) Cutchi Hálái and (2) Sindi, though traces of the other divisions are still to be found. As the names imply, the two divisions are now only territorial. The Sindi Bhátiás are supposed to be the descendants of that branch of the Yadu stock that came from Misar (modern Egypt), the country of the legendary king Bánásur, the branch of Ushnika, son of Sánita.

About 35 to 40 years ago the young men of Sind, being inconvenienced by the small range of selection for marriageable girls, cast their eyes towards their brethren of the Himalayan Valley, while the aged Cutchi and Hálái Bhátiás from Bombay turned towards Dharangam, Vejapur and Telva in the Manmád district, and Hardwár in the Punjab, and brought girls therefrom, the latter paying high bride prices, *viz.*, Rs. 10,000 to Rs. 15,000. These pioneers were welcomed by their respective communities of their places by excommunication. However, the Sindis kept up the agitation and ultimately succeeded in having the whole question investigated and decided favourably. Those marrying from Dharangam, Vejapur and Telva managed to make their way back into the community, but the position of the Hardwár marriages is still disputed by certain caste members in Bombay City.

Regarding the origin of the Visa and Dasa divisions, tradition asserts that in the year 1324 A.D., there lived in the city of Multan a Lohána gentleman named Náru, who had a very handsome daughter by name Moti. Being disgusted with the food she ate daily, Moti once complained of some dishes of their diet to her brother's wife Suján, who retorted that if she was so particular about her food, she would do well to marry a Bhátia. At this Moti made a vow that she would either marry a Bhátia or die a virgin. Learning of this vow, a Bhátia named Manu came forward and married her. The offspring of this union were allowed to remain in the Bhátia caste, but the orthodox section in the community looked down upon them and termed them Dasás (ten) as opposed to Visás (twenty), implying them thereby to be half-caste.

The divisions Visa, Dasa, Panja, Trágadi and Diváni in course of time became hypergamous, that is the Visás married girls from Dasás, but did not give their daughters in marriage to them, and so on. This is suggested by the very names of the divisions, the term Visa meaning twenty, Dasa meaning ten, Panja meaning five, and Trágadi meaning three. The meaning of Diváni is not known. According to some, the divisions Dasa, Panja, Trágadi and Diváni were formed of those families of Bhátiás that were admitted into the caste after the formation of the eighty-four *nukhs* of the caste. The distinctions mentioned above have almost died out, instances of Visás marrying their daughters to Dasás and others being of frequent occurrence. The Cutchi Hálais and Sindis neither eat together nor intermarry.(1)

The exogamous divisions of the caste are known as *nukhs*. They very nearly correspond to clan titles. The *nukhs* are eighty-four in number and are as follows :—

Anadhar.	Babla (of Thali).	Bada.
Asar.	Babla (of Gátha).	Bibal.

(1) A fresh division has recently (1914) arisen from a dispute over the position of Bhátiás who visit Europe, on their return to India.

Baláya.
Bhudharia.
Chámuja.
Chhachhia.
Dhaga.
Dhakkar.
Dhadhal.
Dhadhar.
Degchanda.
Deiya.
Dutia.
Farásgándhi.
Gagal.
Gájaria.
Ghagha.
Gokalgándhi.
Guruguláb.
Hariya.
Jaba.
Jia.
Jiya.
Jidhan.
Jabála.
Jujargándhi.
Jágta.
Kodhia.

Koa.
Kándhia.
Kájaria.
Kapur.
Kartari.
Kukad.
Karangota.
Khaira.
Lakhanvanta.
Media.
Mogia.
Malan.
Mochha.
Mota
Mathara.
Multáni.
Nayegándhi.
Nágada.
Nisát.
Panchlodia.
Padamsi.
Pálija.
Panchál.
Pramala.
Potha.
Padhthaga.

Paregándhi.
Pavár.
Prema.
Parájia.
Panvár.
Radia.
Rámia.
Rája.
Rika.
Sapát.
Suraiya.
Suáda.
Saráki.
Soni.
Sonfla.
Sijavla.
Sodhia
Thávan.
Thaba.
Thiran.
Thula.
Tambad.
Udesi.
Vanoda.
Vadhucha.
Ved.

According to some, the above *nukhs* belong to seven *golras, viz.*, Bháradwáj, Devdás, Madhuvádhasoás, Páráshar, Rishivansh, Sánasa and Sundarvansh. Others maintain that these *gotras* have been engrafted upon them by their Bráhman priests, for if they had these *gotras*, it would not have been necessary to form the eighty-four *nukhs* which are exogamous. They state that being descendants of Krishna, they have only one *gotra*, the same as Krishna's, *viz.*, Atri.

Marriage. Formerly it was a rule that a Visa Bhátia should not only marry a Visa girl, but that the girl should belong to the town or village where he resided. Dearth of marriageable girls broke down the rigidity of this rule, and in course of time marriages between members residing in different localities began to take place, although they were confined only to the rich ; as in such cases, the bride-price ranged from Rs. 8,000 to Rs. 10,000. Those who could not afford to pay such a high bride-price, opened up negotiations with the Yaduvanshi Kshatriyas of Hardwár and Tehri Districts and formed marriage connections with them, and in their case no high bride-price was to be paid. These marriages are not looked upon with favour by the community, in the absence of any convincing proof of the origin of these Yaduvanshi Kshatriyas of Hardwár, yet in the course of the last ten years there have taken place over five hundred such marriages, with the result that the penalty of excommunication has been meted out to them.

A Bhátia must marry within his own caste. According to the reform party amongst them, he can marry a woman of the Yaduvanshi Kshatriya caste of Hardwár and Tehri. From what has been stated above about the origin of Dasa and Visa, it would appear that such marriages were allowed with certain restrictions in old times. A Bhátia cannot marry a woman of the section to which he himself belongs. He can marry a woman of the section to which his mother belongs, though such marriages were not allowed about twenty-five years ago. He can marry a woman of his paternal grandmother's section and his maternal grandmother's section. A Bhátia cannot marry his maternal uncle's daughter, his mother's sister's daughter or his father's sister's daughter. He can marry his deceased wife's sister. Two sisters can marry two brothers. A boy given in adoption cannot marry in the family of his original parents, though there would be no objection to his marrying in the *nukh* of his original parents. In Káthiáwár, the practice of double marriages is very common. Polygamy is allowed and practised, the number of wives a man having at a time never exceeding two. Divorce and widow remarriage are forbidden. Polyandry is unknown.

Girls are generally married between nine and fourteen, and boys between sixteen and twenty-five. If a girl attains puberty before marriage, her parents have to perform a purification ceremony. The supply of marriageable girls falls much short of the demand. Consequently, the bridegroom, besides presents to the girl in the shape of ornaments and clothes of the value of Rs. 4,000 to Rs. 5,000, has in some cases to pay the girl's father large sums in the shape of purchase-money. So great is the expense that many Bhátiás remain unmarried, and in many cases, there is a great disparity of age between the bride and bridegroom.

The offer of marriage comes from the boy's side. Amongst the rich the *pallu* or dower to be settled on the girl is not fixed. Amongst the poor it is fixed. The *vadhái* or betrothal is celebrated some days before the marriage. It consists in the girl's father sending to the boy with the family priest a pot full of sugarcandy and an ivory bangle of the girl's. In some places, the girl's father sends four copper coins, a handful of millet, turmeric and betelnuts and some *dro* or sacred grass. The betrothal is then entered in the caste register and the father of the boy pays a fixed sum to the caste fund. For seven days after the betrothal, sweetmeats are sent to the boy's house by the bride's parents. On the twenty-first day after betrothal, the ceremony of *vena* (lit. oral declaration) is performed. The boy's father with his male relations and friends goes to the girl's house, and a ceremony is performed by a Bráhman priest. Formerly, on this occasion, the boy's father was presented with one *kori* (a Cutch silver coin equal to a four-anna piece), and his mother, grandmother and grandfather with half a *kori* each ; and fifty-one cocoanuts were distributed among those present or in lieu thereof two *dokadás* (a copper coin equal to two pice) were presented to each. This rule has been changed by the Bombay Bhátiás, who present rupees instead of *koris* and small silver coins instead of cocoanuts and copper.

The opening day of the marriage ceremonies is called *samurta*. On this day a *chándlo* (red powder mark) is made on the girl's forehead, and preparations for the marriage are begun by five or seven married unwidowed women commencing cleaning *udid* (black gram) and *mung* (green gram). From this day forward, every night, songs are sung by the ladies of the house and by relations and friends who assemble for the purpose. Formerly they were presented with dates and cocoanuts. Now they are presented with silver coins.

After the *samurta* comes the *lagna lakhávavu*. It is celebrated in Cutch a few days before marriage ; and in Bombay on the day before the marriage. The bridegroom's father with male relations goes to the bride's, and the family priest reads the marriage-deed, naming the auspicious time for the different ceremonies. On this day the ladies go singing songs to a potter, and worship his wheel by making red marks on the wheel and earthen pots. On the marriage day the potter brings four sets of earthen pots, which are arranged round the *chori* or marriage altar. The *mandap-muhurta* or *mánakastambh-ropan* is next performed, in which a wooden post called *mánakastambh* is coloured red and planted in one of the corners of the marriage booth. On the day before the marriage, the ceremony of *dudhalakshmi* or *khir chhatna* takes place. In this ceremony, women from the bridegroom's family go to the bride's, present her with costly articles of dress and ornaments, and make decorative marks on her forehead, cheeks, shoulders, palms and arms. The girl then goes to the bridegroom's and sprinkles milk seven times with a leaf on the person of the bridegroom's father. He offers her a number of silver coins of which she accepts only one, the bridegroom's mother makes a red mark on her forehead, and she returns home. Next a ceremony called *manorbandhan* is performed, in which a fish is tied to the door in Sind, where fish is used as an article of food, and wheat cakes at other places. The probable origin of this ceremony seems to be that a fish brought from an opposite direction while one is going on a good mission, is considered a good omen. This ceremony is followed by *chhaki* in which the bride is taken in procession in a sort of palanquin called *chhaki* to the bridegroom's. She is welcomed by the senior lady of the family and returns home.

Next, the bridegroom on his part goes to the bride's in procession on horseback, and is received at the entrance by the bride's mother. He is led into the house, and, with the bride, sits in that part of the house where the family goddess is painted on the house wall. A piece of coloured cloth is placed between the two, with one end of it on the bride's head and the other end on the bridegroom's lap. They then worship the family goddess, the family priest of the bride officiating at the ceremony. When the worship is over, the bride and the bridegroom take from each other one by one several pieces of *juvár* (indian millet stalks) held in the hand. The female relations of the bride drop one after another small cotton bundles on the bride's head, which the bridegroom clears away; and the female relations of the bridegroom drop the same bundles on the bridegroom's lap which the bride clears away. The bridegroom returns to his lodging. This ceremony is most interesting as it affords both delight and encouragement to the parties to exhibit their skill. The bridegroom on the day of the marriage goes with music to the bride's house in procession with men walking in front and women singing songs behind. The procession stops at the bride's house. The bridegroom alights from his horse, and stands near the door, where he is received by the bride's mother. She shows him a model plough, an arrow and a churning handle and pulls his nose. The bridegroom is led into the house, and sits with the bride at the place where the family goddess is painted on the wall. The ends of the bride's and bridegroom's clothes are tied together, and their hands are joined in the presence of their spiritual head, if he lives in the neighbourhood. They are led into the central square or *chori* of the marriage booth, the marriage sacrifice is performed, and the pair walk four times round the sacrificial fire (*saptapadi*), and feed each other with sweetmeats. The bridal pair are then separated, and the bride is presented with a robe and bodice with five finger marks which she wears while a song on Todarmul is sung by the women present. It is said that this ceremony has a history of its own connected with the Emperor Akbar, and that there is a copper plate relating to it which is still preserved at Jesalmere. Next, they go to the bridegroom's house with the ends of their clothes tied together. There they give each other a handful of sesame, and the bride presents a handful of sesame to the bridegroom's parents, who return it to the bride with a silver coin.

A Bhátia girl is sent to her husband's house immediately after her marriage; cohabitation commences a few days after marriage except among the Pavrai section of the community, among whom the girl is not allowed to pass even a single night at her husband's house until she attains puberty.

Bhátiás believe in and worship Hindu gods and goddesses such as Mahádev and his consort Párvati, Ráma and his consort Sita and their faithful servant Hanumán, the monkey god, and visit places of worship associated with their names. Some of them who are Vedántists, Arya Samájists, and Brahmo Samájists pray to the impersonal Almighty. There are a few Theosophists as well, but most of the Bhátiás are worshippers of their ancestor, Shri Krishna, and his four consorts Rukhmani (also known as Luxmi), Satyabháma, Rádha and Jambuvanti, under various names and at different places, such as Dwárkánáthji and his four consorts at Bet and Dwárka in Káthiáwár, Vithoba and Rukhamanai at Pandharpur and visit temples. They look upon Brij territory, about 84 miles round about Muttra and Gokul, with reverence as being the birth-place of Krishna and thus associated with his *Bála Lila* (chivalrous, acts of his childhood). They make pilgrimages to these places in the company of "chobás" who act as their guides, and who acquaint them with each event from Shri Krishna's childhood connected with the said place. Six miles below Muttra is the old town of Mahabun (in old Gokul) on the western bank of the Jumna, celebrated as being the birth-place where Krishna was exchanged with the infant-daughter of Jasoda to avoid the wrath of his maternal uncle Kaunsa who had ordered his death. The village of Gokul on the eastern bank of the Jumna is noted as being the place where Vishnu first visited the earth as Krishna. To the north is the holy city of Brindávan, a most important place of pilgrimage, ranking with great shrines of Puri, Tháneswar and Hardwár. There is an open space in the town known as the Gyán Guori, in the dust of which pilgrims roll, and it is locally held that a mouthful of it conveys perpetual sagacity. The orthodox consider the land so sacred that they do not wear shoes in treading the sacred ground. The river Jumna is looked upon as sacred, and Bhátiás, when there, use its water for making "*Jamnapani*," *i.e.*, drinking from it water in the palm of the hand. They take baths in the Jumna once during their stay.

The Ganga (the Ganges) is used by them for bathing, and baths at Soron and Hardwár are looked upon as expiating sins. It is here that *shráddhas* are performed. The water of the Jumna from Gokul and Muttra is brought back by the pilgrims well packed in air-tight *lotás* (vessels) and is used for years, a drop of it being given to friends and acquaintances by pilgrims on their return. It is also given to a dying man.

Bhátiás also make pilgrimage to Rámeswar, Badrika Ashram, Hardwár, Puri, Benares, and Náthdwára.

In addition they worship the Nág (Snake) known by them as Khetarpál, also as Dado, on *Nágpanchami* day (5th of *Shrávan Sud*). On *Sátam*, the 7th of *Shrávan*, they worship a pot of water. On the 13th of *Chaitra Vad* they worship Sitalámáta (the goddess of small-pox). During *Holi* children worship a stone known as "Godiápir" on the 15th of *Maha Sud*, and on the 15th of *Fálgun*, Bhátiás worship *Holi*. They are known to worship "*Satis*" of their families and on *Dasara* day, as Kshatriyas, they worship the sword and the *shami* (Prosopis spicigera) because on that day the Pándava brothers, under orders of Shri Krishna, took up arms which they had concealed at the time of going into 12 years' exile. On *Nárali Purnim* day (cocoanut day) they, as traders connected with the sea, worship Dariáságar (sea). On *Diwáli* days they worship Luxmi, the goddess of wealth.

Very many Bhátiás are Vaishnavas and now worship Shri Krishna as laid down by Vallabh and his descendants, who are known by various names, Achàryas, Gosámis and Mahárájás. In *Samvat* 1797 (A.D. 1741) the Bhátiás of Cutch Mándvi appointed for the first time Diksitji of Vallabh descent as the first religious head. Vallabhácharya, by which name the sect who worship Shri Krishna as laid down by Vallabh, son of Laxman Bhat, known also as Shri Vallabhácharjee, Shri Acháryaji, Shri Maha Prabhuji (Vallabh was born in *Samvat* 1535) is known, is a new sree.

It is a new sect inasmuch as it has selected the god Shri Krishna in one of his aspects, that of his adolescence (Bál Gopál Lila), and raised him to supremacy in that respect. It is also a new sect in so far as it established the *pushtimárg* or the way of enjoyment. Latterly the Mahárájás filched the worship from Shri Krishna and directed it to themselves, and began to be worshipped as "gods," but without being godly, and this evil became so great that in Cutch Mándvi the Gosái Runchhorji under the order of the Cutch Darbár was sent away from there as undesirable, and the Bhátiás of Bombay in 1855 passed a resolution restricting the hours of visit of their females to the Vaishnava Temples to such time as the Acháryas were supposed to be busy in worshipping the "gods." Things, however, did not improve, and this led to a crusade against the misdeeds of the Mahárájás and which culminated in the *cause célèbre* known as the Mahárája Libel Case (being Suit No. 12047 of 1861). In the words of the Honourable Mr. Justice Arnould, one of the trying Judges, "*it taught some to think, it led many to enquire*," and the authority of the Mahárájás since then has been crippled and is slowly decaying. Their priests are Pokarna Bráhmans. Gujarát Bráhmans do not eat with Pokarnas.

Death ceremonies. When a man is on the point of death, he is laid on a freshly cowdunged space on the floor strewn with *darbha* grass and *java* grains. The old sacred thread on his neck is removed, and a new one is put in its place. The water of the Jumna river is poured into his mouth. When life is gone, the body is tied to the bier, which is carried by the mourners after they have bathed. The body is burnt in the same way as among other high class Hindus. If a person meets death by drowning, an idol is made in his name, and the funeral rites are performed thereon.

They mourn twelve days. On the eleventh day wheat flour balls or *pindas* are offered to the deceased, and thrown in a running stream. They feast Bráhmans on the twelfth and the caste-fellows on the thirteenth.

Occupation. A large number of Bhátiás are merchants, traders, bankers and brokers; and within the last fifty years, they have become a very wealthy and important class. Numbers have moved either permanently or for a time to Bombay and many of them are settled to the west, in the ports of the Persian Gulf, the Red Sea and Zanzibar, and east as far as Japan. In Cutch they are traders, clerks, bankers and shop-keepers. Some of them are landowners.

Bhátiás are strict vagetarians except in some parts of the Punjab and Sind. The highest well known caste who eat from their hands are the Lohánás. Vániás will not eat from the hands of the Bhátiás, neither will the Bhátiás eat from Vániás. Food.

BHATIA HAJAM.—A sub-division of Hajáms.

BHATNAGRA.—A sub-division of Káyasths.

BHATYARA.—*See* under Minor Musalmán Castes.

BHAVAIYAS or Targálás, that is performers of *bhaváis* or comedies, numbering 5,617 (1901), including 3,052 males and 2,565 females, are found mostly in North Gujarát. They are said to be the descendants of a Bráhman by a Kanbi woman. They wander from place to place performing *nátaks* or religious dramas as well as *bhaváis* or plays of common life. Some cultivate land during the rains. In the Panch Maháls they have the right of levying a tax of one rupee on every girl's marriage. Their profession is rapidly declining with the advance of the native drama and more elaborate staging. They have two divisions, (1) Vyás and (2) Bhávaiyás, who do not eat together or intermarry. Marriages are not allowed among the descendants of collateral males on the father's side, but they are allowed among the descendants on the mother's side when they are three to seven degrees removed. Widow re-marriage and divorce are allowed. Their chief object of worship is the goddess Bahucharáji. Their priests are Audich Bráhmans. Every boy is girt with a sacred thread when he is between seven and eleven, but does not always continue to wear it. Bhávaiyás are strict vegetarians and do not drink liquor. The Vyás do not eat with castes lower than Kanbis while the Bhávaiyás eat with Kolis. Their marriage, death and other ceremonies do not differ from those of Kanbis.

BHAVAGUNA.—A synonym for Bhandári.

BHAVIK GURAV.—A synonym for Konkani Gurav.

BHAVINS(1) and Devlis, sometimes known as Náikins and Náiks, numbering 12,979 (1901), including 6,519 males and 6,460 females, are chiefly found in the Ratnágiri and Kanara districts and the Sávantvádi State. They are said to be descended from the female servants of the Sávantvádi or Málvan chiefs, to whom the chiefs presented lands after dedicating them to the service of village gods. This statement does not apply to all the Bhávins as many can trace their descent to an earlier period. It is, however, a fact, Name and origin.

(1) Compiled from information supplied by Mr. S. R. Nigudkar.

that their number was largely increased by the addition of the female servants of these chiefs.

In this caste, which is naturally somewhat loosely knit, the males are known as Devlis or Náiks, and females as Bhávins or Náikins. The caste is formed chiefly of women from two castes, Maráthás and Bhandáris. Women from certain other Shudra castes are allowed to become Bhávins by the simple ceremony of pouring oil on their head from the god's lamp in a temple.

When a Bhávin girl attains puberty, she has to undergo a form of marriage known as the *shesha*. The bridegroom is represented by a god from the temple. On an auspicious day Ganpati is worshipped and the ceremony of *punyáhavachan* (holy-day-blessing) is performed both at the girl's house, and also in a temple by the Gurav or Rául of the temple. The Gurav and other servants of the temple then go in procession to the girl's house, taking with them a dagger and the mask of the god. The marriage ceremony is performed with the same details as an ordinary marriage, the mask taking the place of the bridegroom. The *homa* or marriage sacrifice is also performed. The ceremony ends with a feast to those assembled. The performance of this ceremony involves no little expenditure. It is frequently dispensed with for this reason. In such cases the young girl performs the worship of Ganpati, and dressing herself in her best attire, goes to a temple to the beating of drums, accompanied by a party of Bhávins and temple servants, taking in her hands a cocoanut and a packet of sugar. She places the cocoanut and sugar before the image of the god and bows to him. The Gurav and other temple servants then invoke on her the blessings of the god and the ceremony ends.

The Bhávin practices prostitution and differs from the common prostitute only in being dedicated to the god. From her children she chooses two or three to succeed her as temple servants. In the social scale she ranks below the Kalávant and is not allowed to sing or dance in public, nor may regular musicians accompany her.

Except those dedicated to the gods, the daughters of Bhávins are married to the sons of other Bhávins, *viz.*, Devlis. The Devlis have neither sub-divisions nor surnames. The names of men are Bábi, Kushna, Ládu, Rám, Sháb, Lakshman, Vithoba, Venkti and Yesu, and of women, Shewantu, Devku, Gunai, Bhiku, Puttu and Chandri. Their home tongue is Konkani. Their marriage and other ceremonies resemble those of the Konkani Maráthás. Widow re-marriage is allowed but a widow may also become a prostitute with the consent of the caste people.

Bhávins are Hindus and worship the ordinary local and Bráhmanical gods, the objects of their special devotion being Mhálsa, Venkataráma, Rámnáth, Ravalnáth, Máhuli, Mallikárjuna, Nirankár and the powers or *Shaktis*. They observe all the Hindu holidays and offer goats and fowls to the village gods and the *Shaktis*. Their religious teacher is the head of the Shringeri monastery. They have great faith in soothsaying, witchcraft, evil spirits and omens. Their priests are local Bráhmans. Those who can afford it burn the dead, the rest bury.

Bhávins are employed in temples to sweep and cowdung the floor and wave the fly-whisk before the god. The Devlis blow the temple horns and trumpets morning and evening, and are paid partly in cash and partly by a share of the offerings. They also attend and blow horns at marriages. Some of them work as husbandmen and labourers, holding land on permanent lease. Some are strolling players and drummers.

The staple food of the caste is rice, pulse and vegetables. They eat fish, mutton, fowls and other articles of food consumed by the Maráthás. Bhávins and Devlis eat food cooked by Maráthás. They do not eat from Sonárs, Sutárs, Jingars, Thákars and other low castes. Some Maráthás eat food cooked by Bhávins, Devlis and Kunbins. Food.

BHAVNAGRI.—A sub-division of Lohárs.

BHAVSARS, numbering 30,761 (1901), including 15,805 males and 14,956 females, are found all over the Gujarát districts and Native States, Poona and Karnátak. They are chiefly found in Kaira, Ahmedabad, Surat, Káthiáwár and Mahi Kántha. Of the total number 4,467 were returned as Musalmáns and 6,139 as Jains. In Gujarát, Bhávsárs are also known as Chhipa or Chhapgar, and the term applies equally to both Hindu and Muhammadan Bhávsárs. Name.

Bhávsárs are divided into two main endogamous divisions—Gujaráti and Marátha. Gujaráti Bhávsárs, besides being divided into Meshri or Hindu and Shrávak or Jain and Musalmán Bhávsárs, who neither eat together nor intermarry, have three sub-divisions—Rewákánthiás living on the banks of the Mahi and the Narbada, Rámdeshis living in Páli and Partápgad and Talabdas living in North Gujarát. The members of these three divisions neither eat together nor intermarry, though Rámdeshis and Rewákánthias do not object to eat food cooked by Talabdás. Some appear once to have been Vánis, but most claim to be of Kshatriya descent and have Rajput tribal surnames Divisions.

such as Bhatte, Chohan, Gohil, Parmár and Ráthod. Like the Kanbis the Bhávsárs are almost certainly of Gurjar origin. Marátha Bhávsárs, who are separately described below, appear to be an offshoot of the parent or Gujarát branch which penetrated to the Deccan through Mungi-Paithan. They still worship Hingláj Máta of Sind, the patron goddess of the parent stock, but for the rest have become identified in language and customs with the population of the Deccan districts in which they are found. According to the caste tradition, during Parshuram's persecution of the Kshatriyas, their ancestors hid in a Máta's temple, and for this act of trust were afterwards known as Bhávsárs because they placed *bháv* or confidence in the goddess. The original home of their ancestors is said to have been Brij Mathura in Northern India, from which they moved to Márwár and thence to Champáner and the country bordering on the Mahi and the Narbada. From Central Gujarát some went to Káthiáwár and Cutch in the north and some to Surat in the south. Certain local surnames bear witness to their former settlements, *e.g.*, Amadabadi, Harsotia, Jamnagra, Masania, Modesia, Parantia and Visnagra.

The following particulars apply to GUJARAT BHAVSARS :—

Marriage. Marriages cannot take place between relatives unless they are removed by from ten to twenty degrees from the common ancestor. Marriage with a maternal uncle's or mother's sister's daughter is not allowed. Marriage with a wife's younger sister is allowed, both during the wife's lifetime or after her death. Two brothers may marry two sisters, but the elder of the two brothers must marry the elder sister. Girls and boys are married before they are twelve years old. Polygamy is permitted but polyandry is unknown.

The offer of marriage generally comes from the boy's father. The father of the girl pays from one to two hundred rupees as dowry. Some receive a bride price, the amount varying from seven hundred rupees to one thousand. Their marriage rites do not differ from those of Vániás, Meshri and Shrávak. Ganpati is invoked and propitiated. The knot tied in the bride's and bridegroom's upper garments on the marriage occasion is loosened before the Hingláj goddess.

Widow remarriage is allowed. A widow cannot marry her maternal uncle's or mother sister's son. She sometimes marries the younger brother of her deceased husband. A bachelor is not allowed to marry a widow. The Bombay Gazetteer states that divorce is allowed among them, but recent inquiries seem to show that divorce is now no longer allowed.

Bhávsárs follow the Hindu law of inheritance and belong to the Hindu religion. They belong to Kabirpanthi, Rádha Vallabhi, Rámánandi, Rámánuj, Santrámpanthi, Shaiva, Swáminaráyan and Vallabhácharya sects. The Shrávaks contain members of the Svetámbar, Digambar and Dhondia sects. Their family goddesses are Ambáji and Hingláj. They visit the sacred shrine of the Hingláj goddess in Sind. The Sunday which falls in the latter half of the month of *Paush* is supposed to be the birthday of the goddess and is observed by them with special reverence. They employ Bráhman priests in all their ceremonies.

Bhávsárs burn their dead. Children under three years of age are buried with their heads to the north. The *shráddha* ceremony for the propitiation of their ancestors is observed.

Bhávsárs are calico-printers and dyers. Many have given up calico-printing and have become confectioners, tailors, washermen and sellers of brassware. Some are husbandmen.

MARATHA BHAVSARS found in the Deccan claim to have come into the Presidency about seventy or eighty years ago from Mungi-Paithan, about fifty miles north-east of Ahmednagar. They have no sub-divisions. Their commonest surnames are Banchhod, Lale, Lokhande, Modgare and Parpati ; those bearing the same surname do not intermarry. The names in common use among men are Bháu, Ráma, Sakhárám, Thamáji and Vithoba ; and among women Gita, Lahani, Rama, Rambai and Thaku. They speak Maráthi.

Girls are married from the time in the cradle up to the age of ten or twelve, and boys from ten to twenty or twenty-five. The boy's father looks for a wife for his son. When he has found a suitable match he takes with him a couple of near relations or friends and formally asks the girl's father to give his daughter in marriage to his son. If the girl's father agrees, the family priest is asked to name a lucky day, and on that day the boy's father goes to the girl's home, taking a few near relations and friends and his family priest. After they are seated, the girl is called, and takes her seat near the priest. The priest marks her brow with red powder, presses her brow with a silver coin, and gives the coin into her hands. Sweetmeats and betel packets are served and the guests retire. This is called the red powder rubbing or *kunku lávne*. Their asking or *mágni* is the same as the Kunbi asking, and the turmeric rubbing lasts five to seven days. The boy and girl are rubbed with turmeric at their homes. On the first day five married women grind turmeric and rub it on the boy's body, and, taking some to the girl's house with a

Marriage.

new green robe and bodice, accompanied by kinswomen and music, rub the girl with it, dress her in the new clothes, and return with a present of a turban and sash for the boy. The turmeric rubbing is repeated both at the boy's and the girl's during each of the next five or six days and during those days no other ceremony is performed. Marriage booths are built at both the houses, and an earthen altar is set up at the girl's with five earthen jars ranged round it. Their marriage guardian or *devak* consists of the leaves of four fig trees—*Ficus religiosa, Ficus glomerata, Ficus indica* and *Ficus infectora*—and of the mango. In the evening of the marriage day, accompanied by kinspeople and friends, the boy goes on horseback to Máruti's temple in the girl's village and takes his seat on the verandah. The girl's party come to the temple, present the boy with a turban and sash, put new shoes on his feet and bring him to the girl's home. Before the boy enters the marriage hall, an elderly woman waves rice and curds round his head and throws them on one side. The girl's father leads him into the marriage hall and makes him stand on a wooden stool, blanket or carpet, in front of the girl, and a cloth is held between them. The priest repeats verses and, at the end, throws grains of rice over their heads, and the boy and the girl are husband and wife. Their right wrists are tied with seven rounds of yellow cotton or *kankan* thread, to which a piece of turmeric root is fastened. The sacred fire is lit on the altar by both the boy and girl and fed with butter and parched rice. The boy's father presents the girl's brother with a turban. He ties together the skirts of the boy's and girl's robes and they are led to the village Máruti's temple, bow to him and return. The day ends with a dinner. Next evening exchange presents of clothes are made between the two houses, and the boy takes his wife in a procession, accompanied by kinspeople, friends and music, to his father's house.

They have house images of the usual Deccan gods, but their chief objects of worship are Bálájì or Krishna and Hingláj Máta. They keep the usual fasts and feasts and believe in the power of spirits and ghosts. Their priests are Deshasth Bráhmans, whom they greatly respect.

Death ceremonies. When a person dies, relations, friends and castefellows are told, the body is brought out of the house and laid on the house steps and warm water is poured over it. A piece of cloth is rolled round its loins, it is laid on a bier and sweet flowers are strewn over the body. The bier is carried on the shoulders of four men, and the chief mourner walks in front, carrying an earthen pot with burning cowdung cakes. On the way to the burning ground the body is rested and pieces of bread are left for the evil spirits to eat. At the burning ground a pile is raised, the body is laid on the pile, and the pile is kindled by the chief mourner. When the pile is completely burnt the chief mourner walks thrice round it with an earthen jar full of water. At the end of the third turn he dashes the jar on the ground and cries aloud, beating his mouth with the back of his right hand. The mourners return home. On the third day the chief mourner goes to the burning ground, removes the ashes, shaves his moustache, bathes and sprinkles cow's urine and dung on the ashes. On the spot where the body was burnt he sets three earthen jars filled with cooked rice, curds, honey and milk, and after bathing returns home. They mourn ten days and on the eleventh the chief mourner goes to the river-side, prepares ten wheat flower balls, offers one to the crows and throws the rest into water. On the eleventh or twelfth day the memorial or *shráddha* ceremony is performed at the mourner's house, and either on the twelfth or thirteenth day the caste is feasted, chiefly on sweet cakes or *puran polis*.

Bhávsárs in the Deccan prepare dyes and print and dye cloth.

BHAVSARGOR.—A sub-division of Audich Bráhmans.

BHERLE.—A sub-division of Bhandáris.

BHIKSHUK.—A synonym for Mánbháv.

BHILS, numbering 559,930 (1901), including 282,345 males and 277,585 females, are chiefly found in Gujarát and Khándesh. The name Bhil is often given to half-wild tribes such as Chodhrás, Dhánkás, Dhodiás, Kátkaris, Konknás and Várlis. The census figures cannot therefore be taken as accurate. Their original home is the hilly country between Abu and Asirgarh, from which they have spread westward and southward into the plains of Gujarát and the Northern Deccan, and lately, under pressure of famine, even to Sind. They are found in considerable numbers in Rájputána and Central India. Name and origin.

The term Bhil, according to Wilson, is derived from *billee* the Dravidian word for a bow,(1) which is the characteristic weapon of the tribe. Sanskrit lexicographers derive it from the root *bhil*, which means to cut. They take it to mean Mlechha, that is, one who has fallen or become degraded. The earliest mention of the word in Sanskrit literature occurs in the Katha-Sarit-Ságara(2) of Gunádhya,

(1) Aboriginal Tribes, 3.

(2) Verses 161—170 of Taranga 1 of the Alamkár-Vahi Lambaka or Taranga 52 from the beginning (*vide* p. 290 of Katha-Sarit-Ságar, Niranya Ságar Edition).

who, according to Dr. Weber, flourished about the sixth century A. D. The passage in which the word occurs is highly interesting since it makes mention of a Bhil Chief mounted on an elephant and opposing in great force the progress of another king through the Vindhyas. This would show that the Bhils in those times were very powerful. Secondly, the passage gives *Dasyu* as another name for Bhil. Now the word *Dasyu* is as old as the Rig-Veda, and if the Bhils are the modern descendants of the *Dasyus* of the Rig-Veda, there is little doubt that the Bhils represent those people who opposed the advancing tide of Aryan conquest in primitive times, and who are described under all sorts of opprobrious names, such as Kirát, Pulinda, Chándála, Sabara, etc., in the earliest Sanskrit literature.

The references to the Bhils in Sanskrit literature are interesting inasmuch as they show that the Bhils were a race both feared and hated, gradually pushed back by the invading Aryan race to the fastnesses of mountains and forests which they eventually occupied. The Hindus troubled little about them until some retaliation on the part of the Bhils caused the chronicler to mention them with abhorrence: no attempt was made to enquire into their origin, but later when they had been pushed back into the tracts of country where they are now found, and no doubt after the Rajput ascendancy, it was felt necessary to account for the Bhils, and they were allowed to be "an illegitimate race(1) descended from the four original classes", in other words, admitted to some of the privileges of Hinduism, and instructed as to their origin by a myth which they were proud to repeat as connecting them with the dominant race. Mahádev had a son by a human wife, who slew his father's bull and was banished to the mountains. This son was the ancestor of the Bhil race. There are various Bhil legends of obviously Hindu origin; which, though interesting historically as showing a desire on the part of the Bhils to connect themselves with the dominant race, throw no light on the origin of the Bhil race.

The Bhils are supposed by some to be the 'Pygmies' of Ctesias (400 B. C.) and the *Poulindai* and *Phyllitæ* of Ptolemy (A. D. 150). They seem to represent an invasion earlier than that of the Aryans either by the north-west or by the north-east routes into India. This invasion no doubt confined the Dravidian race to the south of India. The Bhils have been assigned to the Kolarian race, but Sir G. Grierson

---

(1) In the Smritis the Bhil is spoken of as the issue of the union of a Bráhman mother and a Tiwara father—a Tiwara being a hunter, who is himself variously described as a son of a Kshatriya by a Rajput woman or of a Pundraka by a Chunari woman. In the *Játimála* Bhils are classed with Medhs as one of the seven lowest tribes.

has given good reasons why the race should be called Munda, the term given to it by Prof. Max Muller. There is evidence that the Bhillas, so contemptuously spoken of in Sanskrit literature, were at one time a powerful race owning considerable tracts of country. Both Jodhpur and Udaipur made conquests over the Bhillas, winning tracts of country from them, and the Rajput princes of Dungarpur and Bánswára similarly won land from Bhils. Sir John Malcom is of opinion that the country north-west of Málwa was the original stronghold of the Bhils from which they were gradually ousted and pushed towards the hilly tracts and the country where they are found at the present day. As they had opportunity, their chieftains retaliated by invasion of the plain country ; but from the time that the Bhils came prominently into notice they may be said to have their strongholds among the hills and forests, only extending their dominion over the adjoining plain country as opportunity served. A confirmation of Sir J. Malcom's theory as to the original stronghold of Bhils is found in the yearly visits of Chárans and Bháts from Udaipur to the south. They are the priests of the leading Bhilála families, and besides performing their ceremonies, prepare for them their genealogical trees.

The Rajputs seem to have had more connection with the Bhils than any other Hindu race, and many intermarried with the Bhils. Thus both by amalgamation and conquest the Rajputs gained a great ascendancy over the Bhils. From this connection rose the Bhilálás tracing their descent from the marriage of a Rajput with a Bhil woman. There is no doubt that there was much admixture between these two races, but the leading families of Rajputs were careful to keep their descent—at least nominally—pure by means of genealogical trees which were kept for them by the Chárans and Bháts.

The tradition lingered long that the Rajput race had demeaned themselves by an alliance with the Bhils, and even among the Bhils themselves anxiety was shown to prove that Rajput blood was in their veins. This pride of race led to a distinction among the Bhils ; those who could prove descent through Rajputs were known as *ujwála* or the "light-coloured", those less fortunate as *kála* or "niggers", a rather amusing circumstance, proving that snobbishness was not unknown even among Bhils. There is one interesting custom which survived to show that the Bhils had originally had much more power than in the time of Rajput ascendancy. At the accession of a Rajput prince, blood taken from the thumb or toe of a Bhil was smeared on his forehead. This was known as *Tika*. The chieftains known as Bhumiás were mostly of Bhilála race.

Appearance. Bhils differ much in appearance. As a rule the Gujarát Bhil is small, light-limbed and active, some having handsome though irregular features. The typical Khándesh Bhil, the wild woodman of the Satpurás, is dark, well-made, active and hardy, with high cheek bones, wide nostrils, and in some cases coarse almost African features. These are no doubt stunted and degraded by want and ill-health, and perhaps by intermarriage with still older and lower tribes. Among the southern and western tribes, who probably more nearly represent the original type of Bhil, are many well-built and even some tall handsome men with regular features and waving hair. The plain Bhils are scarcely to be distinguished from local Kunbis.

Dress and ornaments. The every-day dress of a Gujarát male Bhil consists of a *fenta* or *falia* a headcloth made of a coarse cloth, a *pachhedi* or shoulder cloth and a *potiu* or waistcloth. The Gujarát Bhil woman's every-day dress is over the head and shoulders a short robe *sallo*, an open-back bodice *kánchli* and a petticoat *gágro*. Of ornaments the men wear silver earrings and silver bracelets. The women wear brass and tin head ornaments. three silver brass or tin rings or *vellas* for the upper ear and one silver, brass or wood *lotia* for the lower lobe. Round the neck, in addition to strings of glass and stone beads and shells that often completely cover the breast, is worn a silver or tin ornament called *hánsdi* and sometimes in the nose a nosering of gold, silver, brass or tin.

The hill Bhil in Khándesh has seldom any clothing but a piece of cloth round the loins, and their women a coarse tattered robe. The peasant Bhil wears a turban, a coat and waistcloth, and their women a robe with or without a bodice. Both men and women wear brass or silver earrings, and when they can afford them, anklets.

Language. Bhils speak the cognate dialects of Gujaráti, Maráthi, Rángdi, Mevádi, Hindi, Rájputáni, etc., in accordance with the proximity of the larger languages. These dialects vary much in corruption from the source from which they are borrowed. Some of the words in the dialects are easily recognizable, some with much difficulty. These dialects too are of a fluctuating nature as is only natural when there is no standard to which they can be referred. According to Sir G. Grierson, the dialects classed as Bhili are dialects of Gujaráti. Whether, as was the opinion of Sir James Malcom's Bhil informant, there was an original language which has been displaced by dialects of the people of the plain, is still an open question. The difficulty of collecting reliable specimens of the dialect is very great, both from the fluctuating nature of the dialects themselves and from the difficulty of getting their users to speak them to order. It is only by great care, and occasionally even by accident, that some strange form of speech is come across that seems to point to an original language, now almost lost. It may be noted that the Bhils are exceedingly reluctant to speak their dialects with strangers. They usually know sufficient of the local patois to avoid doing so. On the other hand, when their confidence is gained they are too prone to display their erudition by the introduction of foreign words into a dialect which at other times they could speak naturally.

Bhils are divided into a number of tribes which tends to lessen the underlying homogeniety of the race. The remarks of Sir J. Malcom in this connection show that the process of sub-division has been going on for a long time. He says, "In every province where Bhils were established, I have found the names of tribes, or rather families, increase in the ratio that inquiry was pursued".(1) He instances the Koku Bhils whose signal on plundering expeditions was like the crowing of a cock. There seems to be little doubt that the so-called tribes are merely clans or families, who are differentiated according to the extent to which they have adopted Hindu customs, intermarried with other races, or are affected by local influences. Why this natural process of differentiation should be accelerated by the Bhils themselves is difficult to explain, unless the influence of the caste system be taken into account—a system which was undoubtedly quite unknown to the original Bhil. **Divisions.**

Bhils may be roughly divided into two territorial groups, (1) Gujarát Bhils and (2) Khándesh Bhils. Gujarát Bhils vary considerably, like the Kolis, in the proportion of Rajput blood which they can claim, and the dividing line between them and the Koli clans on their borders is a very shadowy one. In the Panch Maháls, Pateliás, Rávaliás and Báriás are admitted into the Bhil tribe at the cost of a feast, and the similarity of clan names among the higher Gujarát Kolis and Bhils clearly indicates a common origin.

The part Rajput Bhils, that is those with a Rajput strain in their blood, are found in Prántij, Modása and other districts of northern Gujarát. The pure Bhils, except a few in Idar, Rewa Kántha and the Panch Maháls who are part Bhils, are found in eastern and southern Gujarát, but chiefly in Rewa Kántha and the Panch Maháls. Again

(1) Trans., R. As. Soc. I., 81.

the Rewa Kántha and the Panch Mahāls Bhils belong to two classes, (1) hill and (2) plain Bhils who, except that they are more settled and better off, do not differ from hill Bhils in traditions and customs.

Khándesh Bhils may conveniently be classed under three groups, (1) plain Bhils, (2) hill and forest tribes and (3) mixed tribes. The plain Bhils, the largest and most civilized class, found in almost all the villages of central and south Khándesh, are known simply as Bhils in contradistinction to the hill and forest tribes. The latter consist of the following tribes so far as has been ascertained upto the present :—

1 Barda.	7 Mathvádi.
2 Dángchi.	8 Mávchi.
3 Dhánka.	9 Nahál.
4 Dhorepi.	10 Pávra.
5 Gavit.	11 Várli.
6 Khotil.	12 Vasáva.

Of these, all except the Dángchis who are found in the Sahyádris are found in the Sátpudás. The mixed tribes are three :—

(1) Bhilála, half-Bhil half-Rajput or Kunbi.

(2) Nirdhi, half-Musalmán half-Bhil.

(3) Tadvi, half-Musalmán half-Bhil.

The Bhilálás and Tadvis are found in the eastern Sátpudás and the Nirdhis in the Sátmálas in the south.

The description given below deals with the Bhil tribe as a whole, the Bhilálás, Dángchis, Khotils, Mathvádis, Mávchis, Nahāls, Nirdhis, Pávrás and Tadvis being described in brief at the end of the article.

Most of the Bhil tribes in Khándesh admit outsiders except from the impure castes, on payment of a fine of Rs. 10 to the *panch* and on the outsider drinking and eating with the tribe. In some places, the outsider has to be adopted by a Bhil, who, on being presented with a turban and his wife with a robe and bodice, performs the adoption ceremony.

Most of the Bhil divisions, both Gujarát and Khándesh, are divided into an endless number of small clans, some of them such as Ahir, Barda, Bária, Dángi, Gáikvád, Ganáva, Jádhav, Katára, Makvána, Máli, Mori, Parmár, Pavár, Ráthod, Shinde, Sonone, Thákur, etc., arising from a claim of a strain of non-Bhil blood, others, as Vághia and Ghania, taken from the names of animals ; a third set, as Pipalsa, from the names of trees ; and a fourth, of miscellaneous origin, from a forefather's name, a favourite settlement, or some private signal. Of all the clan names the following are interesting as indicating an original totemistic organization and thus supporting the view that the Bhils are of primitive origin :—

Name of clan.		*Its devak or totem.*
1 Ahir	..	A snake-like fish called *ahir*.
2 Bhavare	..	The bird *gangudli*.
3 Bhor-kole	..	The *kohala* (pumpkin).
4 Bijary	..	The *biju* or polecat.
5 Bongade	..	The bird *gangudli*.
6 Borshe	..	*Bore* (a kind of bird).
7 Gáikvád	..	The *pipal*.
8 Gangode	..	The bird *gangudli*.
9 Magar	..	*Magar* (crocodile).
10 Máli	..	Any kind of flower.
11 More	..	*Mor* (peacock).
12 Pawár	..	Pigeon.
13 Pipalsa	..	The *pipal*.
14 Shakere	..	Sparrow.
15 Shinde	..	The *shindi* tree (wild date plam).
16 Sonone	..	*Balde* (a kind of bird).
17 Vágh	..	*Vágh* (tiger).

All these clans show their reverence for the objects of their *devaks* by not cutting the trees and by abstaining from eating the flesh of the animals representing the *devaks*. The Vághs go even further. They worship the tiger and grieve when they hear of a tiger being killed. Cases are known of Bhils of this clan throwing themselves pros trate when they accidentally see a tiger passing. The Bhor-koles worship the pumpkin gourd by smearing it with red lead, and offer slices of it to the gods.

Marriage.

Marriage is prohibited between members belonging to the same clan. A Bhil may marry his maternal uncle's daughter, but not his father's sister's or mother's sister's daughter. In some places marriage with a maternal uncle's daughter is also prohibited. Marriage with a wife's sister is allowed and brothers are allowed to marry sisters. Marriage is adult. Sexual license before marriage is connived at, if it does not result in pregnancy. In the latter case a fine is levied by the *panch* and the parties are sometimes compelled to marry. Polygamy, widow marriage and divorce are allowed and practised. Polyandry is unknown.

It is very difficult to ascertain the customs proper to the original Bhil race, as the tribes belonging to it represent various grades of civilization, from the primitive man to the fully Hinduised Kunbi or cultivator. Again, they vary from place to place. The following details may, therefore, be taken as applying to certain typical localities in which Bhils are found.

Birth ceremonies in Gujarát.

In Gujarát, five days after a birth the child and mother are bathed. In the Rewa Kántha no ceremony is performed. But in the Panch Mahábls the mother makes a circle of flour, piles little heaps of flour on all sides, and sits in the middle of the circle, when her female relations make her presents of money or clothes. On the tenth day the father and mother name the child. On the twelfth day, in the Rewa Kántha, the house is cleaned and a feast is given, but this is not done in the Panch Mahábls. At five years' old the child's head is shaved. The child's aunt takes the hair in her lap, and, wrapping it in her clothes, receives a cow, buffalo or other present from the child's father.

Birth ceremonies in Khándesh.

In Khándesh at the birth of a child a midwife is employed, and besides a bottle of liquor, a rupee is paid if the child is a boy, and eight annas if it is a girl. For four days no one but the midwife touches the mother. On the morning of the fifth day a party of women are called, and both mother and child are bathed in warm water. Just outside the threshold of the hut, the mother cowdungs the ground and traces turmeric lines. In the middle of the drawing she places a lighted lamp, setting round it five flint stones corresponding to the number of days since the child was born. Round these pebbles she lays pieces of cocoa kernel, and over the whole sprinkles turmeric, millet, red powder and liquor. The guests drop a few grains of millet over the mother and child, and then re-enter the house. Next the guests are feasted with wheat and rice bread, mutton and liquor, and the whole night is spent in singing, smoking and drinking. The lamp is allowed to burn for twenty-four hours.

On the twelfth day a dish of boiled millet and split pulse is made ready. Some of it is laid on a brass platter in which are also placed twelve wheaten cakes and lighted lamps, corresponding with the number of days since the child's birth. In another dish a lamp, *árti*, is set, and along with the mother, women go in procession, singing and beating the drum, towards the nearest running water, where the mother arranges the twelve lamps. The cakes are placed in a line between the lamps, and a little of the boiled food is laid on each cake. The mother worships the water goddess, *Faldevta*, throws a little red lead, red powder and some grains mixed with turmeric into the water and on the twelve lamps, and lighting a fire before the lamps, feeds it with oil. They then go home and feast on mixed rice and pulse and oil.

Marriage ceremonies in Gujarát.

In Gujarát, a marriage between a young couple is arranged entirely by their relations. When the parents wish to marry their son, they send friends to the parents of the girl whom they wish to become their son's bride. These make proposals, and present raw sugar and liquor, and if they accept the offer of marriage, the girl's parents eat the sugar. After some time the boy's father visits the girl and presents her with clothes and food. The betrothal is then complete. On the morning of the marriage-day the bride and bridegroom each at their own homes are rubbed with yellow powder. In the south, during the ceremony, the bride's party laugh and jeer at the party of the bridegroom, the men at the men, the women at the women. After the ceremony a fire is kindled, and round it the people dance, the bridegroom taking a few turns with the bride on his shoulder. When the dance is over, the bridegroom gives all a drink before they leave. Then the bridegroom is bathed and afterwards, to guard against the evil eye, his eyes and cheeks are marked with soot or *kájal*. The bridegroom wears a turban, a long coat of country cloth, a waistcloth *dhotar* and a sword. The party start with drums and cymbals for the bride's village. The women follow singing. When they reach the village they stop a couple of hundred yards from the bride's house. Here they are met by the bride's father and a few friends. After saluting, they seat themselves, and the amount fixed as the price of the bride is counted out. The bride's father then goes back to the house, the bridegroom and his party following with music. On reaching the house the bridegroom's party are seated on one side of a *mándva* or booth built in front of the door. The bride is then led in by her mother and seated opposite the bridegroom, their hands are joined, and the hems of their garments are tied. Then, while three women sing songs, the bride and bridegroom walk together twelve times, the bridegroom leading for the first six and the bride for the second six, round a branch of the *shami* (Prosopis spicigera) tree, placed in the middle of the booth. When this is over, the bride's mother leads the bride and bridegroom into the house and lays before them a dish of wheaten bread and molasses, and with this the bride and bridegroom feed each other in turn five times over. Then the knot that fastened their garments is unloosed, and the bridegroom, leaving the bride, returns with his friends to his own house. Here he and his party feed on rice and pulse sent by the bride's father. When the meal is over they return to the bride's. The mother brings out the bride. The garments of the bride and bridegroom are again tied together, and, taking the bride with him, the bridegroom, accompanied by his friends, returns to his house. Among the Mahi Kántha Bhils women, as a rule, choose their husbands. But, on the fair day, at Tosina, in the north of the Mahi Kántha, if a Bhil takes a fancy to a Bhil girl, and can, without being found out, get her to cross the river with him, he can claim her as his wife. If they are caught on the way the man is punished by the bride's father.

Though in theory a marriage should be attended with all this ceremonial, in practice the Bhils are very loose in their marriage relations. A man marries a second or a third wife if the first wife does not bear children, or if she does not get on with him, or if he does not like her, or if he has a large number of children and the work of the house is heavy. A woman marries again, not only if her husband dies but if she falls in love with another man and can get him to take her and pay her husband his marriage expenses. The children, if there are any, remain with the father. An unmarried girl is allowed to live with any man she likes without any ceremony either of marriage or betrothal. If after betrothal a girl goes to live with some other man, her husband has to pay her betrothed the cost of the betrothal ceremony. So, after marriage, if a woman takes a fancy to any man she may go and live with him if he is willing to pay her husband's marriage expenses.

Marriage ceremonies in Khándesh.

In Khándesh, suggestions of marriage come from the boy's house and are taken by the boy's relations to the girl's father. When it is known that a favourable reply will be given, a formal proposal is made by the boy's father, or his nearest relation. When the affair is so far settled, the nearest relations, both men and women, go to the girl's house and there ask that the girl shall be given in marriage to their boy. If her father agrees, the girl is brought out and seated among the guests, and the boy's father or his nearest relation offers her a packet of sweetmeats. This over, they dine together, and the guests, before leaving, talk over the betrothal, and a day or two after, with the help of a Bráhman astrologer, the boy's father fixes the betrothal day.

On the betrothal day the astrologer, the boy, his father, and other relations, taking with them a robe, a bodice, and sweetmeats, go to the girl's house. After resting for a short time, the girl's father calls a council, *panch*, and in their presence agrees to give his daughter in marriage. The boy's father then presents the girl with a robe and bodice. A married woman touches the girl's brow with red powder and gives her some sweetmeats, blessing her and hoping that, like them, her life may be sweet. The whole party then drink from funds supplied by a present of a rupee and a half from each of the fathers. That evening the girl's father gives the guests a dinner, and next morning the boy and his party go home.

There is no fixed interval between the betrothal and the marriage. It may be a month or it may be years. When he is in a position to meet the marriage expenses, the boy's father sends word to the girl's father that he is bringing the dowry, *ghum* or *dej*. On arrival he and his company are given refreshments, and a council is called. The dowry from Rs. 10 to Rs. 20 is settled, and the amount laid before the council in a metal plate. An unmarried woman of the girl's family touches, with red powder, one of the rupees in the plate, and the brows of the boy and his party. The girl is brought out and seated on the boy's father's lap, and the boy's father, taking a rupee, places it inside the top of the folds of her robe. The council then tell her to go into the house, and take two rupees from the plate, to buy liquor for the evening's entertainment. The rest of the dowry is handed to the girl's father. After a feast the evening ends with music and dancing. Next day the father, with a few friends, goes to the family priest, *bhat*, and fixes the marriage day.

Next comes the turmeric, *haldi*, ceremony, when turmeric, mixed with water, is rubbed on the boy's body, and part of it is taken, by a band of relations, to the girl's house, and there rubbed over her. After this, generally for about a fortnight, both the boy and the girl are rubbed morning and evening with turmeric. At both their houses booths are built, and at the girl's house an altar, *bahule*, is raised.

On the marriage day, an hour or two before the time fixed for the ceremony, the boy, riding on horseback with a marriage ornament, *básing*, tied to his turban, starts with a company of relations and friends. On the way he is taken to the temple of Máruti, closely followed by his sister, who walks behind him with a water jar, *kara*, in her hands in which five copper coins have been dropped. Halting at the temple all drink from a jar, *ghada*, of water, and one of their number, the leader, *vardhava*, is seated on a pony or on a man's shoulders and taken to the girl's house. Here he is feasted and his face rubbed with soot, *kájal*. Going back to his friends he washes his face, and about sunset the party goes to the girl's house. As they draw near, the boy is pelted with onions and fruit, and when he arrives a cocoanut or a piece of bread is waved round him and either dashed on the ground or thrown away. When he dismounts seven women stand before the booth with full water pots, *lotás*, into each of which the boy drops a copper. After this, one of the women waves a lighted lamp round his face, receiving from him the present of a piece of cloth, *cholkhan*. The boy then sits facing the east. The Bráhman priest sends for the girl, and, seating her face to face with the boy, passes a thread round them both. A coloured cloth is held between them high enough to prevent their seeing each other. The girl, joining her hands together, touches the cloth, and the boy from the other side clasps her hands with both of his. One of each party holds the boy and the girl round the waist, while the priest standing on a raised platform repeats marriage verses, and the guests throw grains of rice or millet over the heads of the couple. After a short time the priest claps his hands, the boy and girl throw garlands round each other's necks, the cloth is pulled aside, guns are fired, music played, and the guests move about congratulating each other. Betelnut and leaves are distributed among the men, and turmeric and red powder among the women. The boy and the girl are seated on the altar ; the laps of five married women are filled with wheat, rice, dates and betelnuts, and round the boy's and girl's right wrists yellow strings with a piece of turmeric are tied. The boy and girl then feed one another and the guests are feasted. After supper, sitting in small groups in and about the booth, the boy's party on one side and the girl's on the other, they pass their time in singing and drinking.

Next morning the boy and girl bathe, standing on low wooden stools, the women of the party all the time throwing water over them. Then comes the lap-filling, *phalbharne*, when the girl is given clothes and ornaments, and her lap is filled with wheat, rice or millet, a piece of cocoa kernel, dates, almonds and betelnuts, and the parents and relations exchange presents of clothes and money. Then, with music, the boy's mother and her relations and friends go in procession to the girl's house, walking on clothes bathed in warm water, and if the girl's father can afford it, glass bangles are put round the women's wrists. Both boy and girl are then presented with clothes. During this time, till the return procession, the boy and girl amuse themselves, biting pieces of betel leaf or of cocoa kernel out of each other's mouths, or searching for a betelnut hid in the other's clothes. While the boy is at his house the girl's father gives two dinners to his caste-fellows and relations. After two or three days, a party from both families, taking the girl on horseback, go to the boy's house, and on the following day the boy's father gives a dinner. After this the yellow threads are taken off the wrists and necks of both the boy and the girl, and they are bathed to remove all traces of turmeric.

Widow re-marriage cere-mony in Gujarát.

Among Gujarát Bhils, when a man wishes to marry a widow, if his proposals are accepted, the suitor is desired to bring to the house of his intended bride such presents as he can afford, which are usually a petticoat of coarse chintz, a robe, a bodice, a necklace of beads, two pots of arrack, sixteen pounds of roasted peas and two pounds of molasses. The match is then considered settled. Taking some friends with him and the materials for a feast, the man goes to the woman's house, where a company of her friends are assembled. Next morning before daybreak the married pair leave the house. Marriage with a widow generally takes the form of an elopement, the bride and bridegroom being received back after the bridegroom has made the bride's friends and the headman a present. The couple pass the day after the wedding in some solitary place three or four miles from the village, from which they must not return till dusk. Their friends send them meat and drink.

Widow re-marriage cere-mony in Khán-desh.

In Khándesh, when a man wishes to marry a widow he sends some of his friends to urge his suit with the woman or with her parents and relations. If his proposals are accepted, the suitor takes to the woman's house a robe and bodice, a bead necklace, two liquor jars and some boiled peas and sugar. The match is then settled. The man takes with him a few friends and the materials for a feast, and they share the food with a party of the woman's relations. The woman dresses herself in the clothes brought to her, and after the guests leave, she and her husband pass the night together. Next morning they start from the house before daybreak, and spend the whole of the day in the field in some lonely place, three or four miles from the village, their friends sending them food. These widow marriages are often preceded by an elopement, which, after the payment of a fee to the head of the community, is condoned by the parents and relations.

Divorce is permitted when the wife and the husband do not agree or when there is cruelty and ill-treatment on the part of the husband, or adultery on that of the wife. If the husband divorces the wife, he tears off the end of his turban and gives it to her, and she is then quit of him. If the wife deserts the husband, she tears off the end of her *sári* and gives it to the husband. He is then quit of her. A woman so divorced may marry again, but the man who marries her has to pay a fine to the *panch*. Part of this fine is spent in drink. Sometimes a woman deserts her first husband and goes to another man's house and lives with him as his wife. She is then called *Ghar-ghushi* or 'one who has entered the house,' and the man who permits her to enter his house is made to pay all the marriage expenses of the first husband. The payment of these expenses is known as *Zagada*. Half of this fine is paid to the first husband and the other half is appropriated by the *panch* for drink. The first husband is made to strike a *Nim* tree twice or thrice, and the divorce is complete.

Religion. It is not easy to describe the religion of the Bhils as they are in all stages of civilization from the wild fetish and nature worshippers having no idea of a divine being to the peaceful peasant who observes most of the details of popular Hinduism. An attempt is, however, made to describe below the religious beliefs of the wilder sections of the tribe, which are fast giving way to the beliefs of the Kunbis, and at no distant future are likely to be wholly replaced by the latter.

Except the Nirdhis and Tadvis, who are now half Hindus half Musalmáns, the original religion of the Bhils was perhaps a form of nature worship, and even now they worship the Vágh-deva or tiger god, Sivariya-deva or boundary god, Nimaji-deva or the god of the *Apta* plant or trees, Dungarya deva or the mountain god, Bárábij or Bárbij the moon, etc. Other minor deities worshipped by them are Káli, Hatipava, Vághácha Kunver, Hal-Kámáta, Khodiyármáta, Devikánai, Behyee, Baji, Ghora Rája, Hallam, Gaukondámáta, Hanivanamáta, Bhadribáimáta, Ghona, Ginva Deva, Shálu Pándar, Páchchhaya, Máta Pánda, Kákásat, etc. They believe greatly in demoniacal influence, witchcraft and omens. Captain Prescott says that they are superstitious beyond all belief. Mr. Willoughby mentions the same characteristics and how they desert villages on the outbreak of an epidemic. "Their religion" he says "is one of fear." Sir J. Malcom is of opinion that the original worship was that of deceased ancestors. Of the gods of their adopted religion they chiefly worship Mahádev, whose fiercer aspects would appeal to original nature worshippers.

Bhils have no temples. Over some of their most sacred images they raise open sheds; but, in general, for a place of worship they choose some tree consecrated by a few large stones set on a mud terrace built round its roots. They respect Musalmán shrines and make offerings to Musalmán saints. Although they worship the deities mentioned above, their chief objects of worship are spirits and ghosts. In the forests near an old tree or well, but often apparently at some chance spot, they offer to ghosts and spirits earthen horses, jars and beehive-shaped vessels. In honour of the spirits in most of these god-yards or *devasthâns* they also raise beams of timber, sometimes as much as twelve feet long, poised on two uprights in the form of a rough seat. Here they offer a goat and a cock, numbers of Bhils coming together to eat the sacrifice and to drink.

The animal held in most veneration by the Bhils is the horse, and in Khándesh also the dog. If a prayer has been granted, they often make small clay horses and range them round an idol or in the spirit-yard. In many of their legends the principal event depends on the assistance or advice of an enchanted horse. Except the Modása and Khándesh Bhils who kill neither the cow nor the blue-bull *Portax pictus*, Bhils have no special feeling for the cow, most of them eating its flesh and freely taking its life. Except in some parts of Khándesh, they do not worship snakes, and kill them when they have the chance. Except a few who reverence the *pipal* or *apta* they have no holy trees or plants.

With Bhils the chief festivals are those in honour of the dead. The only regular Hindu festivals they specially observe are the *Shimga* or *Holi*, the *Dasara* and *Diváli*. Besides these three regular festivals, the Gujarát Bhils perform three sacrifices or *játars*, one on *Dasara* day, the bright tenth of *Ashvin* (September-October), and two, both of them field festivals, one in *Ashád* (June-July) when the green grass shoots, and the other in *Ashvin* (September-October) when the early or rainy season harvest is reaped. On *Dasara* day the sacrifice is offered either to the goddess Kálika or Chámund or to the god Kachumbhar, in *Ashád* to the god Sarsel or Sálun, and in *Ashvin* when the crop ripens, to the goddess Chámund. On all these occasions the sacrifice or *játar* is performed with the same rites. On the day before the *játar*, the village headman cleans his house and at nightfall calls the Badva to recite incantations. The Pujári, or in the absence of the Pujári the Badva, with a loud voice calls the gods to be present. Throughout the night the Badva continues singing. He first invokes the aid of Sárda the goddess of learning, and then sings the praises of Ganpati and other divinities, including the goddess Chámund and the god Kachumbhar. He recites the tale of Jasma, the old woman who rejected the love of king Siddhráj Jaising (A. D. 1100). Early next morning the Badva becomes inspired by the god Kachumbhar. To ascertain if he is really inspired or, as the Bhils say, if 'the breath has entered him' they send the Badva to bathe, and in his absence place in a line on the ground seven *billas* or apples of the *bel* Ægle marmelos tree. On his return the Badva is asked to point out which apple was first laid down. If he chooses the right one, he is believed to be really inspired. Some of those present then ask the Badva questions regarding their future, regarding the cause and cure of some sickness, the next rainfall, or the cattle plague. The people then accompany the Badva outside of the village to the spirit-yard or *devasthán* of the god or goddess in whose honour the festival or *játar* is held. In this spirit-yard the Badva sings, becomes inspired, and is again asked a number of questions. After the breath or spirit of the god has passed, the Badva offers the sacrifice of a buffalo or a goat, generally a buffalo on *Dasara* day. The Badva throws a little water on the head of the sacrifice ; and if the animal shakes its head, the offering is believed to be accepted. The headman then cuts the neck of the animal with a sword. The head is separated from the trunk and placed near the image of the god or goddess. As a libation to the deity the headman pours on the ground a little home-made liquor. The liver of the sacrifice is dropped into the fire, which is kept burning at the time. The head of the animal is taken by the village headman, and the rest of the meat and liquor is distributed on the spot. Sometimes, besides the three regular *játars* to obtain rain or for some other purpose, the Panch Mahál Bhils hold special *játars* in honour of Ghodadev the horse-god whose temple stands on a hill in the Sháhada village of Dohad.

The Khándesh Bhils go to the caves of the hills, in which the Dungarya Deva is supposed to reside, in the months of *Kártik* and *Márgashirsha*. For a fortnight before they approach the shrine, they practise a sort of penance as a preparation for approaching the god. This penance consists in bathing morning and evening each day and living on gram and maize. They keep puffing, and blowing and shivering and chattering as if they were possessed, and at intervals blow aloud and beat their mouth, shouting the name of Dungarya Deva. On the *Paurnima* or full-moon day they ascend the hill. It is supposed that a fissure or passage is made in the hill by their prayers, and a goat or a hen is first driven through the passage ; and if the animal returns with a red mark on its forehead, the god is supposed to be pleased. The chief *Bhagat* or devotee then enters the cave followed by others who have also taken the vow. Then they worship the god and stand with outstretched hands and offer prayers. Then it is said that some cowdung drops into the hands of some and grains of maize into those of others. Some get nothing at all. Those who get cowdung are considered to be blest with cattle; those who get grains of maize feel assured of a plentiful harvest. After this ceremony, they offer sheep, and having fulfilled their vow, return home also puffing and blowing and shouting the name of Dungarya Deva.

Except some of the civilized sections of the Khándesh Bhils who employ Bráhmans as priests, Bráhmans are not held in special respect by Bhils, and do not, on any occasion, take part in Bhil ceremonies. Instead of Bráhmans, three classes of men are held in special reverence. These are *bhagats* or *badvás* devotees and exorcists, *rávals* or priests, and *bháts* or *dholis* minstrels. Of these, Badvás are Bhils by caste, and the Rávals and Dholis are separate castes. Any Bhil who can learn to recite the incantations can become a Badva. The Badva conducts the *játars* or sacrifices and is consulted on occasions of general calamity and individual sickness. Sickness of all kinds is attributed either to the displeasure of some deity or to the evil eye of a witch. In the former case vows are made to the deity; in the latter, the witch is found out, and demands an offering of a he-buffalo, a goat or cock to cure the sick person. If the sick man recovers the animal named by the witch is sacrificed by having its throat cut, and the witch is made to drink its blood. If the sick person dies the witch is driven into the forest. In the Panch Mahále one case is on record of a witch being burnt to death and another of a witch being cut to pieces by a sword.

The Dholis are the Bháts or genealogists of Bhils, and they also supply music at weddings and funerals. Each clan of the Bhils has a Rával attached to it. His chief duty is to officiate at a funeral feast called *kaita*.

When an epidemic breaks out, heads of the villages go to the Badya with offerings and ask him to tell them the cause of their misfortune. He is always ready, after a due amount of mummery, to point out some old woman as the head and fount of the offence. Small mercy is shown to the luckless creature after she is named. She is seized by a crowd of fanatics, swung by the heels and otherwise ill-treated, and unless timely notice is given to the authorities, her life is in great danger.

Death ceremonies in Gujarát.

Among Gujarát Bhils, except in the case of a very young child or when the cause of death has been small-pox, the dead are burnt as they say 'with the sun as a witness', that is, only during the day. When life is gone the relations bathe the body, spread a waistcloth *dhotar* over it, and carry it on a rough bamboo bier to the burning ground. At the burning ground the chief mourners sit near the body while the rest of the party gather wood for the pyre. The son or other next-of-kin sets the pyre alight. When the body is half burnt the mourners bathe. On the way back to the deceased's house the party rest half-way between the deceased's house and the burning ground, place five stones near each other, and to the branch of a neighbouring tree tie a small piece of the deceased's winding sheet. On returning to the deceased's house the party smoke tobacco for a short time and after saluting each other go home. On the fifth day after death ten to twenty friends and relations of the deceased come to the place where the small stones were laid, and without drinking any liquor eat boiled maize *ghugari*. After the meal they throw away the stones and the piece of the winding sheet, and return to their homes. On the fifth day as well as on the day of the *kaita* or death-dinner the Jhálod Bhils have the special practice of shaving their moustaches. In Jhálod, where they are well-to do, Bhils give a death dinner or *kaita* on the twelfth day like upper class Hindus. Among the poorer Bhils the families of five or six deceased persons subscribe and give one combined death-dinner, in some cases two or three years after the death. For this death-dinner much liquor is distilled and a dish called *ghugari* made of Indian corn, gram and wheat boiled together is prepared When the guests, who often number two or three thousand, come together, a Rával pours a quart of milk into a metal salver and in the milk sets a brass horse. Two of the deceased's near relations squat down holding the dish at arm's length above their heads. Then while the Rával plays a one-stringed guitar or *tamburo* with a hand drum accompaniment, the mourners for an hour or two keep throwing into the dish money, rice and Indian corn. At last the salver shakes and the image of the horse falls on its side in the milk. The mourners weep and wail. Liquor is handed round, and, in a leaf, each guest is given a small dole of boiled Indian corn, gram and wheat. When the meal is over, all but relations leave, the Rával taking his perquisites, the brass horse and the salver full of grain. The relations usually bring a goat or young buffalo or a few yards of country cloth as a present for the son of the deceased. If they bring cloth it is given when the villagers leave; if they bring a goat or young buffalo it is at once beheaded and the head thrown on the roof of the deceased's house. The body is taken to a distance, cut up, cooked and eaten, the relations bringing liquor to drink with it. If the deceased was a man of importance, a year or two after his death his relations go to a stone mason and make him cut on a stone slab the figure of a man on horseback with a spear in his hand, paying him by the gift of a cow or a she-buffalo. On the first *kálichaudas* or dark fourteenth of *Ashvin*

(September-October) the stone, with procession and drum beating, is carried in a cart to the deceased's house, where it is washed, daubed with red powder, covered with a white cloth and again placed in a cart, and taken to the village spirit-yard or *devasthán*. There a goat is killed, its blood sprinkled on the stone, and its flesh cooked and eaten with as much liquor as the party can afford.

Death ceremonies in Khándesh.

In Khándesh, when a Bhil is on the point of death, his relations distribute money among the poor in his name. When he dies, the body is laid on a blanket or on a piece of cloth spread over a blanket. An earthen pot full of cold water is placed near the door of the house and the body is brought out, held in a sitting position outside the door, and water poured over it. The old clothes are taken off, and tying a new piece of cloth round the loins, the body is laid on the bier and covered with a new white sheet, leaving the face bare, and the head covered with a turban. Red powder, *gulál*, is sprinkled over the face, and some red and cooked rice are tied together in a piece of cloth and placed on the bier. The body is then tied with a string to the bier, and carried to the burying ground on the shoulders of four near male relations. In front of them go the sons of the deceased, the chief mourner carrying fire in an earthen jar, and one of the others carrying an earthen jug full of water. Half-way to the grave, the bier is lowered, and some of the cooked food is laid near a bush. The bearers change places, and without further halt the body is carried to the burning ground. Here the bier is lowered and the mourners help in digging a grave, long enough for the body, and to prevent it being opened by wild animals, about five or six feet deep. In this the body is laid, the head to the south and the arms stretched along either side. Cooked rice and bread are placed in the mouth, and the body is sprinkled with water. Before leaving the grave, the man who is last arranging the body tears a small hole in the winding sheet. Then the whole party sit round the grave, so far off that they cannot see the body, and the chief mourner throws a handful of earth on the corpse, and, all joining, cover the corpse with earth. When the body is covered they rise and fill the grave, cutting a small trench round it. In this trench, beginning from the north, they pour water out of an earthen jug, and when the circuit of the grave is complete, drop the jug and break it to pieces. Then the bier is turned upside down and burned, and the funeral party, going to the nearest water, bathe and accompany the chief mourner to his house. In front of his house a fire is lit, and into it some woman's hair is dropped, and each of the funeral party, taking some *nim* Melia azadirachta leaves, throws them on the fire, and passing his open palms through the smoke, rubs them over his face. The mourners are now pure, and after taking a draught of liquor, go to their homes.

On the third day, one of the women of the mourning household rubs the right shoulders of the pall-bearers with oil, milk and cowdung, and washes them with *nim* twigs steeped in cow's urine. Then the four men bathe and are treated to a dinner. In the house the only sign of mourning is that every morning for five days the women wail for about a quarter of an hour.

On the eleventh day the chief mourner goes to a river, and there has his head, beard and face shaved and bathes. Next he makes a dough cow, sprinkles it with red powder, and setting it on a leaf plate, bows to it, and throws it into the water. He then bathes and goes home.

Either on the twelfth or the forty-fifth day, a potter, Kumbhár, is called and a seven-step hemp ladder, *chodhvan*, is set against the wall of the house that the soul of the dead may climb by it to heaven. The priest sits at the foot of the ladder and chants a verse from the *Puráns*, the string by which the ladder is fastened to the ground is burnt, and the ladder pulled down and thrown away. The spot where the ladder was tied is then covered with flour, and a small plate with a piece of bread and cooked rice is laid over it. In the plate is set a small water pot, and alongside of the water pot a lighted lamp covered by an empty bamboo basket with a cloth drawn over it. This day a grand dinner is prepared, and before it is eaten, five mouthfuls are burnt near the basket. The burial rites for a woman are the same as those of a man. When a child dies the father carries the body in his arms and buries it, and on the seventh day a small dinner is given. In some rare cases the Bhils burn instead of burying their dead.

Occupation. Bhils are mostly peasants, labourers and watchmen. In the Panch Mahâls most are peasants, tilling regularly though roughly the same fields, and seldom changing their houses except through necessity ; only a few lead a wandering life in the woods and live by wood-ash tillage. In the Mahi Kántha they are cultivators, robbers and cattlelifters, and village watchmen and guides. In Broach they are almost all village watchmen, and in the forest lands of the south they are charcoal burners, makers of catechu, wood-cutters, day labourers and peasants. In Khándesh they work as husbandmen and field labourers, sell grass and fuel, help the ordinary Kunbi landholder, and when they can get them, gather wax and honey. All Bhils are good hunters, killing with their bows and arrows pigeons, partridges wild cats and hares. They rear fowls in large numbers, especially for sale.

The Bhil is frank, thriftless, timid, fond of spirits, and loathes steady work. At the same time he is simple, faithful and honest, kindly and intelligent. In the Mahi Kántha they go armed with bows and arrows ready to fight with each other or their neighbours either to please their chief or to shelter a criminal. In the Panch Mahâls, where sixty years ago were almost daily complaints of their daring agressions, though they are still poor and somewhat unsettled, they are not as a class given to serious crime. The women, who in former times went to battle sometimes using slings with great effect, have much influence over the men. **Character.**

The Bhils are fond of amusement and excitement, hunting and fishing, playing games of chance, telling stories singing to the accompaniment of a six-stringed fiddle, *chikár*, and dancing.

The every-day food of a well-to-do Gujarát Bhil is rice cooked with salt and mixed with butter-milk, and of an ordinary Bhil, Indian corn and butter-milk boiled with chillies, and sometimes split peas or beans and grain mixed with vegetables. Except the ass, horse, camel, rat, snake and monkey, the Gujarát Bhil objects to no form of flesh, eating animals he has found dead as well as those he has killed. As there is a belief among them that if women eat or even cook a cock or hen they will become witches, they will not let a fowl be cooked in the house or even in one of the household vessels. The men eat and cook them at their spirit yard or *devasthán*. They are extremely fond of toddy and liquor. **Food.**

The every-day food of the civilized sections of the Khándesh Bhils is millet bread, curry, curds, vegetables, fish, and when they can afford it, goat's flesh or mutton. The wilder sections of the tribe eat carrion, animals that have died a natural death, cows, buffaloes, rats, jackals and monkeys. They feed on wild roots and fruits, and on all sorts of vermin and garbage. Like their Gujaráti brethren, all Khándesh Bhils indulge in drink to excess.

In Gujarát, from his indiscriminate fondness for flesh and his want of reverence for life, the Bhil holds a very low place among Hindus, and though his touch does not defile, his is one of the few classes from whom a high caste Gujarát Hindu will not take water. Gujarát Bhils have no objection to eat food cooked by Musalmáns.

In Khándesh, the more civilized sections of the Bhils will not eat pakki or kachchi or smoke with Mahárs, Mángs, Chámbhárs, Mochis, Dhors or Bhangis. The latter will eat the leavings of Bhils. Maráthás and Kunbis will smoke with them, but some will not use their *chchápi* (the piece of cloth through which smoke is inhaled from the chillum).

BHILALAS are found at Dhauli, Vaijápur and Chirmira in Khándesh, and in Nimár and the Sátpuda hills. They claim to be Tilole Kunbis. But, as their name shows, they are generally supposed to be partly of Bhil descent. In Central India they are half Rajputs. The chiefs of the Bhils in the Vindhya mountains are almost all Bhilálás. The Rája of Mándháta, an island in the Narbada about sixty-four miles north of Bhusával, is a Bhilála chief claiming descent from a Chohán Rajput Bharatsing who is said to have taken the island from a Bhil chief in 1165. The Central Provinces Bhilálás are all descended from alliances of Rajputs with Bhils and take the name of the Rajput clan to which they trace their origin.

Bhilálás are small, sturdy and well-featured. In addition to the loin-cloth, *langoti*, for wearing which, according to their story, they were nicknamed Bhilálás, they sometimes wear a waistcloth or trousers and always carry a long white sheet worn as an outer robe. In religion they are Hindus, but are not particular about the presence or service of a Bráhman. They name their own children and have no particular birth ceremonies. They celebrate their marriages at sun-down, one of the caste being set to watch. As the sun disappears the watchman claps his hands, and the young women of both bride and bridegroom's families fasten the bridegroom's waistcloth to the bride's *lugda* robe. Presents are made and a feast follows. Bhilálás are chiefly husbandmen, being the principal cultivators in the native states on the north-west boundary of Khándesh.

DANGCHIS or DANG BHILS, living below the Sahyádris, are the most uncivilized of all the wild tribes, stunted in body by their drunken dissolute life and dulled in mind by hardships and bitter poverty. They are very dirty feeders, eating monkeys, rats and all small vermin, not to mention cattle killed by tigers or by themselves. Even on grand occasions their dress is only a loincloth, *langoti*, and a wisp of rag round the head. They always carry materials for producing fire, flint and steel and some silk cotton in a small gourd hung round the waist by a strong thin cord. They have a very high idea of their dignity, as Rájás' kith and kin. The Konkanás and Várlis are not above helping about camp and carrying loads. But the

Bhil Rájás never condescend to such work fit only for their subjects, and when they are not resting or idling, wander about with bows and arrows in search of small game such as peacocks and hares. Thoroughly unwilling to work, they do very little cultivation, and live on the share they take of the harvests of their so-called ryots, the Konkanás and Várlis. They hold the tiger sacred and worship Vághdev.

KHOTILS are chiefly found along the south face of the Sátpudás and at Dhauli, Vaijápur and in many of the Chopda and Shirpur villages in Khándesh. The Tadvis and people of Sávda call all Bhils Khotils. But they are a distinct class, regarded by the pure Bhil as degraded, because they indulge in carrion and do not hesitate to touch the dead body of the cow. Their common surnames are Ghánia, Ghartia and Takria. Their ceremonies are very simple. The child is named by its parents or tribesmen. When the time for marriage comes, if old enough, the lad himself, or if he is too young, his father, arranges with the girl's father for a certain price. The caste committee, *panch*, and the headman, *náik*, are asked to witness the agreement, and a day is fixed for the ceremony. The officiating priest, a Bhil by caste, known as Mánkar or Chaudhri, is the Náik's minister, *pradhán*. For his service he gets a turban or some other present, or a money fee of Re. 1 annas 4. If the headman is present, he also is paid about Re. 1 annas 8. After, in the ordinary way, the bride and bridegroom have been rubbed with turmeric, on the auspicious evening the minister begins the ceremony by asking the bridegroom the name of his bride. He tells her name and ties his waistcloth or trouser-cloth to her gown *lugda*. Then she is asked the bridegroom's name, and after saying it, ties her robe to his. Thus tied together they turn seven times round, and the ceremony is complete. A feast, costing from Rs. 5 to Rs. 30, follows, and the bridegroom goes to his father-in-law's hut, where he lives from a week to three months or a year, and then takes the bride to his own dwelling. Among the Khotils the marriage tie is loose, and a woman may leave her husband and marry another for comparatively trivial reasons.

Many of the Khotils worship the tiger-god and refuse to join in a tiger hunt. They do not employ Bráhman priests. They bury their dead without form or ceremony, piling a few stones to mark the grave. They are great huntsmen and very fond of liquor. They make their living by catching fish and gathering leaves, lac, honey, wild berries and other forest produce, which they barter for cash or credit.

MATHVADIS, also called Panáris, are found in the north of Taloda, in the Sátpuda Bhil villages and in the trans-Narbada state of Mathvád, from which they take their name, and from which they are said to have come to the Sátpudas before the British conquest of Khándesh. Of ordinary size, they are generally dark with round faces. They allow their hair to grow but shave their beards. Their houses, which they share with their cattle and change once every three years, are generally grass huts with bamboo partitions. They have the regular Kunbi marriage ceremonies, but no priests. They worship Vághdev and the river Narbada. They burn their dead except young children, whom they bury. With the deceased, his clothes and ornaments are carried to the burning ground, where they are taken away by the Mahár. Their chief occupation is husbandry. They eat the flesh of sheep, deer and hens, but never of buffaloes. They drink liquor.

MAVCHI, Mauchi or Gávit Bhils, are chiefly found in the high western Pimpalner plateaus in Khándesh. They are a timid, inoffensive, quiet and well behaved people, rather given to drink, and, especially the wilder ones, truthful. They constantly change their huts and move their settlement. The commonest form of marriage among them is the winning of the bride by serving her father for a term of years. Five years is the usual period, but credit is often given and the girl allowed to live with her husband before the full term is over. The marriage tie is loose, and a woman may leave her husband and marry another for comparatively trivial reasons. The caste committee, *panch*, usually awards compensation, but cases are not rare when the husband does not think it worth his while to apply to the committee, and comforts himself with another wife. Mávchis are very ignorant and superstitious, tracing all disasters to the influence of witches. They worship Astamba, Gavli, Vághdev and Parameshvar. They bury their dead, and often lay the deceased's personal property in the grave with him. Mainly cultivators, some have taken to carting. They eat beef and are excessively fond of drinking liquor.

NAHALS are chiefly found on the north side of the Sátpudás bordering on Holkar's Nimár and the towns of Balvadi, Palasner and Sindva. They are the most savage of the Bhils. They are very dark, small and harsh featured, and wear as shoes pieces of *nilgái* hides tied with strings. Like the Khotils they are regarded by the pure Bhils as degraded, as, like the Khotils, they indulge in carrion and do not hesitate to touch the dead body of the cow. Their customs are much like those of Khotils, and like them the marriage tie among them is loose. Some of them are Musalmáns, but most have no noticeable religion, neither worshipping Hindu idols nor following the Musalmán creed. A few raise a little grain among the ashes of burnt boughs or barter forest produce for cloth, but they are seldom seen beyond the limits of their native forests. They live chiefly on roots, fruit and berries, shun all intercourse, and lead an utterly savage existence. They have an hereditary headman *náik.*

NIRDHIS or Nilde Bhils dwell along the base of the Sátmalás in the Jámner and Páchora *tálukas* of Khándesh. Their creed and ideas are similar to those of Tadvis. In former times they were much dreaded. During seasons of revolt the most atrocious acts were invariably the work of Nirdhis.

PAVRAS are chiefly found in Akrán and parts of Taloda and Shaháda in Khándesh. They are called Pávra Bhils, Pávra Náiks and Pávra Kolis indifferently, but they are more like Konkan sea Kolis than Bhils. They deny that they are Bhils and consider the name a reproach. They are said to be Rajputs who were driven by the Udaipur chiefs from their homes near the hill fort Palagad. They come from the Mathvád state north of the Narbada and are often called Mathvádis. Formerly marriage among Pávrás was generally adult, and the young men chose their brides themselves. Of late the rich marry their boys at ten or twelve. The bride's father is given a bride price of Rs. 110 or more, but if the boy's father is unable to pay this amount he gives his bullocks to the bride's father. Among the poor, marriage by serving the father-in-law is common, the period of service being eight to ten years. During this period the youth lives with the girl's family and is generally married to her when half the term agreed to is over. Marriages are held only during *Phálgun* and *Vaishákh.* On the day before marriage, all the bridegroom's relations go dancing to the bride's village and stop there for the night, perform religious ceremonies next morning, and then, one of them carrying the bride on his waist, they come to the bridegroom's village to perform the marriage ceremonies, which generally take place in the afternoon. First they worship Khandoba, who is represented by a heap of rice with two pice on it. The couple is then seated on a stool, the ends of their garments are tied together, and they throw rice on each other. When this is done, it is a custom with some families to take the pair on their shoulders and dance.

Widow remarriage is allowed. Polygamy is common, and those who can afford to, have three or four wives.

Their religion is simple. They have neither priests, temples, nor idols. They worship a supreme creator, *bhagván*, and strive to please him with sacrifices and offerings. In the forest near each village is a sacred tree, round which, before harvest, the villagers meet and prostrate themselves before the rising sun, offer corn, and sacrifice goats and fowls. The deity to whom these offerings are made is called Báva Kumba. His wife, Ráni Kajhal, has also, not far from her husband's, a sacred tree to which offerings are made. They worship the tiger god *vághdev* but only to propitiate it and prevent it attacking their cattle, or when it has carried off any of their people. Though they acknowledge no household or village deities and reverence no rivers or fire, they are very superstitious, believing in witchcraft and sorcery. Before the British rule, many an old woman had her nose slit under the suspicion of being a witch, *dákin*, the idea being that the loss of the nose destroys all power to work evil. A belief in omens is common. Odd numbers are lucky, but to see a blackbird called *pichi* is most ill-omened. At the beginning of any undertaking they cast omens with a bow and arrows. They salute friends by taking the two hands of the person saluted, and saying *bhaj-bhaj*, that is, worship.

Pávrás have three chief holidays, *Indraja*, *Diváli* and *Shimga* or *Holi*. *Indraja*, apparently in honour of Indra, is held only when the year is good or when a vow has to be discharged. It is celebrated on any Sunday, Wednesday or other lucky day between *Dasara* and *Diváli*. Its chief ceremony consists in planting a *kadamb* Nauclea parvifolia branch in front of a landlord's, *jamindár's*, house, so as to remain one cubit underground and a man's height above. The branch is rubbed with vermilion and worship begins at midnight. A goat and hen are killed and offered, and dancing is kept up till day-break. Next morning at about ten they pull up the branch and throw it into some neighbouring river or pond. On returning they drink and dance, and eat the goat and hen offered overnight.

Diváli, sometimes called *Nágdiváli*, is a yearly festival celebrated in the month of *Posh* (January) on different dates in different villages, so as to last on the whole for nearly a month. Four or five stones are brought from a neighbouring river and placed outside the village but within the limits of the village lands. They are then painted red, and next day at noon worship begins. Liquor is sprinkled on the ground and freely drunk, and goats and hens are killed. Dancing begins at nightfall. Two men, holding two lighted bamboo sticks, go from house to house followed by the villagers. Every housewife comes out with a lighted lamp in her hand, waves it before them, marks their foreheads with lamp oil, and gives them drink. After dancing for a few minutes, the procession passes to another house and there go through the same routine. Next day they feed their bullocks with Indian millet, rice, *banti* and *parál*, and give them drink.

The *Shimga* or *Holi* takes place, as elsewhere, on the fifteenth of the bright half of *Phálgun* (March). Immense crowds meet at Dhedgaon, the central village and police head-quarters of the Akráni territory. A pit is dug, and a wooden rod thrust into it and lighted about ten or eleven at night. Everyone present brings a piece of bread, some rice and a cock. Portions of these are thrown into the fire, and the rest is handed round among friends. Then, with the help of an occasional draught, they dance till dawn.

Except lepers, persons who have died of cholera and small-pox, women dying in child-birth and children under two or three months, who, as a rule, are buried, the Pávrás either burn or bury their dead. So great is their aversion to a leper that, when living, he is kept in a distant cottage, and when dead, is buried by a Mahár untouched by a Pávra. In ordinary funerals a party of them carry the corpse. A rupee, or, if the family be poor, a pice is placed in the deceased's mouth, a little rice, turmeric and red powder *gulál* are rubbed on the forehead, and his sword and bows and arrows are placed on the bier by his side. To the sound of drums and music, the body is carried to the burying ground. The widow wears good clothes on the day of her husband's death, cooks rice in an earthen pot, and after the corpse is carried away, breaks the pot outside the house door, and follows the burial party dressed in new clothes. On her return, she puts on her old clothes, and unless she wishes to marry, never again wears gay clothes or ornaments. All the furniture of the deceased, dishes, cots and pots, except drinking pots, are buried or burnt with him. If the dead did not own these articles, they are bought and laid by his side. His silver ornaments also are sometimes burnt. But shoes, cows and money are given to his sister's son *bhácha*. On the return of the funeral party, some drink, and all bathe. On the eighth day after death, friends and relations meet at the house of the deceased and drink a jar of liquor. Though the death is not considered to have made the family impure, they perform ceremonies on the twelfth day after death. The ground is smeared with cowdung, leaf plates are spread, straws are laid to represent the dead man's forefathers, liquor is sprinkled on the ground, and a dinner of rice, or mixed rice and pulse, is given to the caste-fellows. On that day they drink, but do not dance. It is not obligatory to perform these ceremonies on the twelfth day; if that day does not suit, they can be performed on any day within the month. Till these ceremonies are over, the nearest relations do not wear turbans. Like other Bhils, Pávrás leave a house in which two or three deaths have taken place.

Most of the Pávrás are husbandmen, many of them very skilled. Some are carpenters and blacksmiths, but none barbers or shoemakers. Each man is his own barber, and each family makes its own field tools and basket work. Except for their shoes which they bring from Kakarmunda, and their silver and brass ornaments which are made by Hindu workmen of Roshnál, they have little need of foreign craftsmen. The women gather *mahua* flowers and *chároli* nuts. They are honest and hardworking and robbery is almost unknown to them. They are passionately fond of music and dancing, their music being neither harsh nor untuneful.

Pávrás eat only goats, sheep and fowls. Though they drink a great quantity of *mahua* liquor at their feasts and marriages, in ordinary life they are very temperate.

TADVIS are chiefly found in the villages at the foot of the Sátpuda hills from Asirghad to Chopda. They are said to be the descendants of Bhil women and Musalmán men, and to date from the Emperor Aurangzeb's reign (1658-1707). But though they own that they were formerly Hindus, they do not acknowledge that they are or ever were Bhils. Many of them dress like ordinary Khándesh cultivators, the better-to-do inclining to the dress of the Musalmán *sipáhi*. Their religious beliefs as well as manners and customs are like those of other Khándesh Musalmáns. At the same time, like other Hindu converts, they have a deep regard for certain Hindu deities. They employ the Kázis at their weddings. They make good soldiers and constables, but are poor cultivators, generally living by wood and grass cutting. To the fault of laziness they add the vices of a quarrelsome and vindictive temper, and a great fondness for liquor.

BHIL.—A sub-division of Gopáls and Berads; a sub-division of Kolis.

BHILALA.—A sub-division of Bhils.

BHILAVE.—A sub-division of Kolis.

BHILLAKABBER.—A synonym for Kabbaligar.

BHINGI.—A synonym for Hanam Golla.

BHIRALE.—A synonym for Bhiláve.

BHISTIS or Pakhális, an occupational caste, numbering 2,312 (1901), including 1,122 males and 1,190 females, are found all over Gujarát and Native States and in some parts of the Deccan. Of the above number, 607 were returned as Musalmáns at the census of 1901. Name.

They state that when Parashurám persecuted the Kshatriyas some of them escaped by stating that they were water-fillers. These were the ancestors of the modern Bhistis. Another account relates that they were originally Rajputs of the Yádav stock. At the time of their adversity they took to carrying water in leather bags (*pakháls*) and thus formed a separate caste named Pakhális.

There are no endogamous divisions of the caste. They are said to belong to the Káshyap *gotra*, the common refuge of those desirous of rising in the social scale. They are divided into clans, all of which are found amongst the Rajputs. The chief of these are Chávada, Chohán, Parmár, Solanki and Vághela. Marriages are prohibited between members of the same clan and within seven degrees of relationship. A member of the caste cannot marry his father's sister's, mother's sister's or mother's brother's daughter. Marriages between the descendants of brothers and sisters can take place from the fourth generation. A man is not allowed to marry his wife's sister during the wife's lifetime. Two brothers may marry two sisters. Marriages are prohibited between families residing in different geographical positions, though a few connections of this kind can be traced. Polygamy is allowed and practised, but polyandry is unknown. Divisions.

Girls are married from two to eleven, as a rule before attaining puberty. Maidens committing sexual indiscretions with castemen or members from higher castes can remain in the caste by paying a fine to the caste-people. If the offence is committed with members of lower castes, the offenders are turned out of the caste.

The offer of marriage comes from the girl's father. The boy's father has to pay to the girl a *pallun* (woman's property) consisting of ornaments worth Rs. 25 and clothes worth Rs. 15. The day for the marriage is fixed by an astrologer or by the family priest who conducts the service. The marriage ceremonies of Bhistis resemble those of the Galiárás, in addition to which they perform the *máta vávava* ceremony. If this ceremony is not performed at the time of marriage, it is required to be performed at the time of first pregnancy. From the commencement of the marriage till it is over, the bridegroom holds in his hand a dagger, a knife or a pair of scissors, which is ultimately thrown into a river or well. The binding portion of Marriage.

the marriage service is the joining of the hands of the bride and bridegroom.

The remarriage of widows is permitted with the sanction of the caste *panch*. A widow may marry her late husband's younger brother. A widow remarriage is celebrated on a Tuesday, Thursday or Sunday. The pair to be married and a Bráhman priest are present on the occasion. Unwidowed women are not allowed to attend the ceremony. Ganpati is worshipped, and a lighted lamp is placed in an earthen pot and is covered with a sieve. The sieve is then removed, and the widow and her new husband look at the lamp and throw grains of rice on each other. This completes the ceremony. A bachelor desirous of marrying a widow has first to marry a *shami* bush (Prosopis spicigera).

A husband can divorce a wife on the ground of her misconduct. A wife can divorce a husband if he ill-treats her. A divorced woman has to pay a fine of from Rs. 100 to 200 to the caste-people in order to remain in the caste. Divorce is not much in vogue. The caste follow the Hindu law of inheritance.

Bhistis mostly belong to the Hindu religion; about one-fourth of the number returned at the 1901 census are Musalmáns. The special objects of their worship are the *mátás* or goddesses, to whom liquor and flesh are offered on the fourteenth day of the bright half of *Bhádrapad*, the eighth day of the month of *Ashvin* and at the time of marriages. These offerings are partaken of by the offerers themselves. When an epidemic breaks out, the goddesses are propitiated with offerings of goats. Bhistis observe all the Hindu holidays and make pilgrimages to all the sacred places of the Hindus. The Musalmán saints are venerated. Their religious teachers are Gosávis. Their priests are a degraded class of Bráhmans known as Kayatiyás. The death ceremonies are conducted by the caste elders.

The dead are either burnt or buried. The funeral rites of Bhistis resemble those of Galiárás.

The hereditary occupation of the caste is carrying water in leather water bags. There are no indications of their abandoning this occupation.

Food. They eat fish and flesh, and drink liquor.

MUSALMAN BHISTIS or Pakhális—known in Gujarát also as Mashkis or waterbag-men, numbering 607 (1901), including 313 males and 294 females, are found all over Gujarát and in the large towns of the Deccan and Karnátak. They are said to be the descendants of converts from Hindu Bhois, and, except at Surat, form a separate community, marrying only among themselves and having local headmen, who settle social disputes with the consent of the majority of the caste and punish breaches of caste rules by fines, which generally take the form of caste feasts. They are Sunnis of the Hanafi school, but are seldom religious or say their prayers, and in the Deccan have strong Hindu leanings, worshipping Hindu gods, keeping Hindu fasts and feasts and eschewing beef. They carry water in leathern bags on bullock back and supply water to Musalmáns, Christians, Parsis and a few low-caste Hindus.

BHITRA.—A sub-division of Khedáwál Bráhmans.

BHOI.—A sub-division of Kabbaligars.

BHOIS, numbering 57,904 (1901), including 29,552 males and 28,352 females, are found throughout the Presidency and Native States, chiefly on the banks of rivers. The term Bhoi, besides being the name of a caste, is also used to denote a litter-bearer; and has consequently been appropriated by members of other castes pursuing the same occupation. Thus, there are Mahárs who style themselves Bhois. In some parts of Khándesh the Bhois are confused with Kahárs, an immigrant caste of fishermen from Northern India. In some places they are known by the name of Meharia. They are very often addressed as Kolis on account of the similarity of occupation between the two castes, and they have doubtless been recruited in the past from Kolis and numerous other castes of similar standing. **Name and origin.**

With regard to the origin of Bhois, the Játiviveka calls Bhois Paushtikas, and says that they are sprung from a Bráhman father and a Párásar mother; the Párásar, again, is said to be descended from a Bráhman and a Shudra mother. In the Deccan the Bhois differ little from the Marátha Kunbis in looks, dwelling, food and drink. In Násik they call themselves Kunbis, and some Kunbis eat with them. This suggests a connection with the Kunbi caste, not unlike the relations existing between the Marátha and Koli Kunbis. Their invariably dark complexion and the survival of totemism found amongst them point to their being one of the aboriginal tribes of the Presidency. These totems are found mostly among the Khándesh Bhois. They consist of the leaves of the following trees :—

1. *Arái* = Mimosa rubricaulis.
2. *Bor* = Zizyphus jujuba.
3. *Ruchkin* = Calotropis gigantea.
4. *Shami* = Prosopis spicigera.
5. *Jámbhul* = Eugenia jambolana.
6. *Amba* = Mango.
7. *Utakatiari.*

8. *Aráti* = Mimosa hamata.
9. *Boráti* = Bor ?
10. *Apta* = Bauhinia racemosa.
11. *Umbar* = Ficus glomerata.
12. *Dhumak* = Acacia arabica.

Among the Bhois of Ratnágiri, known locally as Rájabhois, the common totems or *devaks* are the mango, the *kalamba* (Anthocephalus cadumba), the peacock's feather and the axe. The Marátha Bhois have mostly the *pánchpálvi* or leaves of five trees as their totem.

In many cases marriages are regulated by these *devaks*, every exogamous division having a separate *devak*. This system of *devaks* or totems is gradually being supplanted by the more advanced system of prohibiting marriage between members bearing the same surname, and in some places Bráhmanical *gotras* have also been adopted ; but their bearing on intermarriage has not yet been fully recognised.

The Bhois may broadly be divided into five territorial groups, (1) Marátha, (2) Khándesh, (3) Karnátak, (4) Kanara and (5) Gujarát. There are also a few immigrants who follow the occupation of fishing and litter-bearing known as Pardeshi, Káchi, Tarkashi and Telangi Bhois. The Musalmán Bhois, who are described separately, are generally called Zinga Bhois as they chiefly catch *zingas* (shrimps). The five territorial groups of Bhois differ to such an extent that they must be described separately.

MARATHA BHOIS.—The Marátha Bhois of the Poona district have three endogamous divisions, Proper, Varádhi and Kadu. They can dine together but not intermarry. The Varádhis soak and parch grain. Kadus are bastards. In Ahmednagar they are divided into Marátha and Mala, who neither eat together nor intermarry. The Marátha division have also a bastard sub-caste known as Lenkávales with whom they eat but do not marry. In Násik they are divided into those who live north and those who live south of the Chándor or Saptashring hills. In Thána they are divided into Khári or salt water and Gode or fresh water Bhois, who neither eat together nor intermarry. The Bhois of the Ratnágiri district are known as Rájabhois. They are only palanquin-bearers. They do not catch fish. They do not interdine or intermarry with the other Bhois, whom they distinguish by the appellation of *Macchimár* or fish-catching Bhois.

The home tongue of the Marátha Bhois is Maráthi. In the Ahmednagar district they have a dialect of their own. The names in common use among men are Bápu, Bhikya, Chima, Dagadu

Gangárám, Gopál, Hari, Káshirám, Khandu, Malhári, Malya, Mhádu, Náráyan, Fakir, Sahádu and Vithu; and among women, Bhági, Bhimi, Chimi, Ganga, Jamni, Káshi, Ráhi, Párvati, Rangi, Saku, Sávitri, Siti, Tái and Yamani. They have caste councils, and settle social disputes at meetings of the castemen. Breaches of caste rules are condoned by caste feasts, and decisions of the caste councils are enforced under pain of expulsion. The caste councils are highly respected and greatly feared.

There appear to be no exogamous sub-divisions of the caste, above families, members of which have the same surname. The following are some of the commonest surnames :—

1.	Bhokre.	8.	Jádav.	15.	Musale.
2.	Chaván.	9.	Jháte.	16.	Nirmal.
3.	Dáge.	10.	Kámble.	17.	Povár.
4.	Ghatmál.	11.	Káshid.	18.	Sinde.
5.	Gholap.	12.	Káthavate.	19.	Singáre.
6.	Ghume.	13.	Jite	20.	Tilave.
7.	Gunvant.	14.	Mahulkar.		

Many of these surnames, *e.g.*, Chaván, Jádav, Povár and Sinde, are common among the Maráthás. The surname Káthavate has been apparently borrowed from the Deshasth Bráhmans.

Marriage is prohibited within the sub-division covered by one surname. A man cannot marry the daughter of his maternal aunt, though he may marry that of his maternal uncle. Instances of marriage with the paternal aunt's daughter are not wanting, but they are rare, in consequence of the belief that the girl so married does not live long. There is no prohibition against the marriage of two sisters to the same husband. Two sisters can also be married by two brothers. Marriage

The usual practice among Marátha Bhois is to marry their boys between sixteen and twenty-five, and their girls as infants, generally at ages ranging from ten to fourteen years. If the parents are rich and the connection sought is desirable, girls are married in infancy and even while they are still in the cradle. If their parents are too poor to defray the marriage expenses or if they have no proper guardians to arrange for their marriage, girls may remain unmarried even up to their sixteenth year. In such cases the caste council collect subscriptions and marry them to suitable husbands, without exacting any caste dinner. In the case of girls who are not married in infancy, sexual intercourse before marriage is strongly reprobated, and the girls are excommunicated if discovered.

Polygamy is permitted in the event of the first wife being barren or suffering from some incurable disease. In theory there is no limit to the number of wives a man may have. It is rare, however, in actual life to find more than two. Polyandry is unknown.

Marriage proposals as a rule come from the boy's father, the girl's father agreeing to them in the presence of some of the friends. At the betrothal, the girl worships a betelnut placed in a wheat square in the name of Ganpati, and also a metal pot filled with water with betel leaves dipped in it in the name of Varuna, the god of water, with offerings of flowers, sandal paste, vermilion and copper coins. The boy's father presents the girl with a green robe and bodice, marks her head with vermilion, and fills her lap with rice and fruit. Betel leaves are served and the betrothal or *kunku lávane* is over. The Bráhman priest writes invitation cards, and lays one of them before the house gods, and others are sent round among friends and kinsmen. The turmeric rubbing lasts for one to five days before the marriage. The girl is rubbed with turmeric paste first, and what is left of the paste is sent with music and a band of married women to the boy's to be rubbed on him and his parents. The parents of the bridegroom and the bridegroom himself are then seated in a square prepared by the bride's kinswomen, and after a coil of thread has been passed round the necks of four earthen pots, one in each corner of the square, they are rubbed with turmeric and bathed in warm water. A married couple belonging to the boy's house and a second couple belonging to the girl's house, with the hems of their garments knotted together by the priest, each in separate parties, visit the temple of Máruti, carrying the *devak*, lay a betelnut and leaves before the god, and return home with the *devak* covered with a white sheet and held over the head of the pair by two friends, one of whom walks in front and the other behind. On drawing near the house the couple tie the *devak* to the first post in the booth, and lay before it sandal paste, vermilion and food. Friends and relatives of the bridegroom and of the bride are feasted at the fathers' houses. In the evening the bridegroom goes on horseback with music and a band of kinsfolk to the temple of Máruti in the bride's village, bows before the god, and puts up in the temple. Meanwhile an unmarried brother he bride's on horseback with an *abdágiri* or ornamental umbrella held over him, under a shower of onions, is taken by the bride's party with music to Máruti's temple, where he presents the bridegroom with a suit of clothes and decks his brow with a marriage coronet or *báshing*. Lastly, the bridegroom lays before the idol a packet of betel laaves and nuts, bows before the god, and mounts the horse brought for him by the bride's brother. All go to the bride's house, where the bride and bridegroom stand face to face on two low stools, a curtain being held between them by the Bráhman priest, who repeats texts and throws Indian millet over them. They next seat themselves on the marriage altar or *bahule*, from which they throw clarified butter into the sacred fire lit by the priest. Marriage wristlets are tied to their hands. Then comes the troth-plighting or *páni-grahan*, when the bride's maternal uncle pours water into the hollow of the bride's folded hands laid on the bride-groom's (*dháre*) and completes the ceremony by putting a money gift or *dakshina* into the hands of both. Betel leaves and nuts are served and the guests withdraw. Next day they are again seated in the sacred square and are bathed in warm water, throwing at each other *chiksa* or the fragrant mixture of turmeric and Indian millets. Married women then mark their brows with vermilion and wave lights round their faces. Next comes the *phal* or cloth-presenting ceremony. The bridegroom's party go to the bride's with betel, a turban, a robe and a bodice, and uncooked provisions, rice, pulse, molasses and clarified butter, and the priest lays before the bride rice, five half-cocoa-kernels, five dry dates, and five betel leaves with nuts. Her father-in-law presents her with a robe and bodice and jewels, the musicians play their instruments, and the friends and kinspeople, both of the bride and bridegroom, are feasted at the bride's. The bride's mother respectfully asks the bridegroom's mother to visit her house and look at the bride. She goes to the bride's attended by music and a band of friends, takes the bride on her lap, and puts sugar in her mouth, presenting her with jewels. Lastly, the *jhál* or handing ceremony at the girl's house completes the marriage. The bride's parents hold a bamboo basket with four dough lamps laid in it, gently touch the heads of the bridegroom's parents with the basket and formally hand the bride to the bridegroom's parents after seating her on the lap of the bridegroom' father and repeating the words "She was ours up to this time, now she is yours". The pair are then seated on horseback and taken to the bridegroom's, where the bridegroom gives the girl a new name, and the guests are treated to a sumptuous dinner.

The remarriage of widows is permitted, but never with the deceased husband's brother, nor with a man of his surname or her father's surname. Her marriage with the son of her maternal aunt is also prohibited, though not with that of her maternal uncle or paternal aunt. The marriage of a widow is allowed if she is in the prime of her youth or if there is none to protect and feed her, her relatives arranging for the *mhotur* or remarriage. The sanction of the caste *pancháyat* is required, and is obtained by contributing Rs. 7 to the caste fund and paying about Rs. 3 to the members of the *pancháyat* for sweetmeats. On a copper pot are placed five betel leaves, one or more betelnuts and one cocoa-kernel. It is sprinkled over with vermilion and pigment. One betelnut and one cocoanut are placed in a dish and are daubed with vermilion. The widow and her intended husband, in the presence of a Bráhman, take a few grains of corn in their hands and throw them over the copper vessel. They then fall at the feet of the god Máruti. The widow presents her intended husband with a turban and waist-cloth and is in turn presented by him with a *pásodi*, robe or ornaments. A feast to the caste completes the *mhotur*. The ceremony is performed at night time in the dark fortnight, only widowers and widows being present. If the man who marries the widow is a bachelor he is first married to the *rui* plant (Calotropis gigantea).

Divorce is permitted with the sanction of the caste *pancháyat* if the wife proves unchaste or if the husband neglects to maintain her, if either party suffers from an incurable disease, or if a permanent misunderstanding has arisen between them. If a woman is caught in adultery with a man of her caste and thereby becomes pregnant, both are excommunicated; otherwise the man is fined and is free to marry her after she has been divorced from her first husband. Divorced women, except those caught in adultery, are allowed to marry anybody they like by the widow remarriage form. The caste follow the Hindu law of inheritance.

Marátha Bhois profess Hinduism and worship Mahádev, Máruti and Vithoba of Pandharpur. Among Hindu holidays they keep *Shimga* in March, *Sanvatsar pádva* or New Year's day in April, *Akshatritiya* in May, *Nágpanchami* in August, *Dasara* in September, and *Diváli* in October. They also visit Alandi in Poona, Madhi in Ahmednagar, Pandharpur in Sholápur, and Tuljápur in the Nizám's country. Their family deities are Khandoba of Jejuri, Bhaváni of Tuljápur, Bahiroba and Mhasoba.

The offerings made consist of fowls, goats, cocoanuts and cocoa-kernels, which the worshippers consume after making over a portion to the Gurvas of the temples. Their religious guides are the slit-eared or *Kán-pháte* Gosávis, whom they call Bávás. They believe in soothsaying, witchcraft and evil spirits, and employ *devrishis* or exorcists to drive ghosts out of possessed persons. Their priests are Deshasth Bráhmans.

The dead are usually burnt, but those who cannot bear the expense bury them in a sitting position with their face turned either to the east or west. Children under ten years of age are buried. The pebble or life-stone with which the water jar is broken at the funeral is kept in the house for ten days; and for this period the family consider themselves in mourning. On the third day the chief mourner goes to the burning ground, sprinkles milk, curds, butter, cow's urine and dung on the ashes of the dead, and throws the ashes into water. He sprinkles cowdung and water on the spot where the body was burnt, and places two dough cakes—one where the head lay and the other where the feet lay, bathes and goes home. On the tenth day he goes to the bank of a river with the life-stone. Grains of *til* (sesamum) and *sátu* (barley) and one pice are offered to the stone and it is bathed thrice. All the mourners present then bathe in the river, their Bráhman priest afterwards mutters certain prayers and the stone is thrown into the river. Eleven dough balls are made, ten of which are thrown into water, and the eleventh is set for crows to eat. The party do not return home till a crow has touched the ball. The priest is given the metal vessels used in performing the rites, with some money or *dakshina*. On the thirteenth day castefellows are asked to feast on fish, mutton and cakes and they present the chief mourner with a white turban, which he folds round his head. He then goes to the temple nearest his house. The deceased is remembered every year on the day corresponding to the death in *Mahálaya Paksha* or All Souls' Fortnight, when uncooked provisions with cash are given in the name of the dead to a Bráhman and kinspeople are feasted.

Death ceremonies.

One of their chief occupations former was carrying palanquins and litters, but with the opening of roads litters have nearly disappeared; and most of them now make their living by catching fish including tortoises. Some of them are grain-dealers, shop-keepers and messengers. Some are *inámdárs*, *ináms* having been bestowed on them by the *Mahárájás* of Kolhápur and Chiefs of Sángli.

Food.

They eat all kinds of scaly fish except *mus* and *devamása*, and the flesh of sheep and fowls only. They drink liquor, and esteem themselves higher than Mahárs and Mángs on account of their abstaining from beef and pork.

They do not eat *pakki kacchi*, drink or smoke with any lower caste. The higher castes that will eat and drink with them are Kunbis, Sutárs, Támbolis and others of similar standing.

KHANDESH BHOIS.—The Khándesh Bhois speak the Ahiráni dialect. The names in common use among men are, Bhila, Chindu, Kallu, Punju, Tandu, Tuta and Yedu; and among women, Bhágu, Harku, Jija, Rama, Sáitri and Vithi. They have two endogamous divisions, Maharyarla and Tarakshi. There is said to be a third division known as Dhimar or Dhivar who are immigrants from Gujarát. One account states that the whole caste has the same *gotra*, *viz.*, Káshyap, another account gives two *gotras*, Káshyap and Válmika, while according to a third account their *gotras* are Káshyap, Atri and Vishvámitra. The first two accounts assert that the *gotras* do not stand in the way of intermarriage, while the third maintains that sameness of *gotra* as well as of *kul* is a bar to intermarriage. It appears that the caste is in places adopting the Bráhmanical system of exogamy. Sameness of *devak* is in some places still considered to be a bar to intermarriage, but as a rule marriages are regulated by *kuls*, which are identical with surnames. The commonest surnames are as follows:—

1. Bharsákhare.	10. Jávare.	19. Nikaváde.
2. Chaván.	11. Julve.	20. Padval.
3. Dánge.	12. Kámare.	21. Sátote.
4. Dhole.	13. Khedkar.	22. Shivate.
5. Divekar.	14. Kutarmori.	23. Shigare.
6. Phulpagar.	15. Lambolia.	24. Sonavane.
7. Gulimade.	16. Landmori.	25. Távade.
8. Hajaban.	17. Mishál.	26. Válde.
9. Jádhav.	18. More.	

Marriage.

Marriages are prohibited between members of the same *kul*. A member of the caste may marry his maternal uncle's daughter, but not his mother's sister's or father's sister's daughter. Marriage with a wife's younger sister is permitted during the wife's life-time as well as after her death. Two brothers are allowed to marry two sisters.

Marriage is infant as well as adult. Sexual license before marriage is not tolerated. If a girl is guilty of misconduct with a casteman, both are fined, and the girl is allowed to remain in the caste after performing a penance. Sometimes she is married to her seducer if their *kuls* permit. The same penalty is inflicted on the girl if the offence is committed with a member of a higher caste; but if the man involved be of a lower caste, the girl is excommunicated. Polygamy is allowed and practised, but polyandry is unknown.

The offer of marriage comes from the boy's father, who has to pay a bride-price of from Rs. 5 to Rs. 50 to the girl's father, if he is poor. The day for the marriage is fixed by a Bráhman who conducts the service. The principal ceremonies of marriage are as follows :—

1. *Sáyakhada*, *Kunku lávane* or *Sagái* is the betrothal in which a party from the boy's house go to the girl's house and present her with dry dates, dry cocoa-kernels, betelnuts, red powder, a robe and a few ornaments. A Bráhman priest marks the girl's forehead with red powder, and the ceremony is over. A betrothal cannot be broken.

2. *Mándava* and *Belmáthni.*—A marriage booth of the boughs of the mango, *jáman* and *ruchkin* is erected. To the right, at the entrance to the booth, in the inside, two holes are dug by the pair who are to rub turmeric paste on the boy or the girl, Ganpati and Varuna are worshipped, and the *belmáthni* (boughs of the mango tree) is planted in these holes.

3. *Halad* is the ceremony of rubbing the boy and girl with turmeric paste by a married pair selected by a Bráhman priest.

4. *Telan.*—On the eve of the marriage day five married women hold a bamboo basket over the house gods and sing songs. Next, the basket is laid on a slab and songs are sung. It is then placed on the threshold of the house again, held over a lamp set on a cot, and lastly a nose-ring is put into the basket and songs are sung. Next, one of the women ties a *kankan* (a wristlet of wool with seeds of *mahua*, Bassia latifolia, and *jowári*) to the wrist of the boy with a yellow thread. A *kankan* is tied similarly to the girl's wrist at her house.

5. *Devak.*—The *devak* is brought by the sister of the bride or bridegroom and her husband. The ceremony takes place in the afternoon of the marriage day at the girl's house, and on the same day or the day before at the boy's house. The boughs of the tree or trees representing the *devak* are first placed in Máruti's temple, and then divided into five parts, one of which is tied to the *belmáthni*, and the remaining four to the four corners of the marriage pandal.

6. *Lagna.*—The boy starts on horseback with relations and friends for the girl's house. On his way a halt is made near Máruti's temple and the bridegroom is seated on a low wooden stool. A barber brings water, and the girl's father, washing his feet in it, presents him with a suit of clothes, which he puts on (*simanti*). When the party draw near the entrance to the marriage booth, a married woman from the girl's house meets the bridegroom, carrying water-pots on her head. The boy puts some coins into the topmost pot

and enters the booth. He is seated facing the east, and the girl is brought by the barber in attendance and seated in front of him. A cloth is held between them. When the sun is just about to sink below the horizon, the curtain is drawn aside, and the party assembled clap hands. Next, the hands of the bride and bridegroom are joined (*hátola*), they are worshipped by the girl's parents (*kanyádán*), and a money present is made to the Bráhman priest. The pair are again worshipped by the boy's father, who pays to the priest double the amount paid to him by the girl's parents. The hands of the pair are then separated, and gifts distributed.

7. *Chavari-bhavari.*—The sacrificial fire is then kindled and *ghi*, sesamum and barley are offered to it. Next, the bride and bridegroom walk five times round the sacrificial fire. At each turn two betel-leaves with a little *ghi* are thrown into the fire by them. A lucky necklace is then put round the girl's neck by a married unwidowed woman, and the bride and bridegroom feed one another with five mouthfuls of a mixture of *ghi* and molasses (*kasáre*). This ends the first day's ceremonies.

8. On the next day *rukhavat* or sweet dishes are carried from the girl's house to the boy's. In the evening the boy and girl are taken on their shoulders by two persons, and they are moved in a procession through the principal streets of the town, the pair throwing at each other *chiksa* (the fragrant mixture of turmeric and Indian millet ground together). One of the party carries a bamboo basket on his head, in which are placed the clothes to be presented to the girl, and another holds in his hand the clothes to be presented to the boy. This ceremony is known as *zál*. Next, the bride and bridegroom are made to worship Ganpati and Varuna, the bride is dressed in a new robe, and her lap is filled. If the couple are young, two men take them on their shoulders and dance to the accompaniment of drums, the ceremony being known as *zenda*. Next, the pair are seated on a low wooden stool, the girl is presented with a robe, a bodice or an ornament by the boy's parents, the boy is presented with a suit of clothes by the girl's parents, and the girl is handed over. On the following day a feast is given by the girl's father and the boy returns to his house in procession with his bride (*varát*). The turmeric is then washed off and the marriage ceremonies come to an end. The essential portion is the *chavari-bhavari*.

The remarriage of widows is permitted. A widow cannot marry her father's sister's, mother's sister's or mother's brother's son, or a member of her late husband's section. A widow remarriage is celebrated on a dark night of any month except *Pausha* and *Bhádrapad*. The widow's intended husband has to pay to her father a sum of Rs. 20 to Rs. 50. Relations on both sides, the caste *panch*, a Bráhman priest and a barber are present at the wedding. The widow is bathed and dressed in new clothes and ornaments presented by her intended husband. The pair are then seated side by side on two low wooden stools, the hems of their garments are knotted, Ganpati and Varuna are worshipped, and the widow's lap is filled. Next the barber feeds the couple with five mouthfuls of *Kasára* (*ghi* and molasses mixed together), which completes the union. In some places, after the worship of Ganpati and Varuna, a string of black glass beads is tied round the widow's neck and this is considered to be the essential portion of the ceremony. A widow remarriage is celebrated either at the widow's father's house or beyond the village boundary. A bachelor desirous of marrying a widow is first married to a ring or to a *rui* bush (Calotropis gigantea).

A husband can divorce a wife for infidelity or bad temper. Sometimes when a man is suffering from leprosy he is compelled by the castemen to divorce his wife. The marriage expenses incurred by him are paid to him by the wife's parents or by her intended husband, the amount being spent on liquor by the castemen. A deed of divorce is drawn up and registered. The religious ceremony by which a divorce is effected is known as *karma karne*, that is, performing funeral rites in the name of the woman by her husband. A woman taken in adultery with a casteman or a member of a higher caste can remain in the caste by paying a fine or giving a dinner to the caste people. The penalty for misconduct with a member of a lower caste is excommunication. The caste follow the Hindu law of inheritance.

The Khándesh Bhois belong to the Hindu religion. They worship all the leading Hindu gods and observe the principal Hindu holidays. Every exogamous section has a separate family goddess, some having more than one. The following are some of the commonest :—

Name of *kul*.	Name of its family goddess.
1. Dhole	..Chaudhar Ai.
2. More	..Morsái.
3. Sátote	..Chávada Máta, Sanasái, Manasái, Renuka.
4. Távade	..Ekvira.
5. Válde	..Injáti Máta.

These goddesses are worshipped on the *Shrávan* new-moon *Chaitra* new-moon, the *Dasara* day and at the time of a marriage. Once a year a goat is offered to Mariái, the head of which is given to a Bhil and the body taken by the worshipper. Offerings are made also to other minor gods. When the Bhois go to fish, they worship a god Jadhiár. The goddess Kánbai is worshipped by females only, on the fourth day of the dark half of *Phálgun*. Stones smeared with vermilion are installed in the name of persons who meet accidental deaths, and are called *Virs*. They are worshipped on the day following the *Sankránt* (the vernal equinox), the *Akshatritiya* day and the *Mahálaya* days. In some places *táks* or images embossed on gold or silver plates are installed instead of *Virs*. The image of a woman who dies a violent death is styled *Iráni*, that of a woman who dies in child-birth, *Vadadákhin*. The Khándesh Bhois go on pilgrimage to the holy places in the vicinity. Musalmán saints are venerated. When cholera or small-pox breaks out, vows are made to the goddesses supposed to preside over the diseases, and they are propitiated in various ways. The religious teachers of the Khándesh Bhois are Gosávis. Their priests are Deshasth Bráhmans.

Death ceremonies.

The dead are either burnt or buried. The unmarried dead must be buried. At burial the corpse is laid on its back with head to the south. The standard funeral rites in use among castes of similar standing are observed. For the propitiation of the deceased ancestors *pitar* or *mahálaya* is performed in the latter half of *Bhádrapad* and on the *Akshatritiya* day, when uncooked articles of food are given to a Bráhman, and castemen are feasted.

The hereditary occupation of the Khándesh Bhois is catching fish and bearing palanquins and litters. They also parch grain and grow water-melons and cucumbers in river beds. Some keep donkeys and carry grain on their backs from place to place. Some hold land under the *Rayatvári* system. Some are agricultural labourers and are paid either in cash or in corn.

Food.

They eat the flesh of goats, sheep, fowls, hares, deer and scaly and scaleless fish, and drink liquor. They eat food cooked by Maráthás, Kunbis, Rajputs, Phulmális, Dhangars, Kumbhárs, Vánis, Sonárs and Sutárs. They will drink water brought by a Koli. They do not eat food prepared by Shimpis, Nhávis or Telis. They will smoke with those castes from whom they can take water. Kolis, Mahárs, Mángs, Bhils, Musalmáns, etc., eat food cooked by them. Kunbis, Mális, Dhangars and Kumbhárs will drink water brought by them

The KARNATAK BHOIS of Belgaum have four endogamous divisions, Koli, Kár, Masande and Paratgi, who eat together, but do not intermarry. The Kárs are probably Kahár immigrants. The Masandes catch fish but do not carry palanquins. The occupation of the Paratgis is cement-making. In Dhárwár they are divided into Besta, Gangi, Sadar and Karva. Besta Bhois, who are immigrants from Mysore, wear the *linga* and eat from Gangi Bhois but not from Sadar Bhois. They do not marry with the other two classes. Sadar Bhois do not wear the *linga*. They eat from Besta and Gangi Bhois, but do not marry with them. Girls are married before they come of age, the boy's father giving a bride-price to the girl's father. Polygamy and widow marriage are allowed, but polyandry is unknown. The dead are buried and mourned ten days. Rites on behalf of the dead are performed between the eleventh and the thirteenth. They observe all the ordinary Hindu holidays. Their marriages are conducted by Bráhmans and death ceremonies by Gosávis. They eat mutton, pork and fish and drink liquor. They eat from all classes except Musalmáns, Holayás and Madigars.

The KANARA BHOIS have neither surnames nor household gods. Members of the same family stock do not marry. Their home speech is Kanarese, but they can also talk Konkani. They throw the casting net without swinging it over the head as the Ambigs do. Their customs do not differ from those of the Ambigs. They worship all village gods and goddesses, are firm believers in witchcraft and soothsaying, and employ Karnátak Karháde and Havik Bráhmans to perform their birth, marriage and death ceremonies. Their spiritual teacher is Tátiachári, a Rámánuj Bráhman whose monastery is at Govindráj-pattan in North Arcot, to whom they pay tithes through his representative the *párupatyagár* of Ankola. In addition to palanquin-bearing and fishing, some serve as messengers in Revenue offices, some bear torches in village temples, and some hold umbrellas at marriages.

The GUJARAT BHOIS claim to be Rajputs from Lucknow in the United Provinces. They have nine sub-divisions :—

1. Bakoria.	4. Gudia.	7. Máli.
2. Bhathva.	5. Kár.	8. Mela.
3. Gadhedia.	6. Máchhi or Dhimar.	9. Purbia.

Of these, Mális and Bakoriás eat together and intermarry ; Mális, Gudiás and Kárs eat with one another but do not intermarry ; the rest neither eat together nor intermarry. Except the Purbiás, whose home speech is Hindustáni, they speak Gujaráti. They do not perform any ceremony on the birth of a child. After the sixth day some worship the goddess Chhathi. The mother remains impure for fifteen to thirty days. Except among a few, no name-giving or food-giving ceremonies are performed. Their marriage, pregnancy and death rites do not differ from those observed by Kanbis. Marriage between near relations is forbidden. Widows are allowed to marry, and, except among the Bhois of Broach, divorce is easy. Most of the Gujarát Bhois worship Mothers or *Mátás*, though some of them are Bijmárgis, Rámánandis, Shaivás and Vallabhácháris. In the Panch Maháls they keep in their houses Meladi Máta, the image of a deceased woman of the family, who is worshipped when they intend to harass an enemy or to exorcise an evil spirit, in which art several Bhois of Godhra have special skill. In other parts of the province they have no housegods and, except on holidays, do not visit Hindu temples. All but a few in Broach are said to believe in sorcery, witchcraft and omens. Their chief holidays are *Diváso* in June-July, *Gokul Athem* in July-August and *Navrátri* in September-October. Some of them visit the ordinary places of Hindu pilgrimage. Their priests are Modh and Audich Bráhmans, whom they call Pandits and to whom they pay Rs. 2 to Rs. 4 at marriages and deaths.

The Gujarát Bhois make their living chiefly by fishing, growing water-chestnuts, and carrying palanquins or litters. Except in Native States, palanquin-bearing has almost died out. Some till lands and work as field labourers; others tend sheep and goats, and sell grass or fuel and *bábul* tooth-sticks; some are household servants and water-carriers as Pakhális or Bhistis.

They eat fish and the flesh of goats and drink liquor.

BHOI VAIDU.—A sub-division of Dádhichevála Vaidus.

BHOJA.—A sub-division of Ods.

BHOJAK.—A sub-division of Shrimáli Bráhmans.

BHONDE.—A synonym for Hátghade Kumbhár.

BHONDKAR.—A synonym for Hátghade Kumbhárs.

BHOPA.—A synonym for Rabári.

Name. **BHOPES,** also known as Bhute, are a religious order recruited from among Bráhmans and Maráthás. They were returned as numbering 80 at the census of 1901, but many of them must have been entered under the name of the parent caste. They are chiefly found in Poona, Sátára, Kolába and Ratnágiri. Bhopes have the same surnames as Maráthás. They are called Bhope or Bhute because they are devotees of the goddess Bhaváni.

The rules regarding marriage are the same as amongst the Maráthás. Marriage can only take place between those families between whom a connection can be traced within the last four or five generations or earlier. Families entirely unconnected cannot intermarry. There are no exogamous divisions. Marriage.

At Tuljápur in the Nizám s territory there is a temple of the god dess Bhaváni. A family by name Kadam. consisting of about fifty branches, hold the entire village in Inám. They are the hereditary priests of the goddess. They resemble the Badves at other sacred places. They help the pilgrims who visit the place by arranging for their lodgings, food, etc. Bráhman and Marátha families who have Bhaváni for their family goddess visit the place at times, and the offerings made by them are received as a right by these priests. Vákaji Kadam is their head or Pátil, and he has the third share in the offerings.

Bhutes can dine with Maráthás in the same row. They are superior to Gondhalis, who recite religious songs and wear strings of *kavadi* shells. The latter form a distinct and lower caste.

Their head-quarters are Tuljápur, Kolhápur and other places. They stay at Tuljápur for two months, *viz. Ashvin* and *Kártik* (October and November), and go to the fair at Kondanpur on the 15th of *Márgashirsha* (December). They then travel in the districts of Poona, Sátára, Nagar, Thána, Bhor, Phaltan and Bombay for four months begging alms, and return to their native places at the end of *Jeshtha* (June), where they pass the rainy season.

Bhutes admit outsiders into their caste, but only from the Maráthás and Bráhmans. When a Marátha or Bráhman has no issue or his children are short-lived, he makes a vow that if he begets two children he will offer one to the goddess Bhaváni and make him a Bhutya. This child, when grown up, is taken to Tuljápur. There the head Bhute or Pátil Kadam obtains the consent of the goddess to make him a Bhutya, worships her and puts the string of the *kavadi* shells worn by himself round the neck of the new-comer. He then admits him to his caste and makes the fact known to the whole Bhute community. If the new-comer is poor he wears the badge of the goddess and begs in her name.

There are Bhutes among Bráhmans, especially among the Deshasths, who commonly offer their children to the goddess. There are Bráhman families at Dehu whose males as well as females wear strings of *kavadi* shells, worship the goddess and beg in her name at least at five houses on Tuesdays and Fridays, and also keep the *kavadi* string amongst the house gods and worship it. These are Bhutes by vow. They are not professional beggars like the Marátha Bhutes.

Besides worshipping Bhaváni they also worship Khandoba of Jejuri, Bahiroba and Jotiba of Ratnágiri.

The badge of the Bhutes is a string of *kavadi* shells with an image of the goddess in the centre, a torch of rags and a *tuntune* or one-stringed fiddle. They wear the string round their neck and offer it to the goddess and worship it.

The original occupation of Bhutes is begging. They are followers of the goddess Bhaváni and go begging from door to door and village to village with a lighted torch in their hands and playing metal cups or *tals*, the one-stringed fiddle or *tuntune*, and the drum or *samel*. They cover themselves with shells from head to foot, mark their brow with red-powder or *pinjar* and have a square breast plate or *ták* hung from their necks. While begging they dance, sing songs and touch their bodies with the lighted torch or *pot*.

BHORIA.—A sub-division of Rávals.

BHORPIS, also called Bahurupis, a class of strolling dramatic players, numbering 641, including 333 males and 308 females, were recorded in small numbers at the census of 1901 in Ahmedabad, Surat, and most of the districts in the Deccan, Konkan and Karnátak. They look like Marátha Kunbis and do not differ from them in religious and social customs. They live in wattled huts thatched with straw, and while on their wandering tours, in *páls* or small tents. They are Smárts by religion. They worship all local gods, the special objects of worship being Bahiroba, Janái, Jokhái and Khandoba. Their priests are the local Bráhmans. They make their living chiefly as strolling actors, but many of them rear and deal in cattle. They are proverbially honest, putting out of caste persons charged with theft. They eat flesh except beef and pork and drink liquor.

BHUJARI.—A synonym for Bhadbhunja.

BHUKANIA.—A sub-division of Bráhmans.

BHUMIPUTRA.—A synonym for Mahár.

BHUND.—A synonym for Kankália Bhát.

BHUSARE.—A sub-division of Lamánis or Vanjáris.

BHUSHARE.—A synonym for Bhusáre.

BHUSARJIN.—A synonym for Bhusáre.

BHUTE.—*See* Bope or Bhute.

BHUYAL.—A synonym for Mahár.

BID.—A sub-division of Korava.

BIJAPURI.—A sub-division of Gavlis.

BILE.—A sub-division of Ganigs and Berads.

BILE SHRIYA.—A sub-division of Hanbars.

BIRLINGE.—A sub-division of Holayás.

BODA.—A sub-division of Chodhrás.

BOGARS, also called Kásárs, are Jains, who are found in small numbers in Kanara and appear to have originally come from Goa. They were probably recorded under Kásárs at the census of 1901. Their principal occupation is selling glass bangles, but some also make and sell copper and brass vessels, and are hence called Kásárs. Their customs do not differ from those of other Jains.

BOHORAS, numbering 118,307 (males 60,363, females 57,944) at the census of 1901, are found in large numbers in the Surat and Broach districts and Bombay City and, scattered in small numbers, in all parts of the Presidency. They are also found as traders in all the principal trade centres in India. Their headquarters are in Surat, where the high priest of the Dáudi Bohorás, the principal section of the community, resides. Name and origin.

The origin of the name Bohora is doubtful. It is generally traced to the class of Hindu Bohorás who are still found in Márwár, Rájputána and the United Provinces.(1) But as there is no certain record of Hindu Bohorás in Gujarát,(2) it seems better to derive the word from the Gujaráti *vohorvu* to trade, the occupation followed

---

(1) Malcom's Central India, II, III; Tod's Rájasthán, II, 491, Edition 1831; Elliot's Races, I. 44. The Mirat-i-Ahmedi (Pers. Text, II. 87) confirms the Hindu derivation of the name Bohora. It says many Bráhman and Bania traders being called Bohoras retained the name after their conversion. Many Baniás and even Nágar Bráhmans to this day bear the surname Bohora.

(2) There is now no trace of a Hindu Bohora caste in Gujarát, and the passage in the Kumárapálacharitra "There are plenty of Bohorás in Anahilaváda and Birgong" (Viramgám) (Tod's Western India, 149-157) was probably written about A.D. 1150 or some time after the spread of the Ismáili faith among the traders of north Gujarát.

by the first Hindu converts to Islám.[1] However, it must be admitted that neither at present nor under the Musalmán rulers of Gujarát is its use limited to traders or to converts of the special Ismáili form of faith. Besides the traders there is a larger and not less prosperous class of village Bohorás, tillers of the soil and Sunnis by religion. The existence of these two distinct classes is an illustration of the fact that in Gujarát Shiáhism was spread by the persuasion of preachers and Sunniism by the power of rulers. The early Shiáh preachers (A.D. 1067), being treated with much kindness by the Hindu kings of Anahilaváda, settled and made converts chiefly in the great trading centres, while to the Musalmán Governors it was of more political value to bring over to their religion the sturdy and outlying villager than the weak and peace-loving trader. The use of the same name for classes so unlike as the city and village Bohorás would seem to be due to the great division of the Gujarát population into armed *dhárála* and unarmed. To distinguish converts from the armed Rajput and Koli castes the Musalmán governors coined such names as Molesalám, Malik and Sipáhi. For converts of the trading class the word Bohora was in use, and this they extended to converts from all the unarmed castes, Bráhmans, husbandmen and craftsmen.[2]

All Bohorás can be traced to converts made in the eleventh century by Shiáh missionaries of the Ismáili sect. Though settled in many parts of the Bombay Presidency, and in Hyderabad in the Deccan, in Berár, Málwa, Central India and Rájputána, and, as traders, found over almost the whole of India, the high priest and head-quarters of the sect are in Surat. Some of them claim to come from Egyptian-Arab and Yaman-Arab ancestors. Others acknowledge themselves to be entirely of Hindu blood, the descendants of converts

---

(1) Other explanations are from Behrinah, said to be a town in Yaman in lower Arabia, the birth place of the great Bohora missionary Abdulláh : from *bohráh*, the right or good way, because as the Shiáh Bohorás say, the way of their religion is right ; or from *bahuráh* many paths, because, according to the Sunni Bohorás they were converted from many castes ; from the Persian *bahir* meaning trains of camels and thence a horde of camp followers ; and from *bahráj*, a word meaning prudent or business-like. But these are all fanciful and unlikely. The word *vohorvu* is probably from the Sanskrit *vyavahára* which in the modern vernaculars usually has the principle meaning of " trade."

(2) Compare Rás Mála (New Edition, 264) : " The Rajputs forcibly converted by Sultán Ahmed I. (about A.D. 1420) formed a separate caste called Molesaláms ; the Vániás and the Bráhmans converted at the same time joined the sect of the Bohorás." The ordinary Gujaráti use of the word Bohora very closely corresponds with Hindu converts from the unarmed classes. Thus several classes who have a special name from their craft or calling are spoken of as Bohorás, and in some cases, as in Ghánchi-Bohora, the word Bohora is added to the craft name. So, too, the Dhándhári Momnás call themselves Bohorás, and the class of Konkan Musalmáns who take service with Europeans are known in Gujarát as Konkani Bohoras.

to the teaching of Ismáilian missionaries. A certain special look and character support the statements of Musalmán historians that they are partly the descendants of refugees from Egypt and Arabia.(1)

According to the received account of their rise in Gujarát, in the course of the eleventh century about A.D. 1067 (H. 460)(2) Abdulláh, a missionary *dái*, sent from Haras in Yaman by the high priest of the Mustaáli Ismáili sect, landed at Cambay. Abdulláh, who was a man of great learning, is said to have stayed some years at Cambay studying the people. Two stories are told of his first missionary success. According to one story, he gained a cultivator's heart by filling his dry well with water. According to the other, by dashing to the ground an iron elephant hung in mid-air in one of the Cambay temples, he won over some of the priests. After this the missionary is said to have travelled towards Anahilaváda, or Pátan, at that time the capital of Gujarát. The story goes that the ruler of the city, Sidhráj Jaising (A.D. 1094—1143), anxious to see the stranger, sent a force of armed men to bring him to his capital. Finding the saint surrounded by a wall of fire the troops retired. Then the

---

(1) Farishtah and the Mirat-i-Ahmedi. One account gives as early a date as A.D. 870, and another the close of the eleventh century, when the Nazárian Ismáil is becoming supreme in Persia are supposed to have ousted their rivals the Mustaáli Ismáilis. In later times A.D. 1539 the date given for the arrival of the supreme head of the sect from Aden so nearly agrees with the capture of Aden by the Turks that it seems probable that the high priest was accompanied to India by a band of refugees.

(2) Khán Shaháb-ud-din and Briggs "Cities of Gujaráshtra," Appendix IX. The Dáudi prayer book gives A.D. 1137 (H. 532) as the date of the first missionary's death. Conolly (Journal Asiatic Society, Bengal, VI.2.824) gives A.D. 1137 as the date of the conversion, and calls the missionary Muhammad, not Abdulláh. Colebrook's Miscellaneous Essays, II.228. The Mirat-i-Ahmedi (Persian Text, II.87) agrees with Conolly in stating that the name of the first Bohora missionary was Mulla Muhammad Ali. He says the shrine of this Pir at Cambay, known as the shrine of the Pir-i-Rawán or the Ever-alive Saint, drew at the time when he wrote large crowds of Bohorás from all parts of Gujarát. When Mulla Muhammad Ali landed in Cambay the people of Gujarát were ignorant of Islám. A Hindu saint was the object of general faith. The Mulla, considering open opposition to this saint dangerous and impossible, joined the number of his disciples. His intelligence soon attracted the saint's notice. After mastering the language of the country, he studied the saint's holy books and so worked upon his mind as to convert him to his views. Many of the saint's chief followers adopted the new faith. At last news that his minister was a convert reached the Rája's ears. The Rája, finding his minister at his prayers, asked what he was doing. Searching for a snake, said the minister. A snake appeared in a corner and the Rája became a convert though he kept it secret till on his death-bed he ordered his body to be buried. With the establishment of Muhammadan power many Cambay Bohorás settled in the capital (Pátan). When in A.D. 1391 Muzáffar I came from Delhi to Gujarát as governor he brought many priests of the Sunni sect, who were active in turning the people to this branch of the faith. Most of the Pátan Shiáh Bohorás were converted to the Sunni faith and their example was followed by their brethren in the other chief towns though the Bohorás of the country towns and the outlying parts remained Shiáhs. The Sunnis and the Shiáhs both being of the same origin intermarried till in A.D. 1535 Sayyad Jáffar Shirázi persuaded the Sunnis to keep apart from the Shiáhs.

king himself came, and in obedience to the stranger's command the fire opened and let the king pass. Full of wonder, the king asked for one sign more that the new belief was better than the old. His wish was granted ; one of his holiest idols declared that the Arab's was the true religion. Hearing these words the Hindus, king and subjects alike, struck with astonishment, embraced the new faith.(1) For two centuries and a half (A.D. 1130—1380) there was little in the history of Gujarát to check the progress of the Ismáili faith. But with the establishment of Muzaffar Sháh's power (A.D. 1390—1413) the spread of Sunni doctrines was encouraged, and the Bohora and other Shiáh sects repressed. Since then, probably with gradually lessening numbers, they have passed through several bitter persecutions, meeting with little favour or protection, till at the close of the eighteenth century they found shelter under British rule.(2) The chief event in the modern history of the Bohorás is the transfer in A.D. 1539 (H. 946) of the seat of the head priest of their faith from Yaman to Gujarát. Till then the Gujarát Ismáiliás had been under the guidance of a high priest at Yaman, to whom pilgrimages were made, tithes paid and disputes referred for settlement.(3)

Divisions. Bohorás have two main divisions, (1) Shiáhs or trading Bohorás and (2) Sunnis or cultivating Bohorás. The former are further split up into the following divisions:—

1. Alia.
2. Dáudi, who form the bulk of the community.

---

(1) Though Sidhráj (A.D. 1094—1133) would seem to have died a Hindu, his fondness for religious discussions and his tolerance might, without giving up his own religion, have led him to patronise the Bohora missionary. Rás Mála, 172 and 344. Both of Sidhráj's successors, Kumáralála (A.D. 1143—1174) and Ajayápála (A.D. 1174—1177) and Sidhráj's great Jain teacher Hemácharya, at a time when there are no recorded Musalmán invasions, are said to have been converted to Islám. Tod's Western India, 184 and 191 ; Rás Mála, I. 344. If the Khojáh history is correct the conversion of the Hindu king was about A.D. 1240, that is, during the reign of Ajayápála's successor Bhima II. (A.D. 1179—1242).

(2) The Chief Bohora persecutions are said to have been under Sultán Ahmed I. (A.D. 1411—1443) and Mahmud II. (A.D. 1536—1554). Of their troubles in Sultán Ahmad's reign the story is told that the chief Mulla, because he kept the beginning of the month of Ramazán at a different time from the orthodox reckoning and denied that he did so, was killed by order of the king. Even under the more liberal of the Delhi emperors, the Gujarát Bohorás are by a friendly writer described as ever involved in the difficulties of concealment and suffering much persecution at the hands of the wicked murderers (Sunni Musalmáns) invested with public authority. Sayad Nurulláh quoted in Colebrook's Miscellaneous Essays, II. 229.

(3) According to the Bohora accounts there was at the time great want of zeal among the Yaman people and strong faith among the people of Gujarát. This tempted the high priest Yusuf-bin-Sulaimán to come and settle at Sidhpur. Khán Bahádur Kázi Shaháb-ud-din. As already noticed, the success of the Turks (A.D. 1537) in Aden and other coast towns had probably something to do with this movement. Journal Asiatic Society of Bengal, VI-2,842.

3. Jaáfari.
4. Nágoshi.
5. Sulaimáni.

These divisions are described below separately.

ALIA BOHORAS take this name from Ali, who founded the sect in A.D. 1624. He was the son of Ibráhim, one of the sons of Shaikh Adam, the head Mulla. The father, passing over his sons, named one Shaikh Tayyib as his successor, and in spite of the efforts of his sons, who joined in support of Ali's claims, only a very small number refused to accept Shaikh Tayyib as their head. The Aliás resemble the Sulaimáni Bohorás in appearance and customs.

DAUDI BOHORAS are the richest, best organised and most widely spread class of Gujarát Musalmáns. They are also called Lotiás from *lota*, a waterpot, because their turban is shaped like a *lota*.(1)

Though active and well made, few Dáudi Bohorás are muscular or even robust. Their features are regular and clear, the colour olive, the expression gentle and shrewd. They shave the head, wear long thin beards, and cut the hair on the upper lip close. Many of the women are said to be beautiful and fair-skinned with delicate features. Following the precept and to some extent the example of the prophet, they are careful to keep their eyelids pencilled with collyrium, their teeth blackened with *missi*, an astringent powder, and the palms of their hands and the soles of their feet reddened with henna. Their home tongue is Gujaráti marked by some peculiarities of dialect, and the use of several Arab words well pronounced even by women who have not learned Arabic. Except a few, who, having performed a pilgrimage to Karbala or returned from a voyage to China or some foreign country, have of late years adopted the Arab costume, a Dáudi wears at home a silk or white cotton skullcap, a jacket of white cloth, a shirt falling below the knee, and trousers of white or stripped cotton cloth loose above and tight near the ankle. Out of doors he wears a small white turban, a waistcoat, a Hindu shaped coat *angarkha*, trousers the same as those worn in the house, and long shoes called *Ujjaini*. The Dáudi woman wears a red-dark-blue or yellow cotton silk scarf *odna*; in North Gujarát a light tight-fitting silk bodice and in South Gujarát

(1) Faria (A.D. 1664) speaks of the Musalmáns of Gujarát as Lauteas partly strangers, partly native converts (Ker's Voyages, VI. 229).

a silk jacket *dagli*, a silk petticoat, and shoes of wood in the north and of leather in the south. Their holiday dress is very rich, of embroidered silk and brocade. Out of doors, over the dress they wear a large dark-coloured silk veilrobe called *burka* passing over the head. This covers the face, leaving small net openings in front of the eyes, and drapes in loose folds to the ground shrouding the whole figure. Both Hindu and Musalmán ornaments are worn.

Daudi Bohorás are Shiáhs of the Mustaálian division of the great Ismáili sect. They are attentive to their religious duties, many—both men and women—knowing the Kurán. They are careful to say their prayers, to observe *Muharram* as a season of mourning, and to go on pilgrimage to Mecca and Karbala. They abstain from music and dancing and from using or dealing in intoxicating drinks and drugs. The chief points of difference between their beliefs and practices and those of regular Musalmáns are that they pay special attention to Ali and his sons Hassan and Hussain, and to their high priest the Mulla Sáhib of Surat; that they attach special importance to circumcision; that they reject the three Caliphs Abu Baker Sidik, Umar and Usmán; and that at death a prayer for pity on the soul and the body of the dead is laid in the dead man's hand. They would seem to share all the ordinary Indian beliefs in spirit-possession and exorcism and in charms and omens.

Except for some peculiarities in their names; that they attach special importance to circumcision[(1)]; that the sacrifice or *akikah* ceremony is held in the Mulla's house; that at marriage the bride and bridegroom when not of age are represented by sponsors or *walis*; that at death a prayer for pity on his soul and body is laid in the dead man's hands; and that on certain occasions the high priest feeds the whole community, Dáudi customs do not, so far as has been ascertained, differ from those of ordinary Musalmáns.

The completeness of their class arrangements, the envy of other Muhammadans, is the most marked feature of the Dáudi Bohorás. Their leader, both in things religious and social, is the head Mulla of Surat. The ruling Mulla names his successor generally, but it is said not always, from among the members of his own family. Short of worship, the head Mulla is treated with the greatest respect. He lives in much state and entertains with the most profuse liberality. On both religious and civil questions his authority is final. Discipline is enforced in religious matters by fine, and in cases of adultery,

---

(1) It is mentioned in the Bombay Census Report for 1911, p. 120, that they excise the clitoris of female children.

drunkenness and other offences by fine, flogging and excommunication. Every considerable settlement of Dáudis has its Mulla or deputy of the head Mulla. He is their leader in religious matters and when disputes arise he calls a meeting of the chief members and decides the point. From this decision an appeal lies to the head Mulla in Surat.

Besides the head Mulla or *Dái* there are Mullas of four grades. Mázun or literally the permitted (to rule), Mukásir or the executor, Masháikh or the elder, and Mulla or the guardian. They do not depend for support on their people, but earn their livelihood as school-masters or by practising some craft. Any well-behaved youth with a good knowledge of Arabic may be admitted into the lowest grade of Mullás. and, as he shows himself worthy, is raised in rank next to the head Mulla. To train youths for the duties of Mulla a college was in A. D. 1809 founded in Surat, and is still, though on a greatly reduced scale. kept up at a yearly charge of about Rs. 10,000. Besides the central college, every Dáudi settlement has its school, where, under the charge of the Mulla and generally by a Sunni Musalmán teacher, boys and girls are taught to read the Kurán. Besides on education the head Mulla spends large sums in feeding and clothing strange and destitute Dáudis, and in helping the poor among his people to meet the expenses of marriages and other costly ceremonies. The funds to meet this outlay and to support the state of the head Mulla are raised from fines, from a special subscription of a fifth part of their income called *khums* and from the regular Musalmán alms *zakát*.

Almost all Dáudi Bohorás live by trade. Some are merchants having large dealings with Arabia, China, Siam and Zanzibar, others are local traders in hardware, silks and hides, and horns and live cattle; but most are town and village shopkeepers, selling hardware, cloth. stationery, books, groceries and spices, and a few, especially in Ahmedábád, Baroda and Surat, are confectioners. The inhabitants of a few villages in Dholka in North Gujarát are peasants and a few are in Government service.

Except that they are sparing in what they eat, taking care that nothing is wasted; that because of its cheapness many of them use beef: that with them fish, like other animals, must, to be lawful food. die under a Musalmán's knife; and that they are specially scrupulous to use no intoxicating drug or stimulant, in their food and way of eating, Dáudis do not differ from ordinary Musalmáns.

JAAFARI BOHORAS are found in considerable numbers in all the towns and chief villages in Gujarát. They are called

Jaáfari after Jaáfar Sherázi who converted them to the Sunni faith. They are also known as Pátanis after their head-quarters. Other synonyms are Badi Jamát, the large body, derived from their following the Sunni faith which is followed by the majority of the Musalmáns of the Bombay Presidency, and Chár Yári or believers in the Prophet's four companions *as-hábs.*

Jaáfari Bohorás are the descendants of those Dáudi Bohorás who went over to the orthodox faith on the advent of Muzáffar I as Governor of Gujarát in A.D. 1391. The Dáudi Bohorás and the Jaáfari Bohorás kept up their marriage relations until their connection was severed by Sayad Jaáfar Shirázi about A.D. 1535.(1) This Sayad Jaáfar Shirázi was one of the ornaments of Mahmud Begada's reign. He is still considered by the Jaáfari Bohorás as their *Pir* and his descendants are still their spiritual guides.

Jaáfari Bohorás differ somewhat from the Dáudis, resembling Memans and other Sunni Musalmáns. In dress they differ from ordinary Musalmáns only by their round narrow-rimmed brown or black turbans. Except the Surat Sunni Bohorás who intermarry with all classes, Jaáfaris marry only among themselves and celebrate their marriage without any processions. Each settlement has its headman and forms a fairly organized body, the rich members meeting at intervals and subscribing to help the poor. They are Sunnis in faith and are religious, most of them, even the women, knowing the Kurán and saying their prayers. They have no special religious head, but many follow spiritual guides. A considerable number of them are known as Kabriás from being devoted to the *Kabar* (tomb) of Pir Muhammad Sháh at Ahmedábád. Their occupation is trade and some of those who trade with Arabia follow many Arab customs. Some are pedlars, and in Ahmedábád and Pátan, silk weavers.

NAGOSHIS or Non-fleshites are, according to the account generally given by the Dáudis, a very small schism not earlier than A.D. 1789. The founder is said either to have been excommunicated or to have been drawn from the Alia sect because he held certain peculiar doctrines, the most prominent among which was that to eat animal food was sin. The Nágoshis are now almost extinct.

SULAIMANI BOHORAS are the descendants of the converts which were made in Arabia in the sixteenth century by a missionary

(1) Mirat-i-Ahmedi Persian Text. II. 87.

sent by a Surat Bohora. These, besides by the regular name of Ismáil, from the priests' title Bizái the fair, became known as Bizái Bohorás. For a time they would seem to have considered the Gujarát high priest their head. But about the close of the sixteenth century (A.D. 1588) Dáud bin Ajabsháh, the high priest of the Gujarát Bohorás, died. Upon his death the Gujarát Bohorás chose as his successor one Dáud bin Kutub Sháh, sending news of the appointment to Yaman. Meanwhile one of the Yaman priesthood, Sulaimán by name, on the strength of a letter said to be from the high priest, was by the people of Yaman accepted as the successor. He came over to Gujarát, but finding his claim rejected by all but a very small body, retired to Arabia. Such of the Gujarát Bohorás as upheld his claims were called Sulaimánis.

Sulaimáni Bohorás do not differ much from the Dáudi Bohorás in look, belief and customs. They associate but do not intermarry with the Dáudis though they have begun to intermarry with regular Musalmáns. They have almost given up the Gujarát Bohora dress and turban. Their high priest lives in Najran in the Hejas in Arabia, they have taken to English education, and some of them are barristers, engineers and doctors.

SUNNI BOHORAS are found in large numbers in Broach, in the Olpád and Mándvi *tálukas* of the Surat district, east in Baroda, and to a less extent north in Ahmedábád and Káthiáwár.

Sunni Bohorás appear to be the descendants of Hindu converts of the unarmed castes who adopted Islám at the close of the fourteenth and during the fifteenth centuries. "Besides under Muzáffar Sháh (A.D. 1390—1443), when they became a separate body, the Sunni Bohorás probably received additions, both from Hindus and perhaps from the ranks of the Shiáh Bohorás, during their conversion under Sultáns Ahmed I (A.D. 1411—1443), Mahmud Begada (A.D. 1459—1513), and Mahmud II (A.D. 1536—1554). Many peasant Bohorás know to what Hindu caste their forefathers belonged. A large number settled in Sárod in Broach claim descent from Manchárám, a Bráhman of Morvi in Káthiáwár, who was converted by Mahmud Begada. Some Bohorás in Dhandhuka, Kavi and Jambusar are Ráwaliás, some in Bharkodra are Vániás, some in Deodi are Rajputs, some in Tankária are Bhátiás or Lohánás, some in Khánpur are Dheds, some in Achodi are Chamárs, some in Mora are Khatris and some in Akola are Modh Ghánchis. The distinction was still kept up in 1898. Those who claim high caste descent refuse to give their darghters to lower class Bohorás.[1]

In addition to their Hindu origin, the look and manner of Sunni Bohorás would, at least in Broach, seem to show that they include some considerable foreign element.

All who have studied the Broach peasant Bohoras have dwelt on their peculiar appearance and character. But what the non-Gujarát element is has not yet been settled. They have been called Arabian Jews and some among the cultivators claim descent from Ismáil, the son of Abraham.[2] Captain Ovans in one of the note books of the first Broach Survey (A.D. 1818), gives an account which he had from the Tankária Bohorás, and of the truth of which he was confident. According to this account the Emperor Jehángir (A.D. 1618), finding some Márvári prisoners-of war enslaved by a Hindu chief, gave them their freedom. To show their gratitude, the Márváris became Muhammadans, and in reward were settled in waste lands in Gujarát. Some of the Kaira cultivating Bohorás give almost the same account, and though these Márvári converts cannot have been the original Bohorás, they may at one time have been a distinct class like or the same as the Kákápuris. As far as features and manners go, a Márvári element would very well explain the Broach Bohora's special looks and ways. This Márvári strain may be a trace of the special Gurjjara settlement in Broach (A.D. 580—808).

Sunni Bohorás have strong burly muscular frames with fair complexion and high regular features. They shave the head and wear the beard long and full. The women are tall, stout and fair with good features.

In North Gujarát a cultivating Bohora wears a large loose turban, a jacket *bandi*, a waistscarf *pichodi*, and trousers like a Káthi's, loose above but tight under the knee and buttoned at the ankle. In Central Gujarát he wears a full turban though less large and loose than in the north, a coat, and a waist cloth tied round the body without being passed between the legs. South of the Narbada, he generally has on a patchwork padded skullcap, a long coat and loose trousers *tammán*. Prosperous Bohorás settled in South Gujarát cities and in Bombay have adopted the Meman dress or the Arab coat and overcoat with the gold-bordered or silk-embroidered arched turban. Except in and near some of the chief towns, where

(1) K. B. Fázal Latfulláh.

(2) (Vaupel in Trans. Bom. Geog. Soc. (A.D. 1840) VII 46).

they have adopted Musalmán fashions, over the whole of Gujarát peasant Bohora women dress like Hindu women in an upper scarf, bodice and petticoat. Shoes are worn by all, both men and women. Men wear silver necklaces, wristlets, rings and sometimes anklets. The ornaments of women are peculiar, very massive and heavy, in make partly Hindu, partly Musalmán. They are more particular than the women of most local classes to avoid ornaments that ring or tinkle.

Except among the Ankleshwar Bohorás, who speak half-Hindustáni, half-Gujaráti, their home language is Gujaráti with less peculiarity of dialect than among the Dáudis. The home language of the prosperous among them settled in cities and in Bombay is gradually undergoing a change from Gujaráti to Urdu.

Except in the case of some rich men settled in Surat and Bombay, Sunni village Bohorás seldom marry with any one not of their own class. The villagers north of the Narbada do not marry with those to the south. In Dhandhuka some families claiming the title of Desái hold aloof from the common Bohora villagers, and in several parts of Broach, houses of Bráhman or Rajput descent, though they allow their sons to marry with them, refuse to give their daughters to families whose forefathers were Kolis, Rávaliás or Dheds.

They are Sunnis in faith and religious, some knowing the Kurán and many of them careful to say their prayers. Almost all have spiritual guides, *Pirzádás*, whom they treat with great respect. Most peasant Bohorás still keep some Hindu practices. Some of them call their children by Hindu names, Akuji or Bájbhái, and others have oddly changed Musalmán names, as among boys Ibru or Ibla for Ibráhim and Ipsu or Isap for Yusuf, and among girls Khaja for Khálija and Fatudi for Fátima. Two or three days before marriage in honour of a special deity Wánudev they distribute dishes of two kinds of pulse, *láng* and *wál*, boiled together. At death their women beat the breast and wail like Hindus, and they also give death and marriage dinners as among Hindus. Some of them have become followers of the Gheir-Mukallid teachers of Wahabi sect. These have taken to strict Musalmán customs.

Almost all Sunni Bohorás are landholders and peasants : if poor, their women helping them in field work : if rich, they maintain *halis* or farm-slaves, who are usually of the Chodhra or Dubla or other aboriginal tribes. They eat fish and flesh like other Musalmáns, but abstain from liquor.

BOJGAR.—*See* under Minor Musalmán Castes.

BOLE.—A sub-division of Mahárs.

BOMBILVIKE.—A synonym for Rávjin Vanjári.

BORICHA.—A sub-division of Ahirs.

BORIVALE.—A sub-division of Kaikádis.

BORSADA.—A sub-division of Bráhmans.

BOVAR.—A sub-division of Kabbaligar.

BRAHMA BHAT.—A sub-division of Bháts.

Name. **BRAHMA KSHATRIS,** numbering 3,305 (1901), including 1,715 males and 1,590 females, are found chiefly in Ahmedábád, Broach and Surat, and a few in Káthiáwár, Cutch and Junágad. The term Brahma Kshatri means Kshatris or warriors of the Brahma, that is Bráhman, class, and has its origin in the tradition that when Parashurám, the Bráhman warrior, had subdued the Kshatriyas and was determined to extirpate their race, some of the Kshatri women who were pregnant sought the refuge of certain Bráhmans, and when detected, were saved by the protectors by giving the persecutor to understand that they were Bráhmans. The tradition further asserts that in verification of their statement the Bráhmans ate food cooked by the women. As a proof of the truth of this tradition, the Brahma Kshatris point to the fact that their priests, the Sárasvat Bráhmans, partake of food cooked by them even to the present day.

Origin. Apart from the above tradition, which is put forward by many castes claiming a Kshatriya origin, the facts that they are the same as the Punjáb Kshatris, who have been admitted to belong to the original Kshatri race, and that though now engaged in peaceful occupations they have not wholly lost their martial spirit, tend to prove that they were originally Kshatriyas. Their identity with the Punjáb Kshatris is established by the similarity of some of their customs, by their being called Khákha Kshatris like the Punjáb Kshatris, and by the custom of the Sárasvat Bráhmans—who are priests to both—of eating cooked food at the hands of the caste.

History. When and under what circumstances the Brahma Kshatris came into Gujarát is not known. The tradition is that about 500 years ago they emigrated from the Punjab and settled at Chámpáner in the Panch Maháls. On the capture of Chámpáner by Mahmud Begada (A.D. 1484) the Brahma Kshatris are said to have moved to Ahmedábád, where they occupied the quarter of the city at present known by the name of Khadiyu. The oppression of the Musalmáns compelled them to migrate to other parts of India. Some of them went as far as Hyderabad in the Deccan, where a few families still marry with Gujarát Brahma Kshatris. Some who went to Benáres and Lucknow are now known as Gujarát Kshatris.

They are a handsome fair-skinned class, some of them with blue or gray eyes, in make and appearance like Vániás, only larger and more vigorous. Except at their weddings, they dress like other high caste Gujarát Hindus. The only special marks are, among the men a small tightly-wound turban, and among the women a heavy cloth veil or hood sometimes worn in public to hide the forehead. Appearance.

Brahma Kshatris speak Gujaráti with a few Hindustáni words, such as *roti* bread for *rotli*, *chacha* uncle for *káka*, *bua* father's sister for *phoi*, *nána* mother's father for *ájo* or *vadvo*, and *barát* marriage-procession for *ján*. Language.

Brahma Kshatris have six endogamous divisions as follows :— Divisions.

1. Brahma Kshatri Proper.
2. Chudgar.
3. Dakhani.
4. Dasa.
5. Nátrávála.
6. Pancha.

None of the above divisions except the Brahma Kshatris Proper and Dakhanis eat together or intermarry. The latter have interdining and intermarrying relations. Dasás and Panchás are said to be the offspring of a Brahma Kshatri and a woman of another caste. Nátráválás and Chudgars are functional in origin, the first following the occupation of making idols' eyes and the second; bangles.

Brahma Kshatris have *gotras* or exogamous sections like Bráhmans. Marriages are prohibited between members of the same *gotra* and also within seven degrees of relationship. Marriage with two sisters is allowed. Widow marriage and divorce are forbidden.

The ceremonies and customs of Brahma Kshatris differ in some particulars from those obtaining among the higher castes of Gujarát. They are as follows :—

On the evening of the day on which a child is born the mother's breasts are worshipped and the child suckled. Among a few families in Káthiáwár a woman while in confinement eats only fruit and roots or such food as is used on fast days. On the sixth day after birth the goddess of fortune *Vidháta* or *Chhathi* is worshipped. The first giving of cooked food or *botan* takes place in the sixth month after birth. The rite of hair-cutting or *mudan* takes place between the age of five and seven, when girls as well as boys have their hair cut. Like Birth.

thread-girding and pregnancy ceremonies, hair-cutting is performed at the place sacred to the family-goddess. Except in Káthiáwár, at the first hair-cutting a minor ceremony called *devka* is performed. The child's mother and father go to the mother's house with music and a following of women. There the pair tie the ends of their garments together and bathe, and then wait in their wet clothes until some woman of the mother's family whose husband is alive spots with saffron the clothes of the father's maternal uncle and gives him sweets to eat. When this is done the mother and father put on fresh clothes, return home, and worship the family-goddess.

Three, four or five days before the hair-cutting, as also at thread and pregnancy ceremonies, the family-goddess is worshipped. A black male kid five or six months old is bought, kept in the house, and fed with green grass and grain till the last day of the ceremony. On that day the family priest slits the kid's right ear and touches with blood the forehead of the child, its parents, and other members of the family. The kid is then let loose in one of Devi's temples and allowed to roam at pleasure. This custom is kept by many families. In a few families during the eight or nine days of the ceremony six or seven male black kids are brought every day and their foreheads marked with red powder. The priest kills the kids, and the flesh is cooked, offered to the goddess, and eaten by the members of the family, friends and relations, including the priest himself. In almost every family one or other of these customs is kept.

The thread-ceremony is performed when the boy is between six and eight in mainland Gujarát and between six and eleven in Káthiáwár. Betrothals generally take place two or three years before marriage. At betrothals the boy, accompanied by the women of the family, is brought on horseback to the girl's house. Here he is taken by the girl's mother, and if young is set in her lap and fed with sugarcandy and almonds. In some families the betrothal ceremony is performed on the booth-consecrating *mándva murt* day, that is three days before the marriage-day. During the time between betrothal and marriage, presents are exchanged ; and on holidays the boy is asked to dine at the girl's house or the girl at the boy's house.

Marriage ceremonies. Three days before the marriage, booth-consecrating *mándva murt* and Ganesh-invoking ceremonies are performed. The day before the marriage at the boy's house the *sákranman* or sweet-curd ceremony is performed. Two big clay pots, one containing 1 cwt. 3 qrs. 4 lbs. and the other 1 cwt. 8 lbs. (5 and 3 *mans*) are filled with curds mixed with sugar and a little clarified butter. An old woman whose husband is alive and who is a relation of the bridegroom stirs the curds with her hand. The family-priest worships the pots, and presents are made to the woman who stirred the curds. Next the priest takes the pots, accompanied with music, to the bride's house and there gets the bride to worship them. The big pot is kept at the bride's house and the little pot is sent to her maternal uncle, and the contents of both pots are distributed among the caste-people. When this is done the priest brings what is called *dahiani* from the bride's house. This *dahiani* consists of a brass dish with two clay pots *kodia*, a letter naming the day and hour of marriage, and a certain amount of cash. After these presents the betrothal cannot be broken. On the wedding-day, shortly before the marriage hour, the bridegroom, his face covered with flower garlands and wearing a long tunic and a silk waistcloth *pitámber*, escorted by the women of his family, goes to the bride's house on horseback in procession. Here, in presence of a company of the bride's friends, he stands at the central square of the marriage-hall, and looking down into a large earthen pan full of water, from their reflection in the water, touches with the point of his sword four saucers hung over his head. He then goes back to his father's house and after two or three hours his friends, setting him on horseback, escort him to the bride. Before the bridegroom's party arrive, the bride, dressed in a headcloth, bodice and loose Musalmán-like trousers, is seated in a closed palanquin or *balai* set in front of the house. The bridegroom, on dismounting, walks seven times round the palanquin, the bride's brother at each turn giving him a cut with an oleander *karena* twig and the women of the family throwing showers of cakes from the windows. He retires, and while mounting his horse and before he is in the saddle, the bride's father comes out, and giving him a present leads him into the marriage-hall. In Káthiáwár, on the morning of the marriage-day, the bride bathes in water drawn from seven wells. She then puts on *chatudi* or Punjab bracelets sent by her maternal uncle. She wears yellow trousers reaching to the knee, and a red robe. The girl keeps her eyes closed throughout the whole day, not opening them until the bridegroom is ushered into the marriage-booth, so that the first object she sees is her intended husband. On the first Monday, Thursday or Friday after the marriage the bride is hid either in her own or in a neighbour's house. The bridegroom comes in state and with the point of his sword touches the outer doors of seven houses and then begins to search for his wife. The time is one of much fun and merriment, the women of the house bantering and taunting the bridegroom, especially when he is long in finding his wife's hiding place. When she is found, the bridegroom leads the bride to the marriage hall, and they sit there combing each other's hair. After a time the women of the party in sport douse the bridegroom with dirty water. Then the couple have to bathe and sit together on a cot and gamble with dice. Fresh clothes are put on instead of the wedding garments, and the marriage ceremonies are over.

Religion.

Except in Káthiáwár, where the land-owning Brahma Kshatris are Vaishnavs of the Vallabhácharya sect, their favourite objects of worship are Shiva and Shakti. Each household has its family goddess or *Kuldevi*, who is held in high respect. It often happens that when a Brahma Kshatri family has left its former home it keeps the old shrine and on special occasions goes to worship at it. Brahma Kshatris observe the Bráhman rules of religious life. Their priests are Gujarát Sárasvat Bráhmans, who eat with them and on that account are considered degraded by good Bráhmans.

Death ceremonies.

When a Brahma Kshatri is on the point of death he is made to give presents to Bráhmans and others, is shaved, bathed, and laid on a part of the floor of the room which has lately been cleaned with a wash of cowdung. After death he is carried to the burning ground, where the ceremonies are the same as those performed by Bráhmans. Contrary to the Gujarát practice of beating only the breast, the Brahma Kshatri women strike the forehead, breast and knees. For thirteen days after a death women weep and beat their breasts thrice a day, at morning, noon and evening. Afterwards they weep and beat their breasts every evening till a year has passed, not even excepting Sundays, Tuesdays or Hindu holidays. During this year of mourning the female relations of the deceased used to eat nothing but millet-bread and pulse, but this custom is being gradually given up. The cloth-water *kapdepáni* ceremony takes place a month and a half after death, when all the deceased's relations, both men and women, meet, and the women sit down and beat their breasts and all of them eat millet-bread, pulse and dates. This custom also is being gradually given up.

Occupation.

Brahma Kshatris are mostly writers by profession, and several hold places of trust and importance in Government service. Some are hereditary district officers *desáis*, others pleaders and money-lenders.

Food.

Though most of the Brahma Kshatris live on vegetables and drink no intoxicating liquors, animal food and spirits are not forbidden, and of late their use has become more general.

BRAHMANS, numbering 1,052,978 (males 549,639, females 503,339) at the Census of 1901, are found all over the Presidency. The term Bráhman is derived from *brahman*, the Supreme Being, and in its earliest sense denoted one who attained to Him. During the Vedic period it came to denote one who knows or repeats the Veda; and later on as the rituals became more complicated, a 'priest'. The earliest instance of it as a class name is the famous *Purusha Sukta*[(1)] hymn, where society is divided into four classes, (1) Bráhmans who "were the mouth" of the Supreme Being, (2) Kshatriyas[(2)] who "were his arms," (3) Vaishyas who "were his thighs" and (4) Shudras who "were born from his feet." The hymn in question is an account of the general cosmogony of the universe. The *Purusha* is regarded as the elemental life-giving force of the world of men and things. This idea is materialized into a cutting up of *Purusha* as a great sacrifice. In addition to the four classes of men mentioned above, many other natural phenomena were produced, as, for instance, the sun from his eye, the sky from his head, and so on. It seems probable that the four *varnas* of the hymn represented a rough classification of a society not yet split up into rigid endogamous castes, just as in medieval England a classification of society was recognized into barons, knights, squires, yeomen, commons and the like. How far the fourfold classification of the hymn was a generally admitted classification of those early times, or was merely a rough and ready classification of the particular hymn-writer, will never be known. It was crystallized by the author of the *Mánavadharmashástra*,[(3)] who merely repeated the imaginative imagery of the *Purusha Sukta* hymn as a definite fact in the origin of the race. He was cognizant of more than fifty different castes (*játi*), many of them functional groups, and these he fitted into the four *varnas* by assuming an elaborate system of hybridization. Unfortunately, though long abandoned by scholars, the Manu tradition of caste origins lingers on among the people with much the same tenacity as the Biblical account of the creation and the assumption of the "day" of that account as a period of 24 hours lingers on among Christians. The very meaning of the word *varna* as originally applied to the four classes is unknown. Its commonest classical meaning—"colour"—has led some writers to assume that under this name we can detect the fair Aryan immigrant's scorn of the darker aboriginal races.

---

(1) Rig Veda X. 90, 12.

(2) The word in the hymn is *Rájanya.*

(3) Mán. I. V. 31.

Others believe that it is connected with the practice of the different classes wearing clothes of different colour,—white for Bráhmans, red for Kshatriyas, yellow for Vaishyas, and black for Shudras. But this latter tradition is clearly an attempt to explain the word in a fanciful and artificial way.

The origin of castes as endogamous groups is therefore obscure and cannot be here discussed in full. Three things are certain, however,—(1) that the rigidity of caste as a matter of heredity was a late development: this will be discussed with reference to Bráhmans below; (2) that individual castes may arise in various ways, most of which may be termed isolation, *e.g.*, isolation in locality, in function or in religious beliefs; and (3) that while cases of the re-uniting of existing endogamous groups are not unknown, and while the boundaries of some of the larger modern castes are still fluid the usual tendency has been for the segregating off of more and more isolated groups. These groups sometimes retain a sense of cohesion with one another and sometimes lose it. The point of these remarks is to lead up to the interesting fact that, more than any other of the early castes, the Bráhmans have retained their cohesion. Though now broken up into territorial and minor groups, the caste is possessed of considerable solidarity. A Bráhman is a Bráhman everywhere, and would support his castefellows in any social matter though separated from them by colour, sect, customs and language.

To return to the first of the three facts mentioned in the last paragraph, we know that the kernel of the modern caste system, namely, its inflexible hereditary character, did not develop until late. Once a Kshatriya always a Kshatriya was not by any means the case. We find numerous instances as late as the *Mahábhárata* and *Puránic* period of Kshatriyas and persons of the lower classes becoming Bráhmans, and of Bráhmans marrying women of Kshatriya and even lower classes. Thus we find that the descendants of Garga, although Kshatriyas by birth, became Bráhmans.(1) Vishvámitra, by the force of his austerities, became a Bráhman. From Ajámidha, a Kshatriya, sprang Kanva, from whose son Medhátiti the Kánváyana Bráhmans descended. The great sage Vasishtha was born of the womb of a harlot, but became a Bráhman by religious austerities. Vyása, the celebrated author of the great Hindu epic *Mahábhárat*, was born of a fisher-woman, and Parásara of a Chándál woman. The two sons

(1) Vishnu Purán.

of Nábhágarishtha who were Vaishyas attained to the state of Bráhmans.

Later still, in comparatively modern times, there are instances of the creation of certain classes of Bráhmans. "Thus in Partábgarh there is a legend current that the celebrated Oudh chieftain Mánik Chand created Bráhmans wholesale out of various Kurmis, Ahirs and Bhars. A similar case occurred in Fatehpur. In Unáo, again, a story is told of Rája Tilok Chand, that one day while hunting he was very thirsty, and having no attendant he asked a Lodha, who was present there, to fetch him some water, which he brought in his own drinking vessel. The Rája after drinking the water discovered that the owner of the vessel was a low-caste man, and so he asked him to call himself a Bráhman under the title of Páthak of Amtara, as he was watching the mango (*ám*) trees. This title still remains with his descendants, who are acknowledged as Bráhmans. Sir J. Malcom in Central India found many low-caste female slaves in Bráhman houses, the owners of which had treated them as belonging to their own caste."(1)

Again, it has been clearly shown by Mr. D. R. Bhandarkar that members from foreign tribes such as the Abhirás, Magás, Gurjarás, etc., have been absorbed into the Bráhman caste and that the Bráhman castes Maga or Bhojak, Nágar, Karháda, Havik, etc., are of partly foreign origin.(2)

In this connection it is also to be remembered that, according to all Hindu law-givers, the degradation caused by mixture of castes can be washed out in a certain number of generations. According to Manu if a male begotten of a Bráhman by a Shudra female, that is a Parásava, marries a female of the same caste possessing excellent moral character and virtues, the offspring attains to the status of Bráhman in seven generations. Others hold that if the daughter of a Bráhman from a Shudra woman marries a Bráhman, and her daughter again marries a Bráhman, and so on for seven generations, the offspring is elevated to the Bráhman status. In the same way the offspring of a Bráhman from a Vaishya woman regains the status in five generations, and that of a Bráhman from Kshatriya in three. Yájnavalkya also says that the elevation of caste occurs in the fifth or seventh generation.

---

(1) Crooke's Tribes and Castes of the North-Western Provinces and Oudh. Volume II, p. 145.

(2) Foreign Elements in the Hindu Population. Reprinted from the Indian Antiquary, Bombay, 1910.

The above remarks clearly show that originally a man who attained to a certain social and moral status was designated a Bráhman. In the post-Vedic period, when religious rituals became more and more complicated, it was found necessary to have a special class of men trained to conduct them, and the term Bráhman tended to be restricted to the professionals to whom this function was assigned, whatever their origin. The Bráhmans are thus of mixed origin and cannot lay claim to pure Aryan blood. Gradually as the descendants of the original Aryan and other later immigrants spread over the peninsula, in other words, as the whole continent became opened up, two main territorial groups of Bráhmans came to be recognized : (1) Gaud or those to the north and (2) Dravid or those to the south of the Vindhya range. And out of each of these rough territorial groups five other sub-groups were classified, although this fivefold classification was probably never more than artificial. The classification was as follows :—

(I) *Gaud* :—Sárasvat, Kányakubja, Gaud, Utkal, Mithil.

(II) *Dravid* :—Maháráshtra, Andhra or Telugu, Dravid, Karnátak, Gurjar.

The Bráhmans of the Bombay Presidency mainly belong to four groups : (1) Gurjar, (2) Maháráshtra, (3) Sárasvat and (4) Karnátak.

Members of other groups are also found, but they are immigrants. *Theoretically* the above divisions are of no importance. Marriages can take place between any Bráhmans who follow the same Veda and belong to the same *shákha* and claim different *gotras*. Diversity of language and of local practices has, however, imposed further restrictions, and the varying social importance of local groups has led to minute sub-division, which may or may not be supported by the religious heads of the community. So long as the ritual remains unaltered a difference in Veda or *shákha* is a final bar, but social position is continually changing and new groups are formed and small groups are absorbed according to the ceaseless changes of public opinion. Education is rapidly becoming an important factor ; and there are signs that the desire for literate brides may lead to the gradual disregard of subcaste distinctions.

GURJAR or GUJARATI BRAHMANS consist of ninety-three endogamous divisions. A list of these (with the sub-divisions where they exist) is given below :—

1. **Agarwál.**
2. **Agarsindhwál.**
3. **Akshmangal.**
4. **Anávala** (2 sub-divisions).

5. Anodhia.
6. Audich (29 sub-divisions).
7. Ashpura.
8. Balam or Valam.
9. Bhalvi.
10. Bhárgav (4 sub-divisions).
11. Bharthana.
12. Bhukania.
13. Borsáda.
14. Chaun.
15. Chovisa or Chorisa (2 divisions).
16. Dadhich or Dadhichi.
17. Dahema or Dayama.
18. Dareda.
19. Deshawál.
20. Gadiali.
21. Gangáputra.
22. Garoda.
23. Gayáwál.
24. Godhwál or Gorwál.
25. Girnára (5 sub-divisions).
26. Godmálvi.
27. Ghogari.
28. Gomitra.
29. Gomtiwál.
30. Gujali.
31. Gurjar.
32. „ Gauda or Ghoda.
33. Guru.
34. Harsolia or Harsola.
35. Indhvál or Idhavál.
36. Jamu or Jambuvant.
37. Jhárola.
38. Kalinga.
39. Khandolia.
40. Kapil or Kapol.
41. Karbelia.
42. Karkhelia.
43. Khadáyata.
44. Khedawál or Khedwa (3 sub-divisions).
45. Lalat.
46. Madhyáchal.
47. Malikwál.
48. Mewáda (5 sub-divisions).
49. Modh (9 sub-divisions).
50. Madhmaitra.
51. Motála.
52. Nágar (18 sub-divisions).
53. Nandrána or Nandraina.
54. Narsignpura or Narsigpura.
55. Nardik.
56. Namal.
57. Nandora or Nandodra.
58. Nandhána.
59. Napal.
60. Oswál.
61. Paliwál or Palewál.
62. Panjora or Pangora.
63. Parja or Parásar (2 sub-divisions).
64. Parsolia.
65. Porwál or Porwád.
66. Pretevál.
67. Pundwál.
68. Pushkarna or Pokharna.
69. Puwáwál.
70. Rajwál or Rangwál.
71. Raíkula.
72. Raipura.
73. Raisthala.
74. Ráyakwál (2 divisions).
75. Rodhwál or Rotwál.
76. Sáchora (2 sub-divisions).
77. Sanodhra.
78. Sanothia.
79. Sanodia or Sanáth or Sanáola.
80. Sarvaria.
81. Sárasvat.
82. Sevak.
83. Sindhwál.
84. Shrigaud (10 sub-divisons).

85. Shrimáli (5 sub-divisions).
85A. Sonpura or Sompura.
86. Sorathia.
87. Tangmodia.
88. Tapodhan.
89. Udámbara (3 sub-divisions).
90. Vadádra or Valandra.
91. Vainsh Vadhra.
92. Váyada.
93. Yajnikval.

List of sub-divisions included in the above scheme:—

Anávala.

1. Proper or Bhátela.
2. Sajodra or Saghodia.

Audich.

1. Achárya.
2. Barad.
3. Bávisa.
   Bhavsárgor.
   Darbhia or Kayatia or Karatia.
   Káthigor.
   Koligor.
   Khatrigor.
   Luhárgor.
4. Motináth.
5. Maru or Márvádi.
   Mochigor.
6. Pardeshvari.
   Rájgor.
   Sáigor or Darjigor.
7. Sahasra or Sahasravadi.
   A. Ahmedábádi.
   B. Sidhpuri.
   C. Sihori.
   (a) Gohilwádi.
   (b) Jadhia.
   (c) Kharedi.
   (d) Proper.
   (e) Simaria.
   (f) Talagia.
   (g) Unevál.
   (i) Charia.
   (ii) Malharia.
   Tolakia.
8. Vanjhágor.

Bhárgav.

1. Bharuchi.
2. Dasa.
3. Ramreha.
4. Visa.

Chovisa.

1. Motha.
2. Nána.

Girnára.

1. Baradi proper.
2. Chorwádi.
3. Dámodarji.
4. Madhavpura.
5. Sankhi Bardai.

Khedawál or Khedwa.

1. Báj proper.
2. „ Darmaria.
3. Bhitra.

Mewáda.

1. Bhát.
2. Chorási.
3. Rahduri.
4. Ráwal.
5. Tarvádi or Tiwári or Trawádi or Triwádi.

Modh.

1. Agyána or Ayara or Agarsa.
2. Chaturvedi.
3. Dhinoja.
4. Jethimal.
5. Khichadya.
6. Tandalya.
7. Tangalia.
8. Tripala.
9. Trivedi.

Nágar.

1. Bárot.
2. Chitroda proper.
3. „ Bárad.
4. Krashnora proper.
5. „ Bárad.
6. Prashnora proper.
7. „ Bárad.
8. Sáthodra proper.
9. „ Bhikshuk.
10. Sáthodra Bárad.
11. Vadnágra proper.
12. „ Bhikshuk
13. „ Dungarpura.
14. „ Bárad.
15. Visnagra proper.
16. „ Ahmedábádi.
17. „ Bhikshuk.
18. „ Bárad.

Parja.

1. Proper.
2. Patania.

Rayakval.

1. Motha.
2. Nána.

Sáchora.

1. Dasa.
2. Visa.

Sárasvat.

1. Sorathia.
2. Sindhava.
   (1) Cutchi.
   (2) Halái.
   (3) Goghari.
   (4) Broachi.

Shrigaud.

1. Juna
2. Khambáti.
3. Kharola.
4. Málvi.
5. Medatvál or Metwál.
6. Nava.
7. Parvalia.
8. Tamboli.
9. Trivedi.
10. Verola.

Shrimáli.

1. Aboti.
2. Bhojak.
3. Daskoshi.
4. Sámvedi.
5. Yajurvedi.

Udámbar.

1. Abhuankar.
2. Lád.
3. Potachor.

Of the above divisions many have their counterparts in the sub-divisions of other large functional castes. A list of these and of other sub-divisions of this nature common to many castes, with the castes in which they are found, is given below :—

Name of sub-division.	Castes in which found.
1. Agarvál	.. Bráhman, Vánia.
2. Ahmedábádi	.. Ghánchi, Mochi, Káchhia.
3. Broachi	.. Khárva, Ghánchi.
4. Champáneri	.. Ghánchi, Kansára.
5. Deshávál (Desávál)	.. Bráhman, Vánia.
6. Gujar	.. Darji, Soni, Sutár, Cháran, Dhed, Kumbhár, Vánia.
7. Harsola	.. Bráhman, Vánia.
8. Jhárola	.. Do.
9. Káchela or Parjia	.. Luhár, Soni, Cháran, Bráhman.
10. Khadáyata	.. Bráhman, Vánia
11. Kapol	.. Do.
12. Khambáti	.. Luhár, Mochi, Kumbhár, Káchhia, Khárva.
13. Lád	.. Vánia, Kumbhár.
14. Maru	.. Darji, Kansára, Soni, Suthár, Cháran, Dhed.
15. Meváda	.. Bráhman, Vánia, Soni, Suthár.
16. Modh	.. Bráhman, Vánia, Ghánchi.
17. Nágar	.. Bráhman, Vánia.
18. Nandora	.. Do.
19. Osvál	.. Do.
20. Palivál (Palevál)	.. Do.
21. Patni	.. Ghánchi, Dhed, Soni.
22. Porvád (Porvál)	.. Bráhman, Vánia.
23. Rámdeshi	.. Bhávsar, Darji.

Name of sub-division.	Castes in which found.
24. Shrimáli	..Bráhman, Vánia, Soni.
25. Sihora	..Kansára, Luhár.
26. Sorathia	..Bráhman, Vánia, Kumbhár, Luhár.
27. Surti	..Ghánchi, Luhár, Mochi, Dhed, Khárva.
28. Váyada	..Bráhman, Vánia.

It would appear that most of the above names are of a geographical nature which, as pointed out by the late Mr. A. M. T. Jackson, (1) have their origin in the political jurisdiction of ancient Hindu kings. He has clearly shown in his 'Note on the History of Caste System' that during the days of independent Hindu rule Indian society consisted of a hierarchy of castes, at the head of which stood the Bráhmans and the king, that the royal authority was constantly called in to keep each caste to its proper functions, and to prevent what the law books technically call *varnasankara* or confusion of castes. He wrote :—

"The natural result of this exercise of the royal jurisdiction in caste questions would be the gradual establishment of a body of caste customs ; and if a caste lived in an area so extensive as to be subject to more than one political jurisdiction it would tend to split up into sections whose customs differed in detail owing to the divergent decisions of the kings to whom it was subject. Thus the customs of the Bráhmans of Kosala would differ in detail from those of the Bráhmans of Magadha, and so on. Now, the political condition of ancient India was such as to favour in a high degree this splitting up of the original caste, for, as far back as our knowledge goes, we find the country divided into small tribal kingdoms. Megasthenes (B.C. 300), as reported by Arrian, had before him a list of 118 of these, covering the whole area of India. The Buddhist scriptures show us the same state of things existing at an earlier date (*see* Oldenberg's Buddha, 1897, Exc. 1, and Rhys David's Buddhist India) and we can follow it still further back as far as the Rigveda itself (*see* Zimmer, Alt Indisches Leben). As Prof. Macdonell says (Sanskrit Literature, 157-8) : '.... the Vedic Aryans were split up into numerous tribes, which, though conscious of their unity in race, language and religion, had no political cohesion. They occasionally formed coalitions it is true, but were just as often at war with one another. The tribe, in fact, was the political unit, organised much in the same way as the Afghans are at the present day, or the Germans were in the time of Tacitus.' Each

(1) Journal and Proceedings, Asiatic Society of Bengal (New Series), Vol. III. No. 7, 1907, pp. 509-515.

tribe, being under a different king, would tend to diverge from all the others in the matter of caste customs, owing to the different jurisdiction to which it was subject. The tribal kingdoms did not lose their identity even if they were conquered and incorporated into larger empires, for it was the Indian custom to place on the throne of a conquered province a member of the old royal family. For instance, Manu says (VII. 201-3, Buhler's translation): When he has gained victory, let him duly worship the gods, and honour righteous Bráhmans, let him grant exemptions, and let him cause promises of safety to be proclaimed. But, having fully ascertained the wishes of all the (conquered), let him place there a relation of the (vanquished ruler on the throne) and let him impose his conditions. Let him make authoritative the lawful (customs) of the (inhabitants), just as they are stated (to be), and let him honour the (new king) and his chief servants with precious gifts.' Similarly the Vishnu Smriti says (III 47-9, Jolly's translation): 'A king having conquered the capital of his foe, should invest there a prince of the royal race of that country with the royal dignity. Let him not extirpate the royal descent.' The passage from Manu, in particular, shows most clearly that the jurisdiction in caste questions remained unaffected by foreign conquest.

" But it may be asked, if the multiplication of castes dates back as far as the days of the old tribal kingdoms, how is it that so few of the existing sub-castes are mentioned in Indian literature? The answer is that the name of the sub-caste is used only when it has to be distinguished from another sub-caste. Thus, a writer living at Kanauj naturally speaks of a Kanaujiya Bráhman as a Bráhman simply, just as a writer in England might speak of an attorney as a lawyer, while a writer in Scotland might use the same word for a 'writer to the signet.' In the Census Reports it is often found that portion of a sub-caste, which is still settled in its original home, returns itself under the caste name only, *e.g.*, as Bráhman only or as Banya only, without giving the sub-caste name at all, so that it might seem as if the sub-caste did not exist at all in the very place which is known to be its chief centre.

" It will be noticed that, while some sub-castes take their names from the kingdom, others take it from that of the capital city. The latter is especially common in the case of the trading and artisan classes.

" Another means of testing the correctness of the theory put forward in this paper, as to the jurisdictional factor in the history of caste, is to look for sets of sub-castes bearing the same geographical names. Each of the old tribal kingdoms would naturally have had its own section of Bráhmans, traders, carpenters, etc., and we should expect to find traces of these complete sets of castes surviving at the present day. We do, in fact, find such traces, though in many cases the sub-castes are now named from cities which are known to have been founded after the arrival of the Muhammadans in India. This may be due either to the fact that the caste organization in these cases is really of later origin, due to the imitation of the higher classes by the lower ; or to the jurisdiction over caste offences having passed, on the fall of the Hindu kings, to the craft gilds, who naturally made their principal seats in the largest cities, and were quite ready to migrate from an old capital to a new one, whose name they would then adopt as their own. Thus in Gujarát we find castes with Ahmedábádi and Surati sub-divisions, though these two cities did not exist before the 15th century."

Of the remaining groups some are immigrants from Northern India, while others claim descent from holy seers, or are connected by tradition with some holy place chosen in early times by Aryan settlers from Upper India. Except Anávalás, who are all theoretically laymen or *grahastha*, each of these divisions is theoretically either entirely priestly, that is *bhikshuka*, or contains two classes, *bhikshuka* and *grahastha*.[1] Except Bhárgavs, Nágars and a few other Bráhmans who have among them families believing in one of the other Vedas, all Gujaráti Bráhmans are generally followers of the Yajurveda. Each division includes from five to twenty-five exogamous *gotras* or family stocks, each stock theoretically claiming descent on the male side from one of the *rishis* or seers. Except among Nágars, religious and lay families, if not of the same stock, may intermarry. A man's position as priest or layman is hereditary and is not affected by his actual business or profession, being purely theoretical and having no basis in present-day fact.

Except the fair and regular featured Nágars and Bhárgavs, most Gujarát Bráhmans, compared with the trading and other high caste Hindus, are somewhat dark, rough-featured and strongly made. Except in Cutch, where some men wear long flowing Rajput-like whiskers, and except some who in fulfilment of a vow allow the hair on the head and face to remain uncut for a few months

(1) Originally the life of a Bráhman was divided into four ásrams (periods or orders) : (1) *Brahmacárin* or student of the Vedás, (2) *Grihastha* or householder, (3) *Vánaprastha* or dweller in a hermitage in the woods, and (4) *Bhikshuka* or *Sanyásin*, religious medicant or abandoner of wordly concerns. *Bhikshuka* in the sense of priestly is not classical.

or a year, Bráhmans as a rule retain the hair of the head only over a space that could be covered by a cow's hoof. This hair is generally long and tied in a knot from behind, especially when engaged in religious worship. Women have their forehead marked with a circular *kanku* (red powder) dot; the men's forehead is marked with a sandal or *kanku* circle or two or three horizontal lines.[1]

Unlike Vániás who are always amply and cleanly clad, the every-day dress of most Bráhmans is little more than a turban and a waist and shoulder cloth, and the every-day dress of most of the women is simple and cheap. Still all have some store of good clothes; the man a rich turban and silk dining dress, the women at least two good robes, one of them of silk. Compared with other high caste Hindus, the men have few ornaments. But the women have nearly as large a store of jewels as the women of any other caste.

All Gujarát Bráhmans, except a few who belong to the Svámi-náráyan sect, are followers of Shiva. Their social and religious customs are chiefly ruled by the Mayukh, the Mitákshara and the Dharma and Nirnaya Sindhu. Of the sixteen[2] Vedic *sanskárs* or sacraments, Gujarát Bráhmans observe only four at their proper time: *Simanta*[3] or parting of the hair at pregnancy, *Upanayana* or thread girding, *Viváha* or marriage, and *Svargárohana* or funeral ceremonies, literally "heaven-climbing," some of the remaining being observed along with one or other of these, some being not performed at all.

Marriages are prohibited between *sapindas* and between members belonging to the same *gotra* and *pravara*. *Sapindas*[4] are those who are within five degrees of affinity on the side of the mother and seven on that of the father. The person himself constitutes one of these degrees; that is to say, two persons stand to each other in the *sapinda* relationship if their common ancestor, being a male, is not further removed from either of them than six degrees, or, being a female, four degrees. The *pravara*, also called *ársheya*, are those sacrificial fires which several *gotras*[5] had in common. So persons of those *gotras* which

---

(1) Generally speaking worshippers of Shiva use horizontal and worshippers of Vishnu vertical marks.

(2) Some authorities make 12 only; others 40.

(3) Also *Simantak* or *Simantonáyana*.

(4) *Sapinda*, lit. having the same *pinda*. The *pinda* was the ball of flour or rice offered to the Manes in the *shráddha* ceremony.

(5) *Gotra* means literally a cow-pen, and hence any enclosure; *pravara* excellent, chief, and hence of the founder of a race; *ársheya* of or belonging to a *rishi*. The sense of sacrificial fire is not classical.

had a common *pravara* cannot intermarry. Marriage with a father's sister's, mother's sister's or mother's brother's daughter is not allowed. A man may marry his deceased's wife's sister. Except among Nágars whose girls are seldom married before they are thirteen, Gujarát Bráhmans generally marry their girls between seven and eleven irrespective of the bridegroom's age. Besides a dowry the bridegroom receives presents with his wife. In regard to the dowry, the practice among most divisions of Bráhmans is fixed. Except among some degraded Bráhmans, widow marriage is not allowed. Divorce is strictly prohibited. Polygamy is permissible, but polyandry is unknown.

ANAVALAS, also known as Mástáns and Bháthelás, numbering 30,325 (males 16,036, females 14,289) at the Census of 1901, are found in the Surat district and the neighbouring Baroda territory. They are the best cultivators of south Gujarát. The name Anávala is derived from Anával, a Gáikwár village about forty miles east of Surat, famous for its hot spring. The origin of the names Mástán and Bháthela is uncertain. Mástán, according to one account, means proud or overbearing, a meaning which agrees well with the character of the former revenue farmers and village managers of this class. According to another account, Mástán is a shortened form of Mahásthán or Great Place, a name supposed to be the record of some former settlements of the tribe. But it probably means the chief community of the south Gujarát as such phrases as Soni Mástán the goldsmith community, and Khadáyata Mástán the Váni community, are in common local use. Of the term Bháthela two explanations are offered; one would connect it with the tribe of Bháts, the other would from *bhát* rice, translate it rice-man, a name well deserved by the Anávalás, the most successful rice-growers of south Gujarát. But besides the difference in letters, the name Bháthela is always considered disrespectful. It was probably given by some of the later Bráhman settlers from North India and seems to be a corruption of Bhrashthela or Fallen. According to local tradition, Ráma on his return from the conquest of Ceylon halted at a place called Pátarváda in the hills of Bánsda, about forty-five miles south-east of Surat. Determining to hold a sacrifice, he required the services of a large body of priests. He searched the country round, and failing to find priests enough, collected eighteen thousand of the hill-tribes and made them Bráhmans. The legend that certain classes were made Bráhmans by Ráma, Krishna and other heroes and demigods is found in all parts of India. The usual explanation is that in early ages when the greater part of the continent south of the Vindhya mountain was under forest, bands of Bráhmanic Hindus, pressing southwards, ousted the earlier tribes from their forest clearings and established a more regular mode of life and tillage. In later times fresh bodies of Bráhmans, bringing with them from the north a more elaborate social and religious system, found the descendants of the early settlers opposed to them in many points of faith and practice. Unable to deny their claim to be Bráhmans, the newcomers, by the device of some local legend, strove to show that the original settlers were Bráhmans of a lower order than themselves.(1) In the present case it seems probable that the founders of the class were Bráhmans who gathered round some early settler who had chosen the Anávala hot springs as the place of his hermitage. That Anávala Bráhmans are the earliest Bráhman settlers in south Gujarát is supported by the fact that, unlike other Bráhmans, the whole body of the Anávalás are laymen or *grahasths*, and that it was under their management the south of Gujarát was redeemed from forest and brought under tillage.

Almost all Anávala Bráhmans worship Shiva. But as a class they are lax in religious observances and careless in enforcing caste rules. Though obstinate and somewhat rough and quarrelsome, they are a contented and orderly community, enterprising, friends to education, hospitable and liberal. Fifty years ago almost all were peasants, and though tillage is still the occupation of most, a considerable number learning to read and write have become village accountants and schoolmasters. Some have become lawyers and others traders in articles of food, and some entering Government service, have risen to posts of trust and responsibility. Socially, Anávala Bráhmans are divided into an upper or *desái* class, the original colonists of south Surat, afterwards revenue farmers and superintendents and still holders of grants of money and land, and a lower or *bháthela* class, the ordinary cultivators. Before and for some years after the introduction of British rule, as farmers of land revenue and as village managers the *desáis* enjoyed considerable power and wealth, claiming the rank of superior landlords, with the titles of *zamindárs* and *tálukdárs*, and possessing households of as many as four hundred dependants. Under cover of their office they levied taxes on their own behalf, and for a time the bulk of the peasants were practically

(1) However, the instances given above of persons of other *varnas* becoming Bráhmans, and the trenchant arguments of Mr. Bhandarkar (op. cit.) showing that many Bráhman groups are not Aryans at all but Shakás, Gurjarás, etc., must not be lost sight of.

their tenants-at-will or their bondsmen. The gradual extinction of the practice of farming the land revenue (A. D. 1803—1812), and the establishment of the mass of cultivators as direct holders from Government, took away from the *desáis* the source of much of their wealth. Many of them are said to have sunk into poverty, and, falling into the hands of money-lenders, have been forced to mortgage their lands and houses.

In spite of these changes a marked social distinction is still maintained between the representatives of the *desái* families and the ordinary peasants or *bháthelás* and among the whole community three houses still receive special respect as *pedhiválás* or men of family. Though the large establishments of *hális*(1) or farm-slaves are now much reduced, a few well-to-do *desái* families still leave to their dependants the heavier parts of field work. They eat with all the members of their caste, but object to marrying their daughters into any except *desái* families. Successful men among the lower class of *desáis* and the richer *bháthelás*, anxious to improve their social position, try hard to marry their daughters into rich *desái* families. This rivalry for the hands of men of good family has led to some unusual practices. Polygamy is not uncommon. A *desái* who finds himself in difficulties marries another wife, receiving from the bride's father money enough to enable him to pay off his debts. Another result of the rivalry is that expenses consequent upon marriage such as payments in honour of the bride being sent to her husband's house, in honour of pregnancy, of the birth of a child, and on other occasions, are made not by the husband but by the wife's father. So heavy are these charges and such large sums are required as marriage portions, that among the *desáis* some families, where daughters have been numerous, have fallen into debt and been forced to mortgage their lands and houses. In other cases, after the marriage ceremony has been performed, fathers have been unable to meet the expense of sending their daughters to their husband's houses. Cases have occurred in which, for this reason, girls have remained at their father's house till they have reached the age of eighteen or twenty. Under these circumstances the birth of a girl in a *desái's* family is looked on as a calamity.

Free from such special expenses, the position of the ordinary *bháthela* peasants has improved under British rule. Though less frugal and hardworking than the Kaira Kanbis, they are successful

---

(1) The *hális* of Gujarát are life-servants. Their status differs in practice little from that of slaves. They are maintained not only by Anávla Bráhmans but by Sunni Bohrás and other well-to-do landlords.

cultivators. In the best Surat villages the largest holdings, the richest crops, the finest cattle, and the best built houses belong to Bháthelás. It was reported that during ten years A.D. 1886—1896 important changes were taking place in respect to marriage customs. Nearly 300 families had bound themselves to reduce marriage expenses, to stop polygamy and to marry their girls among themselves without reference to *kul* or family. The movement was so successful that most of the *desáis* did not at that time get large sums of money on account of their son's marriages.(1)

AUDICHYA or Audich Bráhmans, numbering 178,254 (male 91,753, females 86,501) in the Census of 1901, are found all over Gujarát. According to the local saying all Audichyás are seers, *Audichya sarv Rushiya.* The name Audichya or Northerner shows that they entered Gujarát from Upper India. According to their caste traditions they were invited to Gujarát by Mularája, king of Anahilaváda (A.D. 961—996), to help him in holding a sacrifice. When the sacrifice was over, the king offered them presents and grants of land to induce them to stay in his country. Some agreed, and others at first refused till they were persuaded by the grant of a spot of special holiness at the mouth of the Mahi. Those who first agreed were a thousand strong and so became known as the Sahasra or Thousand Audichyas ; those who first refused were, because they formed a band or *toli,* known as Tolakia Audichyas. The Sahasrás are again divided into Sihorás and Siddhapurás from the towns of Sihor near Bhávnagar in east Káthiáwár and of Siddhpur near Mehsána in north Gujarát, which Mularája is said to have bestowed on their ancestor.

Most Audich Bráhmans live on alms ; a few of them are cultivators ; the rest are cooks or family or village-priests, and of late years members of clerical professions. Many are particularly successful as exorcists, fortune-tellers and magicians. A few in Cutch are horsebrokers *dháraks.* The question of the amount of dishonour that attaches to a Bráhman who acts as family priest to low-caste Hindus has caused dispute and division among the Audichyas. In north Gujarát the practice is held so degrading that those who follow it have been excommunicated ; but in south Gujarát the practice is allowed. In the northern districts family priests excommunicated for serving low-caste people have given rise to several sub-divisions. Of these the chief are Kanbi-gors(2) who serve cultivators, Darji-gors who serve tailors, Gandhrap-

(1) Bombay Gazetteer, Volume IX, Part I, pp. 4-6.

(2) The termination *gor* is probably a corruption of *guru.*

gors who serve musicians, Hajam-gors who serve barbers, Koli-gors who serve Kolis, and Mochi-gors who serve shoemakers.

A special branch of cultivating Audichyas is settled in Vágad in Cutch. This branch, because they carry cooked food to the fields, smoke the *hookáh* and allow widow marriage, are held degraded and treated as out-castes. Still they are allowed to give their daughters to Audichya Bráhmans of Hálávád in Káthiáwár, whose daughters again marry with Dhrángadra Audichyas, and the daughters of Dhrángadra Audichyás with the Audichyás of Viramgám, Ahmedábád and Siddhpur, who are the highest Gujarát representatives of their caste.(1)

BALAMS or VALAMS, numbering 3,082 (1901), including 1,506 males and 1,576 females, take their name from Valam, a town in the Pátan sub-division in the Gáikwár's territory. They are chiefly found in Ahmedábád and Kaira. Most of them are beggars and peasants.

BHARGAVS, numbering 1,564 (1901), including 783 males and 781 females, are chiefly found in Broach and Surat, a few being residents of Mándvi and Kamlej in the vicinity of Surat. They claim descent from Bhrigu Rishi, the reputed founder of Broach.(2) They have the divisions *Dasa* and *Visa*,(3) who do not intermarry. Marriages are also prohibited between the Broach and Mándvi Bhárgavs.

BHOJAKS, also known as Magas,(4) are found in considerable numbers in Káthiáwár and Cutch. They were originally Shrimáli Bráhmans who adopted the Jain faith for a living. They are called Bhojaks or eaters because they dine with Osvál Vániás. Bhojaks act as priests to the Jains and eat with them. They allow widow marriage.

BORSADAS, numbering 1,087 (1901), including 542 males and 545 females, are found chiefly in the Kaira district. They take their name from the town of Borsad. According to the local tradition

---

(1) Bombay Gazetteer, Vol. IX, Part I, pp. 6-7.

(2) It is, however, probable that *Bharukaccha* is the earliest spelling of Broach; and that *Bhrigukaccha* and the legend referred to in the text are due to later false analogy.

(3) These terms, like the sub-division names given above, are common to several Váni sub-castes also.

(4) Bhandarkar (op. cit. pp. 11 ff.) identifies the *Magas* with the Iranian Magi, their reputed ancestor *Jarasástu* with Zoroaster (*Jaratusta*), and the girdle which they wore, and called *avyanga* with the Avestan word *Aiwyáonghán*. They were sun worshippers and were imported into North India by a king named Samba to cure him of leprosy by erecting a sun-temple. They came from Sákadvipa, the land of the *Sakás*.

they are descendants of Bhadrasiddha and his followers by women of the Rabári tribe. Another account states that they are called after a certain Varáhsiddha who along with others of the Siddha tribe is said to have settled colonies in this part of Gujarát marking them by the tribal name Siddha, which appears as *Sad* in Vásad, Visad, Borsad, etc. Borsádás are hereditary agriculturists, many of them being headmen of villages.

CHOVISAS, numbering 369 (1901), including 190 males and 179 females, are found in Káthiáwár and Baroda. They have two divisions, *motha* (large) and *nána* (small).

DADHICHAS, named after the sage Dadhichi, numbering 778 (1901), including 420 males and 358 females, are found in Kaira and Broach. They state that originally they belonged to the Audich Sahasra stock, and obtained their present name by settling in the village of Dehvan near Bijápur where there is an *áshram* or hermitage of Dadhichi. Most of the Dadhich Bráhmans are village headmen, money-lenders and cultivators.

DESAVALS, numbering 22 (1901), including 8 males and 14 females, are found chiefly in Surat and Ahmedábád. They take their name from the town of Deesa in Pálanpur and are priests to the Desával Vániás.

GAYAVALS, numbering 35 (1901), including 16 males and 19 females, are an offshoot from the mendicant Bráhmans of Gaya.

GARODAS, numbering 12,899 (males 6,404, females 6,495) in the Census of 1901, are found in all parts of Gujarát. They act as priests to all unclean castes, including Bhangiás in central Gujarát but except Bhangiás in south Gujarát. They claim to be Bráhmans who, according to one account, were degraded because the head of their tribe married the daughter of his religious teacher or *guru*; according to another story, because they agreed to act as priests to the Dhedás; according to a third story, at a sacrifice they ate a piece of the victim; and according to a fourth, they are the descendants of the Bráhman priest who was given to the Dhedás by Siddharája. Their surnames Dave, Joshi, Nágar, Shrimáli and Shukal point to a Bráhman origin, but a few bear the Rajput surnames of Gohel and Gandhiya. Except in the Panch Mahál s, where there are two divisions, *shudh* or pure and the *káyatia* or impure, who eat together but do not intermarry, there are no sub-divisions among Garodás. Girls are generally married before they are twelve. Divorce and widow marriage are allowed. They worship the ordinary

Bráhmanic gods, especially Rám, the basil plant, and Devi, and they keep the Bráhman fasts and holidays. Many are followers of the Rámánandi and Parinámi sects. They go daily to worship Krishna's crown or *mugat* which is placed on the Bhágvat book in their temples. As among Bráhmans a few men called *Shukals* act as their priests. Their dead are burnt. They perform the *shráddha* and hold themselves impure for ten days. As priests of Bhangiás, Dhedás, Chamárs Shenvás and Turis, all of whom style them Bráhmans, they efficiate at marriages and deaths, receiving on each occasion gifts of Rs. 3 or less in cash. Some till, others weave and a few act as tailors to Dhedás. Most of them can read, and a few understand, Sanskrit, reciting and explaining hymns and passages from the Puráns. They eat with Dhedás and join them in any food.(1)

GIRNARAS, numbering 3,674 (1901), including 1,906 males and 1,768 females, are found chiefly in Káthiáwár and Cutch. They have a tradition that they were settled at Girnár by Krishna. According to the *Prabháskhand* they came originally from the foot of the Himálayás. They are Vaishnav temple priests, beggars, traders, money-lenders, cooks and husbandmen. They have the monopoly of the office of priests to pilgrims visiting Girnár and Somnáth Pátan.

GOMTIVALS, numbering 2,201 (males 1,020, females 1,181) in the Census of 1901, are found in Ahmedábád and Rewa Kántha. They take their name from the old city of Gomti among the Barda hills in south-west Káthiáwár. Most of them live on alms.

GUGLIS, numbering 1,025 (1901), including 529 males and 496 females, are found chiefly in Dwárka. They are said to take their name from Gokula sacred to Krishna near Mathura. According to another account they are named after *gugal* or incense, by offering which they succeeded in scaring away a demon who prevented them from settling at Dwárka. Guglis are priests in the temples of Krishna at Bet Dwárka and Dákor. Many of them are servants to the Vallabhácharya Mahárájás.

HARSOLAS, numbering 243 (1901), including 109 males and 134 females, named after Harsol in the Ahmedábád district, are found in Ahmedábád and Surat. Most of them act as family priests to Harsola Vánis.

JAMBUS, numbering 517 (1901), including 259 males and 258 females, named after the town of Jambusar in the Broach district, are found chiefly in Broach and Baroda. They claim descent from

(1) Bombay Gazetteer, Vol. IX, Part I, pp. 344-45.

Yájnavalkya. They appear to have been the first colonists of Jambusar, where copper plate grants show that they were settled as early as the beginning of the fourth century. They are family priests and astrologers.

JHALORAS, numbering 47 (1901), including 27 males and 20 females, take their name from the town of Jhálor in Márwár. Most of them act as family priests to Jhálora Vánis.

KANDOLAS, named after the village of Kandol near Thán in the Jhálávád division of Káthiáwár, numbering 903 (1901), including 479 males and 424 females, are found chiefly in Káthiáwár and Baroda. They act as family priests to Kapol and Sorathia Vánis and as cooks to Rajput chiefs.

KAPILS, numbering 242 (1901), including 113 males and 129 females, are found chiefly in the Broach district. They claim descent from the sage Kapil and are mostly cultivators.

KHADAYATAS, numbering 243 (1901), including 135 males and 108 females, are found principally in Kaira. They take their name from Khadát, a village near Prántij in Ahmedábád. They serve as family priests to Khadáyata Vánis from whom only they take gifts.

KHEDAVALS, numbering 15,887 (males 8,181, females 7,706) in the Census of 1901, are found in large numbers in Kaira, and take their name from Kheda or Kaira, the headquarters of the Kaira district. Their chief settlement is at Umreth in the Anand subdivision of the Kaira district. According to their tradition they are descended from a band of Tripravari and Panchpravari Bráhmans, who, under the lead of Shankar Joshi and Shod Dave, moved from Shrirangapatam in Mysore and settled in Khed during the reign of a certain Mordhvaj, a Rajput of the lunar stock. The truth of this story is supported by the fact that Khedáváls are still connected with Shrirangapatam. Khedávál Bráhmans are divided into outsiders *báj* and insiders *bhitra*. The origin of the division is said to have been that the Kaira chief, anxious to have a son, once offered them gifts. The greater number, refusing his gifts, left the town and settled outside in twenty four villages, all ending in *li*, like Ghumteli, Khadáli, Saudli and Sureli. The few who accepted gifts settled in the town and became known as *bhitra* or insiders. Unlike most Gujarát Bráhmans, Khedáváls are robust, hardworking, thrifty and pushing, and have a special name for stinginess. Their women do not join marriage processions or caste dinners. They wear a necklace *chitak* and earrings *káp* of the same shape as those worn by Deccani Bráhman women, and, like them, their widows dress in white. The insiders or *bhitrás*, of whom there are but few, are as a class poor, most of them with the name Dave, acting as family priests to the Lád Vániás, to whom, according to the proverb, the Dave is as a sharp axe to a dry tree. The *báj* or outsiders boast that they never take presents and, as large landholders, money-lenders and traders, are most of them extremely well off. Keeping their connection with Kaira, many of them, as jewellers and traders, are settled in Madras, Bengal and other parts of India. In Mahi Kántha, Khedávâls of both divisions are found. Though not at present connected with them, the Mahi Kántha Khedávál community is, according to their tradition, of the same stock as the Khedávál Bráhmans of Kaira. At the same time they trace their name to Khed Bráhman in the Idar State, not to the town of Kheda.(1)

MEVADAS, numbering 23,776 (males 11,567, females 12,209) at the Census of 1901, are found throughout Gujarát. They take their name from Mewár in Rájputána. They have five endogamous sub-divisions. They are mostly beggars, family priests and a few of them peasants. There is a curious custom among the Trivedi Mevádás: before marriage the bridegroom reposes on a cot and the bride applies molasses to the navel of her husband, after which he goes to the marriage hall.

MODHS, numbering 26,281 (males 13,505, females 12,776) at the Census of 1901, are found throughout Gujarát. They are said to take their name from Modera on the banks of the Vatrak river, but this is an extremely unlikely derivation. The word Modh, which is common to other castes also (v. *supra*), is probably an old racial or tribal name. They have nine sub-divisions, of whom the Jethimals are wrestlers in the service of Native States and they permit widow marriage. Except a few peasants, all those of the other sub-divisions are family priests and beggars They are the commonest Bráhmans to be employed for marriages and other ceremonies at the present day, This is probably largely because they have not taken to education to the same extent as the other Bráhman sub-castes. Modh Bráhman officiating priests are usually quite ignorant, and repeat the *mantras* without any idea of their meaning.

MOTALAS, numbering 1,420 (1901), including 701 males and 719 females, are found chiefly in Surat. They take their name from the village Mota, about sixteen miles south-east of Surat. They appear

(1) Bombay Gazetteer, Vol. IX, Part I, pp. 10-11.

to be originally Deshasth Bráhmans, for the following reasons :—They look more like Deshasths than Gujarátis : their family goddess is the Mahálakshmi of Kolhápur ; at the time of marriage and for four days after, the bride keeps her head uncovered and fastens the end of her robe from left to right ; the marriage wristlet is made of wool instead of cotton thread ; and they belong to the Kánva *shákha*. According to one account, they came into Gujarát on account of the cruelties of Malik Káfar (A.D. 1306). Another account puts their arrival in Gujarát somewhat later, and gives as the reason the pressure of the great Durga Devi famine (1396-1408 A.D.). It is stated that they were accompanied by the Jambu and Kapil Bráhmans, all of whom originally belonged to the same stock. This seems probable since the customs of the Motálás, Jambus and Kapils are mostly alike, and a century ago intermarriages took place between the Motálás and Jambu Bráhmans. One peculiar custom among the Motálás is that their marriages take place on the same day every fourth year. They act as family priests only to men of their own caste. The laymen are chiefly engaged as clerks in Government and private offices.

NAGARS,[1] numbering 21,617 (males 11,591, females 10,026) at the Census of 1901, are chiefly found in Surat, Ahmedábád, Cutch, Káthiáwár and Mahi Kántha. There are several traditions current among them about their origin. They all connect them with the Nágs in one way or another. These traditions are of little value as they have no historical foundation, and are merely attempts to explain away the name Nágar by connecting it with the word *Nág* because the former closely approaches the latter in sound. Later discoveries, however, throw a flood of light on this subject. The late Vallabhji Haridat Achárya of Rájkot was fortunate enough to find three MSS. of the *pravarádhyáy* of these Bráhmans. One of these is nearly 200 years old and distinctly states that the *gotras*, *pravars*, etc., which are therein specified are those which were in existence before Samvat 1283, *i.e.*, A.D. 1226. This MS. thus gives a list of thirteen *Sharmans* which were in vogue amongst the Nágar Bráhmans 700 years ago. They are (1) Datta, (2) Gupta, (3) Nand, (4) Ghosh, (5) Sharman, (6) Dás, (7) Varman, (8) Nagadatta, (9) Trát, (10) Bhut, (11) Mitra, (12) Dev and (13) Bhav. To each of these *Sharmans* have been assigned two or more of the *gotras* that are at present prevalent among them. This list is not a fiction, but has a foundation in fact. For no less than three of these *Sharmans* have been traced in the copper-plate grants of the Valabhi kings who ruled

(1) Contributed by Mr. D. R. Bhandarkar, M.A.

over Káthiáwár and North Gujarát from A.D. 509 to 766. They are Mitra, Trát and Datta, and are found appended to the names of Bráhman grantees. That these Bráhmans were Nágars is clearly proved by the fact that they are said to have originally belonged to Anandpur or Anartpur, which are both old names of Vadnagar. Again, the *gotras* mentioned of these Bráhman grantees exactly agree with those assigned in the *pravarádhyáy* to the three *Sharmans* just referred to. There cannot, therefore, be even the shadow of doubt as to these Bráhmans being Nágar. And this shows that the Nágars make their appearance in Káthiáwár and Gujarát for the first time with the Valabhi kings in the sixth century A.D. Now, these *Sharmans* cannot possibly be mere name endings. For in the first place they themselves always follow the name suffixes. Even now at the time of performing religious ceremonies, it is customary to say, *e.g.*, Bhagwánlál Trát and Manishankar Gupta instead of mere Bhagwánlál and Manishankar. The *Sharmans* Trát and Gupta here follow the name suffixes *Lál* and *Shankar*. Secondly while name suffixes like *Lál* and *Shankar* pertain merely to individuals, each *Sharman* was and is the peculiar property of a certain separate group of individuals. There can, therefore, be no doubt that these *Sharmans* are clan indicators. Further, it is worthy of note that out of the thirteen *Sharmans* of the Nágars no less than ten are found as family names among the Káyasths of Bengal. These are : Datta, Gupta, Nandi, Ghosh, Sharma, Dás, Barma, Bhut, Mitra and Deb. This points to a racial identity or affinity between both these castes. The Káyasths of Bengal are, according to traditions, supposed to have come from Kanauj in the time of Adishur. And there can be no doubt that the Nágar Bráhmans also come from the north. The facts that Nágars are found in numbers among the Gurjars of Bulandshahr and that Nágars appear as Nagres among Játs seem to show that both the Nágar Bráhmans and Vániás were not indigenous to Gujarát but came from the north. Again, it is obvious that both these Bráhmans and Vániás are called Nágar obviously because they originally belonged to Nagar, just as the Shrimáli Bráhmans and Vániás were so called because their original habitat was Shrimál or Bhinmal. Though, from the Vadnagar inscription of the Solanki sovereign Kumárpál (1143-1174 A.D.), this place appears to be called Nagar, that was not really its old name, which was Anandpur or Anartpur as attested by the earlier inscriptions. It was when the Nágars were settled in this town that they seem to have given Anandpur the name Nagar. And when Vishnagar was founded and some of the Nágars settled there, the old place came to be called not simply Nagar, but Badá-Nagar, the old Nagar which was sanskritised into Vriddha-Nagar as well as Vat Nagar. There seems to be no reason for Anandpur being called Nagar except the fact that the place from which the Nágars of Gujarát originally emigrated was itself called Nagar. There is abundant evidence to show that various tribes as they migrated southwards brought with them the names of the places and countries which they originally inhabited. So the question is whether there was any town in north India of the name Nagar in olden times. Doubtless there was a town of this name, and it has been mentioned, *e.g.*, by the authors of the *Káshika* who flourished in the seventh century. Further, it deserves to be noticed that the Prashnora, a sub-division of the Nágar Bráhmans, call themselves Ahichhatrás or Ahichhatrajnátiyás. This shows that Nagar was either another name of, or in the close neighbourhood of, Ahichhatra. For, if this had not been so, the Prashnorás and the other Nágar Bráhmans would not have belonged to the same stock, and consequently the former, when they emigrated from Ahichchhatra and came into Gujarát, would have not been admitted to the claim of being called Nágar. Ahichchhatra has been correctly identified by Cunningham with Rámnagar in Bareilly district, United Provinces. It thus appears that Nagar, which was either Ahichchhatra itself or in its close proximity, was the cradle of all the Nágars, including Gurjar Nágars of Bulandshahr, Ját Nágres, and in all likelihood also of the Bengal Káyasths. From Ahichchhatra the latter probably migrated to Kanauj which is to its south and not far off, before they repaired to Bengal and spread themselves there.

Nágars are divided into six main sub-divisions: Chitroda, Krashnora, Prashnora, Sáthodra, Vadnagra including Dungarpura. and Visnagra. None of the sub-divisions intermarry or dine together except that food cooked by Vadnagra Nágars is eaten by all the other classes. Of the six divisions, Sáthodrás, Vadnagrás and Visnagrás are again divided into *Grahasth* or laymen and *Bhikshuk* or priests. Among them there is a further division called Bárads consisting of men who, unable to procure wives in their own communities, have taken wives from other castes and lived apart. Chitrodás and Krashnorás are not found in Gujarát. Prashnorás are found chiefly in Káthiáwár as *vaids* (medical practitioners) and readers of *puráns* (holy books). Sáthodrás, who take their name from Sáthod, about twelve miles from Dahboi, are numerous in Ahmedábád and Kaira as clerks, money-lenders and landholders. Visnagrás, who take their name from Visnagar in Baroda territory, are found chiefly in Ahmedábád, Surat and Baroda territory, as money-lenders, cultivators and servants. Vadnagrás are found all over Gujarát and hold an important position among Bráhmans. They are handsome, intelligent and pushing and have played an important part in the politics of Káthiáwár.

NANDVANAS, numbering 913 (1901), including 443 males and 470 females, are found chiefly in Cutch and Káthiáwár. They claim descent from the sage Nandi who, when officiating at a horse sacrifice, was cursed by Brahma's wife Sávitri. Blighted by this curse his descendants lost all scripture knowledge, but by the kindness of their family goddess Vankal at Viráni in Márwár they regained their knowledge and are now admitted to be priests. They are traders and cultivators.

NANDORAS, numbering 857 (1901), including 456 males and 401 females, are found in Kaira and Rájputána. They take their name from Nádod or Nándod, the capital of Rájpipla. To this class belong the family priests of the Rajput chiefs of Rájpipla and Dharampur. The rest, except a few cultivators, live chiefly on alms.

NAPALS, numbering 227 (1901), including 129 males and 98 females, take their name from Napa, a village in the Borsad sub-division of Kaira. They are chiefly cultivators and say that they originally belonged to the Audich stock.

PALIWALS, numbering 4,785 (1901), including 2,457 males and 2,328 females, are found in Ahmedábád, Cutch and Káthiáwár. They belong to the Kányakubja division of Bráhmans and take their name from Páli, a chief trade centre of Márwár. Some are cultivators but most are traders and merchants.

PARAJIAS, numbering 2,291 (males 1,182, females, 1,109) at the Census of 1901, also called Parásars or Ahir Gors, are found in Cutch and Káthiáwár. They originally belonged to the Audich stock. They take their name from Paraj near Junágad. They are priests of Ahirs and Chárans with whom they eat. They allow widow marriage and are a degraded class.

PUSHKARNAS or POKARNAS, numbering 5,929 (males 3,164, females 2,765) in the Census of 1901, are found in large numbers in Cutch and Káthiáwár. They take their name from the Puskar or Pokar lake about eight miles north-west of Ajmir. They act as family priests to Bhátiás and like their patrons are willing to follow any calling. They are chiefly engaged as husbandmen, confectioners, contractors and clerks. They are followers of Vallabhácharya and their family goddesses are Lakshmiji and Chámunda in Márwár. They sometimes wear the sacred thread, putting it on with little ceremony, generally at a relation's marriage or at some place of pilgrimage. Gujarát Bráhmans do not dine with Pokarnás, who eat cakes and sweet balls (*laddus*) cooked by Bhátiás. On the sixth day after a birth the women of the family, singing as at a marriage, bring a clay horse from the house of the mother's father to her husband's house. At marriages the men dance in the procession and the women sing immodest songs.

RAYAKVALS, numbering 1,589 (1901), including 785 males and 804 females, are found chiefly in Ahmedábád and a few in Baroda, where they have a name as teachers or *shástris*. They take their name from Raika near Dhanduka, about fifty miles from Ahmedábád. They have two sub-divisions, Motha or great and Nána or small. Except a few Ráyakváls engaged in service, the majority support themselves by cultivation and begging.

RAYASTHALAS, chiefly found in Lunáwáda, Pátan and Harsol, are said to have come to Gujarát from Márwár. They take their name from *Ráyasthal* or royal place, that is, dwellers in capital towns. They are mostly beggars.

RUNDWALS, numbering 702 (1901), including 333 males and 369 females, found chiefly in Ahmedábád, are cultivators and beggars.

SACHORAS, numbering 1,347 (1901), including 720 males and 627 females, found chiefly in Cutch and Káthiáwár, take their name from Sáchor in the south of Márwár. They are divided into Visa and Dasa and do not eat food cooked by other Bráhmans. Though some are cooks in the Vallabhácharya temples, beggars and traders, most are cultivators.

SAJODRAS, found chiefly in Broach, take their name from Sajod, a village in the Ankleshvar *táluka* of the Broach district. Tradition asserts that Ráma made them Bráhmans to assist him in the performance of a sacrifice, but their occupation, appearance and customs support the view that they are of the same stock as the Anávalás They are cultivators.

SARASVATS,(1) numbering 6,544 (males 3,267, females 3,277) at the Census of 1901, are found chiefly in Cutch and Káthiáwár. They are split up into two sections (1) Sorathia Sárasvats and (2) Sindhava Sárasvats, who neither eat together nor intermarry.

(1) Based on an article by Mr. A. J. Jetli in the All India Saraswat Quarterly. Vol. I, No. 1.

Sorathia Sárasvats are few in number and are found mostly in Jámnagar and Karáchi. Widow remarriage is permissible among them, but is not popular. They are priests to the Brahma Kshatris.

Sindhava Sárasvats like the Sorathiás, are mainly priests to the Brahma Kshatris, from whom they accept cooked food. They are divided into four sub-sections (1) Cutchis, (2) Haláis, (3) Gogharis and (4) Broach Sárasvats, the first three of which eat together and intermarry. In addition to being priests to Brahma Kshatris they also officiate at the ceremonies of the Lohánás, Káyasths and Depalás. Except among the Broach Sárasvats, widow remarriage is permissible, but not much in favour.

Cutchi Sárasvats, so named from their original home Cutch, are found chiefly in Bombay, Karáchi and Mándvi. They are an enterprising people and take a leading part in the sea-borne trade of Gujarát, Cutch and Káthiáwár.

Halái Sárasvats, coming originally from Hálár in Káthiáwár, are mostly met with at Porbundar, Jámnagar, Khumbalia, Bombay and Karáchi. They are engaged mostly in piece-goods trade, working independently or in service.

Goghari Sárasvats, whose original home was Gogha district, near Bhávnagar, Káthiáwár, are few in number and are chiefly found at Bhávnagar, Junágadh, Bombay and Karáchi. They are priests by profession and are generally poor.

Broach Sárasvats, who form a small community by themselves, are confined mostly to Broach, Surat, Amod, Junágadh, Ahmedábád and Hyderabad (Deccan). They claim the Punjab as their original home, both tradition and their social customs, which resemble those of the Punjab Sárasvats to a considerable extent, supporting this view. The Jetlis, one of the sub-sections of Broach Sárasvats, still worship Jwálámukhi "Flame-mouthed," the renowned deity of the Kángra temple, as their patron goddess. The traditional account of the migration of these Sárasvats from Upper India says that when Akbar the great, the Mughal emperor of Delhi, sent an army to conquer Gujarát in 1572, a number of army officers and soldiers of the Brahma Kshatri caste came to reside permanently in Gujarát. The priests who accompanied these Brahma Kshatris were the ancestors of the Broach Sárasvats. The first place where these Sárasvats settled down is not definitely known but it is believed that Chámpáner, the city now deserted, between Baroda and Godhra, was one of such places. Some of the Jetlis are still known as "Chámpáneria"

After the decline of Chámpáner, these Sárasvats migrated to Broach, which at that time was a great port.

At the time the Sárasvats settled down in Broach, priesthood was their chief, if not sole, vocation. As time went on they accepted private or Government service ; and at the present day there is not a single Sárasvat who is dependant for his livelihood on priesthood alone. While not giving up their right to be the priests of Brahma Kshatris, the Sárasvats, when need arises, engage other Bráhmans as their substitutes to officiate at ceremonies.

Gujarát Sárasvats must not be confused with the Sárasvats of the southern part of the Presidency. Though originally of the same stock they have now nothing in common.

SEVAKS, numbering 377 (1901), including 251 males and 126 females, are ministrants in Vaishnava temples. They are considered degraded.

SHRIGAUDS, also called Godmálvis or Ashtamanglás, numbering 5, 964 (males 3,022, females 2,942) at the Census of 1901, are found all over Gujarát. They belong to one of the five classes of Gaud Bráhmans, who abound in Rájputána. They have ten sub-divisions, most of which are local in origin. They are employed as family priests and doctors.

SHRIMALIS, numbering 17,398 (males 9,263, females 8,135) at the Census of 1901, are found all over Gujarát, Cutch and Káthiáwár. They take their name from Shrimál, about fifty miles west of Mount Abu. They have five sub-divisions. They act as family priests to Jains of the Osvál and Porvád divisions and to Shrimáli Sonis and Vánis.

SOMPURAS, numbering 955 (1901), including 533 males and 422 females, are found chiefly in Káthiáwár. They take their name from Somnáth in South Káthiáwár. They are priests and beggars, the descendants of the priests that used to minister in the famous temple of Somnáth.

SORATHIAS, numbering 34 (1901), including 10 males and 24 females, are found chiefly in Káthiáwár. They are considered degraded, because they eat with their clothes on and do not observe the Bráhman rules of purity. They are labourers, water-bearers and servants.

TAPODHANS, also called Bhaidas, numbering 10,786 (males 5,209, females 5,577) at the Census of 1911, are found all over Gujarát. They are ministrants in Mahádev, Máta and Jain temples. They do not act as family priests, and as they are guilty of the sin of using the offerings made to Mahádev, they are held degraded. Those not engaged in temple service are husbandmen, labourers and a few bricklayers. They allow widow marriage.

UDAMBARAS, numbering 515 (1901), including 230 males and 285 females, found chiefly in Kaira and Panch Maháls, are said to take their name from the sage Udambara. They have three sub-divisions. They are family priests and beggars and a few are cultivators.

UNEVALS, are found chiefly in Baroda and Káthiáwár and are said to take their name from Una, a village in Káthiáwár. Most of them are cultivators and beggars.

VADADRAS, numbering 2,521 (1901), including 1,162 males and 1,359 females, found mostly in Kaira, take their name from Vadad, about fourteen miles north-east of Ahmedábád. They are beggars, husbandmen and money-lenders.

VAYADAS, numbering 21 (1901), including 14 males and 7 females, are found all over Gujarát. They are priests of the Váyada Vánis and are said to have originally come from Bet Island in West Káthiáwár. They take their name from Váyad, a village near Pátan, about forty-four miles north-west of Ahmedábád.

VEDANTS, numbering 386 (1901), including 187 males and 199 females, are found chiefly in Cutch. They claim descent from the sage Vedavyása. According to tradition they are the descendants of two Shrimáli Bráhmans who were outcasted because they dined with Osvál Vánis. Even now Vedánts dine with Vánis and are considered degraded on that account. They are mostly husbandmen, a few being priests and school masters.

MAHARASHTRA BRAHMANS, consist of twelve divisions, (1) Chitpávan, (2) Deshasth, (3) Devarukha, (4) Golak or Govardhan, (5) Javal or Khot, (6) Karháda, (7) Kást, (8) Kirvant or Kramvant, (9) Palshikar, (10) Sámvedi, (11) Saváshe, (12) Tirgul or Trigarth. All of these except Golaks, Javals, Kásts, Palshikars, Savúshes and Tirguls eat together, but do not intermarry. This statement must, however, be qualified in the case of the Palshikar or local Bombay group of Deshasth Bráhmans who have recently established marriage relations with the Deshasth Bráhmans of the Central Provinces and are successfully establishing their claim to be considered Shukla Yajurvedi Deshasth Bráhmans of the Mádhyandin *Shákha*. Poona Deshasths still refuse recognition. Golaks, Kirvants and Tirguls are commonly held to be degraded. Of these the Kirvants are rising to the position of equality with strict Bráhmans, and marriage connections are occasionally formed between them and Chitpávans. As among the Gurjar Bráhmans only the principal *śanskárs* are performed by Maháráshtra Bráhmans. The ceremonies of the different sub-divisions do not differ in any essential detail. Except Javals who eat fish, they do not take animal food. Widow remarriage and divorce are forbidden.

CHITPAVANS,(1) numbering 113,605 (males 58,150, females 55,455) at the Census of 1901, are found in all parts of the Deccan and Konkan. They are also known as Chitpols, Chiplunás and Konkanasths. The names Chitpávan, Chitpol and Chipluna appear to come from the town of Chiplun in Ratnágiri, their original and chief settlement, the old name of which is said to have been Chitpolan. They began to call themselves Konkanasths about 1715 A.D. when Peshwa Bálájí Vishwanáth rose to importance in the Marátha kingdom. Their worship of Parashurám, the slayer of the Kshatriyas and the coloniser of the Konkan, on Parashurám hill close to Chiplun, the fact that they are called *Parashurám srishti* or Parashurám's creation, and the meaning 'pure from the pyre' which the sound of their name suggests, to some extent explain the curious legends of which they are the subjects. According to the Sahyádri Khand, Parashurám was so defiled by the slaughter of the Kshatriyas that Bráhmans refused to perform any ceremonies for him. At that time the bodies of fourteen shipwrecked foreigners happened to be cast ashore by the sea which then washed the foot of the Sahyádri hills. These corpses Parashurám purified by burning them on a funeral pyre or *chita*, restored them to life, taught them Bráhman rites, and made them perform ceremonies to free him from blood guiltiness. Parashurám wished to reward his new priests, and as the Deccan had already been given to Bráhmans he prayed the sea to spare him some of his domain. The sea agreed to retire as far west as Parashurám could shoot an arrow from the crest of the Sahyádris. The arrow was shot and reclaimed a belt of land about thirty miles broad. The banks of the Vashishthi, about forty miles north of Ratnágiri, were set apart for the new Bráhmans, and in memory of the process by which they had been purified they were called Chitpávans and their settlement Chitpolan. After establishing this colony Parashurám retired to Gokarn in North Kanara. Before leaving he told the Bráhmans, if they were ever in trouble, to call on him, and he would come to their aid. After a time, fearing that they might be forgotten, one of the

(1) Mr. D. R. Bhandarkar draws attention to the striking similarity between certain Chitpávan names and the name, of places in Palestine.

Bráhmans feigned death and the rest called on their patron to come to their help. Parashurám appeared, and, disgusted with their deceit and their want of faith, told them that they would lose the power of meeting in council and would become servile. Accordingly they are said to have married Shudra women and become degraded. The historic value of this legend is hard to estimate. The writer of the Sahyádri Khand was hostile to other local Bráhmans as well as to the Chitpávans. He dishonoured the Karháde Bráhmans by a story that they are descended from the bones of a camel which was raised to life by Parashurám. This story, probably, arose from a play on the words *khar* an ass and *hád* a bone. As the two stories are so similar it seems probable that the Chitpávans were called after the old settlement of Chitpolan, and that the resemblance of that word to *chita* a pyre suggested some parts of the legend. At the same time it seems probable that the Chitpávans did not, like the bulk of Konkan Bráhmans, enter the Konkan by land. Their fair complexion, the extent to which they use the Konkan dialect in their homes, and the legend of their arrival as shipwrecked sailors seem to show that they came into the south Konkan from beyond the sea. Whether they were foreigners is doubtful. The legend of the shipwrecked sailors being foreigners or *mlenchhas* is to some extent supported by the low position which the Chitpávans formerly held among Bráhmans and by the commonness among them of the light or grey eyes. The Chitpávans have a tradition that they came from Amba Jogái in the Nizám's country about 100 miles north of Sholápur. They say that they were originally Deshasth and that fourteen Bráhmans of different family-stocks accompanied Parashurám to the Konkan and settled at Chiplun. This does not seem probable as they differ greatly from Deshasths in complexion and features. Until the rise of Báláji Vishwanáth Peshwa, who belonged to this class, the Chitpávans held a low position and were known chiefly as spies or *harkárás*. Even after several generations of power and wealth with strict attention to Bráhman rules, the purer classes of Bráhmans refused to eat with them ; and it is said that when Bájiráv, the last Peshwa (1796-1818), was at Násik he was not allowed to go down to the water by the same flight of steps as the priests. Whatever disqualifications may in theory attach to the Chitpávans, their present social and religious position is as high as that of the Karháde or any other branch of Deccan Bráhmans.

Chitpávans are generally fair, well-made and handsome with greenish grey eyes. The women are small and good-looking but many of them delicate and weak-eyed. In the Konkan in their homes they use a peculiar dialect in many respects not easily followed by Maráthi speaking Deccan Hindus. This dialect is fast dying out, and in the Deccan is known to but few

Chitpavans are either Apastambas or Rigvedis and belong to the Smart sect. They are followers of Shankaráchárya. Their family goddess is Jogái or Jogeshvari. They have fourteen *gotras*. Unlike most castes of the Deccan, a Chitpávan is not allowed to marry his maternal uncle's daughter. They admit outsiders into their caste, but only immediately after birth and before the navel cord is cut off. They are Government servants, lawyers, engineers, doctors, bankers, priests, writers, landowners and husbandmen.

DESHASTHS, numbering 155,305 (males 298,158, females 142,853) at the Census of 1901, are found throughout the Deccan and Karnátak. The word Deshasth is generally taken to mean a resident of the plain or upland Deccan as distinguished from the hilly tract of the sea board Konkan; but as the bulk of the Bráhmans of the Bombay Karnátak even as far south as Dhárwár are Deshasths, it is possible that Sir W. Elliot's explanation that Deshasth means people of the *desh* or country, in the sense of local Bráhmans, may be correct. Deshasths appear to be the earliest Bráhman settlers who migrated to the south of the Vindhyas. They have two main divisions, (1) Rigvedi and (2) Yajurvedi, who eat together but do not intermarry There is also a third division known as Atharvans, the followers of the Atharva Veda, who are found mostly in the eastern part of Sátára. The Rigvedis are sub-divided into (1) Smárts or followers of Shiva and (2) Mádhvas or Vaishnavs, followers of Vishnu. Some of the stricter Vaishnavs do not give their daughters in marriage to Smárts because the two rituals are different and incompatible, but there is generally a good deal of intermarriage between Smárts and Vaishnavs in the Karnátak. Mádhvas are divided into eighteen sub-divisions after as many sects of the school, who eat together, and three of them, *viz.*, Satyabodhas, Rájendratirths and Rághavendras, also intermarry. The Yajurdvedis are split up into (1) those who follow the black Yajurved and (2) those who follow the white. They do not intermarry. Except among the Yajurvedis, marriage is allowed with a maternal uncle's daughter. In some places a man can marry even his sister's daughter. Marriage with a father's sister's daughter is not allowed. They eat with Chitpávans, Karhádas and other classes of the Dravid Bráhmans of the south; but on certain occasions treat them as inferiors. A Deshasth Bráhman will never ask a Chitpávan to dine at his house for a *shráddha* feast or to officiate at any of his ceremonies, while a Chitpávan has no corresponding objection. They are priests, writers, bankers, traders, landowners, beggars, etc. Most of the village accountants or *Kulkarnis* of the Deccan belong to this caste.

DEVARUKHAS, numbering 9,047 (males 4,322, females 4,725) at the Census of 1901, are found chiefly in Kolába and Ratnágiri. They take their name from Devarukh in the Sangameshwar *táluka* of the latter district. They assert that they were originally Deshasths, from whom they separated on their going and settling at Devarukh. Dr. Wilson suggests that they may be remnants of the Devarshis, a *shákha* of the Atharva Veda. They hold a low position among Maháráshtra Bráhmans. It is believed that dining with them brings ill-luck. Consequently many Karhádas Deshasths and Chitpávans object to dine with them. Their religious and social customs do not differ from those of Deshasths. Most of them are cultivators, a few being engaged in trade and Government service.

GOLAKS or GOVARDHANS, numbering 5,417 (males 2,823, females 2,594) at the Census of 1901, are chiefly found in Ahmednagar, Khándesh, Thána and Sátára. They are said to be people from Govardhan in Mathura or from Govardhan near Násik who were ousted by Yajurvedis from Gujarát and by Deshasths from the Deccan, possibly because they continued to practice widow marriage after the later Bráhmans had ceased to allow it. The term Golak which has no connection with *go* a cow, but means " a ball ", is an ancient Sanskrit word and is used in the Mánava-Dharma-shástra of the offspring of Bráhman widows. Govardhana was the mountain which Krishna was reported to have held up as an umbrella to keep rain off the Gopis. It is impossible to ascertain now which was the original name nor why and how it was acquired. Whichever was the original, the other was no doubt given by false analogy, as also *Goumukh,* cow-mouthed, which is also sometimes applied. They claim to be Deshasths, but other Bráhmans do not take water from or eat food cooked by them. They are divided into four sub-divisions. In ceremonies and customs they follow Deshasths. They are husbandmen, money-lenders, money changers and traders, and some act as priests to Kunbis and other lower castes. The Golaks of Thána are said to have the right to mark the time (*ghatka ghálne*) at Bráhman and Prabhu weddings.

JAVALS, numbering 1,324 (1901), including 676 males and 648 females, are found chiefly in the Ratnágiri district. They are also known as Khots or farmers of village revenue. They are said to be descendants of a shipwrecked crew who landed at Javal Kher half way between Harnai and Dábhol in the Ratnágiri district.[1] They always claimed to be Bráhmans ; but their claim was not recognized till 1767, when Parashurámbháu Patwardhan, a relation of the Peshwás, in return for some services, established them in the rank of Bráhmans. Though they are now admitted to be Bráhmans, other Bráhmans do not eat with them. Except that they eat fish, their customs do not differ from those of Chitpávans. Some of them are employed by other Bráhmans as water bearers but almost all are cultivators.

KARHADAS, numbering 32,426 (males 16,813, females 15,613) at the Census of 1901, are chiefly found in Sátára, Poona, Kolába and Ratnágiri districts and the Sávantvádi State. They take their name from the town of Karád in Sátára, the sacred junction of the Koina and Krishna. They claim to be Rigvedi Deshasths. There are various traditions regarding their origin, all of which connect their creation with camel bones. The late Sir James Campbell states—

" The third case of lost Gujars is the Ratnágiri and Sátára community of Karháde Bráhmans. That the Karháde Bráhmans have a strong stranger element is borne out by the unfriendly story that Parashurám made them out of the bones of an ass *karhád*. This, though doubtless an example of unfriendly meaning making, implies in the community some foreign or irregular origin. And that till lately (A.D. 1800) the shadow of human sacrifice attached to the Karhádes supports the story of their special descent. The name is from Karád, the sacred meeting of the Krishna and the Koina in the Sátára district of the west Dakhan. The old (second century A.D.) name both for Karhád and for Kolhápur is closely alike. Karaháta and Karahátaka apparently called after Kshaháta or Khagaráta, that is, the family or stock name of Nahapána, who, a Sáka or Pahlava from the north about the beginning of the second century (A.D. 78-120) conquered Málva and the Konkan, and the Dakhan at least as far south as Karhád. His success and the magnificence of his religious gifts made Nahapána a centre of legend, and the mace on his coins seems to have raised the suggestion that he was a re-birth of the famous mace-bearing hero Parashurám. His great public works in the Konkan and the arrows besides the mace on his coins seem to combine in the tale that by shooting his arrows seaward he reclaimed the Konkan. The fact that they took their name from Karhad makes it probable that the Karháde Bráhmans were Bráhmanised strangers or had at

(1) The etymology of the name is probably quite lost. There is a Konkani word *javal* meaning a storm ; but there seems no ground for connecting the two.

least a Sáka strain and further that they moved down the Kumbhárli pass to Chiplun and from Chiplun colonised the Rájápur and south Ratnágiri coast. In the sixth century when the White Hunas or Gurjjaras were in power and sending forth colonies, or during the seventh century when they were hard pressed in northern India and in Sindh by Turks and Arabs and by the revival of the local chiefs whom they had conquered, White Huna or Gujar settlements seem to have been formed along the Konkan, Goa, and Kanara coasts. When the colonists or the refugees settled in Alibág and in Ratnágiri they would find a common northern strain in the Karhádes, and, combining with the local tribe, seem to have added a new division which adopted the name of Gurjjara. The surname Gurjjara is common; among the Rájápur Karhádes it is almost universal. Its early adoption is proved by the form of the word, which is Gurjjara not Gujar. That it is a name which the clan consider somewhat discreditable is shown by the tales invented to explain its existence. Besides the sameness of name, inquiry has satisfied Mr. Mahipatrám Ruprám that the house and family guardians of the Karhádes are the same as the Gujar guardians. The commonness of the name Gurjjara among Karhádes shews that it is something more than a special surname held by the descendants of individuals employed in Gujarát, and that the fact that the surname is common on the coast, especially in the Rájápur sub-division, and is rare in Dakhan families, and that where it occurs it can in most cases be traced to a connection with the Konkan, all support the view that the Karháde Bráhmans of Ratnágiri are largely of Gujar origin."(1)

Karhádás look like Chitpávans but are somewhat darker, and none of them have blue grey eyes. They speak Maráthi but in the Konkan have certain peculiar words and expressions of their own.

All Karhádás are followers of the Rigveda and belong to the Smárt sect. Their family goddesses are Mahálakshmi, Durga, Mhálsa, Bhaváni, etc. Their priests are men of their own caste. Under the early Peshwás they are said to have offered human sacrifices to their household goddesses. The practice was severely repressed by the third Peshwa Baláji Bájirao (1740-1761). They have twenty-four *gotras*. They occasionally marry with Deshasths. They are writers, priests, pleaders, husbandmen, bankers, etc.

KASTHS or KASTS, numbering 35 (1901), including 20 males and 15 females, also known as Káyasths in Násik, are found in small numbers in Poona, Násik and Sátára. They claim descent from

(1) Bombay Gazetteer, Vol IX, Part I, pp. 497-498.

Káttyáyani, son of Yádnyavalkya by his wife Káttya, and call themselves Káttyáyani Shákhi Bráhmans, that is, Bráhmans of the Káttyáyani branch. Other Bráhmans do not associate with them. They are husbandmen, traders and Government servants.

KIRVANTS or KRAMAVANTS, numbering 162 (1901), including 100 males and 62 females, are found chiefly in the Kolába and Ratnágiri districts and in the Sávantvádi State. The name Kirvant is said to mean insect (*kide*) killers, because while working in their betel gardens they destroy much insect life; but this is of course fanciful and absurd. Another explanation is that the proper form of the name is Kriyávant, and that they were so called because they conducted funeral services, *kriya*, an occupation which degraded them in the eyes of other Bráhmans. According to one account, the Kirvants originally belonged to the Sárasvats of the Sáshti Pránt of Goa, and were priests by profession. Some of them objected to perform ceremonies in the houses of the lower castes, and abandoned the practice of going to such households. The rest, who had no such scruples, formed a separate class and were called Kriyávant or those who performed rites. The Sárasvats kept up the connection by intermarriages for a considerable time, but such marriages are now unknown. The Kirvants of Kolába appear to be a distinct community from the Kirvants of Ratnágiri and Sávantvádi, and generally marry with Deshasths and sometimes with Chitpávans. They are cultivators, money lenders and priests.

PALSHIKARS or PALSHES, numbering 478 (1901), including 251 males and 227 females, belong to the Mádhyandin *shákha* of the Yajurvedi Deshasth Bráhmans and are found principally in the Thána district. They derive their name from the village of Palsavali in Kalyan *táluka* of the Thána district, which according to the Bimbákhyán, was presented by Bimba to his family priests, who belonged to this caste. They are generally believed to have come in 1297 A.D. from Mungi Paithan on the Godávari with Bimba. But it seems that they formed part of the large settlement which from Gujarát supplied the foreign element to the Thána district. They claim to be Vájasaneyi Bráhmans like the Yajurvedi Deshasths of the Deccan. Their claim to be Deshasth Bráhmans has been stoutly denied by the Deccan Bráhmans, especially by Chitpávans, who refuse to interdine with them though they are allowed at places to officiate as priests with other Bráhmans. They support their claims to be Bráhmans by citing *sanads* granted to them by the Peshwás, and recently their claims have been acknowledged by the Smárt Pontiff Shankaráchárya. They are priests, physicians and astrologers and a few of them in Bombay are Government servants.

SAMAVEDIS are found only in the Thána district, where they chiefly grow garden crops.

SAVASHES (1) are found mostly in Sátára, Dhárwár, Kolhápur and Miraj. They are described in the Bombay Gazetteer as Sávashe, which appears to be a corrupt form of Sahavási. The Gazetteer describes them as descendants of Bráhmans who lost caste; but this appears to be inaccurate. According to accounts furnished by them, they are called Sahavási after the *Sahavásis* or companions of Ráma in his exile, from whom they claim descent. This seems to be merely an inference based on the identity of the two terms. They claim to be Deshasths, and this claim has been admitted by two High Priests of the Vaishnav followers of Madhvácharya. Dining with other Deshasths in the same row appears to have been allowed in the Rághavendra, Udpi and other *Maths*. They are Mádhva Vaishnavs, being the disciples of the Shri Rághavendra Swámi *Math* of Madhvácharya. Their religious and social customs resemble those of other Vaishnav Deshasths. They are priests, pleaders and bankers and of late have taken to Government and other services.

TIRGULS or TRIGARTHS, numbering 1,905 (1901), including 1,061 males and 844 females, are found chiefly in Poona and Sholápur. The name Tirgul or threefold is derived by some from the Sanskrit *trikula* (of three families), in support of which it is stated that the Tirguls are the descendants of a Bráhman by three wives, a Bráhman, a Kshatriya and a Shudra. Another account states that they are the descendants of the illegitimate offspring of Bráhman widows and wives sent to Pandharpur during the time of the Peshwás. The Tirguls assert that they were originally Deshasths and became degraded on account of taking to growing betel vines, which involves the destruction of insects. In religion and customs they follow Deshasths. They are betel vine growers, cultivators and moneylenders.

SARASVATS, also called Gaud Sárasvats or Shenvis, numbering 76,422 (males 39,834, females 36,588) at the Census of 1901, are found chiefly in the Ratnágiri, Kanara and Belgaum districts and the Sávantvádi State. They are also found in large numbers in South Kanara, Malabár and Goa. They trace their descent to the sage Sárasvat who lived on the bank of the Sarasvati near Tháneshvar

(1) Information regarding this sub-division was supplied by Mr. G. P. Jámbale of Poona.

in the Punjab and preserved the *Vedas* by living on fish during a great famine which lasted for twelve years and carrying away thousands of Bráhmans, threatened the total extinction of the race. It is stated in the *Sahyádrikhand* and other works that the Sárasvats were brought into the Konkan by Parashurám who granted them the beautiful and fertile province of Gománchal (Goa). They were originally distributed over ninety-six villages, from which they spread themselves over the northern districts of Bárdesh, Pedne and Kudál Mahály and other parts of the Goa province and South Konkan. Their original distribution over ninety-six *Shahánnava* villages has, according to some, led to their being called Shenvis. Others hold that they got the name Shenvi because the number of families originally brought by Parashurám was ninety-six. There are others who maintain that the term Shenvi is derived from *Shánbhog*, meaning a village accountant, in which capacity many of the Gaud Sárasvats have been employed for many generations in Kanara, Goa and the southern part of the Ratnágiri district and the Sávantvádi State, their chief centres. Shenvi is also a surname of many families in Kanara and Goa and is often used as a term of respect in addressing respectable members of the caste.

It is stated in the *Mangeshmáhátmya* that the original colony of the Gaud Sárasvats was further reinforced by Bráhman immigrants from Kányakubja or Kanauj led by (1) Devasharma, (2) Lomasharma and (3) Shivasharma. It is stated that these Bráhmans had started on a pilgrimage to Rámeshvar, but during their halt at Goa *en route* they were so enchanted with the place that they abandoned the idea of going to Rámeshvar and became permanent residents of the locality. The memory of the Sharmás is preserved by means of figures installed before the images (in Goa territory) of the god Mangesh and the goddess Shántádurga, which the Sharmás are supposed to have brought from Tirhoot in Bengal.

Most of the Gaud Sárasvat men are of the middle height, and, except those of the Kudáldeshkar section, have well cut features. The skin of all except the Kudáldeshkars, who are generally dark, is generally wheat-coloured, but some are fair. The women are shorter than the men. They are generally graceful, with dark lustrous eyes and black hair. The Kudáldeshkar women mostly resemble Deshasth women. This difference in colour and features between the Kudáldeshkars and other sections of the Gaud Sárasvats have led some to believe that the Kudáldeshkars are probably local Bráhmans like the Deshasths, and have no connection with the Gaud Sárasvats.

How and when they came to be looked upon as a subdivision of the Gaud Sárasvats is not known. They themselves prefer to be called simply Gaud Bráhmans, and although they interdine with the Gaud Sárasvats many of them claim to be quite an independent community.

Gaud Sárasvat Bráhmans are split up into the following endogamous divisions :—

1. Bárdeshkar.
2. Bhálávalkar.
3. Divádkar.
4. Gaud Sárasvat proper or Shenvi including Sásashtikar or Konkani.
5. Kajule.
6. Khadape.
7. Kirloskar.
8. Kudáldeshkar.
9. Lotalikar.
10. Narvánkar.
11. Pednekar.
12. Rájpurkar.
13. Sárasvat, Kushasthali or Shanaipaiki.

Of the above, the Shenvis are most numerous. The Sárasvats and Kudáldeshkars stand next, while each of the rest number only a few hundreds. Some of the above are local in origin while others are due to caste disputes and fission. About fifty years back the Sásashtakars formed an endogamous group by themselves, but they have now completely merged into the Gaud Sárasvat group by intermarriage. Of late, attempts are being made to amalgamate all the sub-castes, and there is reason to believe that they will be crowned with success at no distant date, as the movement is backed up by the most advanced and educated members of all the sub-castes. A few marriages between members of some of the sub-castes have already taken place. However, in the Census Report of 1911, p. 204, it was mentioned that *pari passu* with the movement for amalgamation there was discernible a movement of fission resulting in two factions, the *Londonwálás,* or those who had been excommunicated by the Swámi for dining with Europe-returned and excommunicated members, and the *non-Londonwálás*, or orthodox.

Except the Sásashtikars and Bárdeshkars, who are Vaishnavs, all the Gaud Sárasvats are Smárts. They are followers of the Rigveda. They have eighteen *gotras.* Their family deities are Mangesh, Shántádurga, Mahálakshmi, etc., the shrines of all of which are in Goa. They have their own *swámis* or spiritual heads who have monasteries at Kavale in Goa, Gokarn, Násik, Benáres, etc. In Goa, Kanara and other centres of the caste they have priests of their own caste. In other places, Karhádás, Chitpávans or Deshasths officiate at their ceremonies. They eat fish, and in the Deccan eat food cooked by Deshasths, Chitpávans and Karhádás, who do not eat food cooked by Gaud Sárasvats. In their own home land they do not take food from any Bráhman caste except their own. They are landlords, merchants, bankers, government servants, pleaders, doctors, etc. Many of them are hereditary village accountants (*kulkarnis*).

THE KARNATAK BRAHMANS found in the Bombay Presidency belong to three main divisions, (1) Habbu, (2) Havik and (3) Karnátak.

HABBUS, numbering 229 (1901), including 130 males and 99 females, are found chiefly in the Kanara district. They are said to have been brought into Kanara with their priests by Mayurvarma in the eighth century. There are some families of Deshasth Vaishnav Bráhmans in the Dhárwár district bearing the surname of Habbu, which seems to show that they were originally Deshasths. They appear to have been at one time an important community, and there are, to this day, villages in Goa and the Kárwár *táluka* known as Habbu Sthánás bearing testimony to their former greatness. In the famous temple of Malikárjuna at Kánkon in Goa and in some other temples in Kárwár *taluka*, at the yearly festivals, a cocoanut is first offered to the Habbus as a token of respect. They are still called *gáonkars* or village headmen. It is stated that their present low status among Bráhmans is a result of a curse imposed by one of the *swámis* of the Shringeri monastery. They belong to the Karnátak branch of the Dravids, but although other Dravids eat together, none eat openly with Habbus. Most of them hold large landed properties, which they either cultivate themselves or lease to tenants.

HAVIKS or HAVIGS, also known as Haigas, numbering 40,571 (males 21,518, females 19,053) at the census of 1901, are found chiefly in the Kanara district and in north-west Mysore. The name Havik is derived by some from *havis* (oblation), others trace it to *havu* or *hai* a snake. According to Buchanan, Parashurám created Haiga at the same time as Tulava and Malabár and gave it to Bráhmans called Nágars and Máchis. The *Sahyádrikhand* relates that probably about 700 A.D. Haviks were brought by Sikvarma, father of Mayurvarma, the founder of the second dynasty of the Banavási Kadambas, to supplant the Bráhmans of Parashurám who had been degraded by their champion in consequence of their want of trust in his promises. Haviks claim as their original seat Ahichhatra, an ancient and ruined city in Rohilkhand in upper India, now best known as Rámnagar. Mr. D. R. Bhandarkar(1) supports this view and states that they were first established by Mayurvarma in Talgund in the

(1) Foreign Elements in the Hindu Population, p. 21.

Shimoga district of Mysore. He further remarks that they are said to have made an effort later to leave the province but were brought back again, and in order to prevent a repetition of the attempt were compelled to leave a lock of hair on the forehead as a distinguishing mark. The Haviks of north-west Mysore still wear their hair in this fashion, and their fair complexion and features support the tradition of a northern origin. But they eat stale food left overnight, and their women wear a *langoti* under the *sári*, which would point to their belonging originally to a non-Bráhman cultivating caste raised to Bráhmanical rank by the Aryan or Scythian invaders. It is still a common tradition among Halvakki Vakkals, one of the leading cultivating castes in Kanara, that their women intermarried with the early Havik settlers, and there is evidence to show that this tradition is not improbable. (See HALVAKKI VAKKAL.)

The Havik men are fair, short and spare with well-cut intelligent features; the women are like the men except that they are fairer. Their home speech is an incorrect and unidiomatic Kanarese with so strong a Malayáli element both in words and tone that Kanarese people who do not know its peculiarities do not understand it. Many understand Tulu, the language of South Kanara, in which in Malayáli characters their books and family records are written by their family priests. This Malabár element in the Haviks is not easy to explain. It may either show that their connection with the south is closer than they acknowledge, or it may show that before its conquest by inland Kanarese-speaking rulers the Malabár language and letters were in use in Kanara.

Haviks have four sub-divisions, (1) Haviks, (2) Kots, (3) Saklápuris and (4) Shivális. Except the Saklápuris, all eat together but do not intermarry. They are further divided into priests and laymen, who eat together and intermarry. They are mostly Yajurvedis of the Bodháyana Shákha. They have eight *gotras*. They are Smárts and have their own monasteries at Rámchandrapur, Honnalli, Nelemare, Bhankuli, Kyadgi and Apsarkond. Their chief patron deity is Ganesh, whose chief shrine is at Idagunji six miles east of Honávar. They regard certain village *ammás* or mothers as their family goddesses, the chief of which are Durgamma, Honávaramma, Karkiamma, Kumtámma and Bhairamma. Fruit and flowers and sometimes fowls and sheep are offered to these goddesses.

Amongst the Haviks there is a dearth of marriageable girls. Partly owing to this, and partly because they are skilful gardeners, a Havik has to pay for his wife, the amount of the price varying from Rs. 500 to Rs. 3,000 according to the circumstances of the parties and the age of the bridegroom. This has led to the marriages of young girls with old men and widowers, with the result that there is a large number of child widows. Such of these widows as are detected leading immoral lives are sent to the *math* or monastery, where they have to perform menial service. These widows can be obtained from the *math* on payment of a certain amount and are employed as maid servants as outcaste members in the family.

More than half of the Haviks are priests. When not engaged in religious duties they work in their palm and spice gardens, their wives doing much of the work except that they do not climb the trees. Most of the laymen are husbandmen and skilful gardeners, growing fine pepper, cardamoms and betelnuts. Some are in Government service as clerks, some are village headmen and some are traders and money-lenders. They are vegetarians and eat with all Dravid Bráhmans.

KARNATAKS, described as Joishis in the Bombay Gazetteer, are found only in the Kanara district. They are Yajurvedis of the Bodháyana Shákha and are followers of Shankarácharya. They hold the same social position as Haviks, though the two classes neither eat together nor intermarry. They are astrologers, cultivators and family priests to Komárpaiks, Habbus and other middle class Hindus.

BRINJARI.—A synonym for Vanjári.

BUDBUDKI JOSHI.—A synonym for Joshi.

BUDHLEKARI.—A sub-division of Dhors.

BUDLIGAR.—A synonym for Budhlekari Dhor.

BUNDELE-GAWLHERE.—A sub-division of Kacchis.

BUNDELI BHOI.—A synonym for Kahár.

BUNDELKHANDI.—A sub-division of Dhors.

BUNKAR.—A sub-division of Mahárs.

BURUD.—A sub-division of Mángs.

Name and origin.

BURUDS are also known as Medars, Ghánches or Gháches and Vánasfodás. The origin of the term 'Burud' is obscure. Medar (Kan. *Medár*) is derived from Medarket or Medarkyat, a follower of Basava, the Lingáyat hero of the 12th century, who apparently converted many of the Buruds in the Karnátak to Lingáyatism. The term 'Medar' seems properly to signify Lingáyat Buruds, though all Medars do not wear the *ling*. The terms 'Ghanche' and 'Vánasfoda' are mere synonyms suggestive of the caste occupation, which is splitting and weaving bamboos, of which they make mats, baskets, winnowing fans, etc.

Buruds number (1901) 19,055, including 9,784 males and 9,271 females. At the Census of 1901 only 430 returned themselves as Lingáyats. But it is probable that many Medars were entered as Hindu Buruds, and the figures must therefore be accepted with reserve. The Bombay Gazetteer (vol. XVII, p. 116) describes the Buruds in Ahmednagar as wearing the *ling.* A reference to the 1901 census return for this district, however, will show that all the Buruds of Ahmednagar are classified as non-Lingáyats.

Divisions.

There are a few Ját and Telangi Buruds from other parts of India resident in the Presidency, but the bulk of the caste can be divided into—

(1) Buruds proper or Maráthi-speaking Buruds,

(2) Medárs, or Lingáyat and Kanarese-speaking Buruds,

each with an *Akaramáse* or *Kadu* sub-division for those who transgress caste rules. These divisions neither eat together nor intermarry. From the craft they pursue it is highly probable that the Buruds represent one of the early tribes of the Deccan and Karnátak. In the Deccan they occupy socially an inferior position. In the Karnátak their adoption of the levelling doctrines of Basava appears to have raised them somewhat in the social scale, and the Medar therefore is the social superior of the Burud. It must be remembered that in the Deccan Medars would be generally described as Buruds, owing to the want of discrimination on the part of the people in applying caste terminology. It is extremely difficult in consequence to separate from the recorded total the Hindu and Lingáyat divisions. It is probable, from the inclusion of the *Jangam* or Lingáyat priest in the ceremonies of most Buruds, that the bulk of the caste became Lingáyats in the 12th or 13th century, but that many have since abandoned that religion. Basket weavers among Kaikádis, Mángs, and similar tribes or castes are sometimes styled Kaikádi Burud, Máng Burud, etc. But they have no connection with the Burud caste here described, and are omitted from the following account.

The primitive origin of the Buruds is shown by the persistence among them of a system of *devaks* or totems regulating marriages. Families or *kuls* with the same *devak* may not intermarry.

The Marátha Buruds relate the following story regarding the origin of the caste: they were originally Maráthás who were put out of caste because they made a bamboo basket for Párvati's flowers and fruit when she was going to worship the *vad* tree on the *Jyeshtha* full-moon. Another version of the story is that Párvati, on reaching womanhood, was presented by the matrons with the usual lap-filling (*oti-bharan*) offering of wheat, cocoanuts, red and yellow powder, betel leaves and a comb. To make a shovel-shaped winnowing basket to hold these offerings, Shiva called the Buruds into existence and allowed them to cut down five bamboo trees in Párvati's garden. Instead of five the Buruds cut ten trees, and thus, through the wrath of Shiva, lost their caste. It is also stated that they are the offspring of Dhivars or Kolis. In the *Bhágavat Purán* they are described as one of the seven castes of *Antyajas* mentioned by Manu.

The exogamous sub-divisions or *kuls* of the Marátha Buruds are identical with surnames. The common surnames are, Bhovare, Chinchavale, Jagtáp, Kene, Khaire, Dukare, Gádhave, Gáikwád, Ghorpade, Mohite, More, Pavár, Sanavate, Shelke, Shinde, Náge, Sasurve, Deshamukh, Vadatale and Vartab. Every *kul* has a separate *devak*. Some of the *devaks* are as follows :—

Name of *kul*.		Name of its *devak*.
More	..	Peacock feather
Jagtáp	..	*Hola* (ringed turtle).
Pavár	..	A cock.
Suravase	..	A hog.
Sonavane	..	*Tarvad* (Cassia auriculata).
Korade	..	A leaf of *rui* (Calotropis gigantea).
Khaire	..	Wood of *khair* (Acacia catechu).
Chinchavale	..	A leaf of the *pipal* tree (Ficus religiosa).
Vadatale	..	A leaf of *vad* (banyan tree).

age. Marriages are prohibited within three generations of relationship. A member of the caste may marry his maternal uncle's daughter. A man may marry two sisters, and two brothers may marry two sisters. Intermarriages between families living in different villages and districts can take place only if former relationship can be traced between them. Polygamy is allowed and practised, but polyandry is unknown. Girls are married from eight till after puberty ; boys from twelve to twenty-five.

The offer of marriage comes from the boy's father. If both the parties are well-to-do, the girl's father pays a dowry to the boy. If the boy's parents are poor, or there is some defect in the boy, the boy's father has to pay a bride-price. The day for the marriage is fixed by a Bráhman who conducts the service. A Jangam is also present, but he takes no part in the service.

The first ceremony in a marriage is the *Patrika-pujan*, or worship of a piece of paper, on which is written the auspicious time for the marriage and for the application of turmeric paste. Next comes *Kunku lávane*, which is celebrated in the same way as amongst the Kunbis. This is followed by *Halad*, or rubbing the boy and the girl with turmeric paste. On the third day or fifth day from this day the marriage is celebrated. In the morning, the *devak* is installed in the manner prevalent among the Kunbis, a goat is killed, and caste-men are feasted. In the evening the bridegroom goes in procession to the bride's house. He is taken into the marriage booth and made to stand on a heap of rice grains in a basket with face to the west. The girl is brought and made to stand similarly facing him ; a cloth is held between them ; marriage verses are repeated ; and at the end, coloured grains of rice or *jovári* are thrown over the pair by the priest and the party assembled. This is followed by *Kanyádán* and the fastening of the *kankans* or marriage wristlets round the wrists of the bride and bridegroom. The marriage sacrifice is next performed, and the boy, taking the girl on his waist, walks three times round the sacrificial fire, this being the binding portion of the marriage service. The ceremonies which follow resemble those of the Kunbis.

The remarriage of widows is permitted. A widow may marry her maternal uncle's son. She cannot marry a member of her late husband's section. A widow remarriage is celebrated on a dark night except a new-moon day or a Saturday or Monday. A Bráhman priest and widows on both sides are present on the occasion. The widow wears a new robe and ornaments presented to her by her new husband, and, covering her face with an upper garment, sits by his side. The Bráhman priest applies red powder to her forehead, Ganpati and Varuna are worshipped, the widow's lap is filled with wheat grains and fruits, and the hems of the pair's garments are tied into a knot. Next, the pair go into the house, bow before the house gods and return, and the knot of their garments is untied. This ends the ceremony. It is considered unlucky to see the faces of the remarried pair till they have bathed and bowed to the gods on the following morning. Next, a feast is given by the widow's new husband to the party who were present the day before at the time of the marriage. A bachelor is not allowed to marry a widow unless he is first married to a *rui* (Calotropis gigantea) tree. Divorce is allowed. The caste follow the Hindu law of inheritance.

Religion. Marátha Buruds belong to the Hindu religion. Some of them are followers of the Várkari sect. The chief objects of their worship are Khandoba, Jotiba, Bahiroba, Bhaváni, Rám, Máruti and Vithoba. Goats are offered to Khandoba and Bhaváni on Tuesdays, Fridays or Sundays. Images of deceased ancestors are made and worshipped. Musulmán saints are reverenced. When an epidemic breaks out, the goddess Bhaváni is propitiated with offerings of goats and cooked food. The Buruds worship all the animals and plants held sacred by the Hindus, and observe all the Hindu holidays. They make pilgrimages to Pandharpur, Shingnápur, Tuljápur, Alandi, Kondanpur and other places. Their religious teachers are Siddhgiri of Kanheri in Sátára and the head Jangam of the monastery at Manurgaum near Ahmednagar. Their priests are Deshasth Bráhmans, who are received on terms of equality by the other Bráhmans.

Death ceremonies. The dead are either burnt or buried. At burial the corpse is seated with face to the east. The bones and ashes of the burnt are consigned to water. In the case of burial, the funeral rites are conducted by a Jangam. He applies ashes to the forehead of the corpse, and walks before it blowing a conch-shell when the corpse is carried to the burial ground. The other details are the same as amongst the Kunbis. On the third day after death, the chief mourner goes to the burial ground with a winnowing fan containing cow-dung, cow-urine, three small earthern jars, three wheaten cakes, and three balls of wheat flour. Half the way to where the corpse was laid down, he places one jar, one cake and one of the balls. The spot where the corpse was buried is sprinkled over with cow-dung and cow-urine, and the remaining jars, cakes and balls are placed on the spot. The chief mourner then returns home and treats the party who attended the funeral to a dinner. In the case of burning, in addition to this, on the tenth day the chief mourner goes to the bank of a river, makes a small raised seat of mud, and places thereon three earthen jars, each covered with a wheaten cake and a rice ball. He plants near the seat three small flags of yellow cotton rags. When a crow touches one of the jars, he bathes and returns home. The mourning ends on this day. On the twelfth or thirteenth day the caste is feasted. For the propitiation of the deceased ancestors uncooked articles of food are given to Bráhmans and Jangams on the anniversaries of the deceased.

Occupation. The hereditary occupation of the caste is working in bamboo. They make bamboo baskets, winnowing fans, birds' cages, children's cradles, sieves and mats. They also make cane chairs and cots. A few own land.

They eat the flesh of goats, sheep, fowls and fish, and drink liquor. They do not eat beef or the flesh of dead cattle. They rank higher than the Mahárs and Mángs, with whom they do not eat. The Kunbis smoke with them.

The Kanarese-speaking Buruds have no exogamous sub-divisions above families bearing the same surname. The commonest surnames are Chandanigeru, Padseru, Pángeru, Sálunkyavaru, and Pevreru. Other surnames are given below. They differ from the Marátha Buruds in the following particulars.

The marriage service amongst them is conducted by a married unwidowed woman of the caste who is selected by a Bráhman. The essential portion of the ceremony consists in tying a lucky necklace round the girl's neck by the priestess. The family deities of the Kanarese Buruds are Basavanna, Hanumanta, Udchamma, Devamma, and Yellamma. Their chief god is Hulsingrái of Gober near Kulburga. They make pilgrimages to Devarguddu in Dhárwár. Images of deceased ancestors are installed amongst household gods and worshipped. They offer blood sacrifices to the mothers or powers and kill goats in honour of their house gods, on the *Mára-navami*, that is, the day before the *Dasara*, and at the end of marriages. On the last day of the *Muharram* they offer mutton and liquor to their house gods and feast on them. Their religious teachers are a Váder or priestly Kuruba and Gurusiddhaswámi who lives at Hubli. Their death ceremonies are conducted by Jangams.

LINGAYAT BURUDS are non-Panchamsáli Lingáyats without the *ashtavarna* rites. Their exogamous sub-divisions are identical with surnames. They are Dukare, Gáde, Gándhe, Ghorpade, Hátage, Hole, Jamkar, Káte, Khaire, Kharáde, More, Pimpale, Pharáve, Shinde, Sole, Sonavane, and Vartale. Persons bearing the same surname may not intermarry. The marriage ceremonies of the Lingáyat Buruds are the same as those of the Reddis and are conducted by a Jangam, no Bráhman being invited to be present. Polygamy and widow-marriage are allowed and practised, but polyandry is unknown.

The Lingáyat Buruds worship all Bráhmanic gods and goddesses. The special deities of their worship are Mahádeva, the Devi of Tuljápur, and Khandoba of Jejuri. Their family deities are Ambábái of Saptashring in Násik and of Tuljápur in the Nizam's country. They make pilgrimages to Alandi, Dehu, Jejuri in Poona, Paithan, Saptashring in Násik, Tuljápur, and other sacred places. On a child-birth the mother is held unclean for three days, but women are not held unclean in their monthly sickness. They observe three of the leading Hindu holidays, *Shimga*, *Dasara*, and *Diváli*. Their religious teacher is a Jangam Virupáksha of Manur in the Nizam's territory. Their priests are Jangams. Their death ceremonies resemble those of the other Lingáyats. For the propitiation of deceased ancestors, uncooked food is given to Bráhmans and Jangams on the corresponding death days in the latter half of *Bhádrapad*, and caste-men are feasted.

Lingáyat Medars, contrary to the usual practice, eat the flesh of goats, sheep, fowls and fish, and drink liquor. They take food from all high caste Hindus.

BUTTALS, numbering 67 (1901) including 43 males and 24 females, are found entirely in the Kanara district. They seem to take their name from the Kanarese *butti*, a basket. They are deemed impure. They marry their girls between 10 and 13 and their boys between 16 and 25. Widow marriage and polygamy are allowed and practised, but polyandry is unknown. Their marriage ceremony resembles that of the local Chámbhárs. They worship all village gods and goddesses, but the chief object of their veneration is Jatga. They believe in soothsaying and witchcraft, and have a great dread of the spirits of the dead. They respect Bráhmans, but do not employ them to conduct their ceremonies. All their ceremonies are conducted by thier headmen, who are called *kolkar* or sceptre-holders. The hereditary occupation of the caste is basket-making. They also work as field-labourers. They eat all kind of flesh except beef and drink liquor.

CHAG BHAISA.—A sub-division of Kumbhárs.

CHAJGADI.—A sub-division of Bhangis.

CHALGERIBALKI.—A sub-division of Bánjigs.

CHAMADIA.—A synonym for Khálpa.

CHAMAR.—A synonym for Khálpa.

Name and origin

CHAMBHARS,[1] numbering 161,321 (1901), including 81,327 males and 79,994 females, are found all over the Deccan, Konkan and Karnátak. They are also called Chamgárs in Kanara and Samgárs in the Karnátak. All these names, besides being the names of the caste, also signify a worker in leather; and consequently, especially the first, are borrowed by others, pursuing the same occupation. Thus, Chámbhár has been applied to other castes and tribes of this Presidency, such as the Káthis, Kattáis, Jingars, Dhors and Mochis, and to emigrants from other provinces, such as the Hindustánis, Bengális, Madrasis and Márwáris.

---

(1) This article is compiled from materials supplied by Mr. D. R. Bhandarkar.

There are two territorial divisions of the caste Marátha and Kanarese, which will be described below separately.

Regarding the origin of the Chámbhárs, a variety of traditions are current. One tradition represents them as having descended from Harali, a devotee and page of the god Shiva. Another tradition obtaining in the same district alleges that their original ancestor was the sage Márkanda. Their forefathers by their implicit devotion propitiated the god Shiva, who told them to earn their livelihood by making shoes of leather. In the Kolhápur State, the Chámbhárs trace their descent from Arálaya, one of the sons and worshippers of Shiva, who incurred Shiva's displeasure by making a pair of shoes of his own skin, which he presented to the god. As a punishment, he was doomed to be a cobbler for life.

Such are the popular traditions with regard to the origin of the Chámbhár caste but they help us little in determining whether they belong to the Aryan or non-Aryan race. It may be argued that the totemism of this caste stamps them as aboriginal; and, in confirmation of this may also be added the facts that the touch of the Chámbhár, like that of the Mahár or Máng, is thought defiling by the Hindus, and that, as a rule, the Chámbhárs are condemned to live on the outskirts of towns like the aboriginal races. It cannot but be said that there is some force in this line of reasoning; on the other hand, reasons of equal, perhaps greater, force may be adduced in favour of a superior origin, as for instance, that the Chámbhárs are generally fair, and that their women, especially in the Kanara district are celebrated for their extraordinary beauty. This differentiates them from the Mángs, Máhars, Dhors and other non-Aryan tribes in the Bombay Presidency, who are of a dark complexion. Secondly, the calling of leather-working was not only not despised in ancient times, as it is now, but was pursued by the Aryans themselves. The word *charmamna*, which means a tanner, occurs once in a hymn in the Rigveda. In the chapter on *Purushamedh* (man-sacrifice) of the Vájasaneya Sanhita of the Yajurveda, various human beings are mentioned as fit victims to be offered to certain deities, many of which are fanciful; and in the list of such human victims, a *charmamna* (tanner) is included. Limmer, a German scholar of great repute, in his work entitled "Altindisches Leben," expresses the opinion that this profession of a tanner was among the manifold callings followed by the Visas or Aryan people in general, as contrasted with the priests and the nobles. In the Páli Játakas or Buddhist birth-stories, which depict the social life of India long before the rise of Buddhism, various trade-guilds, eighteen in number, are referred to, with which the kings were often in direct contact and intimate relation. All these guilds have their presidents (*pamukha*); and among them the guild of leather-workers (*chammakara*) is mentioned. This clearly shows that in pre-Buddhistic times the calling of leather-working had acquired such an importance that those who pursued it had a recognised guild of their own, with which kings always kept themselves in touch. The present Chámbhárs have still their caste councils and their headmen, who are styled *Mehtars* or *Budvants.* This may be a survival of the trade guild with its president, which the *chammakáras* had in pre-Buddhistic days. About a century after the rise and dissemination of Buddhism, public opinion began to change. There is a passage in the Vinay-Pitaka which relegates leather-workers to the class of those who took to low crafts (*hina sippa*); but even here it deserves to be noticed, as pointed out by Dr. Ficks, that the profession of leather-working is classed under *hina-sippa* and not *hina-jati* (low castes), which comprised the Chándálas, Venás (rush-workers), Nesádas (bird-catchers), Rathakáras (cart-makers) and Pukkusas. The conclusion may therefore be safely drawn that, although the profession of leather-working had begun to fall into disrepute about a century after the prevalence of Buddhism or about 400 B.C., those who pursued it were not yet locked upon as belonging to low castes (*hina-játi*); in other words, leather workers were even then regarded as standing within the pale of the Aryan society. But, once considered debasing, the profession must gradually have acquired more and more disrepute, until those who pursued it were degraded into a low caste and were in popular estimation put on the same level with the aboriginal tribes, such as the Mahárs, Mángs and Dhors; and further, when they were ranked with these non-Aryan races, the Chámbhárs must have consciously or unconsciously borrowed many customs from them, and among these perhaps totemism itself. Such are the arguments that may be urged in support of the thesis that the Chámbhárs were originally Aryans. It is by no means meant that pure unmixed Aryan blood runs through their veins. Such an assertion cannot be made with reference to any caste in India. When Manu and other law-givers lay down that the descendant in the seventh generation of an issue of a Shudra woman by a Bráhman, Kshatriaya or Vaishya, becomes a Bráhman, Kshatriya or Vaishya, there is little doubt that some aboriginal blood is flowing in the veins of all Hindus of the present day. All that is contended is that, if the higher castes of the present day are to be regarded as Aryans, the Chámbhárs must also be considered to have some claims to Aryan descent.

The Hindu legislators, however, offer a different explanation with respect to the origin of the Chámbhár caste. If we identify the Chámbhár with the Káráwára of Manu, then he sprang from a Nisháda, father, and a Vaideha, mother. According to Paráshara, the father of the Chámbhár caste was a fisherman and the mother, a Chándála woman. According to other minor authorities, such as Játiviveka, Játinirnaya, and Játidarpana, they descended from a Dhigvana, father and a Nisháda woman. It will be seen from this that in the opinion of all these Hindu writers, the Chámbhárs are a mixed caste. Their view cannot, however, commend itself to any one, first, because they dogmatically assert that, as the castes were originally four, all others that are now in existence are solely the result of the intermarriages between them. This line of arguments evidently ignores the fact that many causes other than intermarriages between the four original castes, such as race, religion, locality, occupation, and so forth have been in operation, and led to the multiplicity of castes. Secondly, the accounts, which the Hindu writers give of the origin of the Chámbhár, are conflicting. Thirdly, it has just been shown that the occupation of leather-working was considered respectable in days gone by, that it was followed by the Aryans in the Vedic and the pre-Buddhistic times, that the leather-workers had guilds of their own, and that only about 400 B.C. the occupation began to be looked upon with contempt, although even then those who professed it were not considered as belonging to a low caste. The Chámbhárs or Chammakárs were therefore considered in those days as standing within the pale of Hindu society ; and hence the view of the Hindu legislators that they sprang from the non-Aryan races, such as the Chándálas and Nishádas, has little weight. The only views that therefore can be regarded as plausible are (i) that they are a pre-Aryan race, or (ii) that they are of Aryan descent. Between these two views no verdict can be passed with perfect certainty.

MARATHA CHAMBHARS have the following endogamous divisions :—

1. Ahir	3. Dábholi.	5. Harali.
2. Chevli.	4. Gháti.	6. Konkani.

Chevlis are those once residing in Chaul in the Kolába district ; Dábholis derive their name from the town of Dábhol in Ratnágiri, their original home ; Konkanis belong to the Konkan and Ghátis to the Deccan. In the Thána and Kolába districts, Cheulis, Dábholis and Ghátis are found. In Sátáta, they have the Harali and Chevli divisions. Haralis do not mend the shoes of the impure castes, such as Mahárs,

Mángs, etc., which the Chevlis do. They do not eat together or intermarry. In Ratnágiri are to be found the Dábholis and Chevlis, who do not eat together or intermarry. The Dábholis consider themselves superior to the Chevlis, as the latter repair the shoes of Jingars, Mahárs and Bhangis and eat the flesh of dead cattle. The Dábholis in their return are looked down upon by the Haralis of the Deccan as the former tan leather, which is considered to be the work of Dhors. In Khándesh the endogamous groups are Maráthás Ahirs, Haralis and Dábholis. In the Belgaum district, they are split up into Maráthás and Konkanis. In the Kolhápur State, however, they are broken up into endogamous divisions (i) those that make shoes for the higher classes and (ii) those that make shoes for Berads, Mángs and Mahárs. In other districts, the caste do not appear to have any endogamous groups.

There appear to be no exogamous divisions of the caste, except families, members of which have the same surname. The following is a list of the commonest surnames :—

Agávane.	Gáikvád.	Kedár.
Ahirrav.	Girimkar.	Lágchavre
Arkhe.	Hankáre.	Nátke.
Bamne.	Hulamke.	Pavár.
Bansure.	Jádhav.	Pote.
Bhágvat.	Jamdhare.	Sálve.
Bhosale.	Kabáde.	Sátpute.
Chaván.	Kadam.	Shelke.
Damáre.	Kadme.	Shinde.
Deshmukh.	Kále.	Sonavane.
Devre.	Kálge.	Suryavanshi.
Dhorge.	Kámble.	Vágha.
Doiphode.	Kánde.	Vasait.
Durge.	Karande.	
Gádekar.	Kávade.	

Marriage is prohibited within the sub-division covered by one surname. It is also prohibited with those worshipping the same *devak*. Some of the *devaks* are as follows :—

Name of Kul.		Name of Devak.
Ahirrav	..	*Nim* (Melia Azadirachta).
Arkhe.	..	*Hariali* (grass).
Bamne.	..	*Pánchpálvi* (leaves of five trees).
Bhosale	..	***Feather of the Rájahansa.***

Name of Kul.		Name of Devak.
Doiphode	..	*Pánchpálvi.*
Karande	..	Do.
Pavár	..	Do.
Shelke	..	*Vad* (banyan tree).
Shinde	..	*Maryádvel* (Ipomœa Biloba)
Vasáit	..	*Vásanvel* (Cocculus Villosus)

The *devaks* worshipped by the Chámbhárs of the Ratnágiri district are the *Umbar* (Ficus Glomerata), *Kalamb* (Anthocephalus Cadamba), the peacock's feather, the eagle's feather and the *Koya* (a bird).

A man cannot marry into the families related to him on the father's side. He cannot marry his mother's sister's daughter, but he may marry the daughter of his maternal uncle. A man may have two sisters as his wives at one and the same time. Two sisters can also be married by two brothers. Marriage is generally infant; but if the parents are poor, the girls remain unmarried till they are sixteen. Sexual license before marriage is not allowed. Polygamy is permitted, but it is not thought right for a man to marry a second wife, unless the first is dead or is barren. Polyandry is unknown.

Marriage

The form of marriage in ordinary use is the Puránic form of marriage, and the essential and binding portion thereof is an oath on the part of the bridegroom to be ever faithful to his wife and protect and support her till death ; and on the part of the bride, an oath of fidelity and obedience to her husband. After these oaths are taken, the ends of their marriage garments are tied into a knot as a token of their perfect union.

On the occasion of betrothal, ornaments are exchanged between the two houses ; the boy is presented with a turban and sash, and the girl with a robe and bodice. On a lucky day, one to three days before the marriage, the boy is rubbed with turmeric at his house and a little is taken to the girl's by kinswomen and friends, where she is rubbed with it and presented with a robe and bodice. Her lap is filled with grains of wheat, dry cocoa-kernel, dates and a packet of betelnuts and leaves. On the marriage day, the boy is set on horseback and, accompanied by kinspeople and friends, goes with music to the temple of Máruti in the girl's village. Here the marriage coronet or *báshing* is tied on his brow, and his father-in-law presents him with a turban, a sash, a waistcloth, and a pair of shoes, and takes him to his house. When he reaches the girl's house, a piece of bread is waved round his head and thrown away. The boy and girl are made to stand face to face in two bamboo baskets, a cloth or *jámnika* is held between them, and the priest repeats verses and throws grains of rice over the heads of the bride and bridegroom, who encircle each other's necks with garlands of flowers and with yellow threads. Then, on the marriage altar or *bahule*, the sacrificial fire or *lájáhom* is kindled and each near relation and friend waves a copper coin over the heads of the boy and the girl, and sticks grains of rice on their brows. Except near relations and friends, the guests retire with a betel packet and the day ends with a feast. Next day a goat is killed in honour of the goddess Jánái, and a feast of mutton and liquor is made. The boy, seated on horseback with his bride and accompanied by relations and friends and music, goes to his house in procession. On the day after, the boy returns to his house, his yellow necklace and turmeric wristlets are untied, they are rubbed with rice-flour, and all traces of the turmeric are washed off.

In some places, the boy pays the girl's marriage expenses, and at betrothal marks her brow with vermilion, and sticks on to the vermilion an eight-anna piece or a rupee. She is presented with a new robe, bodice and ornaments, and the boy receives a turban and a shoulder-cloth from her father. Her lap is filled with rice and a cocoanut, and the boy's friends and relations are feasted. The Bráhman priest names a lucky day for holding the marriage, and neighbour women meet at the house of the boy and girl, each with a dining dish filled with grain, wave it about the boy and the girl who are seated each in a square marked out with lines of wheat flour by the village Gurav woman, and throw away a copper coin. The grain is gathered in a heap, and the copper coins are given to the Gurav woman. Wheat cakes or *undás* are handed to the guests, and a yellow cloth wrapped round a turmeric root and betelnut is tied to the house grindstone and large water vessel or *ránjan*. Booths are erected before the houses of each, and the *devak* ceremony is performed on the day before the marriage. Five married unwidowed women from the bridegroom's house go to the temple of Máruti, each with a water pot in her hands, followed by a pair with the *devaks*, the man carrying an axe and the woman a vermilion box with sandal paste and turmeric. All bow before the image of Máruti, leave sandal paste, flowers, a copper coin and a betel at the temple door, return home with music and friends, and tie the axe and the *devak* to one of the posts in the booth. A cake is waved round the man while he carries the axe to and from Máruti's temple, and five married girls are feasted. In the Sholápur district, a fish is offered to the *devak*. What follows closely resembles a Kunbi wedding. In the Ratnágiri district, the marriage service is conducted either by a Bhagat, who is a Chámbhár, or by a Jangam. The ceremonies are the same as among Mahárs

The remarriage of widows is permitted. A widow is not allowed to marry her husband's brother, nor any man of his surname, or her father's surname or her mother's father's surname. She cannot also marry her maternal uncle's son; but she may marry her sister's husband. The form of the marriage ceremony is called *gándharva* or *mhotur*, and differs from the first by the non-performance of *homa* or worship of the sacred fire, which is invoked as a witness at the first marriage. The essential and binding portion thereof consists in taking oaths of mutual fidelity. In some places, the ceremony consists in seating the pair side by side, worshipping Ganpati and Varuna, and knotting together the ends of the couple's garments. In Ratnágiri, rice grains are applied to the forehead of the widow and to the knee of the widower. In some places, a sum of money is required to be paid to the widow's father by the intended husband, in others, the relations of the widow's deceased husband are also required to be paid. A bachelor is not allowed to marry a widow, unless he first marries a *shami* plant (Prosopis spicigera).

Divorce is permitted on the ground of impotence in the case of man, of adultery in the case of woman, and of the loss of caste in the case of both. Divorce is also allowed on both sides if any permanent misunderstanding arises. In the latter case alone divorced wives can marry again. Divorce is effected simply by public declaration. In some places funeral rites are performed in the name of the divorced wife.

The caste follow the Hindu law of inheritance and profess Hinduism. They belong both to the Shaiva and Bhágvat sect. The deities of their special devotion are Bahiroba, Jánái, Jokhái and Jakhái. In Ratnágiri, a cocoanut is installed among the house gods in the name of the deceased ancestors. The cocoanut is renewed every year, the old one being broken and the kernel distributed as *prasád*. The offerings made consist of a hen, a goat and grain, which the worshippers consume. In the Poona and Násik districts, they have a *báva* or spiritual teacher belonging to their caste, whom they hold in great reverence. In Ahmednagar, however, their religious teacher is a Lingáyat priest, before whom they bow and to whom they give a money present. They worship snakes, and at some places, the Musalmán saints.

Speaking generally, the caste employ Bráhmans for religious and ceremonial purposes, and these Bráhmans do not suffer degradation for associating with them. Their funeral ceremonies, however, are carried out by Kumbhárs in Thána and by the Jangams in Ahmednagar.

Death ceremonies.

The dead are generally burned; but those that cannot bear the expenses bury them on their backs with their heads to the south. In the case of burial the bodies are allowed to lie where they are interred; but in the case of cremation, the ashes are thrown into a river or stream. Well-to-do persons throw the bones and the ashes into the Ganges. In Khándesh, they bury the unmarried and burn the married. Propitiative ceremonies are performed on the tenth, eleventh and twelfth days after death, on the bank of a stream or well. On the thirteenth day the castemen are feasted. The ceremonies of *shráddha* and *paksha* are performed annually, when money and grain are given to the officiating Bráhman priest.

The original occupation of the caste is that of making shoes, and even now their main calling is the same; but some of them cut and dye skins and make bridles, whips, sandals, ropes and waterbags. Some earn their living as cartmen, tent-pitchers and cotton-weavers. Some hold State grants or *inám*, some are occupancy as well as non-occupancy rayats; but the majority are landless day labourers.

Food.

They eat fish and the flesh of sheep, fowls, hare and deer. They do not eat any other animals, nor the leavings of other people. They drink liquor; and esteem themselves higher than Mahárs and Mángs on account of their abstaining from eating beef and the flesh of any animal dying from natural causes. This, however, does not apply to Chevli Chámbhárs, who eat dead buffaloes in all circumstances.

CHAMGARS or Kanarese Chámbhárs have two divisions, Proper and Mochi, who neither eat together nor intermarry. The former profess Hinduism, the latter are Lingáyats. The former have the following exogamous divisions :—

Name of division.	Family god.	Locality.
1. Boryekár ..	Navadurga ..	Goa.
2. Gadkár ..	Mahádev ..	Hosali.
3. Halankár ..	Bhomkádevi, Ravalnáth and Vetál.	Goa.

Name of division.		Family god.		Locality.
4. Kudalkár	..	Lakshmi	..	Goa.
5. Málvankár	..	Shivnáth	..	Málvan.
6. Nandgadkár	..	Venkatarama	..	Angdi.
7. Pávshekár	..	Bhoomkádevi	..	Goa.
8. Revankár	..	Revánáth	..	Do.

Marriages are prohibited between brothers' and sisters' children. **Marri**
A brother's daughter can be married to a sister's son; but if a sister's daughter is to be married to a brother's son, a hanging lamp is carried on the occasion of marriage. Girls are generally married before maturity; boys from twenty to twenty-five. If a girl attains puberty before marriage, her parents lose the right of giving her in marriage. In such cases the ceremony is performed by a near relation of the girl. Sexual license before marriage is neither recognised nor tolerated. Polygamy is allowed and practised, but polyandry is unknown.

The offer of marriage comes from the boy's father, who has to pay a bride-price of from Rs. 16 to Rs. 64 to the girl's father. The marriage ceremony lasts six days. When a match is settled, the fathers of the boy and girl, with some friends and relations, go to a Bráhman priest, either a Joshi or a Havig, ask him to fix the time for the ceremony, and pay him two annas rolled in a couple of betel-leaves. From the priest, all go to the bridegroom's, where plantains and molasses are handed round. They then go to the bride's house with not less than a hundred fried cakes or *vadás*, a cooked fowl, a bodice, a robe, Rs. 2 in cash, flowers and betelnuts and leaves. The price of the girl is settled, and the girl dressed in new clothes. The party then go to a tavern, where they spend Rs. 2 brought by the bridegroom's father, and, on their return to the bride's, are feasted with rice and cocoanut milk brought from the bridegroom's, and go home. On the day fixed by the Bráhman, the bridegroom is rubbed with turmeric paste, bathed in warm water, and dressed in a waist-cloth, shoulder-cloth and head-scarf. Then holding in his hands some betel-leaves, a betelnut, a cocoanut and a dagger, and wearing the marriage coronet, he goes in procession to the bride's house. He is received with the same forms as among high-class Hindus, enters the booth, and stands opposite the bride, separated from her by a cloth. The head of caste calls out: *sávadhán*, that is, take care; the curtain is pulled aside, and the couple throw garlands of flowers round each other's necks. The bride's parents join the hands of the bride and bridegroom and pour water over them (*dháre*). They then sit on a bench called *sávo*, and each guest waves a coin round their heads and drops it in a tray at their feet. After this ceremony is over, the guests are treated to a meal, the chief dishes in which are *páisa* and *vadás*. On the second day the bridal party goes to the bridegroom's, and the ceremony in all other respects does not differ from that of other low castes. The auspicious post of the marriage booth at the girl's house is made of the *kindal* tree (Termanalia paniculata), and that at the boy's, of *Jámba* (Psidium guyava.) The *devak* of all the sections except Halankars is the *Rumad* (Ficus glomerata). The *devak* of the Halankars consists of the *Rumad* and the *kalamb* (Anthocephalus cadamba).

The remarriage of widows is permitted with the sanction of the caste headmen. Only a widower or a married man may marry a widow. The widow has to return to the relations of her deceased husband the amount of her bride-price and the ornaments and clothes received from him. She bathes and takes these things to the house of her deceased husband, and places them at the root of the sweet basil plant, saying that from that day she ceases to belong to his family. Her intended husband presents her with a robe and bodice in the presence of male members of the caste and widows, who alone can attend the ceremony. A dinner to the party ends the ceremony. Divorce is not allowed in Kanara, but it is allowed in the Karnátak. The caste follow the Hindu law of inheritance.

Religion. Chamgárs are Hindus of the Smárt sect. Their patron god is Venkataráma, whose temple is at Manjguni in the Sirsi *táluka* of the Kanara district. Their chief objects of worship are Sirsiamma, Honávaramma, Ankleámma, Mahámáyi, Mahádev or Shiva, Ganpati, Játka, Hanumán and the Nág or Cobra. They never go on pilgrimages. Their holidays are *Shivarátri*, *Yugádi*, *Nágpanchami*, *Dasara* and *Diváli*. They believe in witchcraft, sooth-saying and ghosts, and offer blood-sacrifices to the village-spirits. Their priests are either Karháda or Havik Bráhmans, whom they employ at marriages. In the Karnátak, Lingáyat priests are employed to conduct the funerals.

Death ceremonies. The dead are burnt in a sitting position with face towards the north. The mourning lasts for eleven days. On the twelfth day, if the deceased be a male, his son-in-law or sister's son is invited and presented with the deceased's clothes, silk girdle, a copper-pot, a dining-dish, etc. If the deceased be a female, her daughter is invited and presented with an ornament and a robe belonging to the deceased. This is repeated on every new moon day for one year. The ceremony of *shráddha* is not performed. Only the *Mahálaya* is performed for the propitiation of the deceased ancestors.

The coast Chamgárs tan hides after they have been cleaned by Mahárs, and make sandals. The upcountry Chamgárs are better off than the coast people, earning money as husbandmen, labourers and cartmen as well as by working in leather.

They eat mutton, fowls, fish and pork and drink liquor. They do not eat from the hands of Jingars, Sonárs, Devalis, Bándis, Gudigars, Nhávis, Holayás and Kotegárs. They rank with Mádigs and Holayas and their touch is held to defile. Food

CHAMBHAR.—A sub-division of Devángs and Lamánis or Vanjáris.

CHAMGAR.—A synonym for Chámbhár.

CHAMPANERI.—A sub-division of Ghánchis and Kansárás.

CHAMTHAS, numbering 190 (1901), including 70 males and 120 females, are found principally in Káthiáwár. They allow widow marriage and bury their dead. The chief object of their worship is Khodiád Máta. Some are professional dancers. Others deal in hand-mills.

CHANCHI.—A sub-division of Kolis.

CHANDLAGARA.—A sub-division of Mochis.

CHANDRAVANSHI.—A synonym for Bhátia.

CHANNA HOLIYA.—A sub-division of Mángs.

CHANTALA.—A sub-division of Chodhrás.

CHAPALSANDE.—A sub-division of Mángs.

CHARAN.—A sub-division of Lamánis.

CHAPARBAND.—*See* CHHAPARBAND.

CHARANS, numbering 32,852 (1901), including 17,267 males and 15,585 females, are found all over Gujarát except the Surat district, in Cutch, Káthiáwár and Sind. They are also called Gadhavi, Báhrot, Bárath or Bárahatta, and Mángan. The term Cháran is derived by some from *chár* to graze, as a large number of the tribe were originally graziers. According to others, it is derived from *char* to spread, as the Chárans are bards and genealogists attached to royal courts and spread their fame by singing their praises. Both these derivations are acceptable, as they are indicative of the two main divisions of the Chárans, the graziers and the bards. The word Báhrot with its varients Bárath, Bárat́ and Bárahatta is variously interpreted. It is stated by some to be Bahurat, *i.e.*, those who speak much. Name.

Another explanation is that the appellation Bárahath was given to the Cháraus because they have *hatha* obstinacy of twelve kinds (*bálahat*, *rájahat*, *strihat*, etc.). A third party hold that Bárath is a corruption of the Sanskrit *varishth*, *barishth*, *barath*, *bárath*, just as *sheth* is from *shreshth*. These three derivations are mere puns on the word Báhrot or Bhát, which means a bard and has been adopted from the Bhát sections of the Rajputs and Maráthás (*see* BHAT). The epithet Gadhavi, the Chárans explain, is applied to them, because they are often the owners of *gadhas* (forts) villages, or because formerly they lived at the courts of twenty capital forts, the original word being Gadhavisa. This explanation is obviously fanciful. Commonly Gadhavi at present means a headman. According to a bardic account, the origin of the term Gadhavi is that a son was born to an unmarried girl of the Dhedhi clan of Rajputs. To hide her shame the girl abandoned the boy, as soon as he was born, behind a fortress *gadh*. The boy was saved and called Gadhavi, by which name the Chárans are still known in parts of North Gujarát. The boy is said to have been also called Cháran because he used to tend a potter's donkey. Two facts are quoted in support of the story that the Chárans were originally donkey graziers. The potter is still known all over the province of Gujarát by the compound name of Kumbhár-Cháran. Till the time of Sidhráj Jaysing (A.D. 1094—1143) the Chárans of Anhilaváda used to levy a tax of Rs. 16 on the marriage of every Kumbhár girl, which was so heavily felt by the Kumbhárs that many girls remained unmarried till they were over twenty-five years old. When the Kumbhárs' grievance was brought to the notice of Sidhráj he called the Chárans and told them to choose one of two richly caparisoned animals, a donkey and a horse. The Chárans chose the horse, and from that day they made the Rajputs their patrons and ceased to levy the tax from the Kumbhárs. The antipathy between Chárans and Kumbhárs is still so strong that no Cháran is allowed to be present at a Kumbhár's wedding.

The term Mángan means a beggar, and is a generic term applied not only to Chárans but to others as well following the same profession, such as Bháts, Bhangads, etc.

Traditions of origin. There are several other traditions concerning the origin of Chárans. In Sind it is said that Sarasvati, the daughter of Brahma, used to worship Mahádev. One day whilst dancing and singing she laughed and in doing so dropped a flower from her mouth, which assumed the form of a boy. When the boy grew up Shiva employed him to graze his bullock. Once while grazing the bullock on a river bank, he came across the clothes of some fairies who were bathing into the river. Taking the clothes the boy ran off to Mahádev. The fairies followed him and complained to Mahádev of the insolence and impudence of the boy. Mahádev referred both parties to his consort Párvati for a decision. Párvati ordered the boy to return the clothes to the fairies; but he declined, saying that he would not do so, unless one of them agreed to be his wife. They agreed and he was married to one of them named Avari. He had two sons by Avari, who are supposed to be the ancestors of the Chárans. It is further stated that Rája Prithu, king of Oudh, was at this time engaged in performing a sacrifice. He went to Shiva and implored him to be present at the sacrifice. Shiva ordered the two Cháran lads to accompany the king, but they declined to do so unless the king made some provision for their livelihood. The king accordingly imposed a tax upon Khatris, payable to the Chárans on every marriage or other solemn occasion. This same tradition, with slight variations, is current in North Gujarát, where it is stated that an idol was made by Párvati with the dirt of her body, which was inspired with life by Shiva and employed to tend four animals of incongruous dispositions, a lion, a serpent, a cow and a goat. The lion attacked the cow and the serpent attacked the lion, but the herdsman by the gift of some of the flesh of his arm quieted them and brought them to Shiva, who in reward gave him the name of Cháran or grazier. The fairies mentioned in the Sind tradition are here represented as serpent girls, to one of whom Cháran was married under the same circumstances as stated in the Sind tradition. The Cháran had two sons and one daughter from the connection. The sons were named Nág and Tamar, of whom Tamar remained with the god Indra and Nág came on earth. Chárans are the descendants of the latter.

The same tradition prevails in Cutch, but the original Cháran is stated to have been born to Shiva of Ganga, and his wife is stated to have been Avad, the daughter of the Shesh Nág (the chief of the Nágas). It is a common practice of the Chárans of Cutch to address the Ahirs as *máma* (uncle), for the latter are said to be descended from Ahi Nág, a son of Shesh Nág. Another son of Shesh Nág, Karkotak Nág, is believed to be the common ancestor of the Káthis.

Some accounts in Cutch give **Nád or Nánd** as the name of the son of Ganga, while one account states that it was not Ganga but Párvati, of whom the original Cháran was born.

In Káthiáwár, the tradition is told in a somewhat different way. It is stated that both the original Cháran and his wife Avad were created by Párvati by her supernatural powers. The Charan was married to her on condition that if he talked to her, she would leave him. Three sons were born of this marriage, Nara, Chauva and Chorado. Avad had conceived a fouth, but (before the time for delivery arrived) Avad scolded Cháran, who was milking a buffalo with the mouth of the vessel downwards. He replied, thinking it was impossible for Avad to leave him, as she had already three sons by him. But as fate would have it, immediately he spoke, she dropped the earthly body (in the womb) and left him.

It is obvious from these traditions that the Chárans were originally graziers. The Máru Chárans, however, at least an intelligent part of them, do not think much of the traditions, and say that they were originally superhuman spirit-beings ranking with the other half-divine fame-spreaders the Siddhas, that is the knowing ones, and the Vidyádharis or female scientists, news agents, and god-messengers. In time, like certain other angelic classes, the Chárans settled on earth, and became the bards of kings and chiefs. After Parshurám's dispersion of the Kshatris, the Chárans accompanied them in their southward flight. In those troubled times, the Chárans took charge of the supplies of the Kshatri forces, and so fell to their present position of cattle-breeders and grain-carriers. In support of their claim to divine origin, they give numerous quotations from various Sanskrit works such as the Rámáyan, Mahábhárat, Matsya Purán, Padma Purán, etc., in which the Chárans are mentioned as the fame-singers of the gods and heroes. They are even referred to in the literature of the Jains. Thus, in the Pallavanáji Sutra the Chárans are classed among the celebrities, *viz.*, *Arihants*, *i.e.*, Tirthankars, *Chakravartis*, *i.e.*, sovereigns, *Vidyádhars*, etc.

The question is whether the Chárans mentioned in the ancient literature and who are undoubtedly represented by the modern court poets are the same as the rough cattle-guarding Chárans. The present difference in appearance between the ordinary Cháran grazier and the Rajput chief's Cháran bard and reciter is so great as to render this doubtful. It has been suggested that the court reciters are distinct from the herdsmen, a set of Chárans of courtly Bráhman or part Bráhman origin who were Chárans or Fame-spreaders, and only from the sameness of sound were supposed to be Chárans or graziers. It has also been suggested that the handsome high class Rájputána graziers whom Colonel Tod so greatly admired may be the forefathers of the courtly Cháran. Neither of these suggestions seems necessary. In spite of their present special appearance, among the courtly reciters are families who belong to all the four main divisions of village Chárans, Gujars, Káchhelás, Márus and Tumers. This fact proves that the court reciters are not a distinct class but are descended from Chárans of all divisions whose talents or good looks raised them to the favour of the local chiefs, and whose present special appearance is due to their having for generations married almost entirely with Cháran families who, like themselves, have long enjoyed the easy well nourished life of court bards and reciters. Though aided by their gifts of paralysing their chief's enemies with their curse and of inspiriting their chief's troops with their songs, the Chárans probably mainly owed their success to their unflinching readiness for martyrdom. This surprising devotion of whole families, old women, men in their prime, and young children, proved to the people the truth of the Cháran's claim to be inspired. When it was well established, the Chárans found that the belief that they were god-possessed opened to them several well paid forms of employment: begging, since the people prized their blessing and dreaded their curse; caravan-guiding leading to caravan-owning and the Cháran's close alliance, if not identification, with the Vanjárás; and debt-insuring, opening an escape from the narrow path of self-sacrifice to the highway of snug common-place money-lending.

Appearance, dress and ornaments. The Chárans, both men and women, are a tall good-looking fair-skinned tribe. The men are like Rajputs, strong and well made. They wear the moustache and long whiskers, and in Central Gujarát they wear the beard. Some have the hair of the head cut at the temples. A man's dress consists of a pair of trousers, and over the trousers a waist-cloth, a jacket, a loose short cotton coat, and a Rajput-like turban or a piece of cotton cloth four cubits long wound round the head. A woman dresses in a petticoat, or in Rewa Kántha a pair of trousers, a bodice or a jacket, a robe, and, except in Central Gujarát among those who are not connected with Rajput families, a black woollen blanket over the head. Among men, the well-to-do wear a silver anklet on the left foot, gold finger-rings, a gold necklace and gold ear-rings. In the Panch Mahúls, no Cháran woman wears ivory bracelets. Well-to-do women wear silver wristlets, silver anklets, a silver or gold necklace, a gold nose-ring, and gold or silver ear-rings.

Language. The Gujar Chárans speak Gujaráti, the Káchhelás Kachhi or Gujaráti or Ahiri, the Márus Márwári or Gujaráti, and the Tumers Kachhi or Gujaráti. The typical names of male members among the Máru Chárans are Haridán, Khubdán, Lakhadhir, Hamir and Shivadán; and of females, Jivanbái, Ládubái, Párvati, Rájabái and Rukman. Among the Tumbel Chárans, the common names of males are Devidás, Jivráj, Khimráj, Keshav, Mánek and Náran ; and of females, Ashbái, Jetbái, Málbái, Nágbái and Rájbái. The names in common use among the Káchhela men are Káno, Rámsur, Sájan, Shivo and Umro. The names of the Káchhela women are similar to those of the other divisions.

A son whose elder brother has died is often given an opprobrious name. Some of the opprobrious names are Ukardo or Ukedo meaning "dung hill," Vachhio meaning "a calf," Gábho meaning "a calf," and Nathu meaning one whose nose is bored.

Community. Some divisions of Chárans have an hereditary head called senior or *ghardero* who settles social disputes in the presence of a large company met at some high feast ; in other divisions a few respected men settle disputes in consultation with the caste people. Breaches of caste rules are punished by fine, and eating with forbidden persons by excommunication. An excommunicated person is readmitted after he has feasted the caste people.

Divisions. Chárans have six distinct sections as follows :—

1. Gujars.
2. Káchhelás from Cutch, also called Parájias or outsiders.
3. Márus or Márwár Chárans—from Máru the Sanskrit name of Márwár.
4. Tumers or Tumbels—probably from Sind.
5. Sorathiás from Sorath or Káthiáwár.
6. Suchia.

Members of all these divisions except the Gujars and Sorathias are found in Sind.

In Gujarát, none of the divisions eat together or intermarry. In Cutch interdining is allowed between the three divisions found there, *viz.*, Máru, Káchhela and Tumbel, but not intermarrying. In Sind, the Márus regard themselves superior to the other sub-divisions inasmuch as they consider it derogatory to give their daughters in marriage to them, though they do not object to taking their wives from among them. The other divisions freely intermarry.

Of the Gujar Chárans little has been learnt. They are said closely to resemble Márwár Chárans many of whom were probably originally Gujars. The Káchhelás are the largest division of Chárans. Besides in Cutch, they are found all over Káthiáwár, and form the bulk of the Cháran population both in North and in Central Gujarát. They are closely allied to the Káthis who in Káthiáwár are their chief patrons, and to the Ahirs, whom, as noticed before in the Cutch tradition, they address as *máma* or maternal uncle and whose dialect closely resembles the dialect spoken by the Káchhela or Parájia Chárans. Within the last twenty-five years, a considerable body of Káchhela Chárans has moved from East Káthiáwár to the forest land in Hálol to the north and east of Pávágad hill in the Panch Mahâls. The Tumers, though sometimes included in the general term Káchhelás, are a distinct class. The Pávágad Káchhelás tell the story that the Tumers got their name from *tumadi* a gourd, because the founder of the caste was shortly after birth placed in a hollow gourd and left to float down a river by his mother, a *vidyádhar* or angel who had loved a mortal.

The Chárans commonly speak of their tribe being made up of three and a half clans (*sádá tran pádá*, *pádá* being the word used for a clan). These *pádás* or divisions are variously named. According to some they are (1) Nara or Taro, (2) Chorâda, (3) Chaunva, (4) Tumbel, the last being considered half a clan, because it has sprung from a child who was undeveloped at birth, as noticed above in the Káthiáwár tradition. According to others, these *pádás* are endogamous divisions, *viz.*, (1) Máru, (2) Káchhela, (3) Tumbel, (4) Nesái or Agarvachha, the last being considered half a division, from the inferiority of their occupation, Nesái meaning those who are graziers. According to the latter, these divisions are said to have been fixed by about the thirteenth century by one Rájbái Máta, a celebrated Cháran woman, who became afterwards deified.

The clans Nara, Chorâda and Chaunva are found only among the Káchhelás. Of these, Chaunvás have twenty-two stocks, Chorádás have fifty-two and Naras have seventy-six.

The Máru or Málwa Chárans include twenty clans with 300 sub-clans or stocks. They are as follows :—

1. Asia with forty branches.
2. Badhva with nineteen branches.
3. Baratrohádia with twelve branches.
4. Bati with thirteen branches.
5. Budhda with four branches.
6. Dhadhania with eleven branches.
7. Dadhvádia with nineteen branches.
8. Gelva with six branches.

9. Háda with ten branches.
10. Jula with thirty-one branches.
11. Khadia with thirty-six branches.
12. Kharol with two branches.
13. Máda with two branches.
14. Mahiaria with eleven branches.
15. Nádhu with twenty nine branches.
16. Ratanu with one branch.
17. Sandhayach with sixteen branches.
18. Siyál with none.
19. Soda with thirty-three branches.
20. Vijál with one branch.

The clans common among the Timber Cháráns are the following :—

1. Alsura.
2. Bárot.
3. Báti.
4. Bhán or Luna.
5. Buchar.
6. Gágia.
7. Ghilva.
8. Gogar.
9. Gungada.
10. Jivia.
11. Kária.
12. Kesaria.
13. Mundhuda.
14. Nándhán.
15. Ságar.
16. Sákhara.
17. Sikhadia
18. Vánaria.
19. Vária.

The Sind Cháráns have 120 exogamous divisions of which the following are the most common :—

1. Ahda.
2. Aliga.
3. Ambe.
4. Anuva.
5. Bansur.
6. Barsara.
7. Barshada.
8. Bati.
9. Beka.
10. Bhansur.
11. Chiba.
12. Dechia.
13. Dekal.
14. Detha.
15. Dewag.
16. Gadan.
17. Gaddia.
18. Gir.
19. Gohar.
20. Iba.
21. Hasa.
22. Jachi.
23. Jenovebra.
24. Jethor.
25. Kanta.
26. Kanval.
27. Kanya.
28. Kapari.
29. Kole.
30. Ladhuva.
31. Lambe.
32. Lunag.
33. Lawan.
34. Mahro.
35. Manraj.
36. Manoha.
37. Manuva.
38. Maya.
39. Mesan.
40. Nadhu.
41. Nara.
42. Naya.

43.	Odha.	49.	Rendhir.	55.	Taparia.
44.	Ontal.	50.	Sarore.	56.	Teja.
45.	Perjia.	51.	Shaha.	57.	Vachia.
46.	Rara.	52.	Shobha.	58.	Vadgama.
47.	Ratno.	53.	Sindhiach.	59.	Vasa.
48.	Rohada.	54.	Sorira.	60.	Vijhal.

For matrimonial alliances the Cháraus group their families into two classes the *Bha* or brother families, *i.e.*, those belonging to the same exogamous sub-division, and *Bháneja* or sister's son's families, *i.e.*, families of other exogamous sub-divisions. So when the Chárans arrange a betrothal, they take care to avoid *Bha* or brother families and arrange it with a *Bháneja* family ; and old men of the caste know by heart a number of brother families and a number of other families, though the lists are not exhaustive, and hence it happens that sometimes families belonging to the same exogamous divisions are unknowingly joined in a matrimonial alliance. Originally, it appears each of the three section Nara, Chorāda and Chaunva had their own *Bháneja* division, but later on, they became mixed up and the three became exogamous divisions.

A Cháran must marry within his own endogamous division and at the same time must not marry into his own exogamous division. A Cháran can marry a woman of the section to which his mother belongs, of his paternal grandmother's section, or of his maternal grandmother's section. Máru Chárans do not marry a father's sisiter's, mother's brother's, or mother's sister's daughter ; while Káchhelás and Tumbels marry a mother's brother's daughter and among the former there was formerly a practice of marrying a mother's sister's daughter. Marriage with a wife's sister is allowed either during the wife's lifetime or after her death. Two brothers are allowed to marry two sisters. In Sind, marriage is not allowed between maternal kindred within seven degrees of relationship nor with two sisters at a time. On the death of a wife or in case of her being barren, insane or attacked by a loathsome disease, it is open to a Cháran to marry his wife's sister during the wife's lifetime.

In Gujarát, girls are generally married from one to fifteen, as far as possible before coming of age. In Cutch and Káthiáwár, they are married between twelve and twenty, and in Sind, at about the age of fifteen. Sexual license before marriage is strongly reprobated in all places. Polygamy is allowed on the grounds of failure of issue, want of harmony or even a fancy for a second wife. In some parts of Gujarát, a man is required to obtain the permission of his first wife in order to marry a second.

Birth ceremonies. No ceremonies are performed on the day of a birth. On the sixth day the goddess Chhathi is worshipped. Except among the Panch Maháls Káchhelás, a reedpen, an inkstand and a dagger or a knife or a sword are struck in the ground before the goddess. Among the Panch Maháls Káchhelás, friends come bringing rice or wheat and lay it before the child's cradle or sheetswing. In return each is given some *gugari* or boiled spike millet which they take to their homes and give to children. The child is named on the sixth day after birth or on any other day chosen by the astrologer. The child is bathed, richly clothed, and marked with red powder on the forehead. It is laid on a white cotton sheet, the four corners of the cloth being held by four girls if the child is a girl, and by four boys if the child is a boy. In this cloth-cradle the child is rocked *jholi polied* thrice and named by the father's sister. The boys or girls are feasted and the child's father makes the father's sister presents in cash or in cloth. After childbirth the mother remains impure from twenty-one to forty days, and in the Panch Maháls for about twelve days. Among most Chárans, the ceremony of giving the first cooked food takes place when the child is about a year old. Chárans do not regularly wear the Bráhman thread. In Pálanpur, the goddess devotees wear a black woollen thread, and a few in Rewa Kántha wear the Bráhmanic thread only when they perform a *Shráddha* ceremony.

Marriage. The offer of marriage comes from the boy's father. In Káthiáwár and Gujarát, the dowry called *des* or *pallu* conferred on the girl varies from Rs. 50 to Rs. 300. A portion of the *des* is paid on the day of the betrothal, which is called *Sagái* or *Vesvál* and goes in Káthiáwár by the name *dudh pivun* (milk drinking, perhaps suggestive of their original pastoral life). The remaining portion of the *des* is paid on the marriage day. In Cutch, among the Káchhelás and Tumbels, the bride's parents receive a sum of money of from Rs. 75 to Rs. 100 for the marriage expenses. In Gujarát this sum varies from Rs. 50 to Rs. 150 and is accepted by all classes of Chárans, though some refuse to take it. The marriage ceremonies of Chárans resemble those of Kanbis, the essential portion consisting in going round the sacrificial fire four times (*Fera farva*).

Widow remarriage is not allowed among the Máru Chárans It is permitted among the Káchhelás, Tumbels, Gujars and Sorathia Chárans. Among Sind Chárans none of the divisions allow it. In Cutch, both the Káchhelás and Tumbels allow the widow to marry the deceased husband's younger brother, though she is not forced to do so. Among the Káchhela Chárans of Káthiáwár, *derwatun* (living in connubial relations with the deceased husband's brother) is enjoined, though the widow is not barred from marrying elsewhere if the *der* (brother-in-law) does not insist on his right. The *derwatun* prevails also in Gujarát. The widow's intended husband has to pay a sum of money to her parents. The ceremony takes place at night on a Sunday or Tuesday and is conducted by the family priest. The widow is presented by her intended husband with clothes and ornaments and three sets of ivory bangles. The brows of the pair are marked with red powder, and rice grains are thrown on them, which completes the union. In Káthiáwár, the widow receives a *des* of from Rs. 100 to Rs. 200 and molasses are distributed among those present. The newly married widow is not allowed to enter her new husband's house by daylight, as that is supposed to bring in evil. In Cutch, the heads of the pair are brought into close contact with one another before an image of Máta in the presence of a Bráhman, and this is the only ceremony. In Gujarát, widows having children do not remarry. Usually a bachelor does not marry a widow. If he does, the ceremony is the same as in the case of a widower marrying a widow.

The rule about divorce is not uniform. In Central and North Gujarát, neither the wife nor the husband can divorce each other, though in some parts of Central Gujarát the husband is allowed to divorce a wife. In Káthiáwár, divorce though very rare, is allowed. Adultery on the part of the wife or constant bickerings would justify a divorce by the husband. If however he effects it in order to facilitate bringing in a new wife, he cannot divorce the first wife, except by allowing her *jiwai*, *i.e.*, maintenance (food and raiment). A divorced woman does not lose caste. She may remarry by the widow remarriage form. In Cutch, divorce is not permitted among the Máru Chárans. Among the Káçhhela and Tumbel Chárans, divorce is permitted if the husband is impotent or disabled, or sometimes on account of disagreement between the husband aud wife. The divorce is effected by a deed which the husband passes to the wife under his signature, mentioning the bride-price, or sometimes more, which he expects to be paid in case the woman marries again. Generally the caste settles the bride-price and enforces the payment of the same from the man who marries the divorced woman. In Sind, the very idea of divorce seems shocking to the community. Divorce.

Chárans folllow the Hindu law of inheritance with slight modifications. Among none of them does the custom of female succession Inheritance.

prevail in preference to male. As a rule, in the absence of male children, clansmen become heirs of the deceased. In Káthiáwár and Rewa Kántha, this rule is relaxed. There a man, even though he may be a member of an undivided family, is allowed by will to leave his immoveable property or *girás haks* to his daughter or daughter's son.

Religion. Most of the Chárans are Shaivas and are devotees of the consort of Shiva under many titles, both in her well-known forms of Amba Bhaváni and Párvati and under local names such as Kálika, Khodiár, Bahucharáji, Varái, Bobadi, Totadi, Limbadi, etc. Their devotion for her is so great, that the Cutch Chárans even call themselves *Devi bálak, i.e.*, children of the goddess. Some are Bijmárgis, Kabirpanthis, Rámánujas and Swáminaráyans. They worship in their houses the images of Mahádev, Máta, and Vishnu, and are careful to visit the village temples. In Cutch, they also worship such deified heroes as Váchharo and Pábu, and also Hanumán, Bhairav and Kshetrapál. Váchharo and Pábu are worshipped on Monday with offerings of sweet dishes, cocoanuts or molasses; and Bhairav and Hanumán on Saturday with an offering of *til* or a preparation of *til* sesamum. The other Hindu gods are also respected and the usual Hindu fasts and feasts are observed. The devotees of goddesses fast for nine days during the *Navarátri* and sacrifice a goat on the tenth day. On this day as well as on the seventh day of *Mágh* the Sind Chárans sacrifice either a goat or a buffalo, pour the blood of the victim on the altar of the goddess, and divide the flesh among those present. They believe in omens, witchcraft and sorcery. In the Panch Mahále, that some uneasy family ghost may not harass them, some men wear round the neck a plate stamped with a human face. Of animals they worship the cow, the cobra, and in Cutch the *nilkanth* or jay. Of plants and trees their favourite guardians are the *tulsi* or holy basil and the *pipal* Ficus religiosa. They make pilgrimages to Dwárka, Girnár, Prabhás Pátan, Alláhábád, Benáres, Gokul and Mathura. The sect mark on the forehead of the goddess devotees is an *ád* or horizontal red line or streak made with oxide of lead. The priests of Chárans are Audich, Meváda, Parájia, Rájgor, Sárasvat, Shrigaud and Shrimáli Bráhmans. In Cutch, the priests of Máru Chárans are a class of Bráhmans called Márváda Rájgor Bráhmans, those of the Káchhela Chárans are Chárania Bráhmans or Parájia Bráhmans, and those of the Tumbel Chárans a class of Bráhmans who style themselves Ismália Audich Bráhmans. None of these three classes of Bráhmans are received on terms of equality by Bráhmans of the highest rank. The priests of Máru Chárans do not dine with the Márus. The priests of the

Káchhelás dine with their patrons, and so also the priests of the Tumbels dine with the Tumbels.

The Cháran women are supposed to have supernatural powers, and in Cutch are even now addressed by the lower classes as mother or goddess mother. Several of the most popular goddesses of North Gujarát are the spirits of Cháran women who sacrificed themselves to guard the privileges of their caste.

Death ceremonies. The dead are burnt. Children under two years old and persons dying of small-pox, cholera or leprosy are buried. In Cutch, the Vadava and Sirácha sections of the Tumbel Cháraus bury their dead. Those who have made a pilgrimage to Hingláj are buried in a sitting position. In Rewa Kántha, on the evenings of the second, third and fourth days after death, the chief mourner places a jar holding milk and water on the roof of the house. Their other ceremonies do not differ from those of local Kanbis. The nearest relations of the deceased remain impure from seven to thirteen days. In the Panch Mahàls, male members are not required to shave the moustache; instead of shaving they rub their heads with oil like Musalmáns. *Shráddha* ceremonies are performed for eleven days from the second to the thirteenth, and in some places, for four days from the tenth to the thirteenth. In Cutch, a ceremony called *Náráyan Bali* or *Bávani Kriya* (fifty-two ceremonies) is performed for the propitiation of childless ancestors and men who have died a violent death, generally at some place of pilgrimage, in the month of *Kártik* or *Chaitra*.

Occupation. Chárans follow various callings; some are bards keeping genealogies of Káthis and Rajputs and reciting their praises and the exploits of their forefathers in short rude pieces. Some hold large grants of land(1) and sometimes whole villages, some are poor and unskilful husbandmen, some are traders and money-lenders, some serve in the irregular forces kept up by the chiefs, and some are beggars receiving presents at all feasts and marriages.(2) Most of them, especially

(1) About A.D. 714, on the death of Rám Parmár of Telangana, Cutch is said to have been given to the Chárans. Tod's Rájasthán, I. 84. The date favours the view that the Chárans who overran Cutch early in the eighth century were refugees from the Arab conquerors of Sind. See Elliot and Dowson, I.

(2) In Central India in the beginning of the last century (A.D. 1800) Chárans, particularly of the Máru class who are mendicants, attended at feasts and marriages in great numbers. At marriages they were in the habit of extorting large sums by threatening to sprinkle their blood over the marriage party. About A.D. 1818, when the Rável of Bansváda was on a visit to Sir John Malcolm, Bhimsing, the son of the Rája of Baglu, settled to marry a lady of the Bansváda family. The marriage was delayed on account of a preliminary demand that Bhimsing should satisfy any Chárans and Bháts who might attend the wedding. Bhimsing told Sir John Malcolm that this stipulation might ruin him. Once pledged, the extravagance of the Cháran's demands and their violence in enforcing them were likely to leave no option but poverty or disgrace. Central India, II 135—36.

the Káchhelás, are graziers, cattle-sellers and pack-carriers. As graziers and cattle-sellers they move in companies of about twenty men during the eight fair months, grazing and selling cows, bullocks, buffaloes, camels and clarified butter. Formerly like Bháts they acted as guards to travellers and goods. No traveller could journey unattended by these guards, who for a small sum were satisfied to conduct him in safety. These guards, called *valávás*, were never backward in inflicting the most grievous wounds and even causing the death of their old men and women[1] if the robbers persisted in plundering those under their protection; but this seldom happened as the wildest Koli, Káthi or Rajput held the person of a Cháran sacred. Besides becoming safeguards to travellers and goods they used to stand security to the amount of many *lákhs* of rupees. When rents and properties were concerned, the Rajputs preferred a Cháran's bond to the bond of the wealthiest banker as the Cháran could enforce the payment of a debt to himself or a claim for which he had become security by cutting or killing himself. They also used to stand security for good behaviour called *fail* or *chálu zámin*, and for personal attendance called *házar zámin.* The ordinary *trága* or self-mutilation went no further than a cut on the arm with the *katár* or crease; the forearms of those who were in the habit of becoming security had generally several cuts from the elbow downwards. The Cháraus, both men and women, wounded themselves, committed suicide and murdered their relations with the most complete self-devotion. The guardian-stones or *páliyás* which are scattered all over Káthiáwár, show that Cháraus preferred death to dishonour, and that even women did not hesitate to kill themselves when the honour of the family or tribe was concerned.[2]

(1) The Cháran who accompanies travellers likely to be attacked by Rajput robbers, when he sees the robbers approach, warns them off by holding a dagger in his hand, and if they do not attend to him, he stabs himself in a place that is not mortal, and taking the blood from the wound throws it at the assailants with imprecations of future woe and ruin. If this has not the desired effect, the wounds are repeated; and in extreme cases one of the Cháran's relations, commonly a female child or an old woman, is made a sacrifice. Central India, II. 134—35. Further on (page 137) Sir John Malcolm says: " I collected a number of well authenticated cases not only of individuals but of families; and in two instances I found that the Cháran inhabitants of a village had sacrificed themselves. Instances of people dipping their clothes in oil, setting fire to them, and dancing in the flames till they were burnt to ashes were not uncommon. In one case a boy of fourteen had a spear-head thrust through his cheeks. To take it out the father had to place his knees on the boy's head. But he showed no signs of pain. He confessed it hurt him, but said if he had cried out he would have been considered a useless and unworthy wretch with nothing of the Cháran in him.

(2) Near the entrance of almost every village in Káthiáwár stand guardian-stones or *páliyás* which have been set up to perpetuate the memory of Cháran men and women who, usually with success, have performed *trága* to prevent the carrying off or to recover the cattle of the villages from the predatory Káthis. The name of the Cháran, the date, and the reason for committing *trága* are engraved on the stone, while a rude sculpture marks the way in which the *trága* was performed. Men are shown on horseback wounding themselves with a sword or spear, and women running a knife through their arms.

As was the case with the Bhát and the Bráhman, the source of the Cháran's power lay in the widespread fear that a Cháran's blood brought ruin on him who caused the blood to be spilt. The ground of this fear was the belief that the ghosts of Bháts, Bráhmans and Chárans are specially terrible. How strong was the dread of a Cháran ghost is shown by the Cháran suicide Bahuchara becoming one of the most dreaded and therefore most popular goddess in North Gujarát. In all three classes, Bháts, Bráhmans and Chárans, the reason why their ghosts are specially dreaded is that the castes are believed to be possessed. Some have thought that the Cháran's fairness of skin, made more notable in the case of the women by the wearing of black, helped the belief in their ghostliness. Only to a very limited extent can this be true. Nor can the Cháran's sanctity be traced simply to their connection with the worshipful cow. The main and probably the original reason for the belief that the Cháran was possessed was the reckless daring with which, as the Káthiáwár tombstones show, both men and women threw their lives away in defence of the cattle and villages entrusted to their charge. That respect for his ready self-sacrifice was a chief element in the honour paid to the Cháran is shown by the god Shiva's humorous application of the name Cháran or grazier to the man who fattened his mixed herd on his own body. Besides this of inspired courage the Cháran enjoyed the two great god-gifts of cursing and song. These three inspirations seemed sufficient proof of the Cháran's right to the proud name of *devputra* or sons of god, the favourite dwelling of the guardian spirit. It was the fact that the Cháran was possessed that gave this special power to his blessing and curse which were laden with the spirit which possessed the curser. It was the belief in his posses sion that made the murder of a Cháran the lètting loose of the engaged unhoused spirit of a god or goddess as well as of a man, and therefore made the forcible death of a Cháran so hideous and so heavily punished a sin. As the worship of Bahuchara shows, the fear was greatest in the case of a suicide Cháran. How strong and widespread is the dread of the suicide's ghost is seen in the long continued English efforts to keep the suicide ghost from walking by burying it nailed with a stake at the meeting of three roads. If the dread of the ghost of a suicide man is so keen, who can set bounds to the horror of incurring the wrath and vengeance of a suicide god?

The ordinary food of Chárans is wheat or millet bread, rice and pulse. In Rewa Kántha, Pálanpur and Cutch, on holidays or when they can afford it, besides the ordinary food-grains, they eat the flesh of sheep, goats, antelope, hare and partridge, and fish, except Food.

in Cutch, where only Tumbel Chárans eat it. In Káthiáwár, some Chárans who are the devotees of a goddess, eat the flesh of sheep and goats when the animals are sacrificed. In Pálanpur, two or three he-buffaloes are sacrificed on *Dasara* Day, and their blood is drunk by a Cháran woman. The Sind Chárans also eat pork. All Chárans, except in Central Gujarát, drink liquor. In Cutch, they eat from the hands of Rabáris, Ahirs, Khavás, Luhárs and Darjis. Their priests, the Prajia Bráhmans, and Rajputs eat at their hands. In Káthiáwár, Rajputs, Káthis, Ahirs and Mirs eat with them. In Sind they eat with the Sonárs and Darjis

CHARANIA.—A sub-division of Meghváls.

CHARDOS.—A caste of Native Catholic Christians.

CHAROTARIA.—A sub-division of Dheds and Shrimáli Sonis; a tribe of Kolis.

CHASIA.—A sub-division of Dheds.

CHATAIVALA.—A sub-division of Vaidus.

CHATLA.—*See* under Minor Musalmán Castes.

CHATUR.—A sub-division of Shimpis.

CHATURTHA.—A sub-division of Jains in the Southern Marátha Country.

CHATURVEDI.—A sub-division of Modh Bráhmans.

CHAUN.—A sub-caste of Bráhmans.

CHAWTA.—A sub-division of Vághris.

CHELKAR.—A sub-division of Mahárs.

CHEVLE.—A sub-division of Gavlis.

CHEVLI.—A sub-division of Chámbhárs

CHHADIA.—A synonym for Khálpa.

CHHAPGAR.—A synonym for Bhavsar.

CHHAPPARBANDS, numbering 103 (1901), including 39 males and 64 females, are found chiefly in Poona and Sátára. The word Chhapparband means a thatcher, the occupation of the caste being thatching and the making of false coins. As a criminal tribe, they have lately been taken under control and settled on the land by Government. They claim a Rajput origin. They appear to be immigrants from Upper India, and speak Hindustáni at home, employing Upper India Bráhmans as their priests. They marry their girls between ten and twenty and their boys between twelve and twenty-five. The remarriage of widows is permitted. The chief object of their worship is the goddess Bhaváni. They burn their dead. They eat fish and flesh, and drink liquor.

CHHARA.—*See* under Minor Musalmán Castes.

CHHATRI.—A synonym for Kiliket.

CHHEBRODA.—A sub-caste of Vániás.

CHHETRI.—A synonym for Khetri.

CHIGRI BETKAR.—A synonym for Haran Párdhi.

CHIK KURVINS.—A sub-division of Devángs.

CHILMI-AGNI.—A sub-division of Banjigs.

CHIPLUNA.—A synonym for Chitpávan.

CHITAR.—A sub-division of Jingars; also a synonym for Gudigar.

CHITMIT.—A sub-division of Raddis.

CHITPAVAN.—A sub-division of Bráhmans.

CHITRAKA.—A synonym for Gudigar.

CHITRAKATHI or Picture Showmen, numbering 757 (1901) including 388 males and 369 females, are residents of the Násik district, a few families being found in the adjacent districts of Thána, Poona and Sátára. They take their name from *chitra* a picture, and *katha* a story, and exhibit pictures of heroes and gods, entertaining their audience by reciting stories from the *puráns*. They are wandering beggars who claim to be Maráthás by origin. When settled, they live in wattled huts thatched with grass; and when travelling, in small tents or *páls*. A tradition still exists in the caste that they came from Singnápur and Nátepute in the Sholápur district during the reign of Sháhu Rája. **Name and origin.**

There are no endogamous divisions of the caste, and no exogamous sub-divisions are found above families bearing the same surname. The commonest surnames are Jádhav, More, Povár, Sálunkhe, Shinde, Thombare, Ingale, Ambale, Bhosle and Supalkar, which seem to suggest a probable Marátha origin for the caste. **Divisions.**

Marriages are prohibited between members having the same surname. Sameness of *devak* is a bar to intermarriage. Examples of the *devaks* worshipped by different families are given below. A member of the caste cannot marry his father's sister's or mother's sister's daughter. He may marry his maternal uncle's daughter. A man may marry two sisters, and brothers may marry sisters. Polygamy is allowed and practised, but polyandry is unknown. **Marriage.**

Girls are married between three and twenty, boys between three and thirty. If a girl commits sexual indiscretions with a caste-man, each of them is fined Rs. 5 or made to give a dinner to the caste-people. If the offence is committed with a man of another caste, the girl is excommunicated.

The offer of marriage comes from the boy's father, who has to pay a *dej* or bride-price of from Rs. 50 to Rs. 150 to the girl's father. The day for the marriage is fixed by the village priest, who conducts the service. The marriage ceremonies of Chitrakathis resemble those of Marátha Kunbis. The *devak* or marriage guardian is installed at the boy's house on the day before the marriage, and at the girl's house on the marriage day, when a goat is killed and the caste-men are feasted. Every section has a separate *devak*. The *devaks* of some of the principal family stocks are as follows :—

Name of *kal.*		Name of *devak.*
1. Thombare	..	The *shami* (*Prosopis spicigera*).
2. Ingale	..	The *kohála* (pumpkin).
3. Jádhav	..	An ear of *pála* (*Ehretia buxifolia*).
4. More	..	A peacock's feather.
5. Sálunkhe	..	A feather of the *sálunki* bird.
6. Povár	..	A knife.
7. Ambale	..	An *ámba* or mango.
8. Supalkar	..	The *pánch-pálvi* or leaves of five kinds of trees.

The remarriage of widows is permitted. It can be celebrated on any dark night except the new-moon day during any month except *Bhádrapad*. The widow and her new husband are seated on a blanket, red powder is applied to their foreheads by a remarried widow, and they are made to utter one another's name, which completes the ceremony. A bachelor is not allowed to marry a widow.

A husband can divorce a wife on the ground of her misconduct or incompatibility of temper. In the former case the wife is turned out of the caste. In the latter, she may marry after the fashion of the widow remarriage ceremony.

Religion. The caste follow the Hindu law of inheritance and belong to the Hindu religion. They worship all the Bráhmanic and village gods, their family deities being Bhaváni of Tuljápur, Khandoba of Jejuri and Páli, Jotiba of Ratnágiri, and Lakshmi of Kolhápur. They observe all the Hindu holidays and make pilgrimages to Alandi, Jejuri, Pandharpur, Tuljápur and Kondanpur. Goats and fowls are offered to the village gods, which are eaten by the offerers themselves. *Táks*, or images of deceased ancestors, embossed on metal plates, are installed amongst the household gods. Their priests are the ordinary village Bráhmans.

Death ceremonies. The dead are buried in a sitting position. The corpse is bathed, dressed, and seated on a blanket, and carried to the burial ground with some cooked rice tied to one of its corners. On the thirteenth day after death the caste is feasted. For the propitiation of deceased ancestors the *mahál* is performed every year in the latter half of *Bhádrapad*, when caste-men are feasted and uncooked articles of food are given to Bráhmans.

Occupation. The chief occupation of the caste is exhibiting pictures of gods and heroes and reciting their stories in song and verse. They also exhibit wooden dolls which are made to dance and fight in imitation of the contests between heroes and demons. These puppet shows are losing their popularity, and the exhibitions are usually confined to picture shows. A few of the caste work as day-labourers, and are paid either in cash or in corn.

Food. They eat the flesh of goats, sheep, fish and poultry, and drink liquor.

CHITRODA.—A sub-division of Nágar Bráhmans.

Name and origin. **CHODHRAS**, numbering 30,972, including 15,540 males and 15,432 females, are found chiefly in the Surat district and Agency, and a few families are recorded in Ahmedábád and Broach. They claim to be partly of Rajput descent, and according to their own account were once carriers in the Rajput kingdoms of Northern Gujarát, whence they fled south at the time of the Musalmán invasion. There is little evidence in their customs and organization of any element of Rajput blood; but the tradition of their former connection with Northern Gujarát is not improbable. They appear to be one of the aboriginal tribes of Gujarát, and are classed by the higher castes amongst the *Káliparaj*, *i.e.*, dark race, a contemptuous term in general use for all the aboriginal tribes of Gujarát. Bráhmans will not take any part in their ceremonies, and consider that to do so would be to lower themselves in the social scale.

Divisions. There are nine endogamous divisions of the tribe: Bharutia, Chantála, Chokápur, Takária, Valvái, Santala, Mota, Nána and Boda. Of these the Chokápuris stand highest in social rank. They are also called Pávágadia, which shows their former connection with the famous Pávágad hill. Members of all divisions eat at the hands of the Pávágadiás, but the latter will not eat with the other divisions. Among common surnames are: Valvai, Bharotia, Vashi, Rávat, Rajputia, Hajarnia and Desái. Marriages are prohibited within six or seven degrees of relationship, but generally marriages do not take place between members so long as a former relationship can be traced between them. Marriage with a wife's younger sister is permitted though marriage with a wife's elder sister is forbidden. Two brothers are allowed to marry two sisters. Members from higher castes, such as Kanbis or Kolis, are admitted into the tribe. A gathering of persons invited from five or six villages is held, toddy is drunk, and the new-comer is made to smoke a *bidi* or native cigarette which has been first smoked by one of the party. This completes the admission ceremony. The betrothal takes place at the girl's house, when liquor is served by the girl's father to the party assembled, and the girl bows down to the boy's father and other elderly persons of his party. The latter present her with a few coins.

Marriage. Marriage is generally adult. If a girl commits sexual indiscretions with a caste-man, the latter is compelled to marry her; if with a member of a higher caste, her father is fined Rs. 5, which is spent on treating the tribesmen to liquor. If the offence is committed with a member of a lower caste, the girl is excommunicated. Polygamy is allowed and practised, but polyandry is unknown.

The offer of marriage comes from the boy's father, who has to pay a bride-price of from Rs. 45 to Rs. 100 to the girl's father. The day for the marriage is fixed in consultation with both the parties. Any day except a Saturday, Sunday or Tuesday is considered suitable for marriage. The service is conducted by the bridegroom's sister (who should be an unwidowed married woman) or, in her absence, by one of his female paternal cousins.

On the marriage day, stone images of deceased ancestors known as *khatráns* and the goddess Devali are worshipped. Next, the bride-groom's party go to the bride's house for the marriage, where they are first treated to a dinner. Then the bride hides herself somewhere in the house; the bridegroom's party find her, and seat her on a low wooden stool. Her hair is combed and a necklace of black glass beads is fastened round her neck by the bridegroom's sister, who also puts an upper garment over her. Next, the bride is taken out of the hut and the end of her upper garment is tied to that of the bridegroom by the *Anvariun* (bridegroom's sister) who takes the part filled by the officiating Bráhman among castes of a higher social standing. A dance follows to the accompaniment of a drum, in which the bride is taken on her shoulder by the *Anvariun*, and the bridegroom by a male member of the party. Liquor is then served and the day's festivities end. On the next day the bridegroom returns to his house with his bride.

Amongst the Takariâs the bride and bridegroom are rubbed with yellow powder the day before the marriage.

In some places, after the dance is over, the bride and bridegroom are made to walk four times round the kitchen fire Next, they feed each other from the same dish, which completes the ceremony. The essential portion lies in tying the necklace of glass beads round the girl's neck.

There is another and interesting form of marriage which is known as *Khandália*. This is resorted to only by those who cannot afford the ordinary marriage expenses. In a *Khandália* marriage the bridegroom wins the bride by taking service with her father. Marriage by this form is considered respectable on the part of the girl's father ; but the man who is married by it is lowered in the social estimation of his fellow tribesmen. A woman can divorce a *Khandália* (a husband by such a marriage) at her pleasure. She is sent to work with her *Khandália* husband in the field, and if the result of this association is unsatisfactory, he is divorced. It is not considered objectionable on the part of a woman to marry several *Khandália* husbands in succession.

The remarriage of widows is permitted. A widow cannot marry a paternal or maternal cousin or other near relation. She may marry a relative of her deceased husband or even his brother, provided that they are younger than the deceased. A widow remarriage is generally celebrated on a Sunday or Tuesday. Relations on both sides are present on the occasion. The widow's new husband has to pay to her father a sum varying from Re. 1 to Rs. 100. If he be a bachelor, he is taken on a man's shoulder to a *rui* (Calotropis gigantea) or *shami* (Prosopis spicigera) bush. A necklace of glass beads is tied to a twig of the bush, liquor is served, and the party return home. The ceremony consists in the present to the widow by her new husband of a robe and bangles which she puts on. Next, a necklace of glass beads is tied round the widow's neck by a remarried widow, which completes the union. Liquor is served and the party disperse.

Divorce is allowed on the ground of disagreement between husband and wife or infidelity on the part of the latter, with the sanction of relations and of the caste *panch*. If the divorce is wanted by the husband he has to pay the wife Rs. 5, which is spent on entertaining relations and the caste *panch* with liquor. If a woman is taken in adultery with a caste-man or a member of a higher caste, she can remain in the caste by paying a fine of Rs. 5 to the caste people. If the offence is committed with a member of a lower caste, she is required to give a dinner in order to remain in the caste. A divorced woman can marry again by the widow remarriage form. The caste follow the Hindu law of inheritance.

Religion. The Chodhrás do not appear to worship any of the regular Hindu gods. The chief objects of their veneration are Suraj or the sun, Dharati-mátá or the earth, Kákábalio or the small-pox goddess, Bhaváni, and the boundary gods Pálio, Simário and Náderio. They worship trees such as the *ámbo, tád, khájur*, etc., and add the word *dev* or god to their names. Stone images of ancestors known as *khátrans* are installed under trees, and small earthen domes are erected over them by those who can afford it. Amongst these images one is known as *Dábhio Dev* and is supposed to protect the others. Offerings of goats and fowls are made to gods, part being received by the offerers, part by the worshippers. They go on pilgrimage to the hot spring at *Unái*. Of the Hindu holidays they observe only the *Diváso, Holi, Diváli*, and the thirteenth day of the dark half of *Bhádrapad*, when liquor is freely drunk. When an epidemic breaks out, two kinds of vows are made to the goddess Bhaváni—*Chokli*, which consists in worshipping the goddess by throwing reddened rice and pouring milk over the idol of the goddess and lighting a lamp fed with *ghi* before it; and *Meli*, that is, killing a cock or goat before the idol and pouring its blood and some liquor over it. The god Náderio is worshipped for protection against cattle disease, and Hinário for protecting the crops. All the ceremonies of the Chodhrás are conducted by the caste elders.

Death ceremonies. The dead are burnt. Those who cannot afford to burn, bury their dead. Before lighting the funeral pile, cooked food and rice are placed in the corpse's mouth, and it is thought lucky if a crow comes and takes a portion of it. When the corpse is burnt the party return to the house of the deceased. They are entertained with liquor either here or in a liquor shop on the way. On the third day after death cooked rice and pulse are offered on the spot where the corpse was burnt or buried. The mourning ends on this day. The relatives of the deceased come to his house bringing with them cooked *vál* (Dolichos Lablab) and pay each from four annas to a rupee to the mourners, which is spent on treating them to liquor. If the relatives of the deceased are well-to-do they give a dinner to the caste-people. On the fourth day after death a spirit medium, *báhdar havriya,* accompanied by the friends of the deceased, takes a stone, and groaning and shaking as if possessed, sits in the spirit-yard or *devsthán,* a plot of ground set apart near each village for the spirits of their forefathers, in order that they may not wander from want of shelter and company. He kills a fowl, letting some of the blood fall on the stone. Next, he adds grain, butter and liquor, and marking the stone red consecrates it to the spirit of the deceased, covering it in some cases by a quaintly ornamented hollow clay dome. Near the stone the friends set a small clay cow or she-buffalo for a woman and a horse for a man. No other ceremonies are performed for the propitiation of the deceased ancestors.

The hereditary occupation of the caste is agriculture. Some of them are successful growers of the hardier kinds of rice. They are also wood-cutters. Some hold land under the *rayatvári* system. Many are day labourers. They are hunters and catch small game. They also catch fish.

They eat the flesh of goats, sheep, fowls, squirrels, peacocks, parrots, doves, larks and fish, and drink liquor to excess. They consider themselves superior to Gámtás, Koknás, Náikdás, Bhils and others who eat beef. They eat with the Dublás. Food.

CHOKHAMELA.—A synonym for Mahár.

CHOKHAPUR.—A sub-division of Chodhrás.

CHOR.—A synonym for Dhuntale Kaikádi.

CHORAI.—A sub-division of Meváda Bráhmans.

CHORAIA.—A sub-division of Dheds.

CHORIA.—A sub-division of Dublás.

CHORIDA.—A sub-division of Ahirs.

CHORVADI.—A sub-division of Girnára Bráhmans.

CHOVISA.—A sub-division of Bráhmans.

CHUDBUDKI JOSHI.—A synonym for Joshi.

CHUDGAR.—A sub-division of Brahma Kshatris.

CHUDIVALA.—*See* under Minor Musalmán Castes.

CHUGHADDA MUGHAL.—A sub-division of Mughals.

CHUMLI.—A synonym for Malhár Koli.

CHUNAR.—A sub-division of Gavandis; a sub-division of Lingáyats.

CHUNARIA.—A sub-division of Vághris.

CHUNDADIGIRA.—*See* under Minor Musalmán Castes.

CHUNE.—A sub-division of Lonáris.

CHUNWALIA.—A sub-division of Kolis.

CUTCHI HALAI.—A sub-division of Bhátiás.

CUTCHI MEMAN.—A sub-division of Memans.

DABGAR.—A synonym for Khálpa.

DABHOLE.—A sub-division of Gavlis.

DABHOLI.—A sub-division of Chámbhárs.

DABKAR.—A sub-division of Mángs.

DABKE MADIG.—A sub-division of Mángs.

DADHICH.—A sub-division of Bráhmans.

DADHICHI.—A synonym for Dadhich.

DADHICHEVALA.—A sub-division of Vaidus.

DAFALI.—A synonym for Abdáli.

DAGAD.—A sub-division of Ods.

DAHAMASE.—A sub-division of Joháris.

DAHEMA.—A sub-division of Bráhmans.

DAIVADNYA.—A synonym for Devángan and Konkani Sonárs.

DAKALERU.—A sub-division of Mángs.

DAKALVAR.—A synonym for Dhakalvár.

DAKHANI.—A sub-division of Bráhma Kshatris.

DAKKALGAR.—A synonym for Dhakalvár.

DAKOJI.—*See* Sárodi or Dákoji.

DALAL.—*See* under Minor Musalmán Castes.

DALAYA.—A sub-division of Mángs.

DALE.—A sub-division of Gujar Kanbis.

DALSINGAR.—A synonym for Jingar.

DAMANI.—A sub-division of Dublás.

DAMODARJI.—A sub-division of Girnára Bráhmans.

DANDAVATI.—A sub-division of Kudavakkals.

DANGCHI.—A tribe of Bhils.

DANGE.—A sub-division of Dhangars.

DANGI.—A sub-division of Kanbis.

DARBHIA.—A sub-division of Audich Bráhmans.

DAREDA.—A sub-division of Bráhmans.

DARJIS or Tailors, numbering 73,083 (1901), including 37,229 males and 35,854 females, are found all over Gujarát, Káthiáwár and Cutch, chiefly in towns and large villages. They are also called Meráis, Pipávási, Sais, Suis, Sai Sutárs and Thálávádi. The term *sui* means a needle and describes the occupation of the caste, *viz.*, sewing. The origin of the term *meráj* is not known. The name Sai Sutár is in use in Cutch, and is said to be applied to the caste on account of some of the families following the occupation of carpentry. Name and origin.

According to one account, the founder of the caste was Pipa, a famous saint, many of whose sayings have passed into popular religious aphorisms. It is not known when Pipa flourished. The majority of the caste claim a Kshatriya descent, and state that at the time of Parashrám's persecution of the Kshatriyás, they were given shelter by Pipa in a temple, of which he was the priest. Pipa gave them a needle and thread and told them to sew the clothes of the goddess of the temple. From that day they came to be called Pipávási, dwellers with or under the patronage of Pipa. Traces of their being connected with Rajputs are to be found in their surnames.

About fifty years back, a Lohár was admitted into the Darji caste in Cutch.

Darjis have eight endogamous divisions, which neither eat together nor intermarry. They are as follows:— Endogamous divisions.

Dhandhayás.	Dungarporás.	Maris.	Rámdeshis.
Dosis.	Gujars.	Rájkalis.	Shimpis.

The Rámdeshis, who are found in north Broach, were originally Márwári Garásias, and dress like Pátidárs. The Shimpis are emigrants from the Deccan. In Cutch as the Darjis of Vágad interdine with Ahirs and other kindred tribes, the town Darjis do not intermarry with them. The Darjis residing in the villages of Abdasa have also no intercourse with the town Darjis. This is likely to result in two more endogamous divisions of the caste in Cutch.

The exogamous divisions of Darjis are represented by surnames. The common surnames are— Exogamous division.

Ajaráni.	Dhámecha.
Chávda.	Dhandukia Pithadia.
Chohán.	Dhegáma Pithadia.
Dabhi.	Gabda.

Gohel.	Ráthod.
Koecha.	Sáchula.
Lakadia.	Sáveda.
Lolária Pithadia.	Sodha.
Makvána.	Solanki.
Mándlia Pithadia.	Sonára.
Parmár.	Vághela.

Of the above, Ajaráni, Koecha, Sáchula and Sonára are local or communal in origin. Lolária, Dhandukia, Mándlia and Dhegáma are named after the villages of those names in Káthiáwár, and the term Pithadia is derived from Pithal, the tutelary goddess of these sections, whose shrine is in Bálámbha in Jámnagar State. The rest are Rajput clan names.

Marriage. Marriages are prohibited between members of the same surname and within five degrees of relationship on either side. A Darji can marry a woman of his mother's, paternal grandmother's, or maternal grandmother's section. He may marry his maternal uncle's daughter, but not his mother's sister's or father's sister's daughter. Marriage with two sisters is allowed, and brothers are allowed to marry sisters. Polygamy is allowed and practised, but polyandry is unknown. Except in parts of Kaira and Panch Maháls, divorce is allowed. A woman divorced for other reasons than adultery can marry again by the widow remarriage form. Adultery is punished by fine or expulsion from the caste.

Girls are generally married from eleven to fourteen years, boys from twelve to twenty. Except that they are less detailed, the marriage ceremonies of Darjis are like those of the Kanbis, the essential portions being the *hastamelap* or joining the hands of the bride and bridegroom, and *chorifero*, that is, walking four times round the sacrificial fire.

Except in parts of Kaira, the remarriage of widows is permitted. Except in Ahmedábád and Cutch, where a widow is not allowed to marry a member of her deceased husband's section, the levirate is permitted. The ceremony of widow remarriage is very simple. It is performed in a room in the presence of a few castemen. A Bráhman priest, who officiates, marks the forheads of the pair with red powder. Next, he joins their hands and serves them sweets in one dish, from which they feed one another. Their heads are then brought together, and the ceremony is over. A feast is given to the caste people.

Darjis are Hindus of the Madhváchári, Parnámipanthi, Radhá-Vallabhi, Rámánandi, Shaiva, Sváminaráyan and Vallabhácharya sects. Hingláj is the family goddess of most of the Darjis of Káthiáwár and Cutch. The family goddess of some is Pithal. They worship such minor deities as Gátrad, Chámunda, Satiár, Ker, Pabu, Sitala or the small-pox goddess, Kshetrapál or the snake-god, and deified ancestors under the names of Purushas and Satis. The offerings consist of sweet rice, sweet bread, sesamum, cocoanuts, milk, etc. Darjis keep the regular Hindu holidays and believe in witchcraft, exorcism and omens. They visit the usual places of Hindu pilgrimage. Their priests are the Pushkarna Bráhmans. In their absence, Audich and Modh Bráhmans are also employed. Religion

The dead are burnt. The death ceremonies of Darjis do not differ from those performed by Kanbis. The *Shráddha* and the *Mahálaya* ceremonies are performed for the propitiation of the deceased ancestors every year. The ceremony of *Náráyanbali* is performed for the propitiation of childless ancestors, and of those who have died a violent death, generally in the month of *Kártik* or *Chaitra*. Death ceremonies.

Darjis are hereditary tailors. Though in Cutch some are carpenters and in Káthiáwár some have given up the needle for the plough, the bulk of the class keep to their original employment. Many Darjis from Cutch have settled in Bombay and Karáchi, and some have gone as far as the African ports. Many have thriving millinery establishments in Bombay and Karáchi.

Except in Surat, where they eat fish and flesh of goats and fowls and drink liquor, they are strict vegetarians, though some of them in Kaira refrain from eating carrots. Food.

Darjis eat food cooked by Kumbhárs and Lohárs. Rajputs will eat food cooked by Darjis. Throughout most of Gujarát they hold a middle position in society. In south Gujarát, in the absence of Bráhmans, a Darji officiates at Bharvád marriages. On the other hand, in the Panch Mahâls and Rewa Kántha, besides tailoring, Darjis blow trumpets at marriage and other processions, and hold so low a position that even Dhedas object to eat their food.

DARVESHI.—*See* under Minor Musalmán Castes.

DASA.—A sub-division of many Bráhman and Váni castes.(1)

(1) Dasa is probably the word *das*, *i.e.*, ten, and is applied in Gujarát to the inferior sub-division of a caste, the superior being styled Visa from *vis*, *i.e.*, twenty. In some cases we find below the Dasa division a Panch and Adhich, meaning 'five' and 'two and a half.' In the Deccan a similar system gives the name of Akaramáse or eleven measures to the inferior or irregularly recruited sub-division of a caste, of which the main body is styled Bára-máse, *i.e.*, twelve measures. In the case of the Johári caste, there are sub-divisions known as 'twelve measure,' 'eleven measure' and 'ten measure,' the equivalent of the Gujarát 'twenty', 'ten' and 'five' divisions.

Name and origin.

DASAS, returned as numbering 4,683 (1901), including 2,364 males and 2,319 females, are found mainly in the Karnátak and in small numbers in Kolhápur and the States of the Southern Marátha Country. They are a class of mendicant beggars belonging to different low castes of Hindus and Lingáyats. In Madras they numbered 32,035 at the Census of 1901. They are Vaishnavaites in religion, the Lingáyats only being Shaivas. A man is either a hereditary *dás* (servant of god) or becomes so by vowing to devote himself to the god Venkatráma of Tirupati. A man who has made such a vow goes to Tirupati, where he is initiated, and subsequently makes a pilgrimage to the shrine of the god every year, unless he is prevented by illness. When a *dás* dies the yearly pilgrimage is kept up by his heir. Though the Dásás form one religious order, the members who belong to different castes neither eat together nor intermarry. Examples of such castes are Bánjig, Bedar, Golla, Holia, Korava, Kshatri, Mahár, Valu, Vakkal. The only point of difference between the Dásás and the lay members of their castes is that the Dásás support themselves by begging, and abstain from flesh and liquor on Saturdays, new-moons and fast days.

In addition to begging, some sing and play music, and others perform dramatic plays. The women frequently live by prostitution. Some of them are hereditary temple servants and own *inám* or rent-free lands. They sweep the temple yard, but are not allowed to pass within the door. Besides the produce of rent-free lands they receive the dressed food offered to the village Máruti. The women of the Holia Dásás carry the goddess Murgava in procession, and live by prostitution.

Divisions.

Each caste division of the Dásás has two sub-divisions, Tirmal and Gaud, who eat together, but do not intermarry. The cause of the split is that Tirmal Dásás allow their women to practise prostitution and to take part in plays and dances ; while the Gaud Dásás in acting give the women's parts to boys and have no unmarried women. When a Dása has a family of daughters and no son, he keeps one of his daughters unmarried, to be a prostitute or Basavi. Her children inherit her father's property. If a Basavi has all daughters and no sons, she also keeps one of her daughters unmarried for the same purpose.

Buchanan mentions the Dásás in his account of Mysore and Kanara.(1)

DAS AGRI.—A sub-division of Agris.

DASARA.—A sub-division of Vánis.

(1) Buchanan's Mysore, Vol. I, pp. 241, 331, 339 ; Vol. II, p. 55.

DASKOSHI.—A sub-division of Shrimáli Bráhmans.

DASUNDI.—A synonym for Bhát.

DATANIA.—A sub-division of Vághris.

DAUDI.—A sub-division of Bohorás.

DAULE.—A sub-division of Mahárs.

DAURE GOSAVI.—*See* Bharádi or Daure Gosavi.

DAVAR.—A sub-division of Várlis.

DAVARI.—A synonym for Joshi.

DAVARJI.—A sub-division of Jogis.

DAYAMA.—A synonym for Dahema.

DEPALAS,(1) numbering 603 (1901) including 324 males and 279 females, are found only in Cutch and Káthiáwár, in Dhrángdhra, Wadhwán City, Bhuj and Mándvi. They seem to be a branch of the Lohánás, and it is said that formerly inter-marriages between them and the Lohánás were of common occurrence. The Lohánás, except those of Wadhwán and Dhrángdhra, still interdine with them, and their priests are common. They, like the Lohánás, possessed Bháts or Vahiwanchás three generations ago, but these cannot now be traced. Tradition asserts that there were two brothers Lakho and Dámo who came from Lohárgad (Sind) to Shiáli, a village near Limbdi, and thence went to Dhrángdhra by Wadhwán. From Lakho descended the Lohánás, and from Dámo the Depálás. It is further stated that their residence in Káthiáwár has lasted over 300 years. Name and origin.

There are no endogamous divisions of the caste. They have the following sections which are exogamous:— Divisions.

1. Allaiya and Jobunputra.
2. Chaváni.
3. Damani.
4. Popatia.
5. Rághavani.
6. Váláni.

Marriage with a mother's sister's, father's sister's, or mother's brother's daughter is prohibited. Two sisters can be married simultaneously, or one after the other, the elder one being married first. Two brothers may marry two sisters. Boys are generally married between fifteen and twenty, girls between nine and thirteen. Polygamy is allowed, but somewhat restricted, for no second wife can be taken within ten years of the first marriage unless the first wife is dead. Failure of issue is generally the sole reason for taking a second wife. If one marries a second wife in addition to the first, the former Marriage.

(1) From materials supplied by Mr. K. G Pandit, B.A., LL.B.

wife receives *jivani*, *i.e.*, food and raiment, separately provided under the rules of the caste.

The offer of marriage is made by the boy's father, who has to pay a sum up to Rs. 100 or ornaments and clothes worth that amount to the girl, which is known as *samurtun*. The principal ceremonies of marriage are as follows :—

1. *Sagái* or *vaswál*, that is, the betrothal.
2. *Lagna lakhavun*, or sending a note to the girl's father with the priest, stating the time fixed for the marriage.
3. *Lagna vadhávavun*, or welcoming the priest who has brought the note by presenting him with Rs. 3-8-0.
4. *Pithi chodhavavi*, or applying turmeric paste to the forehead and cheeks of the bride and bridegroom.
5. *Fulenkhun*, or the bridegroom's procession.
6. *Samaiyun*, or the reception of the bridegroom at the village boundary by the girl's party.
7. *Ponkhavun*, or welcoming of the bridegroom by the girl's mother in the marriage booth, when she is given Rs. 25 to be presented to the bride (*hárdo*).
8. *Kanyádán*, or handing over the girl.
9. *Fera farva*, or going four times round the sacrificial fire by the bride and bridegroom, which is the binding portion of the marriage.

Widow re-marriage is allowed. The widow's intended husband has to pay her a sum of from Rs. 25 to Rs. 100. The couple are seated on two low wooden stools opposite each other, and an earthen vessel containing a lamp fed with *ghi* is placed between them. Ganpati is worshipped and the pair touch each other head to head and look below at the lamp, which completes the ceremony. Widow re-marriages are generally celebrated in secret as they are held to be degrading. A payment must be made to the relations of the widow's first husband of two-thirds of the *des* paid at the time of her first marriage. This claim never exceeds the sum of Rs. 66⅔. A bachelor is not allowed to marry a widow. Divorce is not allowed. The caste follow the Hindu law of inheritance with slight modifications

Religion.

Depâlás are Hindus of the Swáminaráyan and Rámánandi sects. Their chief god is Narsinhji, an incarnation of Vishnu. Their family deities are Ashápuri, Pithad, Khodiyar, Suro (a deified ancestor in whose name a pillar has been erected), Surdhana and Thákurji. Those who can afford it make pilgrimages to sacred places of note. The offerings to gods consist of red lead and cocoanuts. When an epidemic breaks out, Mátáji is propitiated with an offering of cooked food. The religious teacher of the Depálás is Gangárámji of Dhrángdhra. Their priests are a section of the Gujarát Sárasvat Bráhmans called *bhat* who occupy a statusinferior to the other Bráhmans, who do not dine with them. These *bhats* dine with Lohánás and Depálás.

The dead are burnt, except infants under six months old, who are buried. The ashes are thrown into a pit on the bank of a river. The bones are carried and thrown into the river Rewájia or Narmada. Those who can afford it carry them to Benares to be thrown into the Ganges. The *shráddha* is performed to propitiate the deceased ancestors. Those who have the means marry a male and a female calf by a mock marriage (*nil parnávavi*) in honour of the unmarried dead and childless ancestors. Death ceremonies.

Depálás believe that their ancestors dealt in provisions, particularly grain, and paints, between Málwa and Dholera. They are now house-servants, artisans and shop-keepers. Some are husbandmen and a few are schoolmasters. The artisans work in stone quarries and carve stone.

Khatris (dyers), Bhávsárs, Káyasths and Dhuldhoyas can eat with the Depálás. In Cutch Depálás dine with those with whom Lohánás dine, and do not dine with Bhavsárs or Dhuldoyás. Of those superior to them, the Bráhman *bhats*, Lohánás, Prajia Sonis and the *bhat* Sárásvat Bráhmans eat with them.

DESAR.—A sub-division of Mángs.

DESHASTH.—A sub-division of Bráhmans.

DESHAVAL.—A sub-division of Vániás and Bráhmans.

DESHI.—A sub-division of Báris, Sonárs and Sutárs.

DEV.—A sub-division of Devángs.

DEVADIG.—*See* Suppalig or Devadig.

DEVALAK.—A synonym for Shaiva Gurav.

DEVALVAKIYA.—A sub-division of Bháts.

DEVANGS, also known as Hatkars, Jáds, Koshtis or Sális, numbering 244,445 (1901) including 124,351 males and 120.094 females, are found in all parts of the Presidency and Native States except Gujarát. Of this number, 103,393 were recorded as Lingáyats and 48 as Musalmáns at the Census of 1901. The caste is also known as Nekár, Negár and Neyakar in the Kanarese districts and Vinkar in the Deccan. Neyakar is a Kanarese and Vinkar is a Maráthi term, meaning a weaver. Regarding the origin of the term Hatkar Name and origin.

it is stated that at one time all the Hatkars were Lingáyats. Several hundred years ago, a certain Devángad Ayya persuaded some of them to wear the sacred thread instead of the *linga* and to rub their brows with sandal instead of with cowdung ashes. The obstinacy with which they have stuck to their new religion, from *hat* obstinacy, is generally believed to be the origin of the name of Hatkar. But this is improbable, as Hatkar is also a name of a class of shepherds to whom the epithet obstinate seems to be in no way applicable. The name Hatkar is also traced to *hadgakhram* or ship-mover, because they used to make sails. The term Koshti is derived from the Sanskrit *kosh*, the cod or cocoon of a spider, which is indicative of weaving, the occupation of the caste. Jád is said to mean a great man. Sáli is derived from the Sanskrit *sálika* weaver. Devàng means the body of gods, and is the name of the supposed original ancestor of the caste. It is stated that Deváng was created by Shiva to cover the nudity of mankind. The Koshtis of Poona say that they were Bráhmans, who, for refusing to give the Jain saint Párasnáth a piece of cloth, were cursed and told they would become weavers and never prosper. Some claim the sage Bhávana as their common ancestor. Bhávana married Bhadrávati, daughter of the sun, who bore 101 sons, who are supposed to be founders of so many exogamous sections in the caste. Some claim descent from Vastradhári, the robesman of the gods, whom the gods accompanied on earth in the form of useful tools. According to their sacred books, the founder of their caste was Sumant, who was born from the mouth of Parameshvar, the supreme being. One day Parameshvar asked Sumant to give him a piece of cloth to wear. As Sumant had none, Shiva prayed to the minor gods, who became the instruments of weaving, and for this reason weaving tools have the names of gods and sages.

It appears likely that weaving began with the manufacture of coarse blankets from the wool of the sheep tended by shepherds and was originally a shepherd's occupation. Hence the weaving caste is still known as Hatkar, which is a sub-division of the great Dhangar or shepherd's caste. With the dawn of an era of agriculture, cotton, and later silk, came to be used. The weaving caste then gained many recruits, and became specialised. Later on, it was split up by religious differences, having come much under the influence of Lingáyatism. A great number of these weavers must have once centred at Vijayanagar, where they seem to have leaders Devángayya and Musangayya, to this day. Another division was formerly resident in the Junnar division of the Ahmednagar and Bijápur kingdoms of the Deccan, and still bears the name of Junnare.

Endogamous divisions

The caste have the following endogamous divisions :—

1. Ahir.
2. Arasinapatala.
3. Bángad.
4. Chámbhár.
5. Chik Kurvin.
6. Dev.
7. Deváng or Khatávan.
8. Halabe.
9. Hire Kurvin
10. Jain.
11. Junnare.
12. Kuláchári or observers of family rites, also known as Jánav Deváng as they wear *jánvás* or sacred threads. Some of them wear both the sacred thread and the *linga*.
13. Kurad.
14. Kurnavál.*
15. Marátha, Sakul, Sahakul or Swakul Sáli.
16. Miskin.
17. Nág.
18. Nakul or Lakul.
19. Padam or Padma Sáli.
20. Pad Sáli.*
21. Patnával.*
22. Patta or Pat Sáli.
23. Saguna or Samaya Sáli.
24. Shakuna or Sakuna Sáli.
25. Shiváchári.*
26. Shubra Sáli.
27. Shuddha Sáli.
28. Soma Sáli.
29. Sukha Sáli.
30. Sunta Sáli.
31. Sut Sáli.
32. Tikale.
33. Togati.

Of the above those marked with asterisks are purely Lingáyats. Padam Sális have two divisions, Hindu and Lingáyat. The Hindu Padam Sális of Kanara wear both the *linga* and the sacred thread ; those of the other districts wear only the sacred thread.

In the Poona district are found two of the above divisions, Marátha and Padma, who neither eat together nor intermarry. The Sátára Sális have five divisions, Marátha, Padam and Nakul, Kurnavál and Patnával. The divisions commonly found among the Násik Koshtis are Ahir, Bángad, Jain, Kurad, Marátha, Miskin and Sut Sáli. The Sholápur Sális are split up into six divisions, Bángad, Marátha, Padma, Sukh, Tikale and Togati. Of these the Maráthás are considered to be the highest in the social scale. They do not eat with the others. The rest eat together but do not intermarry. In Ahmednagar are to be met the Chámbhár, Nakul, Padam and Sakul Sális. Of these the Sakuls are supposed to be the pure descendants of the founder of the caste. Lakuls are bastards. The Sakuls do not eat with the other three divisions, who eat from them but not with one another. The main divisions of the Belgaum Sális are Padam, Saguna, Sukh and Sunta. Except the last division all eat together and intermarry. The Sunta Sális are reverts from Islam and are so called, because they still keep up the practice of circumcision or *sunta.* Their customs are partly Musalmán and partly Hindu. The Sális found in Dhárwár belong to the Nág, Padam, Patta, Shakuna, Shubhra, Shuddha and Soma divisions. Six divisions of Sális are found in Bijápur, who may be divided into three groups. The first group is known under the general name Sáli and includes the Padma, Sakul and Sukh divisions. The second group includes the Pad Sális and Soma Sális, and the third group consists of the Shuddha Sális and Dev Sális. All these divisions formerly ate together and intermarried. Since some have become Lingáyats and others lean to Lingáyatism, none but the Padam Sális and Sukha Sális eat together and intermarry. The Sális of Kanara are divided into Arasinapatala, Padam Sális, Pat Sális and Sut Sális. The Pat Sális do not eat with the others. The Arasinapatalas take food cooked by the Padam Sális.

Exogamous divisions.

The exogamous sub-divisions of most of the divisions mentioned above are identical with surnames. The chief of them are as follows :—

Admane.	Davade.	Kharbuje.	Sátpute.
Akáde.	Dhaval-shankh.	Khirode.	Sind.
Ambte.	Dhanik.	Kode.	Shingáre.
Ashkar.	Dhole.	Kuchekar.	Shewáte.
Bade.	Dhotre.	Lákre.	Somak.
Bagde.	Diváne.	Like.	Songe.
Barje.	Divte.	Lol.	Sukale.
Bendre.	Dumane.	Lotke.	Takle.
Bhágvat.	Gajare.	Mahádwár.	Támbe.
Bhandári.	Gháte.	Mardhe	Tálkar.
Bharote.	Ghodke.	Misál.	Tarte.
Bhutkar.	Ghosale.	Mudgal.	Talpushe.
Bitkar.	Gore.	Nichál.	Tálpurush.
Bolke.	Gupta.	Palmár.	Teke.
Burshe.	Hávre.	Párkhe.	Thigle.
Chángle.	Ingle.	Pátak.	Upare.
Chaudhari.	Jedhe.	Pávale.	Valle.
Chavre.	Jháde.	Pore.	Varáde.
Chote.	Kámble.	Ranbhare.	Varu.
Dandavate.	Karme.	Reke.	Yekár.
Dángare.	Kavade.	Rokde.	
Daphal.		Sámal.	

Some of the sections among the Devàng Koshtis take their names from certain functions they have to perform during marriages. They are as follows :—

1. Bhandári : have to offer turmeric powder or *bhandár*.
2. Chavre : hold a *chauri* or fly-whisker.
3. Dhavalshankh : have to blow a conch or *shankh*.
4. Dhole : have to beat a *dhol* or drum.
5. Divate : have to hold a torch or *divti*.
6. Gháte : have to sit fast or *ghat* before the goddess.
7. Jháde : have to *jhád* or sweep.
8. Kalashe : have to set a pot or *kalash*.
9. Kámbale : have to spread a blanket or *kámbli* before the goddess.
10. Tálkar : have to beat the metal cups or *táls*.
11. Tálpurush : have to lay out the two plates.
12. Upre : have to wave incense.

The Marátha Sális of Násik have also adopted Bráhmanical *gotras* in addition to surnames or *kuls*, such as Bháradwája, Dhaumya, Gautam, Káshyap. Kaundinya and Váshishtha.

In the Karnátak, the exogamous divisions are known as *bedagus* which are as follows :—

Aralikatti	Honnungda.
Arshanda.	Kalasda.
Bijjala.	Konappana.
Devena.	Nányada.
Gadgiya.	Pattada
Gundimeya.	Sakkariya.
Honnabáginda.	Shivásáuda.

Surpurada.

The Hire and Chik Kurvins have seventy-six *gotras*, which are arranged in two equal groups, one called after Shiva, and the other after Shiva's consort Párvati. The stock names Ashva, Benni and Dharu are included in the first group ; and Arishiv, Dev and Guru in the second group. The names of some of the other stocks are Are, Bile, Gandi, Koti, Kunchámani, Mail, Mena. Mine. Mulla, etc.

Marriage. Marriages are prohibited between members having the same surname or *bedagu*. In some places, sameness of *devak* is a bar to intermarriage; in others it is not. In Násik, where the caste has adopted Bráhmanical *gotras*, sameness of surname as well as of *gotra* is a bar to intermarriage. But if the *gotra* of a party is not known, the surname or *kul* only is taken into consideration in settling marriages. Among the Kurvins, marriages are prohibited between members of the same *gotra*, and among the Chik Kurvins the family stocks of the bride's mother's father and the bride's father should be different from those of the bridegroom's father and of the bridegroom's mother's father. In most places, marriage with a father's sister's or mother's brother's daughter is allowed; in a few places it is prohibited. Marriage with a mother's sister's daughter is not allowed. A man may marry two sisters and brothers may marry sisters.

Marriage is infant as well as adult. In Sholápur, as a rule, girls are married before they come of age. Sexual license before marriage is not tolerated. Girls guilty of misconduct are excommunicated. Polygamy is allowed and practised, but polyandry is unknown.

The offer of marriage comes from the boy's father. If the boy's father is well-to-do, he receives a dowry with the girl. If the girl's father is poor, he receives a bride-price. In the Karnátak, as a rule, the boy's father has to pay to the girl's father a sum of Rs. 30. The day for the marriage is fixed by a Bráhman priest, who conducts the service The marriage ceremonies of the Kulácháris are conducted by their religious teachers, who belong to their own caste and are called Devángayyás. The marriage consists of the following ceremonies :—

1. *Kunku-lávne* or *Sákhar-sádi* is the betrothal. It is performed a few days before the marriage. The boy's father with friends and kinsfolk goes to the girl's house accompanied with music. A square of wheat grains is formed and the girl is seated over it. The boy's father worships the girl, presents her with a robe, fills her lap with rice grains, sugarcandy, a cocoanut, dry dates, and almonds, puts an ornament on her person, and applies red powder to her forehead. Sandal paste is then applied to the foreheads of the party assembled, betel is distributed, and the ceremony concludes.

2. *Halad* or *turmeric-rubbing*.—On the day fixed for the purpose, turmeric paste is first applied to the girl at her home and then to the boy at his. A cocoanut and a dagger are then tied in a piece of yellow cloth and put into the hand of the boy. The boy must not part with the dagger till the marriage ceremonies end.

3. *Telan* or *oil-sprinkling*.—On the marriage day, a washer-woman sprinkles oil over the head of the bridegroom, singing songs. She receives a gift and retires.

4. *Devak*.—The *devak* consists of the usual *panchapallava* or leaves of five kinds of trees; or of the loom-rope, a stone lamp and a rice cake put together. The *panchapallava* is put in a winnowing fan which is placed in Máruti's temple. The boy's parents, taking a plate containing an offering to the god, go to the temple in procession under a canopy held by four men, with the hems of their garments tied into a knot. The offering is placed before the god, and the party start to return home. On their way they halt at a goldsmith's, take from him idols of gods, place them over the *panchapallava* and return home. The *devak* is installed in a corner of the house. In some places it is tied to a post of the marriage booth.

5. *Lagna or the marriage proper*.—The bridegroom, dressed in marriage attire, with a *báshing* or marriage coronet fixed on his head, is taken on horseback to the bride's village. He stops at the village temple and sends to the bride his brother, who is called *vardhava*. At the bride's, her father presents the boy's brother with a turban to be given to the bridegroom. The best man in return hands a lucky necklace or *mangalsutra* to a woman in the bride's house to be tied round the bride's neck, and returns to Máruti's temple with a suit of clothes, in which the bridegroom is dressed at the time of his marriage. When the bridegroom reaches the bride's house, rice mixed with curds is waved round him. He is led into the booth and he and the girl are made to stand face to face on bamboo baskets placed on low stools, with a curtain held between them. The priest draws aside the curtain, throws the lucky rice or *mangalákshat* over them, and seats them both on the marriage altar or *bahule*. Seven threads are twisted into a cord, which is passed round them, pieces of turmeric are tied to the right wrist of the bridegroom and to the left wrist of the bride, they throw clarified butter into the sacred fire, and the hems of their garments are knotted together. They go into the house and bow before their family deities. The bridegroom steals one of the images and the bride's mother takes it back from him, giving him instead a cocoanut or a silver ring. The guests are dined. Next day a caste feast is given and sugar-cakes and rice-flour boiled in water and mixed with molasses is eaten.

7. *Phal*.—A party of males and females from the boy's house go with music to the girl's house, taking with them rice grains, dry dates, dry cocoa kernels, almonds, cocoanuts, a packet of sugar,

a robe, a bodice, etc The boy and girl are made to worship Ganpati, the girl is dressed in the robe and bodice, and her lap is filled with the other articles. Betel is distributed, sandal paste is applied to the foreheads of the guests, and the ceremony is over.

8. *Zál.*—The women on the boy's and on the girl's side stand on two sides of a curtain. The curtain is drawn aside, and each party tries to win over the other, that is, to drag them on to their side. This game is known as *zál.*

9. *Zenda.*—This is a dance in which a man takes the bride and bridegroom on his two hips and dances to the accompaniment of music.

10. *Varát.*—This is the return procession of the bridegroom to his house with his bride. On reaching the house the pair untie each other's marriage wristlets or *kankans* and caste people are feasted, which terminates the marriage.

The remarriage of widows is permitted. A widow cannot marry her father's sister's, mother's sister's, or mother's brother's son, or a member of her late husband's section. In some places, she is prohibited from marrying a member even of her father's section. A widow remarriage is celebrated on a dark night in the latter half of the month. In Násik, the bridegroom's father goes to the widow's house with caste people, accompanied with music, taking with him a tray containing a robe, a bodice, bangles, turmeric powder, red powder, a lucky necklace and ornaments. A low wooden stool is placed on the ground and a square of grains is made over it. The widow is seated over the stool and is made to wear the robe and bodice brought by the bridegroom's father. The bridegroom then ties the lucky necklace round her neck and applies red powder to her forehead, which completes the union. Next, the widow is presented with the ornaments brought for her, the pair are made to worship a water-pot (*Varuna*) by a Bráhman priest, *pánsupári* and sandal paste are distributed, and the party return to the bridegroom's house. In Sholápur, the widow remarriage is celebrated in a deserted place, where no light is kept burning. The pair to be married and a Bráhman priest, and on some occasions a few castemen, are present. The widow is first bathed, and then her intended husband. The former is seated on a low wooden stool, the latter on a bullock's packsaddle. Both are made to drink sugared milk from the same cup, and the widow's lap is filled, which completes the ceremony. The faces of the pair should not be seen till the following morning. But this custom is dying out. In some parts of Sholápur, the ceremony consists only in tying a lucky necklace round the widow's neck or in applying red powder to her forehead after she has worn a new robe. In Sátára, as in Sholápur, the ceremony takes place in a lonely locality. The foreheads of the widow and her intended husband are marked, first with cowdung and then with red powder, and the widow's lap is filled. Sometimes rice grains are thrown over their heads and they are made to wear new clothes and bow to the house gods, this being the only ceremony. As a rule, a bachelor is not allowed to marry a widow, but in some places he is allowed to do so after marrying a *rui* bush (Calotropis gigantea).

Divorce is permitted with the sanction of the caste *panch*. Incompatibility of temper, the wife's misconduct, the husband's ill-treatment of the wife or his being subject to an incurable disease, are considered to be sufficient cause for a divorce. In some places, the divorce is effected by breaking asunder the lucky necklace round the wife's neck; in others, by performing funeral rites in the name of the wife. A divorced woman is allowed to remarry by the widow remarriage form. In some places, adultery on the part of the wife is punished with excommunication, in others, she is allowed to remain in the caste on her giving a dinner to the caste people. The caste follow the Hindu law of inheritance.

Sális are chiefly Vaishnavaites, though they have no objection to the worship of Shiva. Many are followers of the Várkari sect. A few belong to the Kabir sect. Their family deities are: Khandoba, Bahiroba, Jotiba, Narsoba, Mahádeva, Bhaváni, Jogái, Satvái and Kedárling. They also worship all village, local and boundary gods, and observe all the Hindu holidays. Goats and fowls are offered to the minor deities on Sundays and Thursdays, which are received by the officiating priests of the temples. On the *Dasara* day goats are killed in honour of Bhaváni of Tuljápur, and feasts of liquor and flesh are given to the castemen; and *gondhal* dances are performed. Goats are also offered by some at the time of marriages. Marátha Sális make pilgrimages chiefly to Alandi, Benares, Jejuri, Kedárling, Pandharpur and Tuljápur. Musalmán saints are venerated. *Táks* or silver-embossed plates are installed in the name of deceased ancestors. They believe in witchcraft and soothsaying. Their religious teacher is a man of their own caste, who lives at Benares and visits them once or twice a year. The religious teacher of some is a Hatkar or Dhangar, who lives at Kolhápur. The religious teacher of the Marátha Sális in Khándesh lives at Bangalore and is called Shesh Náik. The religious teachers of the Kulácháris are men of their own caste. The office is hereditary and there is generally one in each *peth* or division of the

Religion.

larger towns. The teachers are called Devángayyás and their chief, who is called Musangayya, lives at Humpi, thirty-six miles north-west of Bellary. He is a married man and his office is hereditary. He is believed to be a direct descendant of the great Deváng, the supposed ancestor of all Hatkars. The priests of the caste are Deshasth Bráhmans.

Death. The dead are either burnt or buried. Persons died of small-pox, leprosy and cholera and the unmarried dead are buried with head to the south. The death ceremonies of the caste resemble those of local Kunbis, with this difference that the corpse is dressed in a loin cloth and turban. The *shráddha* and *mahálaya* are performed annually for the propitiation of the deceased ancestors.

Occupation. The hereditary occupation of the caste is weaving cotton and silk robes and bodice cloths, sheets, quilts, waist-cloths and turbans. Some act as servants to weavers. Their women help them in cleaning yarn and spinning. Some are shop-keepers, a few are employed in Government service, and some are agricultural labourers. They have greatly suffered from the competition of European and Bombay machine-made goods and many of them are in debt. The Hire and Chik Kurvins, in addition to weaving, rear goats and fowls, but do not keep dogs, as any one who is found keeping a dog is at once put out of caste. They have a strict rule against gelding bulls and never own bullocks.

Food. They eat the flesh of goats, sheep, fowls, hare, deer and fish and drink liquor. The Kulácháris neither eat flesh nor drink liquor.

DEVANGAN.—A sub-division of Sonárs.

DEVARA-DASMAYA.—A sub-division of Jáds.

DEVARUKHA.—A sub-division of Bráhmans.

DEVA TANAKHI.—A synonym for Lohár.

DEVLI.—*See* Bhávin.

DHADE.—A sub-division of Lamánis.

DHAKALVAR.—A sub-division of Mángs.

DHALGAR.—A sub-division of Mochis.

DHALYA.—A sub-division of Vanjáris.

DHANDARI.—A sub-division of Vághris.

DHANDHAYA.—A sub-division of Darjis.

DHANGAR.—A sub-division of Vaidus, Murlis, Vághes, Gavlis and Kolis.

DHANGARS, also known as Gávadás in the Sátára District, numbering 467,622 (1901), including 232,901 males and 234,721 females, are found all over the Deccan, Konkan and the Southern Marátha Country. Regarding their origin, the Játiviveka asserts that they are descended from a Shudra father and a Máhishya woman; the Máhishya, again, is said to be the offspring of a Kshatriya and a Vaishya mother. According to an old tradition, they were created from the dust of Shiva's body. Another tradition alleges that their original ancestor was the sage Tápa. A third tradition asserts that, while Khandoba was once strolling in a forest, he met their progenitor, whom he struck dumb with awe by the display of his miraculous powers. From that time the Dhangar with his relatives began to worship Khandoba with implicit devotion, and offered his daughter Banái to the god, who accepted her as his wife. Khandoba, being thus propitiated, conferred upon him the boon that he and his descendants would earn a good living by rearing and tending sheep. Name and origin.

The social position of Dhangars is below that of Kunbis, but in point of language, house, dress and food they differ little from Kunbis. Dhangars rank themselves with Maráthás, and do not eat from the Ghisádis, Buruds, Parits and Jingars, whom they consider below them. Dhangars thus claim a fairly high status in Hindu society, but there can be little doubt that they are a pre-Aryan race. Their totemism as displayed by the totem trees which they worship at the time of marriage is an indication of their aboriginal descent; and the same conclusion is indicated by the fact that they are of a very dark complexion, strong and generally coarse-featured. Among the people who are to be avoided at sacrifices offered to the gods and *manes*, shepherds and keepers of buffaloes are mentioned by Manu (III. 616). Thus according to Manu, Dhangars, some of whom rear sheep and some buffaloes, are a despised race. The word Dhangar seems to be non-Aryan. Wilson has, indeed, traced it to what he thinks to be the Sanskrit word *dhenukar*. But such a word is foreign to Sanskrit literature, and is not to be met with even in lexicons.

Dhangars seem to be spread not only over the Deccan and Konkan but also over the Central Provinces, Berar, the United Provinces and Central India, where they are called Dhángars. The Dhángars of the Central Provinces and Berar are, like the Dhangars of the Deccan and Konkan, shepherds and wool-weavers, so that their identity is not at all improbable. The same cannot perhaps be said of the Dhángars of Northern India, who are employed in felling the jungle, and work as labourers and scavengers. Wilson thinks these to be different from the shepherds and wool-weavers of this name in Southern India, although they may be the same as the Dhangar cultivators of Telangana. Sherring, however, supposes that the Dhangars of Northern India are not the same, as the Southern Dhangars are much higher in social rank. But diversity of occupation or social rank is not a strong argument against the identity of the Dhangars of Northern India with those of Telangana, or of either with those of Berar and the Deccan and Konkan. Instances are not wanting of tribes being broken up each into a number of sub-castes as they spread over a large area, following various professions and occupying different social positions in different districts. Again, the very fact that there is no such Sanskrit word as Dhangar, or other word corresponding to it in sound, seems to show that originally Dhangar was a tribal, and not a functional, name. The Dhangars or Dhángars, whether in Northern or Southern India, may, therefore, reasonably be considered to belong to the same race.

In the Deccan and Konkan, however, Dhangar lost its original tribal signification, and came to denote, in addition to Dhangars proper, a heterogenous group of distinct races following the profession of shepherds. The Asal Dhangars or Marátha Dhangars who form an important element in the Dhangar population are in all probability the representatives of the original Dhangars who settled in the Maráthi speaking districts. Another large sub-division known as Hatkar seems to have been of considerable importance in Berar, inasmuch as they held sway in the hilly country round Basim, owing nominal allegiance to the lowland rulers, whether Hindu or Muhammadan. These Hatkars indeed claim to be Barge Dhangars or "shepherds with the spears" But Barges and Hatkars are really two distinct sub-castes of the Dhangar tribe in Ahmednagar and Sholápur. Very little need be said with regard to the Ahir sub-division of the Dhangars. Ahirs are doubtless a foreign race, and are even now a separate tribe from Dhangars. The inclusion of Ahirs in the Dhangar group is to be explained precisely in the same way as the fusion of that foreign tribe into the artisan classes of Khándesh may be accounted for.

Though some of the Dhangar sub-castes have settled down as stationary husbandmen or wool-weavers, there are not a few of their castemen, such as Khiláris, who have not yet given up their nomadic habits. In the fair season they travel long distances westward to the hills, and even to the Konkan, supplying the people of the villages with manure, for which they are generally paid in kind. They come back before the end of the hot weather, when most of them make their way to the east, as, during the rains, the raw damp of the western hills is fatal to sheep. They live in huts with walls of wattled reeds and roofs thatched with straw, but, while wandering, they raise temporary huts of the twigs of trees and wild plantain leaves. Their recognised head-quarters are Jejuri in Poona, Sátára in the Amednagar district, Madhi in the Shevgaon táluka of the Ahmednagar district and Meda in Sátára.

The home tongue of the Dhangars is Maráthi. The names in common use among men and women are the same as among local Kunbis. In Sátára, social disputes are settled by the members of three families, Gavandes, Mánes and Rágjes. If one of them is not at hand, he is sent for, and the dispute stands over till he comes. Breaches of caste rules are punished by making the offender give a caste feast. In Sholápur and other districts, they have a caste council, and settle social disputes at caste meetings. In Ahmednagar, their hereditary headman is called Gávade, Kárbhári, Mirdha (meaning a village overseer) or Pátil. They say he has no authority to settle social disputes, which are generally referred to meetings of elderly castemen. In Kanara, like many other castes, the headman goes by the name Budvant. In Khándesh the office of the headman, who is called Mehetar or Chaudhari, is hereditary.

The Dhangars have the following endogamous divisions :— Endogamous divisions.

1. Ahir.
2. Asal or Marátha.
3. Banaji.
4. Barge, Bande or Methkari.
5. Dánge.
6. Gadage.
7. Gavli.
8. Ghogattunya.
9. Hatkar or Zendevále.
10. Holkar.
11. Kangar.
12. Khikri.
13. Khilári or Thilári.
14. Khutekar or Khute.
15. Kuktekar.
16. Lád.
17. Mendhe.
18. Mhaske.
19. Sangar.
20. Shegar.
21. Shilotya.
22. Utegar.
23. Musalmán.

Most of the above divisions have a sub-division known as Kadu or bastards, to which the illegitimate or excommunicated members of the division are relegated.

The origin of the names of most of the divisions is obscure. The Asals are so called because they are considered to be pure Dhangars, the word *asal* meaning pure. Barges claim to be Maráthás, and were perhaps Bárgirs or mounted troopers during the time of the

Maráthás.[1] The Dánges take their name from Dáng, by which name the wild, hilly and ascending tract of the northern division of the Sahyádris is known. The term Gavli means a milkman and is suggestive of the occupation of the division. The term Khilári is derived from *khillár* a herd of cattle. The Khutekars take their name from the *khunte* or peg which they fix in the ground for weaving purposes. The Mendhes keep *mendhis*, that is, sheep and goats. The Mhaskes rear *mhashis* or buffaloes.

In the Poona district are found four of the abovementioned divisions of Dhangars, (1) Asal Dhangar, (2) Hatkars, (3) Shegars and (4) Thiláris. The first two classes are numerous in the Indápur, Bhimthadi and Purandhar *tálukas*. Very few of these Asal Dhangars or Shegars keep sheep or weave. Most of them are cultivators, *pátils* and soldiers. The Asal Dhangars consider the Shegars inferior, but this the latter do not admit. Neither are at all intimately connected with the Thiláris, who still lead a wandering pastoral life.

In Ahmednagar, they are divided into ten sub-castes:—(1) Ahirs, (2) Banajis, (3) Barges, (4) Gadges, (5) Hatkars, (6) Kangars, (7) Khutekars, (8) Maráthás, (9) Sangars and (10) Shegars. The Hatkars, Shegars and Khutekars eat together but do not intermarry; the rest are entirely distinct, neither eating together nor intermarrying. In Sholápur, their endogamous groups are (1) Barges or Bandes, (2) Hatkars and (3) Khutekars and Khutes. In Sátára, they have two divisions, (1) Hatkars and (2) Khutekars, who eat together but do not intermarry. In Násik, they are of five sub-divisions, (1) Ahir, (2) Hatkar, (3) Khutekar, (4) Lád and (5) Shegar. In Khándesh, their recognized sub-divisions are (1) Ahir, (2) Ghogattunya, (3) Hatkar, (4) Holkar, (5) Kuktekar, (6) Marátha, (7) Shegar, (8) Shilotya and (9) Thilári or Khilári. In Thána, they are distinguished as (1) Khutekari Dhangars, who make blankets, (2) Gavli Dhangars, who keep cows and buffaloes, and (3) Mendhe Dhangars, who are shepherds and goatherds. They eat together but do not intermarry. In Kolába, their endogamous sections are (1) Mhaskes, who rear and tend buffaloes, (2) Khiláris, who are shepherds and goatherds, and (3) Utegars, who are blanket weavers. Mhaskes are the Dhangar proper of the Kolába district; Khiláris and Utegars belong to the Deccan, and visit the Konkan only in the dry season. One half-caste connected with this caste is known as Khátiks, who are sheep and goat butchers. In Kolhápur, they are split up into

---

(1) The term Bargir is still in use in *silledár* cavalry in India. A *silledár* recruit brings his own horse. Bargirs are followers for whom horses are provided by the employer.

Dánge or hill and (2) Mendhe or sheep Dhangars, who eat together but seldom intermarry.

Exogamous divisions

The exogamous divisions of Dhangars are identical with surnames.

The following is a list of the most common surnames :—

1.	Agáshe.	37.	Hirva.	73.	Máne.
2.	Akhád.	38.	Hogade.	74.	Máng.
3.	Ambáde.	39.	Holkar.	75.	Margále.
4.	Bárghah.	40.	Hulvan.	76.	Marle.
5.	Bháge.	41.	Iréle.	77.	Matkar.
6.	Bháleráo.	42.	Irkar.	78.	Mitge.
7.	Bhánd.	43.	Jádhav.	79.	Mote.
8.	Bhágvat.	44.	Jankar.	80.	More.
9.	Bhende.	45.	Jhore.	81.	Nagare.
10.	Bhise.	46.	Káchare.	82.	Pandit.
11.	Bhite.	47.	Kaitakel.	83.	Phanas.
12.	Bhonde.	48.	Kákade.	84.	Phendáre.
13.	Bhusári.	49.	Kámble.	85.	Pingle.
14.	Borshe.	50.	Kámbre.	86.	Pisál.
15.	Bule.	51.	Kánkhare.	87.	Ráhinj.
16.	Chendke.	52.	Kápdi.	88.	Rasinkár.
17.	Chitar.	53.	Kápri.	89.	Ráyarál.
18.	Chormule.	54.	Kasbe.	90.	Rode.
19.	Dagade.	55.	Káshid.	91.	Rodge.
20.	Daphal.	56.	Kátor.	92.	Salgar.
21.	Dháyagude.	57.	Kende.	93.	Sarode.
22.	Dhebe.	58.	Kharáde.	94.	Sávale.
23.	Dhivar.	59.	Kharje.	95.	Shendgar.
24.	Dhoinfoda.	60.	Khátekar.	96.	Shelke.
25.	Dhon.	61.	Khoche.	97.	Shinde.
26.	Duble.	62.	Khutekar.	98.	Shingade.
27.	Gádekar.	63.	Khillári.	99.	Shirole.
28.	Gavandi.	64.	Koke.	100.	Shirsat.
29.	Garále.	65.	Kokre.	101.	Soláte.
30.	Gavate.	66.	Kolekar.	102.	Sonaval.
31.	Gávade.	67.	Kore.	103.	Sudke.
32.	Ghodke.	68.	Lámbháte.	104.	Supne.
33.	Ghume.	69.	Lándge.	105.	Tágad.
34.	Gore.	70.	Madane.	106.	Támbe.
35.	Gurav.	71.	Mahár.	107.	Tándle.
36.	Hajári.	72.	Mandlik.	108.	Táte.

109. Thánere.	112. Tong.	115. Vághmáre.
110. Thombar.	113. Uráde.	116. Vávare.
111. Thorát.	114. Vágh.	117. Virkar.
	118. Yedge.	

Marriage is prohibited within the sub-division covered by one surname. It is also prohibited with those bearing other surnames worshipping the same totem such as the sunflower, the lotus, the *pánchpálvi* or leaves of five kinds of trees, and so forth.(1) A Dhangar cannot marry his mother's sister's daughter, but he may marry his father's sister's or mother's brother's daughter. There is no prohibition against the marriage of two sisters to the same husband. Two sisters can also be married by two brothers. Girls are married as infants, at ages ranging from four months to twelve years, as a rule before the age of puberty. Boys are generally married between fourteen and twenty-five; but instances of boys married even when one year old are not wanting. Sexual intercourse before marriage is strongly reprobated. If a virgin is seduced by a casteman, he is compelled to marry her; if by a member of another caste, she is excommunicated. Polygamy is permitted, but it is not thought right for a man to marry a second wife, unless the first is dead or barren. There does not appear to be any specified limit to the number of wives a Dhangar may marry in this manner. But though there are cases of Dhangars having from three to five wives living at one and the same time, very few Dhangars are known to have more than five wives. Polyandry is unknown.

Brith. In Sholápur, after the birth of a child, the mother is held impure for twelve days. For five weeks she is not allowed to cook or to enter the cook-room. On the fifth day after the birth the goddess Pánchvi is worshipped, and on the twelfth day the child is named. On a lucky day before the boy is three years old, his hair is cut in front of the goddess Satvái. A sheep is sacrificed and a feast is held except by the very poor. A lock of hair is left on the child's skull until a brother or sister is born to him. Seven or eight years later the tuft is removed and a proper top-knot is kept on the crown of the head. In Ahmednagar, on the fifth day after the birth of a child, they slaughter a goat in the name of Satvái and offer boiled mutton to the goddess. The mother's impurity lasts ten days. They name their children on the evening of the twelfth, and distribute boiled grain among their friends and kinsfolk. The children of the Dhangars in the Poona district are named by a Bráhman either on the fifth or on the tenth day after

(1) A complete list of *devaks* is given in the article on MARATHAS.

birth ; and in honour of the ceremony relations and friends are feasted. At six months of age, both boys and girls have their heads shaved. In Khándesh, on the fifth day after the birth of the child an image of Sath embossed on gold plate is tied to the wrist of the child.

The boy's father goes to the girl's and settles the marriage with her father in the presence of some members of the caste. Betelnut and cocoa-kernel are served, and the boy's father pays from Rs. 20 to Rs. 40 in cash and about Rs. 30 in ornaments. The boy is given a turban, a waist-cloth, a pair of shoes, a brass dining dish and a drinking vessel. A Bráhman is called to fix the day most auspicious for the celebration of the marriage. But in case the Bráhman is not available, the favourite method of fixing an auspicious time is by means of a young calf. A cow is let out of the hut, and then the calf. If the calf runs directly to the cow to suck, and in so doing passes by the right hand side of the marrying couple, who are made to sit outside the cottage, the omen is auspicious, and the marriage takes place. But if the calf passes by the left of the couple, the marriage is postponed for an hour or two, the time being considered inauspicious, and the operation is repeated. Marriage.

The marriage ceremonies of Dhangars do not differ much from those of Kunbis. The essential and binding portion of the marriage is an oath by the bridegroom to protect the bride, who, on her part, is made to swear lifelong obedience and fidelity. In some districts the *Dháre* ceremony is common. The ends of their wedding garments are then tied into a knot in token of perfect union. In some places, the throwing of rice or wheat grains over the heads of the bridal pair while marriage verses are being repeated is deemed sufficient to consolidate a marriage.

The chief points in which their marriage customs differ from those of Kunbis are : the porch in front of the girl's house is built, not by her father, but by his neighbours and castemen ; on the marriage day the boy and girl are made to stand on two grindstones, each laid on a bamboo basket, and on the four corners of the basket are set blocks of *umbar* (Ficus glomerata) wood ; after a piece of cloth or *antarpát* has been held between them and a few grains of red rice thrown over them, the Bráhman puts on the fingers of the two a *chhaluni*, *i.e.*, a small ring either of silver or a brass metal. In Sátára, prior to the bridegroom's going to the girl's house for the marriage he is taken to Bahiroba's temple instead of Máruti's as among Kunbis.

The remarriage of widows is permitted. A widow cannot marry a member with her deceased husband's or her father's surname. Her marriage with the son of her paternal or maternal aunt is also prohibited. Money is paid to the first husband's relations, without whose consent the marriage cannot take place. In some places, the consent of the headman of the caste is also required. A widow remarriage is generally celebrated at night time in the dark fortnight. It cannot take place in the months of *Ashádh*, *Paush* and *Bhádrapad*. In the Poona district, except in the month of ***Paush***, it can be performed any day from sunrise to sunset. Unwidowed women are not allowed to attend the ceremony, except in Khándesh, where a widow remarriage is not looked upon with so much disfavour as in other places. The widow wears a white robe and bodice and new bangles and ornaments presented to her by her intended husband. Her lap is then filled, and Ganpati and Varuna are worshipped. Next the Bráhman priest marks the widow's forehead with red powder, and the skirts of the upper garments of the pair are tied into a knot, which completes the marriage. In some places, the essential and binding portion consists in both the widow and her intended husband holding a few grains of corn in their hands and uttering mutual oaths of fidelity in the presence of a Bráhman. In others, a little water is given in the hands of both, and then the head of the one is made to touch that of the other. A bachelor desiring to marry a widow is first married to a ring or a *rui* bush (Calotropis gigantea).

Divorce is permitted on the ground of impotency in the case of man, of adultery in the case of woman, and of the loss of caste in the case of either. Divorce is also allowed on both sides, if any permanent misunderstanding arises. In the latter case alone divorced wives are at liberty to marry again after paying the first husband the marriage expenses incurred by him. With regard to women divorced or deserted for adultery, remarriage is forbidden, unless the adultery committed is with a casteman or a member of a higher caste, in which case the sin can be expiated by giving a feast to the caste. Dhangars follow the Hindu law of inheritance.

Religion. The caste profess Hinduism, and belong both to the Shaiva and Bhágvat sects. Their favourite deities are Vithoba of Pandharpur and Mahádeva of Udgiri in Kolhápur. The minor gods specially worshipped by the caste are Khandoba and Bahiroba. Dhangars say that they have been worshipping Khandoba since the time of their progenitor who, as mentioned above, first began to adore and reverence the god when the latter exhibited his miraculous power in a forest. Bahiroba is their tutelary house god, and his image is buried with the bodies of the well-to-do. The minor deities worshipped by them in Ahmednagar are Máruti, Khandoba, Shani, Satvái, Janái,

Jokhái, Mhasoba and so forth. Máruti is smeared with vermilion on Saturday, and offered a cocoanut and other things. Khandoba is sprinkled with turmeric on Sunday, and offered a cocoanut, betelnut, pice and so forth. Shani is rubbed with oil on Saturday, and offered a cocoanut, cotton and so forth. Satvái, Janái, Jokhái, and Mhasoba are offered a cocoanut, flour, salt and so forth on any day. These offerings are received by the hereditary worshippers attached to the respective gods and goddesses. In and about Mahábaleshwar in the Sátára district the minor god worshipped by the Dhangars are Mhasoba, Beheri, Jolla, Janáni of Gothánera and Janái of Thal. Of these five deities, Mhasoba and Beheri are male deities, and the rest are female. Sunday is the favourite day for the worship of Mhasoba and Beheri and Tuesday for that of Jolla and the two Janánis. Cocoanuts, flowers and fruits are the commonest offerings. On the days of *Játra*, *i. e.*, the feast days set apart in honour of these deities, sixty fowls and sixty *khâruks* (dry dates) and twelve goats are offered to all these deities. The number of fowls offered is sixty because there are supposed to be sixty *bhuts* or ghosts in these five deities, of which twenty-five are to be found in Mhasoba, and the rest in the other four deities. On the death of a man, his soul becomes a *pitar*, and twelve *pitars* make one ghost. Hence twelve is the necessary number for the sacrifice of goats. Only the males and young girls who have not attained puberty can perform the *puja* or worship of these deities. Women, if they are not in their monthly courses can stand at a distance, clad in white or red, and prostrate themselves before the deities; but their *puja* and personal offerings are never accepted by the deities, who bring mishaps and disasters on them if they persist in performing *puja*.

Although they set a stone on the hill where they pasture their herd in the name of any one of the minor gods, and rub it with sandal paste, yet those gods have also certain special places of residence, *i. e.*, Khandoba at Jejuri in Poona, Tukái at Tuljápur in the Nizam's country, Yemái at Mardi in Sholápur, and Bahiroba at Senrái in Ahmednagar, at Kudli near Panchala and Raji in the Indi sub-division of Bijápur.

The minor deities worshipped by the Khándesh Dhangars are Khandoba, Bahiroba, Mhasoba, Ekire, Kanbái, Renubái and Chanya Pachya. The last is the patron deity of the Ahir Dhangars. The worshippers of these deities are called Bhagats. Members of many castes such as Sonárs, Mális, Kunbis, Mahárs and Mángs make vows to perform the marriage of their children before these deities, and Dhangar

Bhagats are paid from five annas to five rupees, the sum being always a multiple of five.[1]

Dhangars worship the ghosts of their deceased ancestors and keep ancestral images in their houses. They have great faith in sorcery and witchcraft. In Sholápur, on the *Dasara* day, they go to the temple of the god Hedamdev in waste lands with music, and one of them gets possessed and strikes himself with a naked sword, but is not wounded. Those who are present throw wool and pieces of cocoa-kernel over their heads, and all dance and sing. They make pilgrimages to Alandi, Jejuri, Kundanpur, Násik, Pandharpur, Tuljápur, Shignapur in Phaltan, and Rasin in Ahmednagar. They observe all the Hindu fasts and feasts, and worship the plants and animals held sacred by Hindus.

Speaking generally, the caste employ Bráhmans for religious and ceremonial purposes, and these Bráhmans are received on terms of equality by other Bráhmans. When Bráhmans are not easily available, the elders of the caste perform the ceremonies. In Kolába, the family priests of the Mendhes are the ordinary village Bráhmans, but the Dánges have priests of their own class, who officiate at their marriages. In Thána, again, some of the Dhangars employ Kumbhárs or Lingáyat priests to perform the funeral rites.

Death Dhangars carry their dead on a bamboo bier with tomtom and music, and burn or bury them. In some places, the corpse is carried hung in a blanket. In the case of cremation, the ashes are removed on the third or twelfth day and thrown into a river or stream, and the bones are gathered and buried. In the case of interment, the dead are buried on their backs with their heads to the south. Some families build a mud tomb over the grave, and set stones on it. In honour of the occasion a goat is killed and a dinner is given of rice, split peas and mutton. A woman who dies in childbirth is usually buried. In some places, such as Mahábaleshwar, they do not burn, but bury their dead in a sitting posture with their faces to the west.

On the death of a Dhangar, his son performs ceremonies for his propitiation on the thirteenth and fourteenth days. He also performs *shráddha* every year on the anniversary of his father's death, and *mahál* or *mahálaya* for the propitiation of ancestors in general in the dark fortnight of *Bhádrapad*, on the date of his parent's death. At each *shráddha*, he gives money and grain to the officiating Bráhman priest, and invites his castemen to a dinner. In some places, on the

(1) The number five is of strikingly frequent occurrence in caste and tribal ceremonies. It seems to indicate an origin in remote times when the limit of enumeration was the five fingers of the hand.

third and twelfth day after a death Dhangars perform what is called the ceremony of giving water. In Khándesh, a little cooked food is buried underground where the deceased breathed his last. On the tenth day they send for a potter, who prepares small images of human forms made of flour and water. He carries these flour images with him and places them in flowing water. The potter also says prayers, playing on drums and bells.

Occupation.

The chief calling of Dhangars is that of shepherds, cattle-breeders, cattle-sellers and blanket-weavers. In Ahmednagar some of them who live in the plains rear horses, which are called Dhangars' horses and are famed for hardiness and endurance. In Kanara they keep a special breed of cows and buffaloes known as Dhangars' buffaloes and cows, which are the largest cattle in Kanara. They also deal in wool, and weave coarse blankets called *chaváles*. During the fair season they graze over the country, and collect considerable quantities of grain in return for folding their sheep and goats in fields which are in want of manure. They have a great name as weather prophets, foretelling rain and other changes of weather by observing the planets. Some of them have abandoned their original occupation and work as bricklayers, petty shopkeepers, messengers, money-lenders and cloth merchants. They are even now noted for their martial qualities and readily become soldiers. A large number of Shiváji's most trusted Mávalis or Marátha footmen were West-Poona Dhangars, and many of the bravest Marátha leaders, among whom the Holkars are the most distinguished, are of this tribe. Not a few of them are agriculturists ; of these, some are Inámdárs, the *ináms* having been given to them by the Rájás of Sátára ; some are tenure-holders, holding lands either by a share or by paying a lump sum for a certain period ; some are occupancy rayats, but no privileges are known to have been given to them in respect of rent ; and some are landless day labourers. The implement characteristic of the Dhangars is their spinning wheel ; that of the Mhaske Dhangars is their churning handle.

Food.

They eat the flesh of goats, sheep and fowls. and drink liquor.

DHANKA.—A sub-division of Bhils.

DHANVAT.—A sub-division of Holayás.

DHARALA.—A sub-division of Kolis.

DHARMIK.—A sub-division of Mahárs.

DHARNICHE PUT.—A synonym for Mahár.

DHASTHALA.—A synonym for Virakta Jangam.

DHAVAD.—*See* under minor Musalmán Castes.

DHED.—A sub-division of Kátkaris and Mahárs.

Name and origin.

DHEDAS, numbering 271,597 (1901), including 140,276 males and 131,321 females, are found in all parts of Gujarát. The Kaira Dhedás state that in the Satya Yuga they were called Satyás; in the Dvápár Yuga they were called Meghás; in the Treta Yuga Eliás; and in the Kali Yuga Dhedás. They have also prophecies of a high future in store for their tribe. The king or leader of the new era, Káyamrai by name, will marry a Dheda woman and will raise the caste to the position of Bráhmans. They hold religious meetings or *ochavas,* and at these, with great excitement, sing songs fuil of hope of the good things in store for them. Like the Mahárs of the rest of the Presidency, Dhedás appear to be broken fragments of primitive tribes dispossessed by invaders, and re-inforced from time to time by outcastes.

According to their own story the Dhedás are the descendants of Kshatriyas who, during Parshurám's persecutions, passed themselves off as belonging to the impure castes. "An old tradition among them points to some relation between the Kanbis and Dhedás. Two brothers Leva and Deva were the ancestors, the former of the Kanbis, the latter of the Dhedás.[(1)]" Each family of Dhedás is closely connected with the house of some landholder or *pátidár.* "This connection seems to show traces of a form of slavery. Rich *pátidárs* have always a certin number of Dheda families whom they speak of as 'ours' *hamára,* and when a man dies he distributes along with his lands a certain number of Dheda families to each of his sons."[(1)]

The Dharadas or hillmen, from *dharad* a hill, a sub-division of Dhangars and neighbours to the Kashmiras, are in the Mahábhárat (B.C. 1400—A.D. 200) mentioned among the Kshatriyas slain by the Bráhman warrior Parashurám.[(2)] Manu (B.C. 800—A.D. 400) speaks of them as Kshatriyas degraded from the extinction of sacred rites.[(3)] They are mentioned by Ptolemy (A.D. 177) as living at the source of the Indus.[(4)] These Dharadas or Dhavads, as they are sometimes called, closely resemble Dhedás. Another tribe who in name and social position closely resemble Gujarát Dhedás are the South Kanara Daerds. These people in A.D. 1801, numbering about 50,000, could be bought and sold, and so long as they were fed by him, were for life bound to their master's service. Unlike Gujarát Dhedás the Kanarese Daerds, except a small section of them, did not eat the flesh of the cow, and were not considered unclean.[(5)] The term Dheda

(1) Rev. J. S. Taylor.
(2) Muir's Sanskrit Texts, I. 458.
(3) Id. 482.
(4) St. Martin's Etude sur la Geographic Grecque et Latine de l'Inde 56. Sec. 216.
(5) Slavery in India (Blue Book of 1828), 548.

is commonly used in the Deccan and Southern Marátha Country as a synonym for Mahár, a class occupying a corresponding social position in those areas.

Campbell relates that at the end of the eighteenth century, in some parts of Kaira, Dhedás used to drag thorns after them, and till lately Dhedás were not allowed to tuck up the *dhoti* but had to trail their dress along the ground. Though traces of the practice have disappeared, an abusive term *Kuladi* or *Kodivála* or spittoon-men, shows that at one time the Dhedás had to hang spittoons round their neck.(1) As long ago as the reign of Sidharája (A.D. 1094—1143) the Dhedás of Anhilaváda, at that time the capital of Northern Gujarát, had to live at a distance from other people, to wear untwisted cotton round their heads, and to keep a stag's horn hanging from their waists. From these marks they are said to have been freed by Sidharája in return for the sacrifice of one of their number as a victim to stop the leak of water from the great Patan tank.(2)

Except that they are darker, and in Central Gujarát slighter, Dhedás, in complexion and figure, are much like Kolis and Kanbis. Some of the women are fair and good-looking. Most Dheda men shave the head, leaving a tuft of hair on the top, and wear a thin moustache and, in North Gujarát and Káthiáwár, the beard or whiskers. A few of the Surtis wear a heavy moustache and whiskers, and arrange the hair of the head in European fashion.

The bulk of the Dhedás are ill-clad. A man's dress consists of a coarse waist-cloth reaching to the knee or a short pair of trousers, a coarse cotton jacket, and a cap or a red or white North-Gujarát turban without golden ends,or a piece of cloth wound tightly round the head. A woman's dress consists of a petticoat, a piece of cloth thrown over the head, and sometimes a bodice. Some men and women wear ill-shaped heavy shoes. A few of the better-off men wear a jacket, a long cotton coat, a cotton waist cloth with an ornamental border or a pair of pantaloons, and a white or red Musalmán-like turban with gold ends. A well-to-do Dheda woman wears a full robe and a bodice equalling in the fineness and price those worn by high caste Hindus. Their ornaments are, among the men, wristlets of brass and silver and ear and finger rings of tin or silver, and, among the women, earings of brass or gold, a necklace of *kidia* or glass beads, small nose-studs of glass beads, and in a few cases silver necklaces,

(1) Rev. A. Taylor.

(2) Rás Mála, I. 112.

silver armlets for the elbow of the left arm, bracelets of wood and cheap ivory, finger-rings of brass and silver, and bands of tin or silver round the ankles and toes.

The Dhedás speak corrupt Gujaráti, with, among a few who are in the service of Europeans, a mixture of English commonly known as Lália English

Every settlement of Dhedás has its headman called *mehtar* in Northern and *patel* in Southern Gujarát. Along with three or four other members of the community, he settles all caste and other social disputes. As a body the Dhedás are somewhat strict in punishing breaches of caste rules, and more than most of the artisan castes they show respect to the opinion of their headman.

Endogamous divisions.

The endogamous divisions are :—

1. Bháliás of north Cambay.
2. Chásiás.
3. Chorásiás or Mahi Kánthiás of Baroda and Mahi Kántha.
4. Charotariás or Talabdás of Kaira.
5. Gujars or Gurjars of Broach.
6. Hádiás or Bowmen.
7. Káhanamiás of the Kahánam tract in Broach.
8. Kusia.
9. Márus or Márwáris of Marwar.
10. Meghváns or Rainmen.
11. Pátaniás of Pátan.
12. Surtis of Surat.
13. Vankars or Weavers.

Of these the two most ancient divisions are the Chásiás and Kusiás. Of these, seven are territorial, three are occupational, and one is a race-name. None of these divisions intermarry. Except that the Márus or Márwáris refuse to eat with the rest, all the divisions freely dine with one another. All except the Gujars eat with the Mahárs the representatives of the caste in the Deccan and Konkan. Two classes, the Márwáris and the Surtis, hold a special position among Dhedás. The Márwáris, who are found mostly in North Gujarát hold aloof from other Dhedás, refuse to eat or drag away dead animals and earn their living chiefly as camel drivers.

Among Dhedás, besides their surnames, are several divisions. The common surnames are as follows :— Exogamous divisions.

Chávda.	Dadiya.	Sarvariya.
Chásia.	Gohel.	Solanki.
Chohán.	Makvána.	Vághela.
Chudásama.	Parmár.	Vála.
Dábhi.	Ráthod.	

These surnames suggest a connection with the Rajputs.

Marriage between near relations is forbidden. The levirate is permitted. Divorce can be obtained almost to an indefinite extent. Before they finally settle to wedded life, most couples have more than once changed their partners. Before the change takes place, there must be a formal divorce recognized by the caste.

Pregnancy.

Some Dhedás observe no lapfilling ceremony ; among others the ceremony takes place in the seventh month of a woman's first pregnancy. On a lucky day fixed by the Gáruda, the parents of the woman send to her husband's house a robe, a petticoat, a cocoanut, some rice, and red powder. The pregnant woman bathes, rubs the red powder on her forehead and cheeks, and dresses herself in the clothes sent by her father. She carries the rice and the cocoanut in that part of the robe which covers her breast, and goes to visit her female relations. She visits her friends one after the other, placing two grains of rice on the threshold of each house. After she has visited all her relations she goes to her husband 's house, and cooks, and, with her husband, eats the rice which remains. In Káthiáwár, the custom slightly varies. The woman does not visit her relations. She carries the rice and the cocoanut in her lap and with her husband goes to worship Ganpati in the village temple or at the house of some relation. When the husband and wife start, the ends of their robes are knotted together, and the husband carries a sword in his hand.

Birth ceremonies.

No ceremonies are performed on the birth of a child. A few women of the caste or a Musalmán midwife attend on a woman at the time of childbirth. Among most Dhedás no *Chhathi* or sixth day ceremony is performed. Where any ceremony is performed in honour of *Chhathi*, it takes place on the fifth day in the case of a boy and on the sixth day in the case of a girl. If the fifth day after birth falls within the bright fortnight of the Hindu month, the child is named on that day ; if it falls within the dark fortnight the child is named on a day within the next bright fortnight. The name is given by the Gáruda, who is paid about four annas for his trouble. From the tenth day after childbirth the mother moves about the house and does her ordinary work, but she does not cook or fetch water till after the fifteenth day. No ceremony is performed when cooked food is first given to a child.

Marriage. Girls are married before they are sixteen and boys before they are twenty-five. The marriage day is fixed by a Gáruda or Dheda priest. Three days before the marriage the bride and bridegroom are rubbed with turmeric. On the marriage day at the house of the bride, and on the third day before marriage at the house of the bridegroom, nine married unwidowed women in the case of the first marriage occasion in the family, and two women in all subsequent marriages, bring to the house nine or ten earthen pots full of water from the village well. On the third day before the marriage at the bridegroom's house, and on the marriage day at the bride's, Ganpati is worshipped and the planets are propitiated. On the day before the marriage the bridegroom goes on foot with friends and relations and with music to the bride's village. At the outskirts of the bride's village the party is met by the bride's parents, who lead them to separate lodgings, where they are feasted. On the marriage day the bridegroom with friends and relations passes from his lodgings to the bride's house. At the bride's house her mother meets the bridegroom, and, presenting him with a miniature plough, a grinding pestle and a churning stick, leads him to his seat and places the bride opposite him on his left. Wreaths of cocoanut shells are put round the necks of both the bride and bridegroom, and they are separated by a piece of cloth. The ends of the bride and bridegroom's robe are knotted together, their hands are joined, and the Gáruda priest recites verses. In front of the bride's house a square or *chori* is made with four brass or copper pots, one at each corner. A shallow earthen pot is set in the centre of the square with fire burning in it. After their hands are joined the bride and bridegroom together walk four times round the square. In the square the bride and bridegroom feed each other with coarse wheat flour mixed with clarified butter and molasses. This completes the marriage ceremony. The Gáruda receives from the fathers of the bride and bridegroom a cash present of Rs. 1¼ to Rs. 10½. The Turis or Dheda musicians also receive small cash presents. When the ceremony is over the bridegroom, accompanied by the bride, goes to his lodgings. The bridegroom's party are again feasted by the bride's parents. On the second day after marriage, the bridegroom, accompanied by the bride and his friends and relations, goes to his village.

Religion. Many of the Dhedás belong to the Bijmárgi, Kabirpanthi and Rámánandi sects or are followers of one Haribáva. A few are Swámináráyans. Though they visit the shrines of Musalmán saints, make offerings to saints' tombs and in Káthiáwár eat with Musalmáns, they reverence most of the ordinary Bráhman divinities, especially Hanumán, Ganpati, Máta and Narsingji. They have no household gods, but in some villages have their own temples in which the images of their favourite gods are enshrined. They have religious teachers or *gurus*, who yearly receive from each house annas 4 to rupee 1. Of plants they worship the basil or *tulsi* daily in the house, holding it in special esteem. They observe the ordinary Hindu fasts and feasts, and do no work either on the bright or on the dark fifteenth of any Hindu month. All believe in omens and some in sorcery and witchcraft. When an ancestral spirit harasses a man or a woman, an exorcist, who is generally a Vághri or a Rabári, is called, and begins to jerk his head to the beating of a brass plate which is held over an earthen jar The exorcist throws grains of wheat to the four corners of heaven, and, after holding a cotton thread over burning frankincense, ties it to the right elbow of the patient. Dhedás treat their priests or Gárudás with more respect than the higher Hindu castes pay to their household priests. They sacrifice neither to the horse nor to the snake. Those who can afford it are fond of making pilgrimages to Ambáji, Dákor, Pávágad and Unái, and to the temples of other local gods and goddesses. Cases of men taking to religious life are not uncommon. The two best known saints among Gujarát Dhedás are Khimo of Pálanpur and Shivo of Broach.

Except a few who are well-to-do, the Dhedás bury their dead. The dead body is carried on a bier to the burial ground, where a lamp is kindled. The mourners, after bowing to the ground, dig a pit and lay the body in it. The lamp is placed in the pit near the body, a leaf of the basil plant dipped in water is laid in the mouth of the corpse, and the pit is filled with earth. The mourners bathe and return to the house of mourning. The nearest relations of the deceased are impure for eleven days. A *shráddha* ceremony is performed by the chief mourner with the help of a Gáruda on the twelfth day, or for four days from the tenth to the thirteenth. Caste people are feasted from one to four days. Death.

The position and occupation of the Dhedás of Northern and Southern Gujarát vary considerably. In Ahmedabad and Kaira, with their large population of Bhangiás and the want of a class of field labourers, the Dhedás are private rather than public servants. They are considered higher than Chámárs, and except that they Occupation.

have to drag away the bodies of dead cattle[1], are seldom called on to sweep or perform other unclean work. Formerly their chief occupation was the spinning of coarse cotton thread and the weaving of coarse cotton cloth and the carrying of treasure and burdens. Spinning and weaving used to support them in tolerable comfort. This occupation is now greatly diminished by the competition of steam power. They do not act as guides or point out boundary marks ; a few of them hold rent-free land, and only to a limited extent are village servants. Each family is closely connected with the house of some landholder or *pátidár*. For his master he brings in loads from the fields and cleans out the stable, receiving in return daily allowances of butter-milk and the carcasses of any cattle that die. The Dheda is inclined to be unruly and submits to his master's demands with a bad grace. This opposition and want of subordination is perhaps the cause of the much stronger dislike shown in North Gujarát to the Dheda than to the more unclean Bhangia. Only Dhedás would seem to have been forced to wear special clothes or badges, to hang spittoons round their necks, and to trail thorns to wipe out their footprints.

Food. The Dhedás live chiefly on the coarser grains, though they have no scruple about eating flesh. As they cannot afford to buy the flesh of sheep and goats and as most of them are scrupulous not to kill animals for the sake of their flesh, they content themselves with the flesh of cattle which have died a natural death. To prevent them falling into the hands of the Dhedás, especially in South Gujarát, traders and the higher class of husbandmen often bury their dead cattle. Though most of them do not eat fish, they will eat the flesh of all animals except horses, dogs, cats, rats, jackals and snakes. Animal food is a luxury rather than an ordinary dish. Most take opium, and all drink liquor, in South Gujarát, to excess.

DHEDHA.—A synonym for Meghvál.

DHIDAMVAR.—A sub-division of Ahirs.

DHIMAR.—A sub-division of Macchis.

DHINOJA.—A sub-division of Modh Bráhmans.

DHIVAR.—A synonym for Mángela.

DHOBI.—A synonym for Parit.

---

(1) The practice in dealing with dead animals in Northern Gujarát is that the Dheda removes cows, oxen and buffaloes, and the Bhangia sheep, goats, dogs and cats. A Dheda who touches a dead dog is put out of caste.

DHOBIS, numbering 56,121 (1901), including 29,196 males and 26,925 females, are found all over the Gujarát Districts and Native States. They claim to be Rajputs (some have returned themselves as Muhammadans) and in support of this statement they point to the fact that Chohan is a common surname in the caste. This, however, is no proof of Rajput origin. **Name and origin.**

They have neither endogamous nor exogamous divisions. Marriage is prohibited when relationship can be traced between two contracting parties. Marriage with a father's sister's daughter, mother's sister's daughter and maternal uncle's daughter is not allowed. A man cannot marry his wife's sister till his wife's death. Two brothers may marry two sisters. Boys and girls are married between five and ten. Sometimes girls of poor men remain unmarried till they become fifteen years old. Polygamy is permitted, but polyandry is unknown.

The offer of marriage comes from the boy's father The service is conducted by a Bráhman priest. The father of the bridegroom pays to the bride as *pallu* a sum of eighty to a hundred rupees. Five to seven days before marriage Ganpati is installed at each of the houses of the bride and bridegroom and they are rubbed with turmeric paste. Then the *graha shánti* or planet soothing ceremony is performed. On the day of marriage the bridegroom's party go to the bride's house in procession, which ceremony is known as *varghoda*. Marriage bracelets are tied round the wrists of both the bridegroom and bride, and the skirts of their garments are tied into a knot. Then the bride's hand is put into that of the bridegroom and a curtain is drawn between them. A Bráhman priest recites verses, and when he has ended, the curtain is drawn aside and their hands are separated. Next, a sacrifice is performed on the square *chori*, and the bride and bridegroom are asked to walk round the fire four times. This ceremony is known as *mangal phero* and is the binding portion of the marriage. The next day the bridegroom goes to his house with his wife, and the ceremony is thus brought to completion. **Marriage ceremonies.**

Widow remarriage is allowed. A widow may marry the younger brother of her deceased husband. A widow remarriage ceremony is performed on Tuesday, Thursday or Sunday. A Bráhman priest conducts the ceremony. The widow and her new husband sit on two low wooden stools opposite each other, worship Ganpati, and throw grains of rice at each other. This completes the ceremony. A bachelor wishing to marry a widow is first married to a *shami* tree with all the forms of a marriage. Divorce is allowed. When a demand for divorce is made by a woman she is required to pay a certain sum to her husband. Dhobis follow the Hindu law of inheritance and belong to the Hindu religion. Some are Kabirpanthis, Rámánujas and Vallabhácháris. Though they respect Hindu gods, they have no house gods and do not go to temples. They keep the ordinary Hindu feast days. They visit popular Hindu places of pilgrimage. When cholera and such other epidemics are prevalent, they propitiate *máta* goddess by performing sacrifices. They respect Bráhmans as their priests.

Death. They burn their dead. Children under eighteen months old are buried with their heads northwards. The ashes and bones are consigned to a river. On the 10th, 11th, 12th and 13th day after death the *shráddha* ceremony is performed.

The hereditary occupation of the caste is washing clothes. A washerman is paid by the number of pieces washed. The women and grown-up children help the men.

Food. They eat the flesh of goats, sheep, fowls and fish. They drink liquor.

Name and origin. **DHODIAS**, numbering 94,381 (1901), including 47,337 males and 47,044 females, are chiefly found in Surat, Thána and Surat Agency. They are one of the largest early tribes and chiefly work as field labourers and hereditary servants, *hális*.

Divisions. There are no endogamous divisions of the caste. Their exogamous divisions, which are known as *kuls*, are as follows :—

Antichobdia.	Dhayádharu.	Obadia.
Atari.	Garásia (Mota).	Ootnia.
Bávisa.	Garásia (Nána).	Panchadia.
Bháboa.	Ghádia.	Parbhu.
Bharulia.	Joshi.	Pársi.
Bhat.	Kanbi.	Rávat.
Bhoi (Mota).	Khaynia.	Váda.
Bhoi (Nána).	Kodaria.	Vahiya.
Bráhmania.	Kodria.	Vákda.
Chhasdhola.	Koknia.	Vánia.
Chobdia.	Kola.	Vanjára.
Desái.	Náyaka (Mota).	Vásfodia.
Dhagdia (Mota).	Náyaka (Nána).	Vatnia.
Dhagdia (Nána).	Nitátalia.	Verági.

They admit members from higher castes into their caste, and from their *kuls*, many of which are apparently other caste names, it appears that the caste is recruited from numerous other castes. Marriage with a maternal uncle's daughter, mother's sister's daughter and father's sister's daughter is not allowed. Marriage with a wife's younger sister is allowed during her life-time or after her death. Two brothers may marry two sisters. Boys and girls are married between five and twenty. Sexual license before marriage is not allowed. If a girl commits sexual indiscretions before marriage with a man of her caste, the fathers of the girl and the man involved are fined five rupees, and if the man belongs to a different *kul*, the girl is married to him. When a girl commits sexual indiscretions with a man of a lower caste, such as a Dubla, a Chodhra or a Náikda, the girl and her father are excommunicated, and are not re-admitted until they offer to the *panch* of their caste a goat, a feast or some fine. In some places, when the girl is re-admitted into caste she is made to drink a mixture of cowdung and cow's urine. Girls committing sexual indiscretions, before marriage, with impure castes like Bhangiás or Dhedás are excommunicated for ever. If a girl cohabits with a Pársi, in some places they purify her by making her drink water in which a Bráhman has washed his toe. Polygamy is permitted, but polyandry is unknown.

Marriage ceremonies

The offer of marriage generally comes from the boy's father. An experienced and respectable person acts as a mediator and is known as *Vastalio*. The boy's father gives him a *dhoti* worth about eight annas or some toddy for his trouble. A sum varying from 16½ to 22½ rupees is paid to the girl's father and is called *Dej*. Marriages are celebrated on Thursday. The service of marriage is conducted by two caste women, who are termed *Verno*. In certain rare cases, parents purchase a girl for their boy and allow the couple to live as husband and wife without going through any ceremony. Similarly, well-to-do men purchase a husband for their daughter. He lives with his proposed father-in-law as a *Khandádia* for five years, when, if the daughter approves of him, the marriage is performed. The following are the different ceremonies of marriage.

The boy's father in company with three or four friends and relatives goes to visit the girl and to make an offer of marriage. The amount of *Dej* is fixed on this occasion. This ceremony is termed *Mágni*. The parents of the girl with kinsmen go to see the boy, as also to enquire after the social status of the boy's family. After the exchange of visits, the betrothal or *Mágni* becomes final. Then some one on the bridegroom's side goes to the bride's house to pay the amount of *Dej*, the ceremony being known as *Dej nakwa javu*. On Wednesday in the afternoon, the marriage bower is erected, and boughs of mango leaves are hung on the main entrace of it. Two leaves of mango are also tied to every post of the marriage booth. Two leaves of mango are tied to two steel arrows, and the bride and bridegroom, before being rubbed with turmeric paste, worship them and bow before them. Then the ceremony of pounding rice in a mortar is performed. The bride and bridegroom are rubbed with turmeric paste. They are again rubbed with it on Thursday and Friday and it is washed off on Saturday. The bridegroom is dressed in new clothes, and is given a sword to hold on his shoulder. The bride is decorated with ornaments, and a string of glass beads is tied round her neck. The bridegroom then sits in the marriage bower, and liquor and toddy is distributed among the guests. Both sexes pass the night in dancing. The bridegroom, if he likes, joins them. On Thursday when the bride's party come to take the bridegroom to their house they are received by two girls, who hold over their heads earthen jars filled with water. When the bridegroom enters the marriage bower he is presented with a churning handle, a lamp and a pestle. This is called *Var Odhade*. Then a *báshing* is tied to the bride's brow. In the marriage booth a blanket is spread on a wooden stool, and over it an auspicious figure is drawn in rice, and thirty-two heaps of rice grains are made, twelve coppers being placed over each. These are covered with another blanket, and the bride and bridegroom are seated over it facing the east. The hems of their garments are tied into a knot. On this occasion the bride is given a string of glass beads and an ornament known as *Valo* to wear. No woman can take off these two ornaments until she is divorced or has lost her husband. Then a person who blows a horn takes some grains of rice and applies them to the bodies of the bride and bridegroom from top to toe and puts their heads together. This is the principal and the binding portion of the ceremony. The bride is then asked to sweep the store-room and to pound rice in a mortar. This is meant to test the physical strength of the bride. Meanwhile the guests continue dancing to the beating of drums. Two grown-up men then take the bridegroom and the bride on their shoulders, and go to make a bow to some temples in their vicinity. The bride and bridegroom prepare a small heap of rice before each god. While returning, they keep on beating each other with sprigs of the mango tree. Then the *báshings* are untied by the brother of the bridegroom. While untying one from his sister-in-law's brow, he asks her "Well, *bhabi*, meaning sister-in-law, would you arrange for my marriage ?" to which she answers in the affirmative, and then he gives her a slap on the face and unties it. They are tied to one of the pillars in the house and preserved permanently. When this is over, the guests on the bride's side take the bride to their house. The next day small balls are made of rice or *rági* flour and are cooked in an earthen jar. Out of these, five balls are thrust into the prickles of the *babul* tree that is nearest to their house. The bridegroom goes there on the shoulder of some one and lops off the branch. The balls are brought to their house in a blanket and are distributed among the guests. The same thing is repeated at the bride's house. On Saturday the turmeric paste is washed off, and the marriage ceremony ends with it. Five days after, the bride goes to her father, and after five days more she returns to her husband.

Widow remarriage is allowed. A widow cannot marry her mother's sister's son, father's sister's son or her maternal uncle's son. She may marry the younger brother or any other younger relative of her deceased husband. A widow remarriage is celebrated on Sunday or Tuesday, and is brought about by a respectable person of the caste, who is known as *Vastalio*. Kinsmen on both the sides are present on this occasion. Two necklaces of glass beads are brought by the bride's party. One is tied round the widow's neck and the other to a sword. This is done on Saturday. On Tuesday the bridegroom unties the necklace that is tied round the widow's neck and ties it to a *shami* tree. The necklace that is tied to a sword is taken off and is tied round the widow's neck. This brings the remarriage ceremony to a close. Some observe a different ceremony. The widow and her new husband are seated on low wooden stools facing the east. The widow's sister's husband ties the hems of their garments into a knot. Then some married lady on the bridegroom's side marks the couples' foreheads with red powder and joins them together. A bachelor wishing to remarry a widow is first married to a *shami* tree with all the forms of a first marriage.

Divorce is allowed. Either the husband or the wife can ask for a divorce, and it is effected when the wife is barren, or when the husband is impotent or when one of them is a lunatic or a leper. A divorce is effected in the presence of the headmen of the caste and also with their consent. When a wife asks for a divorce the bride's price is refunded to the husband by the bride's father, and when the husband asks for it, he pays five rupees to his wife. A divorce is complete when the wife removes the string of glass beads that is tied to her neck on marriage or when the husband tears off a piece of cloth from his turban and the wife from her robe. Divorce is usually termed as *Farkat*, *Chhuta chheda karva* or *Ganthi todvi*. A woman divorced for adultery with a man of her caste or with a man of a higher caste is allowed to marry a second time by paying some fine or giving a dinner to her castemen, and the marriage is effected in the form of widow re-marriage. A woman divorced for adultery with a man of a lower caste is turned out of her caste.

Religion. Dhodias follow the Hindu law of inheritance and are animistic in religion. Their favourite deities of worship are Bharam Dev (Brahmadev), Iria Dev, Diwáli goddess, Kákábalia, Máoli Máta or goddess, etc. They worship these deities with a belief that their devotees are protected from the affection of witches, ghosts, small-pox and cholera. They are inclined to worship gods only when any misfortune befalls them. They visit a place known as Dewli Unai, a hot water spring in the Baroda territory, for bathing. The Dhodias of the Surat District visit the shrine of Sámrádev (Brahmadev) that is situated at Rudvel in Chikhli *taluka* at some time between the months of *Kártik* (October) and *Fálgun* (March). Their leading holidays are *Diváso* in June-July, *Vág Báras* October-November, *Diwáli* October-November, and *Holi* February-March. They make offerings to their gods on a Sunday or a Tuesday which consist of a goat or a hen, a cocoanut, a lamp fed with clarified butter, a flower wreath, frankincense, flags of red or white colour, a small dome or a house prepared of clay. When the offerings consist of a goat or a fowl they are partaken of by the offerers; otherwise they are left before the deities. They worship their dead ancestors and prepare images of wood. These are termed *Bhutada* or *Khatra*. Those of female ancestors are called *Sati* and of male relatives, *Bhut*. They make offerings to them some days before the *Diwáli* holidays. A *Bhuvo*, worshipper of a goddess, is called and he ascertains whether the ancestors are pleased with their offerings or require more. When the offering consists of a goat or a hen the *Bhuvo* takes a few hairs from the animal's body and placing them before the image of a ghost says: "Be pleased with the offering and make us prosperous in agriculture and keep our children and cattle safe". Then the goat or the fowl is taken aside and butchered on a small heap of rice grains. The rice grains that become wet with the blood are mixed with other grains in the house, the belief being that by so doing the quantity increases. A cocoanut is broken and is distributed among the company as the *prasád* or favoured food of the deity. On every feast day a small quantity of all food and drink is offered to the ghosts. They do not worship Muhammedan saints. When cholera is raging they worship Samra Dev. A wooden image of the goddess is prepared and carried in procession in a small wooden cart made for the purpose. The image is worshipped with red lead, and silver coins are offered. A burning hearth is also kept on the cart. A devotee of the goddess follows behind shaking his head. The cart with the image is placed at a spot beyond the village boundary. The inhabitants of the next village carry it on in the same way to avert the danger thus brought on them, and so on, until the image is brought to a desolate place. When small-pox is raging they worship Kákábalia deity. They do not employ Bráhmans for conducting their religious and ceremonial affairs.

Death ceremonies.

They bury or burn their dead. Persons dying of small-pox and cholera are buried, as they believe that by burning the disease spreads. The lepers are buried, not by the castemen, but by Bhangis. Children below one year are buried. The deceased is laid in a grave on his back and the head turned towards the south. The ashes and bones of the dead, when burnt, are thrown into a river. When life is extinct they wash the body with water and rub it with turmeric powder. If the deceased be a female dying before her husband, the line along the sinciput is filled with red powder and the body is attired in a new red robe. A male is attired in a loin cloth. Women accompany the funeral party as far as the bathing station. The bier is put down there and the male and female mourners throw one pice on the body as a last token of remembrance. The money so collected is distributed among the impure caste-men. On reaching the burning ground the body is laid on the pyre with its head northwards. A pice is put into the hand of the deceased and a particle of silver into the mouth. The relatives also put rice and curds into the mouth. Then every mourner throws a piece of wood on the body. The chief mourner then kindles the pyre. After some time the chief mourner takes an earthen pot over his shoulder and takes four turns round the pyre. At the commencement of each round a hole is bored to the vessel and water is allowed to trickle through it. A little of the water is sprinkled over the pyre, and the pot is thrown on the ground. Funeral rites are performed three or four days after death or on any other convenient day. On that occasion a *Bhuva* or a devotee is called. He becomes possessed, shakes his head, and utters the names of dead ancestors. He is given toddy or liquor to drink. The relatives then go to the burning ground taking with them two pipes of bamboo and two of castor-oil plant. Two are filled with, milk and the other two with rice gruel. Ashes and bones are collected. and over the spot a bower of the boughs of a *jámbul* tree is erected A male or a female child is fed. On every holiday food is offered to crows. This ceremony is repeated on a larger scale five or six years after and is known as *Ujavun* or *Parjari*.

The hereditary occupation of the caste is husbandry. Some work as agricultural labourers.

Food. Dhodias eat the flesh of goats, sheep, hogs, deer, squirrels, fowls and fish. They drink liquor. They eat kachhi and pakki at the hands of Dublas, Naikdas, Chodhras, etc. No higher caste will eat anything at the hands of this caste.

DHOKA.—A sub-division of Memans.

DHOL AGRI.—A sub-division of Agris.

DHOLI.—A synonym for Bajánia and Mir.

DHOR.—A sub-division of Mángs ; a synonym for Dhed Kátkari.

Name and origin. **DHORS** or Tanners, numbering 19,089 (1901) including 9,512 males and 9,577 females, are chiefly found in Ahmednagar, Khándesh, Sátára, Sholápur, Belgaum, Bijápur and Kolhápur. The name is probably derived from *Dhor* meaning cattle, as they are tanners of cattle skins.

Endogamous divisions. The Dhors consist of the following endogamous divisions :—

1. Budhlekari or Budligar.
2. Bundelkhandi.
3. Hindustáni.
4. Kankaya.
5. Karnátak.
6. Khetarphadi.
7. Lingáyat.
8. Marátha or Dhor proper.

These divisions neither eat together nor intermarry. Budhlekaris, from *budhlas* meaning the leather vessels prepared by them, Khetarphadis, and Dhors proper are found in Sholápur district. Kankaya, Bundelkhandi, and Marátha or Dhor proper are found in Sátára district. Marátha, Karnátak and Hindustáni Dhors are found in Belgaum district, and Hindustánis, Budligars or Budhlekaris and Dhors proper are found in Dhárwár district. The Bundelkhandi Dhors are supposed to be socially inferior to Kankaya Dhors. The tradition regarding the origin of the Kankaya Dhors professes to trace their origin from Mahádeva ; but the story is a mere play on the words *doha* a pool and *kánkh* the arm-pit.

Exogamous divisions. The founder of this caste is also said to have been the sage Lurbhát, who was born of an Aygav father and a Dhigvar mother. The common surnames are as follows :—

Boráde.	Hotkar.	Kávale.
Darveshi.	Holkar.	Kelgandre.
Gáikvád.	Ingle.	Khandare.
Gajakos.	Kadam.	Mánkar.
Gáware.	Kaikandádre.	Munimáni.
Ghodki.	Katakdavande.	Nánande.
Hasanale.	Kalambe.	Náráyankar.

Návagane.	Sadháphale.	Sinde.
Pole.	Sálunke.	Sonone.
Rájuri.	Sherkháne.	Trimbake.

Surnames have different *devaks*. Persons bearing the same surname do not intermarry. Sameness of *devak* is usually a bar to marriage. Among common *devaks* of the caste are the *umbar*, the *jámbhul*, *mariádvel*, a shrub grown on the sea-shore, and a hatchet. The *mariádvel* is brought from the coast for a marriage of a Dhor of this section. Marriage with a father's sister's daughter and maternal uncle's daughter is allowed. It is forbidden with a mother's sister's daughter. A wife's sister may be married. Two brothers can marry two sisters. Boys are married from five to twenty and girls even after they attain puberty. Sexual intercourse before marriage is not allowed, but it is frequently connived at. On discovery, the girl is married to the man concerned, if he be of a different family stock. Polygamy is permitted, but polyandry is unknown.

Marriage ceremonies.

The offer for marriage generally comes from the boy's father. The father of the boy pays to the girl's father from Rs. 50 to 200 as the bride price. A Jangam or a Bráhman settles the auspicious day and conducts the service of marriage. On a lucky day the *mágni* or asking takes place. The boy's father goes to the girl's house and presents her with a new robe and bodice and a packet of sugar. The priest marks her brow with vermilion, and she is dressed in clothes presented to her by her future father-in-law. Her lap is filled with rice and a cocoanut, and betel-leaves are served to the people who are present. Marriage may then be delayed for some time. The first sign of the wedding is the making of turmeric paste. Some of the paste is rubbed on the bridegroom, and the rest, with a present of a bodice, a robe and flower wreaths, is sent to be rubbed on the bride. Two days before the marriage, the leaves of five trees are taken to the temple of Máruti, preceded by drummers and followed by friends and relations. They are laid before the god, brought back to the marriage booth, tied to one of its posts, and constitute the marriage guardian or *devak*. Goats are slaughtered and friends and kinspeople are asked to dine. On the marriage day an altar or *bahula* is raised. The bridegroom on horse back is led in procession to the temple of Máruti in the bride's village. In Sholápur and Bijápur district the bridegroom rides a bullock. His brother or *vardhava* goes in front to the house of the bride, and returns with a turban for the bridegroom. At the entrance to the booth, rice mixed with curds is waved round him and is thrown as an offering to evil spirits. He passes into the booth. bathes and is seated on a wooden plank with the bride standing fronting him on another plank concealed by a curtain or *jamanika*. A Jangam and a Bráhman priest repeat lucky texts or *mangal shtaks* and throw lucky rice or *mangal kshatkas* over the couple. Five cotton threads are twisted into a cord, and bits of turmeric are tied to each end. The cord is cut in two, one-half being then fastened round the bridegroom's right wrist and the other half round the bride's left wrist, and their heads are decked with a brow horn or *báshing*. The priest lights the *hom* fire. The lucky necklace is then placed on the bride's neck, and she is told to walk five times round the altar with her husband. After the five turns are finished, the hems of the couple's garments are knotted together, and they go to the house to lay a cocoanut before the family deities and bow before them. The bridegroom takes the cocoanut with him, and they return to the booth to sit on the altar or *bahula*. Friends and kinspeople are feasted on fried rice flour cakes or *telachis*. The wedding or *varát* procession starts next morning from the house of the bride. When they reach the bridegroom's, five married women fill the lap of the bride. The couple visit the temple of Máruti and bow before the god. Next day they are rubbed with turmeric paste, and are bathed in warm water. Lastly, each unties the other's marriage wristlet or *kankan*, which is thrown into a copper vessel filled with water.

Widow marriage is allowed. A widow can marry her father's sister's son, maternal uncle's son or any member of her deceased husband's family. She cannot marry her mother's sister's son or her deceased husband's brother. A widow remarriage is celebrated on a dark night. Some think the months of *Ashádh* and *Bhádrapad* inauspicious for widow remarriage. A Bráhman or Jangam conducts the service. The widow is made to wear a white robe, and cowdung is applied to her brow. The priest then leads the new couple to the worship of Varuna and Ganpati, and the widow's brow is marked with red powder. The widow then puts on a new robe and bodice, and her lap is filled. The filling of the widow's lap is supposed to be the binding portion of the ceremony. A bachelor wishing to marry a widow is first married to a *rui* tree.

A husband can divorce his wife on the ground of misconduct or incompatibility of temper. Some pass divorce-deeds, while others break a straw into two parts in the presence of the headman of the caste. A woman divorced for adultery with a member of her caste is allowed to marry again, and her marriage is conducted in the fashion of widow remarriage. A woman divorced for adultery with an outsider is excommunicated.

Dhors follow the Hindu law of inheritance. They believe in sooth-saying, witchcraft and sorcery. When anyone is possessed by an evil spirit, they call in a *devrishi* or seer skilled in incantations and charms. The seer visits the sick person, burns frankincense before him, repeats a charm over a handful of ashes, and rubs them on the sick person's brow, waves a cocoanut round his head, sacrifices a goat or a cock, and the sick man is then expected to recover. Religion.

Their religion is Hindu. In places they have become Lingáyats. Some of them belong to the Várkari sect. Their family deities are Bahiroba, Bhaváni of Tuljápur and Kondanpur, Janái, Khandoba of Jejuri, Mahádev of Singnápur and Vithoba of Pandharpur. They keep the usual Bráhmanic and local holidays and fasts, their great days being *Navrátra* in September-October and *Shivrátra* in January-February. On *Dasara* day they make a sacrifice of goats and fowls. Their religious teacher is a slit eared or Kánphátya Gosávi, who visits their houses and receives a yearly tribute either in cash or in clothes. They worship their deceased ancestors. They also revere Musalmán saints. When epidemics like cholera and small-pox are raging they worship both Mari and Sitala, and sacrifice goats and fowls for their propitiation.

Dhors sometimes burn their dead, but as a rule they bury. After death the body is laid on the bier, and carried to the burying ground on the shoulders of castemen. A married woman who dies before her husband is dressed in a new robe and bodice, and glass bangles are put on her wrists ; these honours are not shown to widows. The son or the chief mourner leads the funeral party holding a fire-pot hanging from a string, and the bearers follow repeating *Jay Jay Rám* Victory to Ram. On the way at a spot called the rest-place or *visávyáchijágá* they set down the bier, leave a copper and some bread on the ground, change places, lift the bier and take it to the burial ground. A pit is dug and the body is buried in the pit in a sitting position facing the east. The right hand is laid on the left hand and the pit is filled with earth. The Jangam drops *bel* leaves over the grave and says that the deceased has become one with Shiva. All bathe, and each gives the Jangam a copper coin who then rubs their brows with ashes. On returning to the house of mourning they cleanse their mouths, sprinkle some cow's urine on themselves with a leaf of a *nimb* tree (*Melia azadirachta*) and go home. On the third day they go to the burial ground with a winnowing fan containing three small cakes of wheat flour rubbed with clarified butter, cocoa kernel, molasses, and three small earthen pots filled with cow's milk curds and Death ceremonies.

cow's urine. A cake is left at the rest-place or *visávyáchijágá*. The two other cakes, with the pots of milk and curds, are set on the grave, and the ground is sprinkled with cow's urine from the third pot. The party bathe and return home. They mourn the dead for ten days. On the tenth, the face of the son or chief-mourner is shaved except the eyebrows, and as directed by the *Jangam* priest he prepares ten wheat flour balls. Of the ten balls, nine are thrown into water, and the tenth is given to a crow. On the eleventh, friends and kins-people are feasted. They are not so very particular about the *shráddha* ceremony, but the dead are remembered on the lunar day that corresponds to the day of death in th *máhálaya paksha* or all souls fortnight in dark *Bhâdrapad* or August-September.

Occupation. The hereditary calling of Dhors is tanning hides. They buy skins from Mahárs, and steep them for four days in an earthen pot filled with lime-water. On the fourth day, they take them out and put them in water mixed with pounded *bábhul* bark and *hirdás* or myrobalans. After three days in the water the skins are taken out and dried in the sun. The women help the men in preparing the lime and *bábhul* bark water. Most Dhors carry on their trade with their own capital. Tanning is brisk all the year round, but the cold weather is better than the hot, as in hot weather the skins rot quickly when dipped in water, and are thus spoiled. They also work in leather and make saddles, shoes, water-bags, water-skins, leather buckets, bridles, horses' mouth-bags and boxes. In Sholápur their leather work is of a superior description. A few Dhors are husbandmen and some work as day labourers.

Food. They eat the flesh of sheep, goat, deer, fish and fowls. They drink liquor. They do not eat the leavings of other people. Dhors in Sholápur district eat *pakki* at the hands of Mahárs and Mángs.

LINGAYAT DHORS of Sholápur district are invested with a *linga* by a Jangam soon after birth. Their teacher or *guru* visits them occasionally, when each family gives him Rs. 1-4-0 in cash. Some well-to-do families give more, and also hold caste dinners in his honour. In their customs they differ little from Maráthás. They bury their dead, do not shave the mourner's moustache and observe no mourning. The Dhors of Kanara, Dhárwár and Bijápur respect Bráhmans but lean to the Lingáyat faith. They do not wear the *linga*. They eat flesh. Such Dhors would be described as non-Panchamsáli Lingáyats without *ashtavarna* rites (see LINGAYAT); but many Lingáyats would now deny that a Dhor can belong to their community at all.

Dublas

DHORAJ BHAVNAGRI.—A sub-division of Memans.

DHOREPI.—A sub-division of Bhils.

DHRONA.—A sub-division of Karad Vániás.

DHULDHOYA.—*See* under Minor Musalmán Castes.

DHULPAVAD.—A sub-division of Bánjigs.

DHUE.—A sub-division of Kattais.

DIDU.—A synonym for Dindu.

DIGVAN.—A synonym for Jingar.

DINDU.—A sub-division of Vániás.

DIAVAL.—A synonym for Desháválá.

DIVADKAR.—A sub-division of Gaud Sárasvat Bráhmans.

DOHOR.—A sub-division of Kattais.

DOM.—A sub-division of Mahárs.

DOMB.—A synonym for Mahár and Dom.

DOMBARI.—A sub-division of Jogis; a synonym for Kolháti.

DONGAR.—A synonym for Mahádev Kolis.

DONI.—A synonym for Mir.

DORAVRE.—A sub-division of Kattais.

DORE.—A sub-division of Gujar Kanbis.

DOI.—A sub-division of Darjis.

DUBLA, numbering 100,775 (1901), including 51,241 males and 49,534 females, are found chiefly in Broach, Surat, Thána and Surat Agency. They are classed among the *Káliparaj*, *i.e.*, dark race, a common term in general use for the aboriginal tribes of Gujarát. The Dublás or weaklings, as their name is said to mean, are a feeble people, soon aged by their hard life and their fondness for liquor. They claim a strain of Rajput blood, speaking of their near relations and connections, the Ráthods. It is stated by some that the ancestors of Dublás and Kolis were originally the same. The Dublás admit Hindus of higher castes such as Rajputs, Kanbis, Káchhiás, Kolis, etc., as well as Dhodiás, without performing any ceremony. Koknás, Naikdás and Chodhrás are admitted, on the member wishing admission paying the cost of feeding and supplying with liquor the people of twenty or twenty-five villages who assemble at the time of their admission. In some places, a fine of from Rs. 10 to Rs. 25 is taken from the new-comer. Persons of higher castes such as Rajputs, Kanbis, Kolis, etc., keeping Dubla women are admitted into the caste, Name and origin.

if they so desire, without any ceremony. A Kanbi of Kátargám is known to have entered the caste in this manner.

Divisions. The tribe contains twenty sub-divisions as follows :—

1. Bába.
2. Balsária.
3. Bárunia.
4. Choria.
5. Damani.
6. Harávia.
7. Isria.
8. Kharcha.
9. Mándvia.
10. Narda.
11. Olpádia.
12. Pália or Khodia.
13. Ráthodia.
14. Sarvia or Sarávia.
15. Sipria.
16. Talávia.
17. Ukharia.
18. Umria
19. Vásáva or Vásávda.
20. Vohria.

The Báruniás are named after their practice of performing funeral rites on the twelfth day after a death, Mándviás after performing funeral rites under a shade (*mándva* = bower) and the Taláviás after their practice of performing the funeral rites on the bank of a pond or tank (*taláo*). The Ukhariás and Choriás are so named on account of their performing the ceremonies on a wooden mortar (*ukhar*) and on a square *chori* (altar). Several of the divisions are geographical, named after Bulsár, Daman, Mándvi, Olpád, etc.

Of the above divisions, the Taláviás are the highest in social rank. They take to wife the girls of the Saráviás, but do not give their daughters in marriage to them. The Taláviás and Mándviás eat together and intermarry. With these exceptions, the members of the abovementioned clans seldom eat together and never intermarry.

Marriages are prohibited when relationship can be traced between the two contracting parties. Marriage with a mother's sister's daughter, father's sister's daughter and maternal uncle's daughter is not allowed. A wife's younger sister can be married during the wife's life-time or after her death, and two brothers may marry two sisters. Boys are married from ten to twenty and girls from ten to eighteen. An unmarried girl cannot openly cohabit with any person. When she has cohabited with a man of a higher, or of her, caste and the fact has gained publicity, the girl is fined. In some places, sexual intercourse before marriage is connived at. When the man involved is of her caste, the girl is sometimes married to him. If a girl is guilty of misconduct with a member of the Kokna, Chodhra or Gámta caste, she can remain in the caste by giving a caste dinner and a fine ; but if with a member of a very low caste such as a Dheda or Bhangia, she is permanently expelled.

Marriage ceremonies. The offer of marriage comes from the boy's father. In some places, the marriage day is fixed and the service conducted by a priest

Dubla women

belonging to the degraded class of Tapodhan Bráhmans, or by a member of any other caste wearing the sacred thread. In others, the service is conducted either by a casteman or by a member of another caste who knows the rites. The boy's father pays to the girl's father from fifteen to twenty rupees. Sometimes the amount, which is known as *Dej*, is paid in the form of grain. The *Khandalia* form of marriage, *i.e.*, by serving the parents of the wife, also prevails. When a marriage is settled, the bride's party go to the house of the bridegroom and throw grains of rice coloured with red powder into his house and present him with as many seeds of castor oil plant as there are number of days intervening between that day and the marriage day. Out of these seeds one is thrown away daily. The day on which the last seed is thrown away is thus held to be the marriage day. Five days before marriage the bride and bridegroom are rubbed with *pithi* turmeric paste. The planet pleasing ceremony is performed the day before the marriage day at the bridegroom's house, and again on the marriage day at the bride's house. In the afternoon, with a company of his friends, the bridegroom, his eyes painted and a spot on each cheek marked black to keep off the evil eye, starts with music and singing for the bride's house. He is led by the bride's father to the square space in the centre of the booth. The bride is brought in, and the skirts of the bride's and bridegroom's garments are tied into a knot. As the sun sets, a Bráhman or a casteman calls out three or four times "*Sávdhán, Kaligranthi Sávdhán*" "Beware of the auspicious knot," and joins the hands of the bride and bridegroom. The bride and bridegroom then walk round the *chori* four times and are fed with sweetmeats and cooked rice. Then they make a bow to their patron deity. Walking round the *chori* and making a bow to the patron deity are supposed to be the binding portions of the ceremony. At night men and women dance together, and the marriage ceremony closes with two dinners, one at the bride's and the other at the bridegroom's house. When the bride's father is a well-to-do man he, like the Gamits or Dhodiás, selects a bridegroom and keeps him at his house. If the girl desires the match, the usual ceremony is performed. The bridegroom in such cases is termed *Ghar Jamai* or *Khandálio*.

Widow remarriage is allowed. A widow cannot marry her maternal uncle's son, father's sister's son, or mother's sister's son. She may marry, if she chooses, the younger brother or any other relative of her deceased husband younger than him. A remarriage is brought a out by the near relatives of a widow and is celebrated on a Sunday, Tuesday or Thursday. At the time of remarriage, kinspeople on both the sides are present. The ceremony is conducted by a remarried widow. The widow wears brass ornaments *Chhali* and *Kalla*. The couple are seated on low wooden stools near each other and their brows marked with red powder. A cloth sheet is held over them by four men, and rice grains coloured red are thrown over their heads by four women. This last ceremony of throwing rice grain is supposed to be the binding portion of the ceremony. Some perform this ceremony in two different ways. (1) The bride stands opposite the bridegroom on a mortar, and two widows, one on each side of her, bring together the heads of the bride and bridegroom seven times, and the bridegroom pays to the bride a sum of annas four. This completes the ceremony. (2) Cocoanuts are placed on the heads of the bride and bridegroom, and their heads are brought together. A bachelor is allowed to marry a widow after first being married to a *shami* tree. In some places, the *shami* tree must be of a different village from that of the bachelor.

Both a husband or a wife may obtain a divorce with the permission of the headman of the caste and of the relatives. Divorce is termed *Chhuta Chheda Karva* or *Fárgati Apvi*. Divorce is allowed on account of incompatibility of temper or when the husband is suffering from some incurable disease or is impotent. The party asking for the divorce has to pay to the other a sum of Rs. 15, and Rs. 5 to the castemen. Even when a divorce is effected without the knowledge of the headman of the caste, the above payment must be made. In some places, a man wishing to divorce his wife ties a sum of Rs. 5 to the skirt of her garment and abandons her, which effects the divorce. A woman divorced for adultery is allowed to marry a second time, when her marriage is effected after the fashion of widow remarriage. A woman divorced for adultery with a man of her caste is fined ten rupees. But when she has committed adultery with a man of a lower caste and is divorced, she is fined one hundred rupees.

Religion.

Dublás follow the Hindu law of inheritance. They believe in witchcraft, sorcery and magic. Every community has a Bhagat or sorcerer, who cures diseases by means of a broom made of the leaves of the *nimb* tree. He is much respected when possessed by a spirit; he nods his head and directs the performance of certain rites to free the patient from his troubles.

The Dublás are animists by religion. They have no knowledge of Shiva and Vishnu nor of the incarnations of the latter. Besides spirits and ancestors they worship Hanumán and different forms of goddesses such as Shikotri, Agashi, Himario, etc. Offerings of goats, fowls, etc., are made to their goddesses during the *Navrátra* or nine nights festival in *Aso* September-October. Stones and holy trees, especially the tree *samer*, which is believed to be the haunt of ghosts, and the *shami* are worshipped. They also worship the cow, the bull, the *pipal*, a scythe, a grinding mill, the serpent, the tiger, etc. Their leading holidays are *Matavi Athem* in *Aso* September-October, *Holi* March-April, *Diváli* October-November, *Makar Sankránt* in January, *Diváso* in June-July and *Balev* in July-August. The *Diváso* holiday is specially observed by them. On that day they make dolls and puppets and marry them. There is a saying that the *Diváso* is the special holiday of Dublas alone. During the *Navrátra* they dance and are called *Gherias*. While dancing they wear the skirts of women, but above their waist they dress like men. They tie a belt of jingling bells round their waist and hold a stick in their hands. They collect subscriptions from the public and spend the amount on a feast. They worship the images of their ancestors. The images are prepared of sandal wood and are called *Khatruns*. Offerings of cocoa-nuts, flowers, red powder and red lead are made to them. Occasionally animal sacrifices also are made for their propitiation, and liquor is poured over the images. They revere Musalmán saints. When cholera and small-pox are raging, they adore the minor deities Káliká-máta and Kákábalia. They treat Bráhmans with respect and, except in a few of the wilder villages, on marriage occasions and sometimes at the time of the naming ceremony make use of their services

Except a few of the poorest who bury, they burn the dead. Persons dying of leprosy, small-pox and such other contagious diseases are buried to prevent the spread of the disease. Children below four years are buried. While burying, they place the deceased in the grave head northwards. When the deceased is burnt, the ashes and bones are washed away with water. On this occasion friends and relatives meet at the deceased's house, the women weep and beat their breasts. When the deceased is an unwidowed woman, the brow is marked with red powder, the eyes are painted with lamp black, and red lead is sprinkled over the sinciput. The body is dressed in a new robe, and covered with a new shroud. If the deceased is a male a white shroud is used. The body is set on a bamboo bier, and is carried by four relatives, who, as they pass to the burning-ground, chant the refrain *Rám bolo bhái Rám*, Call Rám brothers, Call Rám. At the halting station every member throws grains of rice over the corpse. On reaching the burning-ground, which is generally on the bank of a stream, the pyre is made ready. Half a seer of rice is cooked in a jar in which fire is brought by the chief mourner. A ball of cooked rice is prepared and is placed on the mouth of the deceased. Death ceremonies.

Four balls are offered to crows on a leaf of banyan tree. This is called *Vas Mukvi*. Copper coins are placed in the deceased's hands, and a particle of silver is put into the mouth. The chief mourner then kindles the pyre. The party wait till the pyre is consumed, receiving on return a draught of *tádi* palm beer. Ceremonies are performed on the second, fourth and sixth days after death, and on the twelfth a caste dinner is given. A poor man delays the ceremonies to a later date, and when they are performed, an image of *kush* grass is made and burnt in the burning-ground, after which the ceremony is commenced. When funeral ceremonies are not observed owing to the poverty of the relations, they bathe at the *Holi* (March-April) *Diváli* (October-November) and *Diváso* (July-August), and before taking food make offerings of a portion to crows. This is known as *Pandadu Mukvu*.

Every year in the month of *Chaitra* or *Mágh* the following ceremony is performed for the pacification of the *manes*.

A devotee called *jangio* is called. He becomes possessed and utters the names of the deceased ancestors. The members of the family then go to the bank of a river and burn images of *kush* grass in the name of the deceased ancestors. After their return home, funnel-shaped earthen pots are filled with water and placed on the ground, one in the name of each ancestor. If the deceased be a male, the earthen jar in his name is covered with a white piece of cloth, if a female, with a red piece. The mouths of the earthen pots are closed with small earthen cups, and over these cups small earthen pots are again placed. Then the devotee nods, and taking in succession the name of each of the deceased ancestor, says "I a certain ancestor have come" After each time he has repeated a name, the devotee is given water and liquor to drink and a little food to eat. After this is over, all the jars are emptied and the ceremony ends. The Dublás believe that only by the performance of this ceremony the deceased ancestors become satisfied. In some places, wooden images are made in the name of the deceased ancestors ; they are dressed in clothes and smeared with vermilion. In the mornings of Sundays and Tuesdays the images are worshipped with offerings of goats, fowls, toddy and liquor.

Dublás are peasants and labourers, most of them ploughmen or *halis*, the hereditary servants of Bhátelá Bráhmans and other better class cultivators. These men work in the fields, their women acting as household servants in the master's family. They are entirely dependent on their masters for food and clothing, and on the whole seem as well off as those of their tribe who are freer in name. As they mix much with the better class of cultivators, their ways are cleaner and their manners less rough and peculiar than those of most early tribesmen. Between A. D. 1863 and 1866, when labour was dear, many Dublás left the families they formerly served and worked as free labourers. Since then they are said to have found their old position as ploughmen or *halis* securer and not more onerous.

Of animals the Dublás eat sheep, goats, hares and fowls. They will not touch the flesh of the çow nor of any animal found dead. Their favourite game is the quail *labdi* and the iguana *pátlágoh*. So fond of the iguana are they, especially their women after child birth, that the proverb runs "A lizard tired of life makes for the Dubla huts." They drink liquor and eat the leavings of higher classes. By not eating large rats, squirrels and monkeys they consider themselves superior to Gámits. Food.

They do not eat at the hands of inferior castes such as Naikdás Chodhrás, etc. They consider Kolis and Dhodiás superior to them and eat from them. No higher caste will eat at their hands. According to some, the Dublás eat at the hands of Parsis and Muhammadans.

DUDHVALA.—*See* under Minor Musalmán Castes.

DUKRE.—A sub-division of Kolhátis.

DUNGARPORA.—A sub-division of Darjis.

DUNGAT.—A sub-division of Virs.

DURBAR.—A synonym for Bábria.

DURGAMURGI.—A sub-division of Kabbaligars: a synonym for Kare Berads.

FADALI.—A synonym for Abdáli.

FATADA.—A synonym for Pavaya.

GABITS, numbering 24,233, including 11,569 males and 12,664 females, are found on the sea-coast chiefly in the Ratnágiri and Kanara districts and in the Sávantvádi State. A few families reside in the Surat, Kolába, and Thána districts, and the Janjira State. They call themselves Konkani Maráthás and state that they were originally Maráthás and manned the navy of Shiváji. Some of them are still known as *Gurabitándels* or captains of grabs, *i.e.*, small vessels of war. On the conquest of the Peshwás by the British and the consequent abolition of the Marátha navy, they took to fishing, which isolated them from the Maráthás. Before the establishment of the British supremacy at sea (1760), and to a less extent until 1800, when the creeks and Name and origin.

backwaters passed under British control, they caused serious loss by their piracies. They are now chiefly fishermen and sailors. It is curious to find that, contrary to the practice of the Marátha castes in the Deccan, they have in places an organization based on *gotras*. But it seems that they adopted this system in recent times after the manner of many castes who are anxious to ascend in the social scale. Some accounts give Káshyap as the *gotra* of the whole caste, while those accounts which give different *gotras* for the different families state that the rule of not marrying into the same *gotra* is not strictly followed. This, and the traces of *kuls* and *devaks* still to be found amongst them, are a tolerably clear indication of the probable Marátha origin of the caste. The chief *kuls* are Bhude, Dhavade, Ghure, Mote, Náik, Tándel, Sávant, and Vasta. The *devaks* are given below.

The original home of the Gábits is Goa, where they are known by the name of Khárvi. Their surnames of Pednekar, Shiveshvarkar, etc., still indicate their original home in Goa. During the Portuguese insurrection they fled to the coasts of Ratnágiri and Kanara and settled there. Those who remained in Goa were converted to Christianity.

Divisions. There are no endogamous divisions of the caste. According to some accounts they have the following *gotras* :—

Atri	Káshyap
Bábhravya	Kaushik
Bháradwája	Shándilya
Gárgya	Vasishtha
Kapil	Vatsa

According to others the whole caste has the same *gotra*, namely, Káshyap, while it is also stated that they have *kuls* or family stocks as follows :—

Bhosale	Chaván
Jádhav	Kubal
Ghorpade	Távade
Dábháde	More
Dhamále	Nikam
Shinde	

The commonest surnames are Távade, Padte, Khule, Sárang, Máyaba, Lone, Khavale, Kharáre, Kurle, Kolhe, Tári, Dhuri, Girap, Vágh, Bhagat, Poshe, Takale, Joshi, Dhoke, Posam, Parabhu, Lád, Chaugule, Pági, Patkuri, Pangáre, Mánjare, Tonage, and Rede. The rules regulating the restrictions on intermarriage are confused. According to some, marriages are prohibited between members of the same *gotra*. According to others, sameness of *kul* is a bar to intermarriage, while the Bombay Gazetteer states (Vol. XV, Part I, page 305) that persons bearing the same surname cannot intermarry. Sameness of *devak* is not necessarily a bar to intermarriage. A member of the caste can marry his mother's brother's daughter as well as his father's sister's daughter. Descendants of sisters cannot marry within three degrees of relationship. A man may marry two sisters, and two brothers may marry two sisters. Boys are generally married from fourteen to twenty, girls from eight to fourteen. Girls may remain unmarried till after they attain puberty. Sexual license before marriage is not tolerated. Polygamy is allowed and practised, but polyandry is unknown.

Marriage ceremonies.

The offer of marriage comes from either family. If the girl's father is poor the boy's father pays him from Rs. 10 to Rs. 100 for the marriage expenses. If the boy's father is well-to-do he receives a dowry with the girl. The settlement of the marriage day and the ceremony itself are entrusted to a Bráhman priest. The marriage ceremonies of the Gábits do not differ from those of the Bráhmans, except in the installation of the *devak* or marriage guardian, which takes place at the commencement of the marriage. The *devaks* of the caste consist of the *kalamb* (Anthocephalus cadumba), the *pángára* (Coral tree,) the *audumbar* (Ficus glomerata), the *vad* (the Indian fig tree), the *pipal* (Ficus religiosa), the mango, the *palas* (Butea frondosa), and the *pánchpálvi* or leaves of five kinds of trees. The *devaks* appear to have originally been totemistic, and the caste still show their reverence for them by not dining on the leaves of, or cutting or burning the wood of, trees representing the *devaks*.

The remarriage of widows is permitted. A widow cannot marry her mother's sister's son or a member of her late husband's section. A widow remarriage can be celebrated on any day, but Sundays and Wednesdays are considered to be the luckiest days. The ceremony takes place in an uninhabited house on the village boundary, or in a temple of Vetál or Bhutnáth. In order to prevent disturbance from the spirit of the widow's deceased husband, a cock, a cocoanut and rice grains are first offered to him. Glass bangles are then put on the widow's wrists by a Kásár, and she wears a robe presented by her new husband, which completes the ceremony. A bachelor is not allowed to marry a widow. A husband can divorce his wife on the ground of unchastity with the sanction of the caste *Panch*. A divorced woman is turned out of the caste.

Religion. Gábits follow the Hindu law of inheritance and belong to the Hindu religion. Some of them are followers of the Várkari and Rámdási sects. They worship all Bráhman gods, the village gods Ravalnáth, Bhutnáth, Sánteri. Bhadrakáli, Vetál. Puruvansha, Kámákshi, Rámnáth and Bhaváni. A cocoanut is installed amongst the household gods in the name of the deceased ancestors and worshipped daily. Goats and fowls are offered to the village gods, which are eaten by the offerers themselves. The *vad*, the *pipal*, the *audumbar*, the *bel* (Aegle marmelos), and weapons and implements are worshipped. Gábits observe all the Hindu holidays and make pilgrimages to all the sacred places of the Hindus, but chiefly to Pandharpur. They are firm believers in evil spirits, in the spirits of the dead, in soothsaying, and in sorcery. When an epidemic breaks out, loud public prayers are held; and a basket containing a cock, a goat, a cocoanut, cooked food, red lead and red flowers is carried in procession and left on the village boundary. The spiritual guide of the caste is the Shankaráchárya of the Sankeshwar monastery. Their priests are the Chitpávan or Karháda Bráhmans.

Death. The dead are either burnt or buried. At burial the corpse is seated. The ordinary funeral rites are observed. For the propitiation of deceased ancestors, *mahál*s are performed on those days of the latter half of *Bhádrapad* which represent the death days, when uncooked articles of food are given to Bráhmans and castemen are feasted. The *shráddha* is performed annually on the anniversary of the deceased.

The hereditary occupation of the caste is sea-faring and catching fish, which they also sell. Some of them hold land. A few are *khots*. Some are tenants of superior holders. Some are day labourers and are paid either in cash or in kind.

Food. They eat the flesh of goats, sheep, hares, deer, wild boars, fowls, and fish, and drink liquor.

GADA.—A sub-division of Ods.

GADAGE.—A sub-division of Dhangars.

GADARIA.—A synonym for Bharvád.

GADHAVI.—A synonym for Cháran.

GADHAV LONARI.—A synonym for Lonári.

GADIALI.—A sub-division of Bráhmans.

Name. **GADRIS**, numbering 1,337, including 686 males and 651 females, are chiefly found in the Ahmedabad, Broach, Kaira and Panch Maháls districts. Gádris move about in search of pasture during the dry season, and return to their homes during the monsoon.

Woman in the Costume of the Vakkal Castes of North Kanara

Divisions.

There are no endogamous divisions of the caste, nor are any exogamous sub-divisions discoverable above families bearing the same surname. The commonest surnames are Chuván, Mori, Dakharata, Megadi, Násani, Gelot and Gujar. Persons bearing the same surname cannot intermarry.

Marriages are prohibited within four degrees of relationship. A man may marry his deceased wife's sister. Two brothers may marry two sisters. Marriage is adult, girls being married at fifteen or sixteen, and boys a little later. Sexual license before marriage is not tolerated. If a girl commits sexual indiscretions with a casteman, he is compelled to marry her. Polygamy is permitted, but polyandry is unknown.

Marriage ceremonies.

The offer of marriage is made by the boy's father, who pays a sum of Rs. 35 to the girl's parents for marriage expenses. The settlement of the marriage day and the ceremony itself are entrusted to a Bráhman priest. Marriage booths are erected at both houses with posts of *salada* wood ornamented with leaves of *ásopálo* (Polyalthia longifolia). The chief ceremonies in a marriage are *Ganeshpuja*, worship of Ganesh; *Pithi chadhávavu*, rubbing the bride and bridegroom with turmeric paste; *Varghodo*, starting of the bridegroom in procession for the girl's house; and the worship of the potter's wheel. The essential and binding portion of the ceremony consists in the mutual untying of the *kankans* (cotton threads) tied round the wrists of the bride and bridegroom. The *devaks* or marriage guardians of the caste consist of the sword, and the leaves of the *khápara* (Trianthema monogyna), mango, reed (*boru*), *ghatbor* and *mahua*.

The remarriage of widows is permitted. A widow can marry a member of her late husband's section; and may marry his younger brother, but not the elder. A widow's marriage must be celebrated at night on a Sunday or Tuesday. The ceremony consists in putting on new clothes and the tying into a knot of the hems of their garments by an elderly widow. Divorce is allowed. The caste follow the Hindu law of inheritance.

Religion.

They follow the Hindu religion, worshipping Rám and Shakti. Offerings of goats, sheep and fowls are made to Shakti and Ghoddev on Diváli day. Stone images of dead ancestors are made and worshipped during the *Dasara* and *Diváli* holidays. Gádris, make pilgrimages to the Ganges, Dwárka, Dákor and Onkárji. Their religious teachers are Gosávis or Bairágis. They employ Bráhmans to conduct marriage and death ceremonies. The dead are burnt, and the bones and ashes consigned to the water. Those who can afford it, carry a few of the bones to the Ganges. On the eleventh day after death a ceremony known as *Sarávavu* is performed in which a male and a female calf are married and set at liberty. The caste perform the *Shráddha*.

The occupation of the caste is the rearing of sheep. They also cultivate land and work as field labourers.

Food. They eat fish and the flesh of goats and fowls, and drink liquor.

GAIDHAR.—A synonym for Gujaráti Sutár.

GALBHOI.—A synonym for Raikari.

GALIARA.—*See* Bhandhári.

GAMETI.—*See* under Minor Musalmán Castes.

GAM GAVDA.—A synonym for Gám Vakkal.

Name and origin. **GAM VAKKALS**, also called Gámgaudás, numbering 12,401 (1901), including 5,963 males and 6,438 females, are chiefly found in lowland villages between the Gangávali and Shirávati rivers in the Kanara district. They are one of the "Vakkal" or cultivating castes of Kanara, ranking next to the Hálvakki Vakkals in social order. Their name appears to be derived from *gám*, a corruption of the Sanskrit *grám*, a village. Their own tradition is that they were named after Gáma, one of their ancestors, who brought the Haviks from Hayakshátra and gave them Gám Vakkal women in marriage on condition that after marriage the women should not abandon their original fashion of dress. A similar claim to a former connection with the Haviks is advanced by the Hálvakki Vakkals, and is supported by the fact that Havik women dress in the same style as the Hálvakki and Gám Vakkals to the present day (1906). In so doing they set at defiance the recent orders of Havik priests to assimilate their costume to that of other Bráhman women.

Exogamous divisions. The caste contains the following exogamous sub-divisions or *balis* :—

1. Ajjane bali .. ..A tree (*Antiaris toxicaria.*)
2. Ane bali .. ..Ane = the elephant.
3. Arashina bali .. ..Arsina = turmeric (*Curcuma longa*).
4. Chendi bali .. ..Chendi = a tree (*Cerbera odollam*).
5. Devater bali .. ..(Unknown.)
6. Hire bali .. ..Hire = a tree (*Luffa acuntangula*).

7. Honne bali .. ..Honne = a tree (*Pterocarpus marsupium.*)
8. Kadan bali .. ..(Unknown.)
9. Kadvin bali .. ..Kadave = the elk.
10. Nerala bali .. ..Neral = a tree (*Eugenia jambolana.*)
11. Shetti bali .. ..Shetti or Shetli = a fish.
12. Shige bali .. ..Shige = soapnut (*Acacia concinna*).
13. Shire bali .. ..Shire = a tree (*Gnandropsis pentaphyla*).
14. Shivin bali .. ..Shivani = a tree (*Gimelina-arborea*).

These *balis* appear to be true totemistic divisions from the respect that is paid to the emblem after which each is named, and from their being exogamous. Thus, members of the Ane *bali* offer a cocoanut to an elephant. Members of the Kadvin *bali* will not kill the elk nor eat its flesh. Members of the Nerala *bali* will neither eat the berries of the *nerala* nor use its wood for fuel. Similarly, in the case of the other *balis* named after trees, the tree is never cut or damaged by the members of the division. The *bali* is traced through male descent. The Gám Vakkals will not readily disclose the names of their *balis*, and it is probable that they are not satisfied with a totemistic system which is unknown in the Hindu castes of a higher social standing.

The Gám Vakkals speak a corrupt Kanarese, the peculiarities being the same as those of the Hálvakki Vakkals. The names in common use among men and women are those found among the Hálvakki Vakkals, the men suffixing *appa* or father, *náik* or chief, or *gauda* or headman to their names.

The rules regulating intermarriage do not differ from those of the Hálvakki Vakkals.

The habits of the caste are settled. They are divided into groups of villages, each group having a *budvant* or headman, and all the groups having a chief, headman or *yajamán*. Each *budvant* has an assistant called *kolkár* or *kudváli* whose duty is to carry messages to the castemen. Small offences are enquired into by the local *budvants*, and cases of gross misdemeanour by the *yajamán* in meetings of the castemen which are known as *kuts*. Ordinary offences are punished with fines, and grave offences, such as adultery, with excommunication.

The authority of the *kul* appears to be declining, as their decisions are often disregarded, and many of the castemen associate freely with the offenders. Outsiders are not admitted into this caste.

Girls are generally married up to the age of twelve years and boys up to twenty. Polygamy is allowed, some men having even four wives. Polyandry is unknown.

Marriage ceremonies. Their marriage ceremonies resemble those of the Hálvakki Vakkals, the essential portion consisting in joining the hands of the bride and bridegroom and pouring milk over them. This is known as the *dháre* ceremony. The *tera* or bride-price varies from Rs. 16 to Rs. 100.

The remarriage of widows is permitted, but of late generally discouraged. A bachelor is not allowed to marry a widow.

Divorce is allowed with the sanction of the *yajamán* or the chief headman. A divorced woman cannot marry again during the life-time of her husband.

Religion. The caste follows the Hindu law of inheritance and the Hindu religion. Their family god is Venkataráma of Tirupati and Balindra, the ancestral cocoanut. They pay respect also to Hanumán and the local minor deities such as Jatgás and Mhastis. Like the Hálvakki Vakkals, they celebrate the *Haridina* ceremony. They also perform a ceremony known as *panwár* in which castemen are invited, the image of Venkataráma is worshipped as in the *Haridina* ceremony, and the guests are feasted. The plough is worshipped after the harvest with offerings of flowers, plantains and cocoanuts.

Death. They resemble the Hálvakki Vakkals in the disposal of the dead and the performance of funeral rites, except that they observe mourning for eleven days instead of three.

Occupation. The original occupation of the caste is agriculture. Of late some have taken to felling and squaring timber and hollowing canoes. They cultivate paddy, sugarcane and cocoa palms. A few own lands, but the majority are *nagdi* and *chálgeni* tenants, that is, tenants-at-will. The *nagdi* tenants cultivate gardens and receive one-half, one-third or one-fourth of the produce for their labour. Some are field labourers and are paid at the rate of three or four annas a day.

Food. The staple food of the caste is rice, *rági*, fish, fowls and mutton, and when they sacrifice or hunt they eat flesh, except beef and tame pork. Both men and women drink country distilled liquor called *challi*, but seldom to excess.

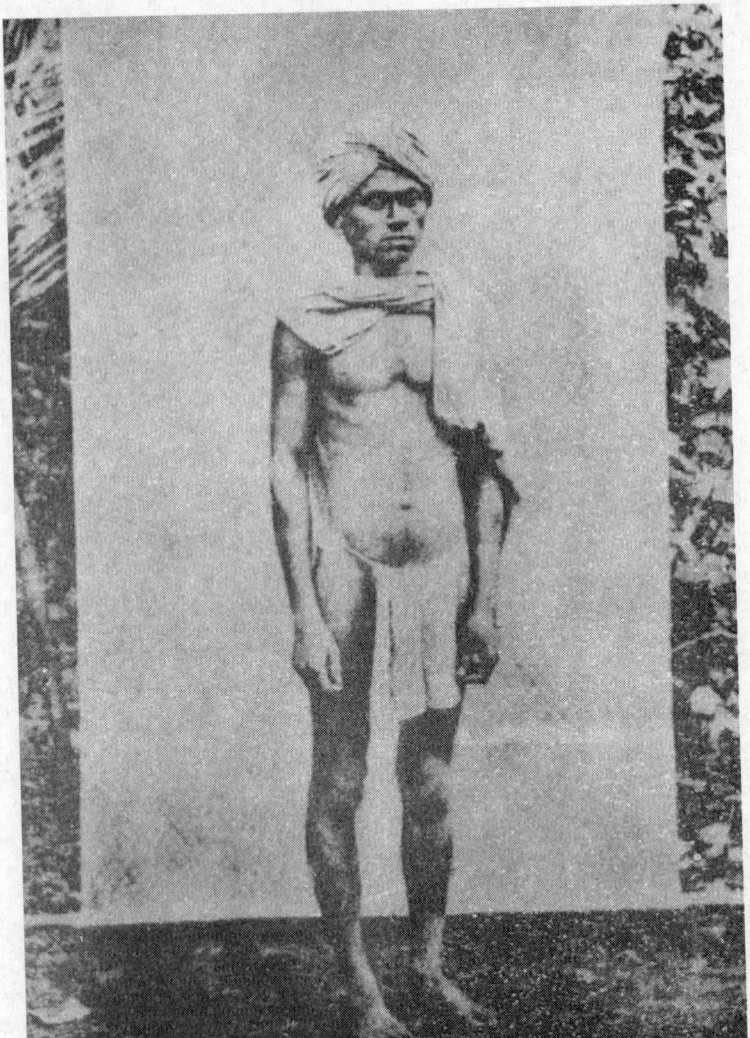

A Gam Vakkal of North Kanara

GAMVASTI BAJANIA.—A synonym for **Bajánia.**

GAN.—*See* Kalávant.

GANACHARI.—A sub-division of Jangams.

GANAKUMAR.—A sub-division of Jangams.

GANDHARIAS[1] numbering 468, including 243 males and 225 females, were recorded at the Census of 1901 only in Káthiáwár; but enquiries show that they are mainly found in Broach, Surat, Baroda and Cambay, a very small number being residents of Bhávnagar. They appear to be a cross between Khárvás and Machhis, the theory being supported by their occupation of tile-turning, fishing and sailing and by the names of two of their sub-divisions, *viz.*, Machhi and Hansoti. **Name and origin**

There are two main divisions of the caste—Sanghádia and Mujphadia. There are three other divisions—Gandhariás proper, who are tile-turners, Machhis, who are fishermen, and Hansotis, who are sailors. Marriages are prohibited between members of the same section and also between those residing in different districts. A Gandharia cannot marry his father's sister's, mother's sister's or mother's brother's daughter. A member of the caste may marry two sisters, and brothers may marry sisters. Polygamy is allowed and practised, but polyandry is unknown. Boys are generally married up to eight and girls up to six years of age. Betrothals are frequently made when a child is still unborn. All marriages in the community must take place at Cambay and the officiating priest must be a Sárasvat Bráhman of Cambay. The caste seem to consider Cambay to be the place of their original abode. Even widow remarriages have to be registered with the *kázi* at Cambay or optionally with a Court of law in the locality. **Divisions.**

The offer of marriage comes from the boy's father. The marriage ceremonies are those in vogue among castes of similar standing in the locality, the essential portion being the *mangalphero* or going four or seven times round the sacrificial fire.

The remarriage of widows is permitted. The levirate is not allowed. The ceremony consists in seating the bride and bridegroom facing each other, placing between them a burning lamp in an earthen vessel, and bringing their heads into close contact. Molasses and liquor are served among those present, and a present of clothes is made to the bridegroom, thus concluding the ceremony. Divorce is allowed, but is very rare. Divorced wives are allowed to remarry.

---

(1) From materials supplied by Mr. K. G. Pandit, B.A., LL.B.

The caste follow the Hindu law of inheritance with slight modifications.

Religion. Gandhariás are Hindus of the Swáminaráyan, Kabirpanthi and Rámánandi sects. Their chief god is Shankar. The Zamorin Báva is their religious preceptor. They observe all the Hindu holidays and sacrifice a goat on the *Dasura* day. *Pirs* are held in veneration. Their priests are Sárasvat Bráhmans, who officiate on all occasions. The dead are burnt. Infants who have not cut their teeth are buried. The standard funeral rites are observed.

Gandhariás were originally a sea-faring caste, but now they are mostly tile-turners. Some make coir ropes, and a few are painters, weavers and carpenters.

Food. They eat the flesh of goats, sheep and fish, and drink liquor. They eat at the hands of Bráhmans, Vániás and Rajputs.

GANDHI.—A functional group, means a grocer; a sub-division of Telis.

GANDHIA.—A sub-division of Vánjhás.

GANDHRAPS or musicians, numbering 99 (1901), including 57 males and 42 females, are found mostly in south Gujarát. They state that they were originally Nágar Bráhmans of the Chitroda division. They play on various musical instruments, and accompany dancing girls in all their performances. Owing to the smallness of their number, marriage is allowed and practised among the children of brothers and sisters. They perform the thread-girding ceremony like Bráhmans, whom they imitate in religious observances and customs. They do not eat fish or flesh or drink liquor.

GANESHIA.—A synonym for Meghvál.

GANGAPUTRA.—A sub-division of Bráhmans.

GANGATIRKAR.—A sub-division of Nhávis.

GANGIMAKKALU.—A synonym for Kabbaligar.

Name and origin. **GANIGS** or Oil-pressers, from *ghána* an oil-mill, numbering approximately 2,502 (1901), including 1,208 males and 1,294 females, are found all over the Karnátak and Kanara. There is a tradition current in the Karnátak that the founder of the caste was a certain Ghánád Kanyapayya, a pious but poor Lingáyat, who is said to have been a devoted worshipper of Revansiddheshvar, an incarnation of Shiva. His chief form of worship consisted in lighting a lamp called *dipárádhan* in Shiva's temple every evening, and in this duty he never failed. He pressed only so much oil as sufficed to light the lamp and maintain himself and his family. To try his faith, Shiva took from him his mill and everything in his house, and left him destitute. Kanyapayya, finding himself bereft of everything, went to the temple, and standing in front of the god, set his long hair on fire and thus lit up the temple. Shiva was so pleased with his devotion that he carried Kanyapayya to heaven.

Gánigs are supposed to have come from Mysore, where they are found in large numbers. The ceremonies of the Bombay and Mysore Gánigs are in many respects similar, and two of the principal divisions of the caste, Kare and Sajjan, are found amongst both, which suggests their original identity.

Division

Gánigs have two main divisions, Hindu and Lingáyat. The former, though professing to be a distinct Hindu caste, appear to be greatly influenced by Lingáyatism inasmuch as they wear the *linga* and follow Lingáyats in most of their ceremonies and customs. Some members of one of their divisions, named Vantiyats, wear both the *linga* and the sacred thread. This article deals with the Hindu Gánigs. The Lingáyats will be found described elsewhere (*vide* Lingáyat).

Hindu Gánigs have nine endogamous divisions :—

1. Bile or white.
2. Kare or black.
3. Kemp or red.
4. Pancham.
5. Pasti.
6. Sajjan or pure.[1]
7. Tilwán.
8. Vaishnav.
9. Vantiyat or men with one bullock.[2]

All except the Vaishnavs eat together, but none intermarry. The Kanara Gánigs are divided into Makkal-Santán or son-heir Gánigs and Aliya-Santán or sister's son-heir Gánigs. The Aliya-Santáns take food cooked by the Makkal-Santáns, but the Makkal-Santáns do not eat with the Aliya-Santáns. The exogamous divisions of the caste are identical with the surnames. Widow remarriage and divorce are allowed except by the Sajjans and Pastis. In Kanara, widows' heads are shaved as among Bráhmans.

Ceremonies.

The birth, death and other ceremonies of the Karnátak Gánigs resemble those of the Lingáyats. The ceremonies of the Kanara Gánigs are similar to those observed by Gudigars.

Gánigs are followers of either Shiva or Vishnu. The Karnátak Gánigs consider it a sin to blindfold their bullocks while yoked to the

(1) These are said in origin to have been Kudavakkals, *see* KUDAVAKKAL.

(2) Vantiyat, from *wondu yettu* Kan, *i.e.*, one bullock.

mill. They have also a belief that it is sinful to work a pair of bullocks, and hence the class of Vantiyats or one bullock men. The Kanara Gánigs pay special reverence to Venkatráma. The priests of the Karnátak Gánigs are Jangams: those of the Kanara Gánigs Havik Bráhmans.

The followers of Shiva bury, and the rest burn, their dead. In the Karnátak, the clothes of the deceased are brought home, worshipped on the seventh day, and given to Jangams.

Almost all the Gánigs follow the hereditary occupation of oil-pressing. A few are husbandmen, cart-drivers and petty dealers.

Food. Except the Vaishnavs, all eat fish and flesh, and drink liquor. Among the Kanara Gánigs the use of liquor is forbidden. They hold themselves to be high class Vaishyas, and will not eat food cooked by any one but a Havik Bráhman.

GAO KASAB.—A sub-division of Musalmán Kasáis.

GAON BHAT.—A synonym for Marátha Bhát.

GARABI.—A synonym for Gábit.

GARANA.—A sub-division of Parjia Sonis.

GARASIA.—A sub-division of Thoris.

GARDI.—A sub-division of Mahárs.

GARETE.—A sub-division of Kumbhárs.

GARI.—A sub-division of Gujar Kanbis.

GARODA.—A sub-division of Bráhmans.

GARODE.—A sub-division of Holayás.

Name and origin. **GARUDI**, also known as Modikars or Madáris from the *Madar* or *rui* plant (Calotropis gigantea), numbering 2,548 (1901), including 1,229 males and 1,419 females, are found in small numbers all over the Gujarát and Deccan and in Kanara. Of this number 233 were returned as Musalmáns. Gárudis are itinerant jugglers and snake-charmers and are said to have formerly resided in Káthiáwár. They speak Gujaráti at home and Maráthi with others. Polygamy and widow marriages are allowed and practised. Bráhman priests are employed to conduct marriages. They are Bráhmanic Hindus and hold the goddess Bhawáni in special reverence. They fast on the eleventh of each fortnight and on the first day of *Navrátra*. They either burn or bury their dead. Crows are fed on the twelfth day after a death. They live by performing with snakes and by begging.

MUSALMAN GARUDIS are converts from the Hindu Gárudis. According to one account they are converts from the Kolháti caste. Their headquarters are at Miraj near Kolhápur. Their home speech is a rough Hindustáni. Their ancestors are said to have been converted by Mir Samsudin, commonly known as Miran Shamna, who died about the middle of the fourteenth century, and was buried at Miraj, his tomb being the scene of a yearly fair. They marry among themselves only and form a separate community under an elective headman. Except circumcising their boys they keep no Musalmán customs, and are Musalmáns in little more than in name. They do not respect or obey the *Kázi* except in employing him as a marriage registrar.

GASRAT GURAV.—A synonym for Kadu Gurav.

GASTI.—A synonym for Assal Máng.

GAUD.—A sub-division of Dásás; a territorial division of Bráhmans.

GAUDA.—A sub-division of Bráhmans and Kabbaligars; a title applied to the members of the cultivating castes of Kanara; a headman of a village.

GAUD CHITRAKA.—A synonym for Gudigar.

GAUDE.—A synonym for Gávade Bhandáris.

GAUDI SANTAN.—A sub-division of Mallavas.

GAUD SARASVAT.—A sub-division of Bráhmans

GAVAD.—A synonym for Halvakki Vakkal.

GAVADA.—A synonym for Dhangar.

GAVADAS, also called Mith Gávadás or Salt Gávadás, numbering approximately 12,370 (1901), including 5,648 males and 6,722 females, are chiefly found in Ratnágiri and Kanara districts and the Sávantvádi State. A few families are resident in Thána and Kolába. The origin of the term Gávada is obscure. A common use of the term is for the village headmen in Kanarese-speaking villages, and in this sense it would seem to correspond to the Maráthi *pátil*. The Maráthás are sometimes called *pátils*, and in the same way, perhaps, the cultivating castes or *Vakkals* of Kanara are known as Gávadás. The Dhangars or Maráthi-speaking shepherds are also known as Gávadás. According to Molesworth, Gávada is derived from *ganv*, a village, and means the village headman. It seems possible that the terms *pátil* and *gávada* were originally applied to the members of the village community possessing the land, in contrast to the labourers and agrestal serfs; the village headman would naturally be chosen from the owners of

Name and origin.

the soil, the various families of which would thus add the title to their name. In the Southern Marátha Country to the present day the Kanarese cultivators greatly favour the suffix *gávada*, a common type of name being, for instance, Basappágávada bin Chanappágávada. Owing to the *Vakkal* or cultivating castes of Kanara styling themselves Gávadás, the census figures for the caste under consideration are unreliable. The Gávada or Mith Gávada of Ratnágiri and Kanara is distinct from the *Vakkal* castes, speaks Maráthi, and is not so conspicuously Dravidian in type.

The caste presents the interesting aspect of a group passing from a primitive totemistic organisation by *devaks* into the Bráhmanical one of *gotras* through the Marátha system of *kuls*. On examination of the different accounts received, it is found that some families of the caste still show their reverence for the trees representing their *devaks* by not cutting or dining on them, or even by not touching the leaves thereof, although the rule of not intermarrying between persons having the same *devak* is fast dying out. Most of the accounts state that Káshyap is the *gotra* of the whole caste, a step further towards the adoption of the Bráhmanical *gotras* after the intermediate stage of the Marátha *kuls*, by which the restrictions on intermarriage are mainly regulated in this caste. One account gives Káshyap, Vatsa and Bháradwája to be the *gotras* of the whole caste and states that the Vengurlekar (those residing in Vengurla) Gávadás belong to the Vatsa *gotra*, the Kubals to the Bháradwája *gotra* and the rest to the Káshyap *gotra*. It also states that intermarriages are prohibited between members of the same *kul* and also between members of the same *gotra*; but members belonging to the Káshyap *gotra* may intermarry, which is inevitable, as most families of the caste have as yet only hit upon this same *gotra*.

ivisions. There are no endogamous divisions of the caste beyond a small group that still make salt and are looked on as socially degraded for that reason. Intermarriage with these is refused. The exogamous sub-divisions known as *kuls* are identical with surnames. They are Chaván, Phátak, Loke, Ludabe, Parab, Rásam, Ráut, Nare, Jogal, Jethe, Rávale, Shetye, Hadye, Dholam, Hadki, Wodye, Bhojane, Dagare, Dhopate and Jare. Marriages are prohibited between members of the same *kul*. According to some, sameness of *devak* is also a bar to intermarriage.

A member of the caste may marry his father's sister's or mother's brother's daughter. He cannot marry his mother's sister's daughter. A man may marry two sisters. Two brothers cannot marry two sisters,

Marriages between descendants of sisters are prohibited for three or four generations. Polygamy is allowed and practised, but polyandry is unknown. Boys are married between 12 and 25 girls before they come of age. Amongst the Gávadás of the Deogad *táluka* of the Ratnágiri district girls may remain unmarried till after they attain puberty, but sexual license before marriage is not tolerated. Girls committing sexual indiscretions are excommunicated, and if the men involved be castemen, they are fined.

Marriage ceremonies.

The offer of marriage generally comes from the girl's father. The day for the marriage is fixed by a Bráhman who conducts the service. If the boy's parents are well-to-do, they receive a dowry up to Rs. 100 with the girl. If the girl's parents are poor, the boy's father has to pay them a bride-price up to Rs. 50. When a match is settled, a feast is given by the girl's father to the kinsfolk and the boy's party, when one of the latter presents the girl with a rupee or a *putali* (a golden coin worth about Rs. 5). Two days before the marriage, the *muhurtamedha* or the auspicious post of the marriage booth is planted, and unhusked rice is ground for the marriage feasts. The *devak* is then brought and installed near the household gods, and Ganpati is worshipped. Next, the bride and bridegroom are rubbed with turmeric paste and oil, and the *Girepuja* is performed, in which the *navagrahas* or nine planets are worshipped by the bridegroom. The *Rukhavat* follows, in which women from the girl's house go in procession to the boy's house, taking baskets filled with sweetmeats, and serve the contents to him. This is followed by *Telsádi*, in which women from the boy's house take oil and a robe to the girl's house, offer the things to the *devak*, dress the girl in the robe, and place the oil by the side of the *devak*. A ceremony of *Phulsádi*, or flowers and a robe, is similarly performed, after which the bridegroom starts in procession for the bride's house. When he reaches the porch of the marriage booth, water is poured on his feet, and a plate containing a lighted lamp is waved around his face. The bridegroom puts a rupee into the plate, enters the booth, and stands on a heap of rice grains. The bride is brought and made to stand in front of him. A cloth is held between the pair, marriage verses are repeated, and when the lucky moment arrives, the bride and bridegroom put garlands of flowers round one another's necks, and sacred grains of rice are thrown over their heads by all assembled. *Kankans* or marriage wristlets are then tied round their wrists, and the *Madhuparka* is performed, in which the bride's father washes the bridegroom's feet, feeds him with curds and honey and presents him with articles of dress. Then comes the *Kanyádán* or handing over of the bride to the bridegroom, which is followed by the marriage sacrifice and *Saptapadi*, the last being the binding portion of the ceremony. The bride and the bridegroom are made to bow to the *devak*, and the bridegroom returns in procession to his house with his bride. The *Kankans* round the wrists of the pair are then mutually untied and the girl is given a new name, which brings the marriage festivities to an end.

According to one account the whole caste has the same *devak*, *viz.*, *kalamb* (Anthocephalus cadumba). According to others, every *kul* has a separate *devak*, that of the Vengurlekars (*i.e.*, those residing in Vengurla) consisting of a sword, seven kinds of earth, seven kinds of flowers, rice grains, cocoanuts, betelnuts, a piece of cloth and a twig of *kalamb*; of the Shirodkars (*i.e.*, those residing in Shiroda), the *kalamb*; of the Ráuts, the *narvel* (Premna integrifolia); and so on.

The remarriage of widows is permitted. A widow cannot marry her father's sister's, mother's sister's or mother's brother's son or a member of her late husband's section. A widow remarriage can be celebrated on any day. It is frequently conducted by a Kásár. The widow and her new husband are seated side by side and then a turban is put on the latter's knee by the Kásár, who applies rice grains and red powder to his forehead. Next, a widow of the party daubs the foreheads of the pair with red powder and applies rice grains thereto, which completes the union. A bachelor is not allowed to marry a widow. A husband can divorce a wife on the ground of her infidelity, with the sanction of the caste *panch* and the caste priest. The divorce is effected by performing funeral rites in the name of the divorced wife. A divorced woman is put out of the caste and generally becomes a prostitute.

Religion. The caste follow the Hindu law of inheritance and belong to the Hindu religion. Some of them are followers of the Rámdási and Várkari sects. They worship all the Bráhmanic and village gods, their family gods being Gávadádev of Vengurla, Raulnáth of Harmal near Goa, and Nágának, also near Goa. All the animals and trees held sacred by the Hindus are worshipped. Goats and fowls are offered to the village gods on the *Dasara* day and on all days except Mondays and *Ekádashis* (11th day of the 1st and 2nd half of a month). The offerings are received by Ghádis, Mahárs or others whose perquisite it is to receive them. In some places cocoanuts are installed amongst the household gods in the name of the deceased ancestors and worshipped daily along with them. On holidays and new-moon days cooked food is offered to these ancestral cocoanuts. When an epidemic breaks out, Jarimari, Sánteri, Pávanái, Máhuli and other goddesses are propitiated with offerings of goats, flowers and cocoanuts. These goddesses are consulted by a rite known as *prasád*, in which rice grains, wheat grains, flowers or betelnuts are stuck with sandal paste to the right and left sides of the idol, and the goddess is requested to let fall the grains or flowers or betelnuts on one side or other according as she approves or disapproves of the petition made to her. If the result of the *prasád* is favourable, a basket filled with cooked food with a burning torch in it, and a cock and a goat are taken in procession beyond the village boundary and left there under the belief that the epidemic leaves the place with the things. Gávadás go on pilgrimage chiefly to Gokarn and Pandharpur, and also to Benares and other distant places if means permit. Their religious teacher is the head of the Shringeri monastery. Their priests are either the Karháda or Chitpávan Bráhmans.

Death. The dead are generally burnt. Those who cannot afford to burn bury their dead. At burial the corpse is seated. The bones and ashes are consigned to water. The ordinary funeral rites are observed. The mourning ends on the eleventh day after death. On the thirteenth day the castemen are feasted. For the propitiation of deceased ancestors, the *shráddha* and *mahálaya* are performed every year, and a crow and a cow are fed on every new-moon and the *Makar Sankránti* day.

The original occupation of the caste was making salt. They are now mostly husbandmen, cartmen and field labourers. Some are Khots. Some have their own holdings, while others are tenants of superior holders, taking land on lease. A few are Government servants. Some are petty traders. Some of them still work on the salt pans, and are held to be degraded on this account, the Gávadás proper not intermarrying with them and none but Mahárs eating at their hands.

Food. They eat the flesh of goats, sheep, wild boars, deer, fowls and fish and drink liquor.

GAVADE.—A sub-division of Bhandáris.

GAVANDI.—A synonym for Pardeshi Kumbhár.

Name and origin. **GAVANDIS,** or masons, numbering 22,105 (1901), including 11,009 males and 11,096 females, are found in small numbers all over the Presidency. Of this number, 826 returned themselves as Musalmáns and were found chiefly in Gujarát. A few Játs were found following the occupation of Gavandis in the Poona district. Some Jingars and Páncháls follow this profession, but they are distinct castes retaining their individuality.

The chief hereditary occupation of Gavandis is working in stone or earth, hewing stones and building walls and houses, ponds and wells. The Ságar and Jire Gavandis also make earth and lime images of Hindu gods and saints and sell Ganpatis. The Gavandis of Bijápur formerly made salt also. Some are husbandmen and labourers.

Divisions. The Gavandis have the following endogamous divisions :—

1. Marátha.
2. Jire.
3. Ságar or Kámáthi.
4. Kanarese.
5. Chunár, Kadiya, Sungar or Gujaráti.

These divisions differ so much in their religious and social customs that they are described separately.

MARATHA GAVANDIS seem to be Marátha Kunbis whose special occupation has formed them into a separate caste. They have the following surnames, which are exogamous :—

Bhonpale.	Ketkar.	Rájpure.
Ghánte.	Pedván	Sindiván.
Kanake.	Ráján.	Sitole.
Kese.		

Polygamy and widow marriage are allowed and practised, but polyandry is unknown. The dead are burnt. All the ceremonies of the Marátha Gavandis resemble those of the Marátha Kunbis. Their family deities are Devi of Tuljápur, Khandola of Jejuri near Poona, Venkatesh of Tirupati in North Arcot, and Viṭhoba of Pandharpur. They observe all Hindu holidays and believe in witchcraft, soothsaying and sorcery. They make pilgrimages to Alandi, Paithan, Pandharpur, Tuljápur and other sacred places. Their priests are Bráhmans. Their religious teachers are Bairágis or ascetics, or *Várkaris* of their own or higher castes. They eat flesh except beef and pork and drink liquor.

JIRE GAVANDIS are found only in Pandharpur and Sholápur. They are called Jire after a former headman's surname, reputed to have been builder to the king of Bijápur. They are said to have been Marátha Kunbis who were put out of caste because they refused to pay a fine of Rs. 150 which their castefellows imposed on them for building mosques for the Adilsháhi kings (1490—1680) at Bijápur. They say Maráthás are willing to re-admit them, but they do not wish to go back, alleging that Maráthás have lately taken to eating, and, in out-of-the-way places, to marrying, with Telis and Sangars. The Jires are said to have come to Sholápur about a hundred years ago to build Sindia's mansion in Pandharpur. They have a *kadu* or bastard division, with whom they eat but do not intermarry. All of them belong to the same family stock, *viz.*, Suryagotra or Suragotra. The common surnames are Kámle, Pavár, Sálunke and Surve. Marriages are prohibited between persons of the same *devak* and surname. Polygamy and widow marriage are allowed and practised, but polyandry is unknown. The marriage, death and other ceremonies are of the Kunbi type. The family deities of the Jire Gavandis are Bhaváni of Tuljápur, Jákái and Jokhái, and Khandoba of Jejuri. They also worship all Bráhmanical gods and goddesses and observe all the Hindu holidays. Their priests are Deshasth Bráhmans and their religious teachers are Gosávis. They believe in witchcraft and soothsaying. They eat fish and the flesh of goats, sheep, rabbits, hares and fowls, and drink liquor, once or twice a year, especially on the last day of the *Shimga* or Holi holidays.

SAGAR or KAMATHI GAVANDIS are found chiefly in the Sholápur district. They claim Kshatriya descent though they admit they have fallen to be Shudras. They assert that they originally came from Benares to the Nizám's territory, whence they are said to have come into the Sholápur district about three hundred years ago. Their castefellows are still found near Hyderabad, some of them wearing sacred threads and dining in silk waistcloths. They occasionally come on pilgrimage from Hyderabad to Pandharpur, when they dine with the Sholápur Ságars, but not unless the local Ságars dress in a silk or in a fresh washed waistcloth. The Sholápur Ságars are divided into Proper and Lenkavalás or *kadus*, who eat together but do not intermarry. All belong to the Káshyap *gotra*. Their surnames are Gadpate, Kalburge, Kálse and Narne, and are exogamous. Girls are married between seven and twelve and boys between twelve and twenty-five. Their marriage guardian or *devak* consists of the *pánch-pálvi* or leaves of five kinds of trees, which are installed near the household gods and worshipped with flowers and rice grains. The marriage ceremonies are of the Kunbi type with this striking difference that, instead of the bridegroom going to the bride's house, the latter goes to the former's for the marriage. Ságar Gavandis are both Smárts and Vaishnavas. They worship the ordinary Hindu gods and goddesses as well as Musalmán saints. Their family deities are Báláji of Giri or Tirupati, Bhaváni of Tuljápur, Jotiba of Ratnágiri, Khandoba of Jejuri, and Yellamma of the Karnátak, whom they sometimes visit to make vows. They observe the usual Bráhmanic fasts and feasts and believe in sorcery, witchcraft and soothsaying. Their priests are Deshasth Bráhmans. The *gurus* or teachers are in some cases Rámánujas and in others Shankaráchāryas. The dead are burnt, the funeral rites being of the usual type. They eat fish and the flesh of sheep, goats, hares, rabbits and fowls, and drink liquor. Those who have become *Várkaris* have given up eating flesh and drinking liquor.

KANARESE GAVANDIS are also known as Ságar Chakravartis, that is, sea-rulers, in Dhárwár. They have two divisions, Pákutras and Trinámádháris, who eat together and intermarry. Their commonest surnames are as follows :--

Bhandigar.	Gudati.	Lania.
Bhamdiyar.	Gansli.	Modena.
Chyámadi.	Kannána.	Rámyana.
Dannána.	Khindia.	Shingri.

Persons bearing the same surnames cannot intermarry. Polygamy and widow remarriage are allowed and practised, but polyandry is unknown. In Kanara, if a girl comes of age before she is married she has to undergo a purifying ceremony. The marriage ceremonies of the Kanarese Gavandis last four days. On the first day a dinner is given in honour of the family gods ; on the second day the bride and bridegroom are rubbed with turmeric and oil, and bathed ; on the third day a Bráhman priest is invited, repeats texts, and the regular wedding ceremonies are gone through ; and on the fourth day the bride and bridegroom are made to sow seeds of five grains in the marriage shed.

The family deities of the Kanarese Gavandis are Hanumán. Tulja-Bhaváni, Venkatarάma, Yellamma and Nandyál Basaveshwar. They also worship the usual Bráhmanic gods and goddesses and make pilgrimages to the shrine of Venkataráma of Venkatgiri in North Arcot and to Tulja-Bhaváni in Tul ápur in the Nizám's territory. They keep almost all the Hindu holidays and have great faith in soothsaying, witchcraft and evil spirits. In the Karnátak, goats are offered to Tulja-Bhaváni on the *Dasara* day. In Kanara, blood sacrifices are not offered. The spiritual teacher of the Kanarese Gavandis in the Karnátak is Tátiáchárya, who lives at Hampi in Bellary ; of those in Kanara the head of the Kalmath monastery at Kittur in Belgaum. The latter is a married man of their own caste, and though not a Lingáyat, wears the *linga*. He officiates at marriages, and lays his feet on the head of the dead. In his absence, the ceremonies are conducted by a Lingáyat priest. The priests of the Bijápur Gavandis belong to the Oshtama caste, though they consult Bráhmans as astrologers. The priests of the Dhárwár Gávandis are Bráhmans, whom they call to conduct their marriages. The dead are either burnt or buried. In Kanara, mourning is not observed for the deceased. They eat the flesh of goats, deer, hare, poultry and fish, and drink liquor.

KADIYAS or GUJARATI GAVANDIS, also known as Chunárs and Sungars, are found in the towns and cities of Gujarát and also in Poona. The latter are greatly influenced by the customs of the surrounding Deccan castes of similar standing. The former do not differ in appearance, dress, ceremonies and customs from the other artisan castes of Gujarát. They belong to the Parnámi, Swámináráyan, Rámánandi and Kabirpanthi sects They keep all the Hindu fasts and feasts and believe in ghosts and spirits. Their staple food consists of millet bread and pulses, and they are said to use in secret flesh, fish and liquor.

MUSALMAN GAVANDIS, numbering 826 (1901), including 447 males and 379 females, are found mostly in Gujarát, a few being recorded in Khándesh and Sholápur. They are descended from local Hindus of the same class, and ascribe their conversion to Aurangzeb. They form a separate community, marrying only among themselves, but have no organization and no headman. They are Sunnis of the Hanafi school, but are seldom religious or careful to say their prayers. They differ from ordinary Musalmáns in eschewing beef, in worshipping Hindu gods, and in keeping Hindu festivals. At the same time they bey the *Kázi* and ask him to conduct their ceremonies.

GAVAR.—A synonym for Cháran Vanjáris.

GAVASE.—A synonym for Gavasi Mahár.

GAVASI.—A sub-division of Mahárs.

GAVIT.—A sub-division of Bhils.

GAVLI.—A sub-division of Dhangars.

GAVLIS, numbering 46,290, including 23,709 males and 22,581 females (1901), are found in the Deccan, Karnátak, Ratnágiri and Kolába. 338 have returned themselves as Musalmán. The te m Gavli means a cow-keeper, *i.e.*, a milkman. It is probable that the census figures cover a number of really distinct castes following this primitive occupation. **Name and origin.**

Endogamous divisions.

Gavlis are divided into the following endogamous divisions, which have nothing in common except a common occupation :—

1. Ahir.
2. Bijápuri.
3. Chevle.
4. Dabhole.
5. Dhangar.
6. Golla.
7. Kunbi.
8. Krishna.
9. Kokni.
10. Kuruba.
11. Lingáyat.
12. Marátha or Khillári.
13. Musalmán.
14. Nagarkar.
15. Pancham.
16. Rajput.
17. Vajarkar.

Of these, Bijápuri, Nagarkar, Pancham and Vajarkar Gavlis are found in Ahmednagar district. The number of Ahir Gavlis found in Ahmednagar district is very small, and Dhangar Gavlis are also rare. Bijápuri, Kunbi and Nagarkar Gavlis are found in Bijápur district. The terms Bijápuri and Nagarkar Gavlis have probably been taken from the former residence of these Gavlis in Bijápur and Nagar districts. The Kunbi Gavlis were formerly in the service of the Bijápuris. They have established themselves as Gavlis, but eat, drink, marry and associate with Kunbis, from whom they differ in no respect. Marátha and Lingáyat Gavlis are found in Belgaum district. Golla, Nagar, Pancham, Lingáyat, Marátha, Rajput, Kuruba or Kanarese Gavlis and Musalmán Gavlis are found in Dhárwár district. The Rajput Gavlis are also known as Ahir Gavlis in Dhárwár district. The Golla Gavlis are the original cowherds. The others seem to be broken fragments of many castes that have taken to the occupation of cowherds.

According to tradition, some four thousand years ago Nanda Gop and his wife Yashoda lived at Gokul or Vraj near the Ganges and the Jumna in Upper India. In their house the parents of Krishna, the eighth incarnation of Vishnu, hid him, when Kansa, King of Mathura, Krishna's maternal uncle, sought his life. Among the Golla Gavlis Krishna was reared and amused himself with 16,000 Gavli women, besides eight legal wives and concubines. His favourite and most beautiful concubine Radha, the wife of Anaya, was a Gavli. For this reason the Golla Gavlis are looked on with great respect. Sir H. Risley[1] identifies Goála with Ahir, and remarks "that at the present day the designation Ahir seems to be confined to Behar and parts of Upper India, Goála being more commonly used in Bengal. The traditions of the caste bear a highly imaginative character, and profess to trace their descent from the god Krishna, whose relations with the milkmaids

(1) H. H. Risley—"Tribes and Castes of Bengal," Volume I, page 282.

of Brindában play a prominent part in Hindu mythology. Krishna himself is supposed to have belonged to the tribe of Yádavas or descendants of Yadu, a nomadic race, who graze cattle and make butter, and are believed to have effected an early settlement in the neighbourhood of Mathura. In memory of this tradition, one of the sub-castes of Goálás in the North-Western Provinces is called Yadu or Jadu-Bansi at the present time. Another story quoted by Buchanan makes out the Goálás to be Vaisyas, who were degraded in consequence of having introduced castration among their herds, and members of the caste who are disposed to claim this distinguished ancestor may lay stress upon the fact that the tending of flocks and herds is mentioned by the authorities among the duties of the Vaisya order. Taken as a whole, the Goála traditions can hardly be said to do more than render it probable that one of their earliest settlements was in the neighbourhood of Mathura, and that this part of the country was the centre of distribution of the caste. The large functional group known by the name Goála seems to have been recruited not merely by the diffusion along the Ganges Valley of the Semi-Aryan Goálás of the North-Western Provinces, but also by the inclusion in the caste of pastoral tribes, who were not Aryans at all." The Ahir, Konkni, Marátha, Nagarkar and Vajarkar divisions are found in the Poona district, of whom Vajarkar are thought to be socially inferior to Nagarkar and Ahir Gavlis as they eat at the hands of the latter two. Dabhole and Chevle are found in the Kolába district. They trace their descent to the Yaduvansha, and say that they came into this district from Mathura. Those that went towards Dábhol are known as Dabhole, and those that lived in parts adjoining the Roha *táluka* are known as Chevle Gavlis. In Bijápur district the Lingáyat Gavlis are known as Nanda Gavlis and the Marátha as Khillári Gavlis. The ordinary milk-sellers in Bijápur were generally Hande-Vazirs, that is, Kurubas by caste, but since the famine of 1876 a few families of Gavlis are found which have come from Pandharpur in Sholápur district.

The Dhangar, Marátha and Krishna Gavlis speak Maráthi. The Lingáyat Gavlis in Kolhápur speak Kanarese. The Rajput Gavlis in Dhárwár speak Hindustáni, and Golla Gavlis, both Maráthi and Kanarese.

Divisions. In Ratnágiri and Kolába there are two endogamous divisions of Gavlis, *viz.*, Dabhole and Chevle, named after the towns of Dábhol and Chaul. The common surnames are Chaugle, Kathle, More, etc. There are no exogamous groups beyond families having a common surname. Marriage with maternal uncle's daughter is allowed.

It is prohibited with father's sister's daughter and mother's sister's daughter. Marriage with wife's sister is allowed during her life-time or after her death. Two brothers may marry two sisters. Girls and boys are married after they become three years old. Sexual intercourse before marriage is neither allowed nor tolerated. If a girl commits sexual indiscretions before marriage, she is turned out of her caste and is not re-admitted into her caste either by paying a fine or giving a dinner to her castemen.

Marriage ceremonies. The offer of marriage generally comes from the boy's father. He goes to the girl's house with his kinsmen to settle a marriage. The kinsmen are given liquor or palm-juice to drink for their trouble. The boy's father pays from Rs. 5 to 150 to the girl's father as the price of the bride when he is very poor, and the payment is known as *dej.* A well-to-do man pays a dowry to the boy's father. A Bráhman priest settles the auspicious day for marriage and also conducts the service of marriage. The common ceremonies of rubbing with turmeric, *mandap sthápan*. the worship of the *devak*, *rukhvat*, the tying of *kankans* or wristlets, the *kanyádán* and *varát* are observed.

Widow remarriage is allowed. A widow cannot marry her father's sister's son, mother's sister's son or any member of her deceased husband's family. The ceremony consists in leading the new couple to worship. The next day the castemen are feasted.

Religion. Divorce is not allowed. A woman accused of adultery is turned out of her caste. They follow the Hindu law of inheritance and belong to the Hindu religion. Their favourite deity of worship is Krishna. Their liking for the worship of Krishna is due to the fact they are of the Yadu *kul*, to which Krishna belonged. They do not go on pilgrimage owing to their scanty means. They also worship local deities and cows, the *umbar*, banyan and *pipal* trees, the scythe, axe, etc., on *Dasara* days. The offerings made to local deities are received by the servants of the deities, who are termed *bhopes*. They do not worship Musalmán saints or their dead ancestors. When cholera breaks out they worship presiding village deities, and when small-pox breaks out they worship Shitala deity at Chaul in Kolába district. Sacrifices of goats and fowls are made for the propitiation of village deities. They employ Bráhmans for religious and ceremonial purposes; and these are received on terms of equality by the other Bráhmans.

Death ceremonies. They bury or burn their dead. Unmarried dead are buried. The ashes and bones of the dead, when burnt, are thrown into a river or are sent to Hareshwar, a holy place near Shrivardhan in Janjira State.

The dead body is taken to the burial or burning ground on a bier covered by a new shroud. Pearls are put into the dead person's eyes and gold particles into the mouth; *gulál*, red powder, flowers, etc., are sprinkled over the bier. The chief mourner walks ahead of the bier taking a cowdung cake in his hand. The bier is put down half-way to the burial or burning ground. The bearers change sides and a stone is picked up. The stone is called *ashma* or the life-stone. The deceased is then placed on a pyre and it is ignited. The face and head of the chief mourner are shaved and the hair is burnt with the dead. The chief mourner, taking a porcelain pot filled with water over his shoulder, then walks three times round the pyre. At the commencement of each round a hole is bored in the porcelain pot by means of the life-stone. After the completion of the third round, the chief mourner throws down the pot and, striking his hand on his mouth, calls aloud. They then go to the dead person's house. There they see a burning lamp placed over the spot where the deceased breathed his last. The mourners are fed by their relatives on the first day. On the third day the ashes and bones are collected, and the spot is washed with cowdung. A triangular mound of earth is raised over it. Three small porcelain pots are placed on the three corners and yellow flags are also pitched near them. Candles of frankincense are burnt. They observe mourning for ten days. Balls of rice are offered to the dead on the tenth day. On the thirteenth day the castemen are feasted. They observe *shráddha* and *mahálaya* during the latter half of the month of *Bhádrapad* for the propitiation of ancestors in general.

Some of them are husbandmen and also work as field labourers. They eat the flesh of goats, sheep and fish. They drink liquor.

KURUBA GAVLIS, like other Kurubás or shepherds, eat flesh and drink liquor. They tend cows and buffaloes in forest and waste land, seldom living in towns or villages. They bring milk, curds and butter to town and sell them there, or dispose of them to Lingáyat and Marátha Gavlis wholesale, who afterwards sell them retail. Their chief holiday is Krishna's birth-day. They eat food cooked by Bráhmans, Lingáyats and Maráthás, but marry with no caste but their own.

Lingáyats.

LINGAYAT GAVLIS. The surnames in use among the Lingáyat Gavlis of Poona are Ganjiwale, Ingmire, Mahankale, Mungle, Alamkhane, Ambarkhane, Bágwán, Dhamkde, Nandarkar, etc. Those among the Bijápur Gavlis are Bhairwádi, Dahinde, Gadyappa, Gháti, Gyanap, etc. Among the Sholápur Gavlis are Agláve, Ajidvani, Bashkar, Baherwádi, Bhágánagdi, Chipkar, Dhajale, Divte, Ghungre,

Langute, etc.; and among the Ahmednagar Gavlis are Atrunkarin, Avasekar, Bahirvade, Chaukáde, Divte, Godalkar, etc. The names in use among men are Bhiwa, Govinda, Satwáji, Shetiba, Dhamu, Máruti, Sávlárám, etc.; and among women are Devkubái, Girjái, Hirnái, Matkani, Bhágubái, Kondábái, etc.

Sameness of surname is a bar to intermarriage. Marriage with maternal uncle's daughter, father's sister's daughter and mother's sister's daughter is not allowed. Marriage with wife's sister is allowed during her life-time or after her death. Two brothers may marry two sisters. Girls are married from seven and boys from twelve upwards. Girls are married among the poor after they attain puberty. Sexual license before marriage is not allowed. If a girl commits sexual indiscretions before marriage with a man of her caste, the girl is fined or compelled to give a dinner to her castemen. The man involved is persuaded to marry her. But if a girl has committed sexual indiscretions with a man of a higher or lower caste she is excommunicated. Polygamy is permitted, but polyandry is unknown.

Marriage ceremonies. The offer of marriage generally comes from the boy's father. The marriage is settled through the mediation of a casteman, and he is called *panch*. A Jangam and a Bráhman priest settle the day of marriage and also conduct the service of marriage. The boy's father and other kinsmen go to the girl's house when the match is settled, and worship a betelnut-Ganpati and present the girl with a robe and a bodice. Both a Jangam and a Bráhman are required to be present at the ceremony. A memorandum is drawn up in which the marriage day and hour are given as well as the day on which the boy and girl should be rubbed with turmeric. Their marriage guardian or *devak* is a *telchi* (a cake boiled in oil), an axe and boughs of the mango tree. The Bombay Gazetteer gives a different *devak* for them. Five earthen jars filled with pond or well water are brought on the heads of five married women and set near the house gods. In Ahmednagar they tie a mango branch as their marriage guardian or *devak* to the first post of the marriage booth at the boy's and at the girl's house. On the marriage day the boy is seated on a bullock or on a horse and taken to the girl's house. Here a piece of bread and curds are waved round his head, and he is taken inside the house and seated on a carpet. The girl is seated near him, and in front of them are set five earthen jars and two lighted lamps. A cloth is held between the boy and the girl, and the Bráhman priest repeats marriage verses, and at the end throws grains of rice over their heads, and they are husband and wife. The boy and girl are seated on an altar. Near relations wave a copper coin over their heads, and the coins are divided between the Bráhman and the Jangam priest. On the following day a feast is held at the girl's house and on the next day the boy goes with his wife to his father's house, and the marriage ends with a feast.

Widow remarriage is allowed. A widow cannot marry her aunt's son and father's sister's son. She may marry the elder or younger brother of her deceased husband or any other member of his family, if she chooses. A widow remarriage is celebrated on any day during dark nights. Both a Jangam and a Bráhman priest are present on this occasion. The widow's new husband gives her new clothes. Then the widow's lap is filled, and this is the binding portion of the ceremony. A bachelor is not allowed to marry a widow.

Divorce is allowed in the case of infidelity on the part of wife or incompatibility of temper, with the sanction of the caste *panch*. A divorced woman is allowed to marry a second husband, and her marriage is effected after the fashion of widow remarriage. A woman divorced for adultery is not allowed to remain in her caste. She is excommunicated.

Death ceremonies.

They bury their dead. In Sholápur women dying in child-birth are burnt. The body is carried sitting in a bamboo frame, the grave is dug, and sprinkled with cowdung and cow's urine and water in which a Jangam's feet have been washed. A Jangam attends the funeral. The body is lowered into the grave, and the Jangam goes into the grave, drops some water, in which his toe has been dipped, into the dead mouth, places the *lingam* which the deceased wore in his clasped hands, and comes out. The grave is filled with earth up to the corpse's neck, then, till the head is covered, it is filled with salt, and above that with earth. The mourning family are impure for three, five, seven or nine days and they are purified by drinking a mixture of cow's urine, dung, milk, curds, sugar and honey. They feed their castemen on the new-moon day, following the death day.

Their chief and hereditary calling is to tend cattle and sell milk, curds and butter. Their women help by making curds and butter and by hawking milk, curds and butter in the streets. Their children graze the cattle.

Food

They are forbidden to use animal food or liquor on pain of loss of caste.

GAYAVAL.—A sub-division of Bráhmans.

GHACHE.—A synonym for Burud.

Name and origin.

GHADIS or Soothsayers, numbering 1,592 (1901), including 724 males and 868 females, are found in the Kárwár, Kumta and Ankola *tálukás* of the Kanara district.

They have neither endogamous nor exogamous sub-divisions. Marriages are prohibited between descendants of a common ancestor. A member of the caste can marry his father's sister's or mother's brother's daughter. He cannot marry his mother's sister's daughter. A man may marry two sisters, and two brothers may marry two sisters. Girls are generally married between nine and twelve, and boys between fourteen and eighteen. Polygamy is allowed and practised, but polyandry is unknown.

Marriage ceremonies.

The offer of marriage comes from the boy's father, who has to give three *khandis* of rice grains and Rs. 12 to the girl's father. The day for the marriage is fixed by the village priest who conducts the service. The betrothal known as *vappalu* takes place two or three days before the marriage, when the girl is presented with ornaments, flowers and articles of dress by the boy's father. In the afternoon of the marriage day the boy starts in procession for the girl's house. At about ten or twelve yards from the house a festoon is hung, under which he is received by the girl's party. He is then led into the marriage booth, the girl is brought and made to stand before him, and they are made to put garlands round one another's necks, this being the binding portion of the ceremony. Their hands are then joined, and the girl's father pours water over them (*dháre*). This is followed by the marriage sacrifice: and the pair finally walk five times round the sacrificial fire. On the following day the boy and the girl are rubbed with turmeric paste and oil, and the boy returns to his house with his bride.

The remarriage of widows is permitted. A widow remarriage can be celebrated on any day except the full-moon and new-moon days from the beginning of *Ashádh* to the end of *Kártik* and in *Poush*. Males and remarried widows only are present on the occasion. The widow has to return to the relations of her deceased husband the clothes and ornaments received by her from him, and her new husband has to pay them a sum of Rs. 6. First, the widow and her new husband are bathed and seated on a low wooden stool or a blanket. Next, the widow wears a new robe and ornaments presented to her by her new husband. Red-powder is then applied to her forehead and her lap is filled. A feast to the party assembled ends the ceremony. A bachelor is not allowed to marry a widow. Divorce is not allowed. The caste follow the Hindu law of inheritance.

They are Hindus. Their family gods are Venkataráma of Tirupati and his attendant Hanumanta, and their patron god is Mahádev of Kárwár. They also worship Dád, Vetál, Jatga, Bhandinás and other minor gods, to whom they offer goats and fowls on all days except Sundays. They observe all the Hindu holidays. They do not go on pilgrimages. Their spiritual teacher is the head of the Shringeri monastery. When an epidemic breaks out, goats, fowls, robes and bodice clothes are offered to Máriamma, Durgamma, and Kálamma. Their priests are the Havig or Joshi Bráhmans. Religion.

Those who can afford it burn the dead; the rest bury. At burial the corpse is laid with head to the north. On the eleventh day after death the caste is feasted. Death.

The hereditary occupation of the caste is soothsaying and slaying animals offered to village gods. They also work as labourers and husbandmen. They do not possess their own land, but take land on lease. Formerly they tilled only *kumri* or hill clearings, but recent restrictions have forced them to take to regular field work.

They take animal food. but do not drink liquor. They rank next to Hálvakki Vakkals. Food.

GHADSHI.—A sub-division of Mahárs and Mángs.

GHADSHIS, numbering (1901) 1,661, including 771 males and 890 females, are found in small numbers throughout the Deccan and the Konkan. Concerning their origin, the Ghadshis relate that when Ráma was being married to Sita there were no musicians; Ráma, therefore, made three images of sandalwood, and breathing life into them, gave one the drum *Sambal*, and the other two the pipes *Sur* and *Sanai*. According to another story, Rávan was their patron and gave the whole of the Deccan to the Ghadshis. Outsiders are not admitted into the caste. Name and origin.

They are divided into two endogamous divisions, Bárámáse and Akarámáse, the latter being the illegitimate offspring of the former. The exogamous sub-divisions of the caste are families bearing the same surname or groups of families with the same *devak* or marriage guardian. The commonest surnames are Bhonsale, Chaván, Gáikwád, Ghorpade, Jádhav, More, Pawár, Rángade, Suryavanshi, Sálunke, Jagtáp, Shinde and Dhumál. Divisions.

A man may marry his father's sister's or mother's brother's daughter. He is allowed to marry two sisters, and two brothers may marry two sisters. Males are generally married between ten and thirty, and girls between two and fourteen. Polygamy is allowed and practised, but polyandry is unknown.

Marriage ceremonies. The negotiations for a marriage are commenced by the boy's father. The settlement of the marriage day and the ceremony itself are entrusted to a Bráhman priest. The marriage ceremonies of the Ghadshis resemble those of the Kunbis, the essential and binding portion consisting in the fastening of the lucky necklace round the bride's neck by the bridegroom. Their *devaks* or marriage guardians appear to be the same as those of the Maráthás.

The remarriage of widows is permitted. A widow cannot marry her maternal aunt's son or a member of her late husband's section. A widow's marriage can be celebrated on any day of the dark fortnight of a month. Unwidowed women are not allowed to be present on the occasion. The ceremony consists in the worship of Ganpati by the widow and by her new husband, the filling of the widow's lap by a Bráhman priest, and the drinking of milk from the same cup by the couple. A bachelor is not allowed to marry a widow. Divorce is allowed. A divorced woman can marry again, adopting the widow remarriage ceremony. The caste follow the Hindu law of inheritance.

Religion. Ghadshis are Hindus and worship all the local and Bráhmanic gods and goddesses, chiefly Bahiroba, Khandoba and Máruti. Images of dead ancestors are installed among the house gods and worshipped daily with offerings of cooked food. The *pipal* and the musical instruments on which they play are worshipped. When an epidemic breaks out offerings are made to Devi. They observe all the Hindu holidays.

Death. The dead are either burnt or buried. Those who have married widows must be buried. The unmarried dead are carried in a blanket or *jholi* on the shoulders of two men ; others are laid on a bier. In other respects their death rites resemble those of the Kunbis.

Ghadshis are hereditary musicians. They play on the drum and pipes and are good singers. Their instruments are the *Sanai* costing Rs. 5, the *Sur* Rs. 2, the *Sambal* Rs. 10 and the kettledrum or *Nagára* Rs. 20. During the marriage season their services are in constant demand, and as wandering minstrels they are much in favour at all seasons. A few own lands. Many are in receipt of yearly allowances from villagers for their services in playing at the village temples. Some are day labourers.

Food. They eat fish and the flesh of goats, sheep, domestic fowls and wild game. They drink liquor.

GHAGARIA.—A synonym for Chhára.

GHATGHADA.—A synonym for Gujaráti Kumbhár.

GHAIJO.—A synonym for Gujaráti Hajám.

GHANCHE.—A synonym for Burud.

APPENDIX.

ETHNOGRAPHIC QUESTIONS.

General Series.

1. Write in English and vernacular the name of the caste with synonyms, if any, noting if any of these are used only by outsiders.

2. Write in English and vernacular the names of the exogamous sub-divisions of the caste, if such sub-divisions exist.

N.B.—By the term exogamous sub-division is meant a group from within which its male members cannot take their wives.

3. Show the endogamous divisions of the caste, if such divisions exist. If these divisions consist of groups of the sub-divisions mentioned in question 2, show the grouping. If they are distinguished by separate names, write the names in English and vernacular.

N.B.—By the term endogamous division is meant a group from outside of which its male members cannot take their wives.

4. State the limits within or beyond which marriage is prohibited, *e.g.*, that a man must marry within the caste, but must not marry into his own or certain other sub-divisions or within certain degrees of relationship or may not marry two sisters.

5. Name any prohibitions on intermarriage based upon (*a*) social status, (*b*) geographical or local position, (*c*) differences of religious belief or practice, (*d*) differences or changes of occupation.

6. State the popular tradition, if any exist, as to the origin of the caste, naming the common ancestor, if any, the part of the country from which the caste is supposed to have come, and the approximate time of its emigration, as marked by the reign of any particular king, or the occurrence of any historical event, together with the number of generations supposed to have intervened.

7. Is the habit of the caste settled or wandering? Have they any recognized headquarters in the province? If wandering, over what tract of country do they wander? Are their migrations periodical or irregular and what are the shape and material of their dwellings?

8. Do they admit outsiders into the caste? If so, from what classes, by what forms and under what conditions?

9. Is marriage infant or adult? If the latter, is sexual license before marriage recognized or tolerated?

10. Is (*a*) polygamy, (*b*) polyandry, permitted; if so, under what conditions and within what limits? In the case of polyandry, must all the husbands be brothers?

11. What form of marriage ceremony is in ordinary use? Name the forms and state the essential and binding portion of the ceremony.

12. Is the remarriage of widows permitted? If so, is the widow obliged or expected to marry her husband's elder or younger brother? If she does not marry a brother, within what limits may she marry? What form of marriage ceremony is used, and what is the essential and binding portion of it?

13. Under what circumstances is divorce permitted, and by what form is it effected? May wives who have been divorced marry again?

14. Do the members of the caste follow the Hindu or Mahomedan law of inheritance, or a tribal custom of their own?

15. To what religion and to what sect within the religion do the caste belong? If Hindus, do they by preference worship any special one of the regular Hindu deities, and are there any reasons for this preference?

16. Name any minor gods or patron saints specially worshipped by the caste. State what offerings are made, on what days of the week, and what class of people receive them. Is the worship of any of these gods or saints confined to women and children?

17. Do the caste employ Brahmans for religious and ceremonial purposes? If so, are these Brahmans received on terms of equality by other Brahmans? If they do not employ Brahmans, what class of people serve them as priests?

18. Do the caste burn, bury, or expose their dead? If buried, in what position? Where are the bodies or ashes finally disposed of?

19. Are any ceremonies performed for the propitiation of (*a*) ancestors in general, (*b*) childless ancestors, (*c*) men who have died a violent death; and if so, of what nature and at what seasons? Is the ceremony of *shráddh* performed or not?

20. Is the caste, or any of its sub-divisions, named after any animal, plant, weapon or implement? Do they show their reverence for any such object either by special worship or by abstaining from killing, eating, cutting, burning, using, or naming it?

21. What do the caste believe to have been their original occupation or group of occupations? To what extent have they or any sections of them departed from it? Describe their present occupation.

22. If they are agriculturists, state what position they usually occupy in the agricultural system, *i.e.*, are they—

(1) Zamindars ;

(2) Tenure-holders, specifying the kind of tenures they hold ;

(3) Occupancy or non-occupancy rayats, stating whether they have or claim any privileges in respect of rent ;

(4) Nomadic cultivators, specifying the mode of cultivation they follow ;

(5) Landless day-labourers, stating the manner in which they are paid ?

23. If their occupation is that of—

(*a*) *Artizans*, what is their industry, and what special material do they work, or abstain from working ?

(*b*) *Hunters*, do they catch game or vermin ?

(*c*) *Fishermen*, do they catch fish only, or also crocodiles and tortoises ?

(*d*) *Sweepers*, do they remove night-soil or not ?

24. Name any implement or mode of working which is characteristic of the caste, and also note whether there is any form or detail of their main occupation by abstaining from which they believe themselves to be raised above others of the same craft ?

25. Do they habitually prostitute their (1) unmarried, (2) married women ?

26. Which of the following articles of food do the caste eat or abstain from eating :—flesh, wine, monkeys, beef, pork, the flesh of cloven-footed or uncloven-footed animals, fowls, scaly or scaleless fish, crocodiles, snakes, lizards, jackals, rats, other vermin, the leavings of other people ? Is there any special article of food their abstaining from which tends in their opinion to raise them above some other caste which does not abstain from it ?

27. Name the lowest well-known caste with which the caste will—

(*a*) Eat pakki, (*c*) Drink.

(*b*) Eat kachhi, (*d*) Smoke.

Name the highest well-known caste which will eat, etc. (as above) with the caste.

Sources of information.—Here should be noted the names, residence (village and thána), profession, caste, sub-caste, and section of the persons who answered the question. If any of them are *ghataks*, genealogists, heads of caste *pancháyat*, or occupy any hereditary official position in relation to the caste the fact should be stated. If the answers to the questions have been derived from any source other than personal enquiry addressed to members of the caste concerned, the source should be stated, and such references given as may enable the officer in charge of the enquiry to test the correctness of the answers.

(Signed) DENZIL C. J. IBBETSON.
(„) JOHN C. NESFIELD.
(„) H. H. RISLEY.